RANADE'S ECONOMIC WRITINGS

RANADE'S ECONOMIC WRITINGS

BY
BIPAN CHANDRA

GYAN

ISBN : 978-81-212-0328-9

Published, 2018

Published by

Gyan Publishing House
5, Ansari Road
Daryaganj, New Delhi-110002
Phone: 011-47034999, 9811692060
www.gyanbooks.com
E-mail: books@gyanbooks.com

GYAN

Printed at: G. Print Process, Delhi.

Preface

Despite the fact that Mahadev Govind Ranade was one of the first major economic thinkers of modern India, his seminal economic writings were not easily available for the last 70 years or so. Some of his economic essays were brought together in a book in 1898, which was reprinted in 1906 and 1920. The totality of his economic writings have been available only to those few who had access to the rare issues of the *Journal of the Poona Sarvajanik Sabha* where nearly all of them were published. The non-availability of his articles, addresses and reviews on economic problems has been widely felt in recent years as there has been renewed interest in the works of Ranade, Dadabhai Naoroji and other nationalist economists of the 19th century.

I have reproduced in this volume all but one of the essays from the earlier collection. The omitted essay dealt with "Local Government in England and India". I have included in the present volume his remaining nine economic essays, three book-reviews and two of the Poona Sarvajanik Sabha memoranda on the Deccan Agriculturists Bill drafted by him. His only major economic writings which could not be included in this volume either because of lack of space or because of their non-availability were: (i) *A Revenue Manual of the British Empire in India: An Epitome of the Fawcett Committee Report of 1877;* (ii) "Lectures on Trade and Commerce", delivered at Poona, 1873; (iii) *Minute of Dissent to the Report of the Finance Committee, 1886;* (iv) *A Note on the Decentralization of Provincial Finance, 1894;* (v) "Plea for Protection: Indian Sugar Industry", three articles contributed by Ranade to the *Times of India*, May-June 1899.

Article number 15 in this volume, "A Protest and a Warning Against the New Departure in the Land Assessment Policy", is incomplete since its last nine pages were missing from the Journal's issue available to me.

All articles, essays or book-reviews are given in the chronological order in which they were published.

In view of the wide diversity then and now, I have kept the spelling, punctuation, italics, capitalization of words, and place names as in the original in the text as well as in the quotations from the text in my introduction. Footnotes in the main text are as in the original. Also all page references within brackets in the introduction are to this volume.

In the end, I would like to express my thanks to Professor Sulabha Brahme, Professor Ravinder Kumar and Sucheta Mahajan for their help in acquiring xeroxed copies of some of the articles in this volume. My thanks are also due to Mridula Mukherjee and Aditya Mukherjee for helping in various ways and to Shri Baweja for typing the introduction. I am grateful to Professor J.S. Grewal and the Institute for Advanced Studies, Simla, for enabling me to stay at the Institute while drafting part of the introduction. As usual, Usha Chandra has contributed in multiple ways, including the editing of the introduction and the checking of the page- proofs of the entire manuscript.

This volume has been a labour of love for its publisher, Mr. B.P. Garg, and thanks are due to him for making this work available to the students of the intellectual, political and economic history of modern India.

Bipan Chandra

CONTENTS

Introduction

I

British colonialism in India was fully structured during the 19th century-Indian economy was integrated with the British and world capitalist economy in a subservient position and India became a classical colony. Early 19th century Indian intellectuals took note of the many negative features of British rule. But ignoring these features and swallowing their patriotic pride and feelings, they supported British rule in the hope that Britain, economically the most advanced country of the world, would transfer its advanced science and technology and production techniques, its fast growing capital and its capitalist economic structure, organization and enterprise to India thus ushering in the industrial revolution and the development of its agriculture and industry. It was this potentiality of creating a modern industrial India which made many of them acclaim British rule as 'providential' for nearly 100 years and to support the British rulers during the Revolt of 1857.

But the consequences of colonialism were very different. India was gradually underdeveloped and impoverished. Its traditional handicrafts were ruined; modern industrial growth was delayed and stunted; Indian agriculture first stagnated and then entered a prolonged period of decline and ruin; large sectors of Indian economy- foreign trade, banking, plantations, transport, energy, modern industry and mining- came under foreign control. At the same time, an indigenous capitalist class did emerge during the second half of the 19th century even though it was cribbed and confined. What was perhaps more important, a nationalist intelligentsia took root during the same period.

The nationalist intelligentsia devoted its energies to diverse fields: politics, social and religious reforms, literature. But it was in the economic field that it excelled, for it was convinced that economic development constituted the essence, and the chief measure, of a nation's progress, that on economic progress depended progress in other fields.

The long term trends and the inner contradictions of colonial economy began to mature and become apparent during the last quarter of the 19th century. The earlier expectations of the nationalist intellectuals remained unrealised. What is worse, instead of progressing the country appeared to regress economically. The intellectuals now began the effort to understand the reasons for these apparently strange and unexpected phenomena.

The nationalist intelligentsia set out to examine through the method of 'the concrete study of the concrete reality' the economic situation of the country, the nature of colonial rule and its impact on the Indian economy, and the quantitative and structural changes being brought about in it—in other words, to try to understand and analyse the causes of India's poverty, the nature of colonial exploitation and their relation to the structure of colonial economy and its inner dynamics. In this inquiry they fully utilised the historical experience of other countries as also contemporary economic theories. Gradually they developed a powerful critique of the economic condition of India and the role of British rule in its making, and of the primary or central contradiction between colonialism and the interests of Indian people.

The nationalists believed that India was extremely poor, was growing poorer, and was in the contemporary context becoming more backward or underdeveloped. They recognized that India was undergoing rapid change, but the change was not for the better. While previously, in the pre-colonial period, India had a well-balanced economy though at a low level of economic development, its economy had become quite unbalanced under British rule. Thus, though India was changing, the transition, they came to hold, was "from traditional, pre-colonial or 'feudal' pattern of backwardness to colonial backwardness where limited modern development, especially in the fields of trade and transport, occurs transforming the country into a raw material producing and processing as well as capital absorbing country, leading to backward agriculture, repressed industry, and foreign domination of economic life. They, thus, evolved the concept of a 'modernizing' economy which was not developing, that is, the concept of a colonial economy".[1] Colonialism was as modern as industrial capitalism; it was, at the same time, as depressing in its impact on economic life as the traditional economic and social structure. This understanding of colonialism and of the primary contradiction between colonialism and the interests of the Indian people was to provide the long-term dynamics of the Indian national movement.

The notion of colonial economy did not emerge full blown at any particular moment. This was an uncharted field. J.A. Hobson, R. Hilferding, Rosa Luxemburg and V.I. Lenin were yet to appear in print. Karl Marx's seminal writings on colonialism in India and Ireland were not available. The challenge posed by the Indian reality was however still met. The analysis of colonialism was the result of the hard political and theoretical practice of many Indian economic thinkers and thousands of early nationalist political activists who debated and discussed nearly every economic issue that arose in contemporary administration and politics. Inevitably this analysis and a fresh conceptual framework to express it developed through gaps, omissions, inner contradictions and wide divergences among the nationalist thinkers. It developed through controversies on the colonial policies regarding trade, transport, currency and exchange, tariffs, finance, role of the state in the economy, land revenue and land tenures, labour and education.

However, a coherent and cohesive analysis of the character of the colonial economy and of its underlying forces based on a common perspective of independent modern economic development had emerged by the beginning of the 20th century. This analysis and perspective and the tradition of such analysis were the work of a large number of nationalist economists—the names of Dadabhai Naoroji, K.T. Telang, G.V. Joshi, G. Subramaniya Iyer, R.C. Dutt, P.C. Ray, Lajpat Rai, and G.K. Gokhale immediately come to mind. Mahadev Govind Ranade, or Justice Ranade as he was popularly called, made a major and original contribution to the emergence of this theoretical and scientific critique of colonial economy.

In 19th century India, economic ideas, analysis and theory were not of mere academic or intellectual interest. They were the very stuff of contemporary politics and journalism. The hegemonic aspects of colonial rule in India were based on two basic ideological notions: (a) that British rule was 'benevolent', that is, the British ruled India in the interests of the Indian people and they were developing and modernizing India[2]; and (b) that British rule was invincible. The 19th century nationalist intelligentsia controverted the first of these notions in a fundamental manner, though they still accepted the second notion. Consequently, defence of colonialism or its basic critique became the chief form of ideological struggle between the alien rulers and the leaders and activists of the rising national movement. The latter had already by the first decade of the 20th century fully and scientifically worked out the main outlines of the nationalist critique of the economics of colonialism in India. The leaders of the later phases of the national movement were to rely heavily on this critique. They propagated it on a massive scale among the common people, but they made hardly any advance over it. Their politics were to be distinguished from the early, moderate politics by greater political militancy and mass mobilization but not by the content of their economic critique of colonialism.

Justice Ranade's economic writings were a major weapon in this ideological struggle between colonialism and the nationalists. The consequence of this struggle was the gradual erosion of the British hegemony over the minds of the Indian people; it was to weaken and then destroy the halo of beneficence around British rule which had led the Indian people to acquiesce in this rule. It was inevitable that in time this erosion would spread to the political field and generate a popular anti-imperialist movement.

To counterpose to the colonial pattern of economic change, an alternative pattern of development was needed. The only alternative available to the Indians at the time was that of capitalist development that was then occurring in Britain, U.S.A., Europe and Japan. Even while noticing the weaknesses of contemporary capitalism—the inequality, the acquisitiveness, the greed, the predatory characteristics, the disruption of existing values and institutions—the nationalist intellectuals opted for, and actively worked for, independent capitalist development; that is, their development perspective remained confined within bourgeois framework—they visualized independent economic development within a capitalist framework. In nearly every aspect of economic life they championed capitalist development in general and the interests of the industrial capitalists in particular. It was not that they were committed to the narrow interests of the capitalist class. It was because they believed that industrial development along capitalist lines was the only way to economically develop the country, or that, in other words, the interests of the industrial capitalist class objectively coincided with the national economic interests of the country. They believed that the capitalist class alone could accomplish the task of industrializing the country which they were advocating in their speeches and writings. They had to look for Indian agents of independent industrial development, otherwise their critique of colonialism would appear to be 'up in the air', hanging in a social vacuum, abstract, unrealistic and utopian, lacking in viability, especially as contemporary colonial administrators and British economists like John Stuart Mill constantly pointed to the relative absence in India of any other agents of modern industrial development except foreign capitalists. The alternative to looking up to an indigenous capitalist class was to look up to the colonial state and foreign capitalists. Who else could have initiated the process of industrialization? To think of socialism in the absence of modern industry and a working class would have been a pure intellectual pastime. (In any case Marx's *Capital* was not available in English till early 1890s). Consequently, the early nationalists came to look upon the Indian capitalists as the class agents or carriers of their anti-colonial programme of industrializing and developing the country. Ranade was one of the chief proponents of this capitalist pattern of independent economic development.

Two other basic aspects of the early economic outlook of the early nationalists were important: (1) They developed an integrated approach towards the problem of economic development. They were primarily concerned with the problem of economic development as a whole and not with economic advance in isolated sectors. (2) They maintained that the core of economic development was the application of modern science and technology to industry and agriculture. Above all, economic development meant rapid industrial development of the country. Consequently, they looked at nearly all contemporary economic issues and policies in their relationship to this paramount aspect of industrialization.

The basic weakness of the early nationalists lay in their politics. Most of them did not adopt a strongly political anti-imperialist position. They continued to believe that their economic and other projects could be realized with the cooperation of the rulers even though it might require a great deal of political agitation to persuade and pressurise the rulers to extend cooperation. Moreover, they still could not get rid of the belief in the invincibility of British rule. Indian people, they felt, were in no position to politically challenge the mighty British empire. Nor could they bridge the wide gulf between themselves and the people. They did not attempt to take their economic and political agitation to the common people, to organize popular agitations and movements and political struggles around their economic demands and policies. At the same time, it may be reiterated that their economic agitation attacked one of the two major pillars of British hegemony over the Indian people and thereby cut at the roots of colonial rule and sowed the seeds of political disaffection and 'disloyalty'. In fact, many of them made the political transition when they realized that there could be no national economic regeneration 'except by their getting rid in the first instance of their European rulers'.

The issue of the political bearings of the nationalist economic agitation was to lead to a major divide among nationalist economic thinkers. Ranade was, in particular, to become a major leader of the 'dissidents' in this respect. While Dadabhai Naoroji and most of the other early nationalists were to pursue their economic critique to its logical political conclusion, to link the failure of the administration to pay heed to their economic advice to the politically dependent status of the country, to conclude that British administration was 'only the handmaid to the task of exploitation', and in the end to point out that control over political power was essential for the implementation of nationalist economic demands, Ranade tried to separate economic issues from politics and reduce his emphasis on economic demands which he felt could not be realized under colonial rule. Thus the *Ranade school of Indian economists* came to be differentiated from the Naoroji school not only in politics but even in emphasis on specific economic demands even while the two shared a common critique of colonial economy.

II

As we have pointed out, Justice Mahadev Govind Ranade was a major member of the group of economists who subjected British colonialism in India to a basic economic critique and helped evolve an alternative path of economic development. He had, moreover, in G.V. Joshi an equally profound co-worker and in Gopal Krishna Gokhale a worthy disciple. Because of his deep learning and wide intellectual reach, extensive writing and speaking, multisided activity which covered almost every area of life from economics and politics to social and religious reform and re-writing of Indian history, and his high moral authority as a nationalist leader and social reformer, *Ranade influenced the social, economic and political thinking of several generations of the Indians.* In the economic field, Ranade covered almost every area, knitting industry, agriculture, finance, foreign trade, currency, tariff, role of the state, and economic theory into a single whole. He thus became the founding father of what came to be known as "Indian Political Economy".

Ranade did not of course make a direct connection between the economic problem and politics. Not that he was unaware of the connection, but he believed that in the then stage of India's social development the economic problem was more important than the political problem.[3]

From his college days, *Ranade took an active interest in economics as a subject.* Economics was one of the subjects he taught at Elphinstone College, Bombay, where he began his working life. His study of earlier and contemporary leading economists was extensive. Adam Smith, Ricardo, James Mill, John Stuart Mill, Malthus, Bastiat, McCulloch, Torren, Jevons and Senior among British economists, Hamilton, Carey among the Americans, Fredrick List among the Germans, were some of the economists whose works he studied critically and mastered. He devoured blue books and government reports. His mastery of contemporary statistics was unmatched. In fact, he initiated the tradition among Indian nationalist economists of trying to acquire mastery of empirical data. The memoranda, petitions he prepared and the articles he wrote were based on unimpeachable data. Nobody was ever able to find a factual or statistical flaw in them. Whenever a young man came to him wanting his guidance in working in the cause of the nation, he would ask him to go through a blue book and prepare its digest. Only those who passed this test were taken under his wings.

As a student of history and of world economy, *Ranade analysed Indian economy in a historical and comparative perspective*; and he constantly tried to correlate Indian economic problems to the historical experience of other countries and to contemporary economic theories. As a wide-ranging thinker he also placed them in their social and political setting.

As in the case of other nationalist economists, the backdrop to Ranade's economic thinking was provided by two fundamental problems. One was India's deteriorating economic condition and the phenomenal and growing poverty of the Indian masses.(270-1)

The other problem was that of the basically unbalanced, dependent and colonial structure of the economy. Referring to the unbalanced economic structure, Ranade wrote in 1890:

> There can be no doubt that, whatever may have been our improvement in other respects, we have in recent times become more than ever dependent upon the single resource of Agriculture, precarious and contingent as that resource is, upon influences we cannot control or count upon with certainty. The coordination of Industries, which regulates the due proportion of men who plough the soil and raise raw produce, with those who manufacture the raw produce, and others still who exchange and distribute it, and the interplay of whose three-fold activities make a Nation thrive, was never a strong factor in our collective Social Polity. We have been all along like most Ancient Nations, more or less exclusively agricultural. But our contact with the world outside, and the freedom of Exchange which has resulted in consequence, have

> produced one most undesirable result. They have aggravated the situation by making us more than ever dependent upon a single and precarious resource. The Industry and Commerce of the Country, such as it was, is passing out of our hands and, except in the large Presidency Towns, the Country is fed, clothed, warmed, washed, lighted, helped and comforted generally, by a thousand Arts and Industries in the manipulation of which its Sons have every day a decreasing share. Foreign Competition, not because it is foreign, but because it is the competition of Nature's powers against man's Labour,—it is the competition of organised Skill and Science against Ignorance and Idleness,—is transforming the monopoly not only of wealth, but what is more important of skill, talent and activity to others. (271)

The balance between the agricultural and industrial sectors of the economy had been disrupted "to a greater extent than it was before". This had led to increasing ruralization - "a distinctly retrograde move" - and forced millions of artisans to fall back upon "the single and precarious resource of agriculture". (340, 281, 277. Also 411-2)

Another consequence, said *Ranade*, was that the country's economic life came more and more under foreign economic domination. Indian market was dominated by foreign manufactures. In addition, "our shipping is not ours, not even the coastal trade is carried on in our bottoms"; "our Banking is not ours, though to a large extent we find the money which finances the Exchange Banks"; "the Insurance and the Freight and the Commission Business are all Foreign Monopolies, and the Foreign Merchant's hand is seen trafficking direct with our producers in the remotest and smallest villages"; "the Railways are admittedly foreign Monopolies". Thus, pointed out Ranade, "political ascendancy is not the only particular vantage ground which we have lost. Commercial and manufacturing predominance naturally transfers political ascendancy, and in this our collapse has been even far more complete". (273) Moreover, even though foreign political domination attracted "more attention", the "unfelt", the more invisible foreign economic domination was more "formidable" and "invidious" because it "paralyzes the springs of all the varied activities which together make up the life of a nation". (410)

Increasingly, noted Ranade, the Indian economy bore a colonial character. It became a producer of raw materials and consumer of foreign manufactures. Earlier North America and other British colonies had performed this function for England. But after the American War of Independence and the granting of political autonomy to other colonies, India had, in the 19th century, taken the place of the old colonies and come to be regarded by its rulers "as a Plantation, growing raw produce to be shipped by British Agents in British Ships, to be worked into Fabrics by British skill and capital, and to be re-exported to the Dependency by British merchants to their corresponding British Firms in India and elsewhere". (411. Also 272)

Overall, the sources of India's national income were being narrowed down and the Indian economy was, consequently, in a precarious condition: "when the whole situation is thus taken in at one view, we feel that we are standing on the edge of a precipice, and the slightest push down will drive us into the abyss below of unmixed and absolute helplessness". (273)

III

Ranade's three major concerns in the economic field were: Industrial development, agrarian structure and agricultural development and political economy. Like other nationalists, he gave intense and undivided commitment to economic development which he saw, above all, as the development of modern industry. As we have seen above he repeatedly pointed to the paralysis of the traditional handicraft industries under British rule. But he also accepted that their revival was no longer possible. "No Hand-made Industry", he wrote, "can hope to thrive in competition with industry moved by cheap natural Agents". (278) The remedy of the existing backward and disrupted economic condition, therefore, lay in modern industrial development which *Ranade advocated* with passion and urgency. The urgent task was to organize "cooperation" as the Indian capitalists had started doing and thus "to compete with the Foreigner" by working up raw materials through modern machines and thus, simultaneously, providing employment to India's working classes. True this would mean working "against great odds", for Indians had to go against old traditions and to compete with advanced countries "whose industrial organization has been completed under more favourable circumstances than our own". (425-6) And so he made one of his rare, fervent exhortations to his fellow countrymen:

> This is the practical work which Providence has set down for us to learn under the best of teachers....We have to improve our Raw Materials, or import them when our Soil is unsuited to their production. We have to organize Labour and Capital by co-operation, and Import freely Foreign Skill and Machinery, till we learn our lessons properly and need no help. We have rusticated too long; we have now to turn our apt hands to new work, and bend our muscles to sturdier and honester labour. *This is the Civic Virtue we have to learn, and according as we learn it or spurn it we shall win or lose in the contest....* I feel sure it will soon become the creed of the whole Nation and ensure the permanent triumph of the modern spirit in this Ancient Land. (Emphasis added.) (425.-6 Also 277-8)

From this point of view, citing Fredrick List, *Ranade pointed out the difference between economic development and economic growth* measured only in terms of increase in national income. "National well-being", he wrote, "does not consist only in the creation of the highest quantity of wealth measured in exchange value, independent of all variety of quality in that wealth, but in the full and many-sided development of all productive powers". (355. Also 336)

Moreover, wrote *Ranade*, in view of the fact that most of the arable land had been brought under cultivation and there was not much scope left for extended cultivation, industries were the only source left through which the pressure of population on land could be eased and the physical needs of the increasing population met. (376, 383)

In any case, it was necessary to put an end to India's further ruralization and its exclusive dependence on agriculture as it was because of uncertain rainfall a precarious source of livelihood. (271, 339, 411) Dependence on agriculture had another negative feature—it was "under the bane of the Law of Diminishing Returns" while modern industries were not subject to any such law. (339) It had also led to the absorption of waste lands and the exhaustion of soil through over-cultivation. (281)

Modern industries had also a vital bearing "on the education of the intelligence and skill and enterprize of the Nation". A purely agricultural country represented a lower stage of civilisation. There was, in it, "a tendency to stagnation and absence of enterprize and the retention of antiquated prejudices". (335) The increasing ruralization of India had meant "its rustication, i.e., a loss of power, and intelligence, and self- dependence". (340) On the other hand, factories and mills could "far more effectively than Schools and Colleges give a new birth to the activities of the Nation". (302)

Industrialization and the consequent urbanization were also necessary for healthy agriculture. Thriving towns and cities would provide the non- agricultural market divorced from which "no agriculture can be really productive". (340) Moreover, industrialization was the only means through which the population pressure on land could be reduced. This emphasis or industry did not mean that agriculture was to be neglected. Ranade repeatedly stressed a proper coordination of the three forms of economic activity—agriculture, industry and trade. (340) In fact, more than half of his economic writing and memorials pertained to agriculture.

As we shall see below in section V, *Ranade rejected the theory of international trade* with its emphasis on international division of labour according to which the natural role of India as a tropical country was to produce raw materials while the European countries were suited to trade and industry.[4] On the other hand, he held that India was fully capable of becoming a major industrial country. For proof, he pointed to the past achievements of India in handicraft manufactures, the wide production of raw materials needed by modern industries, the "natural aptitudes" of Indians for trade and industry and the "undeveloped but unlimited resources", and the existence of "peace and order". (338-9, 350-1, 426)

The need was to strive hard and remove the man-made obstacles from the path. In this context, *Ranade noted with enthusiasm the beginnings of modern industry* in India. He was optimistic that, despite India's struggle for implanting modern industry being "of a very unequal character, a struggle between a Giant and a Dwarf", it was now "gathering up its forces, and marshalling them in order to ward off the evil effects of the first surrender that it had to make by way of homage to British skill capital and enterprise". (412) Already, he wrote in 1893, Indians had in the last 40 years, invested nearly 500 million rupees in manufacturing, plantation, and mining industries. "This is an humble beginning, but it is a very hopeful one", he said . (421) Another ground for satisfaction, however"slight and scarcely perceptible", was the increase of towns and slight increase in the relative proportions of urban and rural populations—in the Bombay Presidency the share of urban population having increased from 17 to 19 per cent from 1872 to 1891. (422 and Article no. 21) Similarly, even though India still in the main exported raw materials and imported manufactures, change was noticeable even here. Exports of manufactured and partly manufactured goods were growing at a faster rate than the export of raw materials, and imports of raw materials were growing faster than the imports of manufactured goods. (414-5)

Giving overt expression to his optimism and concluding his 1893 paper on the "Present State of Indian Manufactures and Outlook of the Same", *Ranade* said that despite having to work against "great odds"—old traditions, poverty of developed resources, "the hostile competition of advanced races, whose industrial organization has been completed under more favourable conditions than our own", and the Free-Trade policy of the Government—"we may win, if we will only persevere in our efforts, and direct them by cooperation on a large scale into the proper channels". (426)

Apart from colonial domination, "the hostile competition of advanced races" and the free-trade policy of the Government, there were certain other obstacles to industrial development. The shortage of capital available for investment was one of these major obstacles: "Just as the Land in India thirsts for water, so the Industry is parched up for want of capital". (299) Why was this so? The accumulated capital and savings of the Indian people were scanty, said Ranade. Moreover, a large part of this potential capital was mopped up by the state through taxation. In any case, the desire for accumulation was rather weak because of the absence of peace and security in the past and the religious ideals of life which condemned the "ardent pursuit of wealth". There was also "an almost complete absence of a landed gentry or wealthy middle class" which, in Ranade's calculation, were the chief agents of accumulation of capital and its use in agriculture, trade and industry. Then there was "the economic drain of wealth and talents" because of foreign domination. (299, 337. Also see 424)

Even so, *Ranade* believed, there was plenty of capital "ready to hand awaiting secure investment". (305. Also see 274-5, 278) The problem was that of its mobilization and utilization. Unfortunately, most of this capital was scattered and immobile. Indian social institutions and laws encouraged "subdivision and not concentration of wealth". (337) The habit of mobilizing the scattered capital resources of the country through joint- stock companies was not developed. Instead, savings were either spent unproductively, for example in purchase of expensive jewellery, or hoarded and buried under one form or another. For example, often they were invested in Government securities and post office banks and were therefore not available for productive investment. India also lacked modern banks and other credit institutions through which scattered savings could be canalized into modern industries. "Hoards of capital" were, of course, "stored up" in the Presidency and other Exchange banks; but they were not available to Indian entrepreneurs. (274-5, 299, 304-5)

The remedy, said *Ranade*, lay in the people taking out their hoardings and turning them to "capital account", and in better organization of capital through the promotion of modern banks, insurance companies, etc., so that those who saved could be brought "face to face" with those who needed capital for investment. (306ff) Above all, since modern industry made "large investments of capital a necessity, and thus handicaps all individual efforts beyond rivalry", Indians must learn to cooperate and combine individual efforts by adopting the institution of joint-stock companies for large undertakings. In this respect, as we will see below, Ranade also pleaded for active state aid and encouragement. (278-9)

The dearth of trained technical personnel was another factor hampering the growth of modern industry. The answer, said Ranade, lay in importing foreign technicians and training Indians in technical institutes in India and abroad and through "the far more practical discipline of Factories and Mills at work". (278) In 1881, through the Poona Sarvajanik Sabha, Ranade appealed to the princes, big zamindars, the rich millionares of Bombay, and other rich Indians to endow scholarships to enable Indian students to go to England, France, Germany, Russia and the United States of America to study their arts and manufacture so that on their return they could help revive Indian economy and society. Citing the example of Japan and

China in this respect, he pointed out that strong efforts to start cotton mills here and there could not compensate for the ongoing industrial prostration for "the mechanical and engineering departments" of these mills were "entirely dependent upon imported skill for their very existence". Modern factories could "never be said to have taken root in the soil till we have a race of men among ourselves fully trained to plan, establish and work every department of manufacturing and trading with efficiency and cheap native skill", concluded the Sarvajanik Sabha appeal.[5]

According to *Ranade*, there was a *positive correlation between industrial and economic development* and a people's social institutions, customs, psychological make up -- "habits of mind"-and culture in general. Change from a rural to an industrial economy presupposed, wrote Ranade, "a change of habits, it postulates the previous growth of culture and a spirit of enterprize, an alertness of mind, an elasticity of temper, a readiness to meet and conquer opposition, a facility of organization, social ambition and aspiration, a mobile and restless condition of capital and labour". All these bourgeois virtues developed over "centuries of Freedom and Progress". But if Indians wanted to develop into a manufacturing country they had to be acquired. (383-4) Similarly, referring to the paucity of iron and coal in India, Ranade said that, though abundance of iron and coal explained the success of foreign competition, far more important than these materials was "the spirit and skill which work them and which conquered India long before Steam Power came into use". "If we but acquire the spirit and the skill", he exhorted, "the resources will be discovered in yet unexplored situations all over the country".(274)

This weakness of the entrepreneurial spirit was, however, believed Ranade, not due to any inherent weakness of national spirit. As we have seen above, he blamed Indian social institutions and laws, the past political condition, the prevailing religious ideals of life and in general conservative habits of mind for the absence of this spirit. Through his historical essays he tried to show how this 'spirit', the qualities of daring and organization, a restless condition of mind, and the facility of organization were to be found in abundance in the days of Shivaji and his successors and how Brahamanical domination under the Peshwas had led to retrogression.[6] The remedy to the present situation lay in the radical altering of the social institutions and social outlook of the people and the imbibing of the new spirit of capitalism. "You cannot have a good economic system when your social arrangements are imperfect";[7] and in his inaugural address at the Allahabad session of the Social Conference in 1892 he put his conception of the changes in the outlook and ideas and social practices in the form of a catechism: "A change from constraint to freedom, from credulity to faith, from status to contract, from authority to reason, from unorganized to organized life, from bigotry to toleration, from blind fatalism to a sense of human dignity".[8]

Ranade was a most consistent and vocal supporter of the idea that the state in India had to play a crucial role in the promotion of industrialization and economic development. He delineated the active role of the state in the economy not only forcefully but even with some originality. *Ranade was convinced that the Indian capitalist class on its own would find it difficult to industrialize the country* for it lacked knowledge, had a weak financial base and faced a narrow internal market and uncertain business prospects. It would, on the other hand, respond positively if state support and protection were extended to it, and if it was covered against early risks of enterprise. Hence he advocated a comprehensive and systematic policy of state aid to individual enterprise. The other side of the model was that the state in an underdeveloped country had a duty, an obligation to actively aid economic development. "The state," he said, "is now more and more recognised as the National Organ for taking care of National needs in all matters in which individual and cooperative efforts are not likely to be so effective and economic as National effort. This is the correct view to take of the true functions of the State." (344. Also 296, 365)

In India, the state's role was enhanced further because of the absence of protection. *Ranade* launched a frontal attack on the validity of *laissez-faire* as a doctrine of state functions, particularly as applied to an economically backward country like India. This doctrinal attack on *laissez-faire* is discussed below in section V. At the same time, he discussed the past and present practices of the Government to show that it had not followed a *laissez-faire* policy and had, instead, taken a direct and active part in pioneering and promoting British industrial and commercial enterprises and granting special privileges to British capitalists in India. (296, 355ff.) It had promoted railway construction by giving state guarantees of profit to private railway companies, and later it had itself taken up the construction of state railway. (295-6, 345) It had pioneered at great state expense the introduction of cinchona, tea and coffee plantations in the country. (297, 344) It had given favourable concessions to iron industry and spent considerable state funds in the form of geological surveys, experimental trials, and subsidies for its promotion. (355. Also 344) It had even worked for a long time several coal mines on its own account. (300. Also 344) There was thus no question of enunciating a new principle in the matter of state aid to industry; "the principle of state-help and guidance in pioneering new enterprize has thus been accepted and acted upon by the Government here." (355. Also 295-6) The question only was that of the form and character of state aid and the nature of enterprises to be aided. The principle should be that of catering to the 'Indian wants'. Instead of promoting plantations and infrastructure in the form of means of transport, as in the past, state aid should now be diverted to the promotion of modern manufacturing industries. (296-8, 301) "Facilities of communication are certainly desirable advantages," wrote Ranade, "but more desirable still is the capacity to grow higher kinds of produce, and develop manufacturing and industrial activities.... A Railway runs from one end of the country to the other, and leaves no permanent impression upon the face of the country, at least none so durable and penetrating as that which surrounds a great Manufactory." (296)

In the choice of industries to be taken up for state support, Ranade suggested certain priorities. A major consideration was to be that of import substitution, availability of raw materials and the needs of further industrial development. Keeping all these factors in view, Ranade recommended that iron and steel industry and coal mining should be assigned the top priority, (300) because iron and steel industry typified "the Resources of wealth on which our future prosperity mainly depends." (350)

India was already importing nearly 250,000 tons of iron and steel, apart from machinery, mill works and railway materials. In 1888-89 it imported nearly 110 million rupees worth of iron and steel goods. On the other hand, India was endowed "more richly with iron ore than almost any other country in the world." Furthermore, India had a rich tradition of iron production in the past when it produced iron of "world-wide fame" and not only supplied its own needs but also exported iron products to other countries. (300, 350-2) Similarly, coal mining was a priority sector. Availability of indigenous coal as a cheap fuel lay "at the bottom of the success of any organized attempt to revive the Industry under modern conditions." In this respect too, nature had been "magnificent in her gifts," India had very large coal reserves. (352)

Among consumer industries, keeping in view the large Indian market and the sensivity of British interests to any curbs on their exports to India, *Ranade suggested that priority be accorded to sugar and oil industries*, for in sugar India competed "not with England, but with China, Mauritius and the Straits Settlements." Similarly, India exported oil seeds on a large scale and imported oil. Here too Indian producers of oil would compete mainly with Ceylon, Mauritius and Straits Settlements. Other industries where, according to Ranade, there was scope for new enterprises on these bases were breweries, woollen manufacturing, tanneries and manufacture of paper and glass. (300-1)

State aid and encouragement to industry and agriculture could take many, varied forms. Following were some of the ways, advocated by Ranade, for the promotion of economic development by the state:

(i) Since according to *Ranade* a major lacuna in Indian industrial effort was the lack of adequate and cheap capital in the hands of Indian entrepreneurs, state aid's most important role was "to supply this want". (299) This it could do, first, by helping mobilize and concentrate the existing scattered capital and transform it into industrial capital through state assisted banks and other credit institutions which should be given facilities for the recovery of loans. (276, 278-9, 364) The Government should also help an industrial company to float its own debentures. (364) Second, and more important, it should directly advance loans to Indian capitalists at low rates of interest and under proper supervision. (279, 297-300, 364) The Government might itself borrow money to make these loans, or it might create special financial corporations which would borrow funds from the Government at low interest and advance them as loans to rural or urban industrialists. Local or municipal boards might also be empowered to perform this function of acting as intermediaries between the Government and the entrepreneurs. Government could lend the savings deposited with it, which were "wholly unproductive", to the local bodies, financial corporations and district corporate banks for this purpose. Thus, "each District might thus have a Fund to develop its resources in its own way, and several Districts might combine together to support a strong undertaking for common advantage". The Government should, of course, exercise proper supervision over the disbursement of these loans, "with judicious supervision the whole face of the Country might be changed in the course of a few years." (301-2)

(ii) The Government should induce investment in new industries by providing security to the investors by giving guarantees of minimum profit similar to those given to railway companies. (364. Also 275, 279, 297, 344, 365) This guarantee was particularly needed for an industry like the iron and steel industry where "no dividend can be expected for the first few experimental years" and where "no capitalist would venture, unless the concessions are liberal, and a subsidy promised on the plan which helped the Guaranteed Railway Companies to obtain their capital." (357-8) The other example held up for emulation by Ranade was that of the Culture System in Indonesia, though he grossly misunderstood the character and economic impact of the Culture System; that however, hardly mattered in his scheme of things, for the only lesson he wanted to draw was that of state support to industrial effort. (Article no. 17) He also advocated, though with lesser emphasis, the grant of state subsidies to new industries "till private enterprise could support itself." (275-6, 279, 297) At the same time, he conceded that the Government should reserve the right to share in the profits of the aided enterprises. (364)

(iii) The Government purchased a large part of stores abroad. These stores constituted a considerable part of Indian imports of manufactured goods. They included such items as equipment for the Indian army and police, materials for water, gas and sewage systems, hospital equipment and medical stores, iron, steel and cement and other materials required for docks, bridges, buildings and roads, telegraph and telephone equipment, stationery and other materials consumed by the administration, and tracks, bridges, rolling stock and building materials for state railways. All but an insignificant part of these stores were purchased in Britain. *Ranade* argued that the Government should purchase these stores in India and thus give a powerful impetus to indigenous industrial efforts. (276, 279,

345, 364) Advocating a radical departure from the policy of *laissez-faire*, he suggested that when some items of these stores were not available in India, the Government should manufacture them in state factories. (276, 279, 345) Generalizing this suggestion, he also asked the Government, though in a rather low key, to pioneer new industries. (279, 344-5)

(iv) The Government should collect and disseminate industrial and commercial information. It should also promote technical education in various ways. And to perform all these functions, it was necessary to set up a separate department of commerce and industries. (279, 344, 364-5)

Even though emphasizing active state assistance, all his life Ranade held that finally economic regeneration must come from Indian people's own efforts; self-help and self-reliance had to be their watchwords. This was the conclusion to his public lectures in 1872; and in his inaugural address to the first Industrial Conference in 1890, he said: "State help is, after all, a subordinate factor in the problem. Our own exertion and our own resolution must conquer the difficulties, which are chiefly of our own creation." (279). And he exhorted Indians: "We have to work with a will, to pull long, and pull all, and to pull till we succeed." (276)

In pursuance of this self-help, *Ranade* undertook or advocated several steps. He pioneered the Industrial Association of Western India in 1890 and the Industrial Conference which first met at Poona in the same year with a view to promoting the creed of industrialism, awaken interest in industrial development, arouse the spirit of enterprise, create a confident and hopeful industrial outlook, and diffuse information regarding the scope and opportunities for various enterprises. His numerous articles and addresses on economic problems had the same objectives in view. He played an important part in the organization of several industrial ventures at Poona—the Cotton and Silk Spinning and Weaving Factory, the Metal Manufacturing Factory, the Poona Mercantile Bank, the Poona Dyeing Company, and the Reay Paper Mill.[9] According to Gopal Krishna Gokhale, "most of the industrial and commercial undertakings that have sprung up in Poona during the last twenty years owe a great deal to his inspiration, advice, or assistance."[10]

Surprisingly, except in the early 1870s, Ranade had little to say on Swadeshi. In his 1872 public lectures at Poona, he popularized the idea of Swadeshi, of preferring Indian goods even if they were costlier or inferior to foreign goods. These lectures so inspired the listeners that several of them, including Ganesh Vasudeo Joshi, popularly known as Sarvajanik Kaka, and Vasudeo Phadke, who later led an armed foray against the Government, took a vow to wear and use only Swadeshi articles. Earlier in Poona, just after coming there, Ranade and Joshi had started a cooperative Company to deal in Swadeshi goods.[11] In 1874 he joined Joshi in organizing on behalf of the Poona Sarvajanik Sabha the first annual exhibition of Swadeshi articles produced in the small-scale factories of Maharashtra.[12] But not a word on the subject is to be found in his later writings and addresses. Perhaps, as brought out below, what he said about the drain and tariff protection of not making vain efforts, also explains his later attitude to Swadeshi.

IV

The agrarian problem occupied a large part of Ranade's intellectual activity. He dealt at length with the relation between the peasant and the colonial state, the peasant and the landlord, and agriculture and industry. He also put forward the broad outlines of a capitalist agrarian structure as an alternative to the existing semi-feudal agrarian structure. In fact, all his analysis was based on the need for 'free' peasants and investing landlords. Articles 1-2, 4-6, 9, 11, 13-15, 18, 24 and 25 bring out his extensive writing on and analysis of the agrarian problem.

x x x x x

During the period of ***Ranade's*** intellectual endeavours, land revenue was the most important source of public income. Since in Bengal, Bihar and Orissa and part of Madras land revenue was permanently fixed at the end of the 18th century and was collected through zamindars and other intermediaries, the problem of relation between the peasant and the state did not concern these areas. Here it was the relation between the peasant and the landlord or the zamindar which mattered. On the other hand, in the Ryotwari areas the state taxed the peasant directly. In these areas and in temporary settled zamindari areas the system of assessment and the pitch of land revenue became the subject of concern and controversy. Ranade was at one with the other nationalist economists and nationalist opinion in a critique of the official land revenue policy as being based on a high rate of assessment, undue upward revision during periodic reassessment and a rigid system of collection. This policy was a major cause, said the militant economists, of the poverty of the peasant and the backwardness of agriculture since it interfered with the full emergence of private property in land and private investment in agriculture.

Ranade initiated the nationalist critique of the land revenue policy in the course of a series of articles in the *Journal of the Poona Sarvajanik Sabha* from 1879 to 1884. Thus, in 1879, he pointed to "the unwelcome truth" that operations of the Bombay Revenue Department "had pauperised the country." (2-3. Also 17-9) In 1881 he contended that "the revenue policy of the Government is responsible to a great extent for the present condition of the agrarian classes", that no other agrarian reform would "lead to any permanent beneficial result as long as the pressure of land revenue under the existing system of assessment continues unabated", and that "the state monopoly of land and its right to increase the assessment at its own discretion are the two most pre-eminent obstacles in the way of the growth of our material prosperity." (176 and 174. Also 178-9)

According to Ranade, a major negative aspect of the revenue system, as it operated in Maharashtra, was the immoderately high pitch of assessment which was continuously enhanced at each recurring settlement to a level which transformed land revenue into a virtual rack rent. (5-9, 159-60, 175-7) For example, he wrote in 1881 : "The only guarantee against excessive enhancement, which is found effective where land is held in private right, is the competition of the landlords among themselves. There is no place for this guarantee under the Indian system, because the land is the monopoly of the State, single and individual. The absence of such a check has resulted in wholesale enhancements all over the country to an extent of which the Government itself is now ashamed". (175) Land revenue thus absorbed more than half the "net or owner's economic rent." (11) In the case of inferior lands, land revenue was even more onerous as it trenched upon the wages of the cultivator and the profits of his capital. As he put it in 1879:

> Further as on all inferior lands the cost of cultivation and of the Ryot's subsistence approaches very nearly the whole value of the crop, no profits are earned by him, as he subsists only because he works on his field. There can be, therefore, no economic rent, and the Ryot pays the Government land-tax, either with borrowed money, or else from income derived otherwise than from his land. (9. Also 342)

Consequently, enhanced assessments in the revised settlements had "destroyed all private property in land." Settlement officials, moreover, disregarded the official provision guaranteeing non-taxation of private improvements in land; nor did they provide for any increase in the standard of life or "the wants of an increased population, with diminished resources of waste lands to fall back upon." In general, the periodic enhancements were "capricious", and full of "defects and fault"; they were made in a "haphazard" manner and "without reference to any principle." The principle of classification of soils followed by the settlement officers was also faulty. These defects and the resulting evil of high assessment were known to the officials and had been brought out by the Deccan Riots Commission; but they were kept up only because of "the strong tie of official comradeship, at once both the strength and the bane of all bureaucratic oligarchies." (3-4) Proof of the severity of the revenue demand lay in the annual remissions and suspensions of the demand that had to be made in the large number of peasant holdings sold for arrears of land revenue, and in the incidents of dacoities and peasant riots. (6-8) Summing up his critique of the periodic enhancements of revenue, Ranade wrote in 1884: "These ever-recurring revisions are a very serious evil, as they, so far from settling, unsettle men's minds, and create uneasiness by reason of their uncertainty. They harass the agricultural classes, and engender discontent by mistakes in assessments, they check expenditure on improvements, deteriorate the standard of agriculture, and involve great delay and heavy cost." (241) Rigidity of the assessment, said Ranade, was another major fault of the revenue system. (8) He also complained that the peasant was made to bear a much larger burden of public revenue than was borne by other classes of society. (178) He recognized that some of the weaknesses of the revenue system had their roots in the Government's adherence to the Ricardian theory of rent and in its belief that the state was the landlord or owner of land in India and that, therefore, land revenue was not a tax but rent in the Ricardian sense. Consequently, he set out to question and demolish both these premises of official policy. This has been discussed below in Section V.

Basic to Ranade's critique of the land revenue system with its high pitch of assessment was the belief that by siphoning off a large part of the ryot's possible savings it checked expenditure on agricultural improvements. (15, 18, 170, 174-8, 241-2) It also prevented capital investment in land by the moneyed classes—"the race of capitalists"—and joint-stock land banks, rendering "cooperation between the labouring and capitalist classes but impossible." (15, 178) Controverting the view widely current among officials that the inherent traits of character of the Indian ryot such as want of energy, ignorance, idleness, habitual improvidence and thriftlessness were responsible for his economic condition, *Ranade* asserted that the ryots could not be "fairly charged with these defects of character." Instead, it was "the precariousness of the seasons and the rack-renting policy of the settlements (which) continue to damp all their energies." (176) By making a comparative study of the condition of the peasants in France, Italy, Hungary, Austria, Switzerland, and Egypt, he argued that they too suffered from these character faults till the institutional conditions, in which they worked, were changed. "The French Peasant," he wrote, "was not always the abstemious and prudent citizen that he now is; there was a time when Arthur Young mourned over the condition of the Agricultural Classes of France. The magic of Property and of Free Institutions have worked all this wonderful change." (194) The high pitch of land revenue also inexorably drove the ryot to the moneylender and to "borrow under great disadvantage." (160, 81-2) The conclusion was obvious to Ranade: there could be no agricultural development or improvement in the condition of the ryot without a proper reform of the land revenue system:

> All that they (ryots) demand is freedom from the oppressive dead-weight of revenue settlements, which paralyse their energies, and dissipate their strength in the hopeless struggle to better themselves in the social scale. Let the weight of this heavy hand be lightened, and the inner springs, activity and elastic power, will surge up in an upward movement of material well-being.... (179. Also 240)

But how was "the weight of this heavy hand" to be lightened? In the short-run, *Ranade favoured reduction in the burden of land revenue*, remission and scaling down in case of failure of crops and scarcity, modification of its rigidity, its payment in kind or at least in the form of a share of the crop, and scrupulous adherence to the principle of non- taxation of improvements carried out by the ryots. (8-10, 41-2, 80-1, 83, 93-4, 243-7, 258-9) In 1879, he recommended 1/16th of the gross produce, which would come to one-half of the economic rent or the letting value of the land, as the utmost limit of assessment for the Deccan districts. (12)

But, in the long run, no tinkering or trifling, no palliatives would work. (175, 177-8) The remedy must deal with the basic problem. It lay in permanently limiting the state demand on land so that "the magic of property" could operate freely in the countryside and the ryot, freed from the grasp of the settlement officer, felt that the land was his own property and exerted himself to save and invest in land, to improve the soil, and to use the latest scientific methods. (13-8, 175-9, 195). The case for the permanent settlement of land revenue was cogently argued by Ranade in nearly all of his early writings. For example, he wrote in 1881:

> ...The Ryots and the middle classes will look upon their lands as their own property, which under present circumstances it is found impossible to induce them to do. All improvements in husbandry suggested by science and experience pre-suppose a great expenditure of capital to be invested in land. The magic of property can alone induce people to incur such expenditure.... If the land-banks have succeeded in other countries so well, most of this success must be undoubtedly laid to the credit of the fact that the peasants in those countries are not tenants of the State, but own the lands they cultivate in absolute right. Without such a guarantee of full property, all endeavours to ameliorate the condition of the Ryots must fail to produce any but a temporary benefit. (177-8)

But what form would the permanent settlement take? Ranade's answer was unequivocal. He wanted permanent settlement of revenue with the ryots; he argued for "a permanent Ryotwari Settlement fixed in grain" and not the

Zamindari settlement on the Bengal pattern. (79) In 1884, he made the authoritative statement:

> ...the views which we have in this journal and elsewhere published from time to time have been too often misunderstood. We have never asked for a subversion of the Rayatwari tenure, or the substitution in its place of a Zamindari Settlement either on the Bengal plan of individual Zamindars, or on the North-West Provinces system of collective Zamindar village holdings. The Rayatwari system has obtained in this Presidency from time immemorial, and it is the only one suited to the democratic constitution of our rural society.... We have agitated for a permanent settlement of the assessment on the Rayat's holding in this Presidency.(254,.Also 5-6,90,195)

It is also interesting that Ranade wanted the benefits of the fixity of tenure to be extended to tenants; only, he added, in this matter "the Tenants of Government" should be extended "the same consideration as those of private Zamindars". (343. Also 95) In parenthesis, we may also point out that Ranade's position on the permanent settlement of land revenue has sometimes been misunderstood because, in other contexts, he welcomed the existence of zamindars and other superior holders because he was opposed to the reduction of "all classes to one dead level of helpless dependence" (2), expected the zamindars to perform the necessary function of the improving zamindars (16-7, 96), hoped that "with the growth of a leisurely and affluent class interested in the agricultural prosperity of the country, other liberal influences, represented by higher education and scientific cultivation, will spread abroad" (95), and refused to believe that the Bengal tenant was worse off than the Bombay ryot. (90)

Ranade was keen to meet the objection that the permanent settlement of land revenue would lead to loss of revenue, especially in case of a price rise. First, he argued that the increase in agricultural production and prosperity would lead to such an increase of government's revenue from other direct and indirect taxes that it would make up any loss due to the permanent settlement. Second, in a spirit of compromise, he suggested a modification under which land revenue would be fixed in perpetuity but could be changed on the sole ground, and to the extent, of changes in prices, whether upward or downward. This result could also be secured by fixing the permanent land revenue in grain, to be commuted into money every twenty or thirty years according to permanent changes in prices. (79, 96, 177, 240-6, 255-6)[13]

We may take note of two other aspects of *Ranade's thinking on the permanent settlement of land revenue*. Firstly, though the settlement was to continue with the ryot, he hoped that men of money—"capitalists"—would start investing in land either by buying the land of "the indifferent and lazy ryots" and then developing it or by financing the sturdy and efficient ryot to make the necessary improvements. (16) Second, it must be accompanied by other measures such as elementary and higher education, industrial development, and reduction of taxes, of the "extravagant" cost of Government, and of the "ever-expanding tribute" which India was paying to England. (97)

In the zamindari areas of Bengal, Bihar, Orissa, the North Western Provinces and Awadh (later U.P.), the Central Provinces (C.P.) and in parts of Punjab and Bombay, the actual cultivator was a tenant who paid rent to the zamindar out of which the latter paid land revenue to the Government. In the ryotwari areas, the peasantry was getting indebted and losing land to moneylenders, traders and professional classes and being reduced to the status of tenants-at-will on their own land. During the early 1880s, the Government undertook tenancy and rent and debt legislation to give some relief to the rack-rented, debt-ridden and disaffected tenantry. Ranade's attitude towards the agrarian structure was basically evolved during his discussion of this legislation as also of the land revenue problem. In general, Ranade opposed the existing semi-feudal agrarian relations in the zamindari as well as ryotwari areas and advocated their restructuring on an entirely new capitalist footing. In this he was powerfully influenced by land legislation in Prussia, Russia and France.

At the narrower plane of the official tenancy and land legislation, *Ranade supported it on grounds of equity and social justice*. In 1892, he provided the following justification for state intervention in agrarian relations:

> The Advanced Theory expounded by the Modern School fully justifies the attempts made by the Government here and in England to check the abuse of Competition among poor tenants by conferring Fixity of Tenure, by adjusting rents judicially for a term of years, and imposing limitations on its increase. In this matter the Tenants of Government claim the same consideration as those of private Zamindars. The justification of this active interference is as valid in regard to Agricultural Labourers and Tenants, as it is in the case of Factory Labourers and Miners in Europe. These people are unable to combine for self-protection, or at least their combination is not so effective as that of the Employers of Labour.... In the same spirit, the regulation of the Freedom of Contract in regard to the fixing of rates of interest in transactions between the poor disunited indebted class and the moneylenders, and the protection of immovable property from being sold away for improvident debts, not secured on the same, are all legitimate forms of protection of the weak against the strong, and not affect the real freedom of Distribution. The Advanced Theory concedes freedom where the parties are equally matched in intelligence and resources; when this is not the case, all talk of equality and freedom adds insult to the injury. It is in this spirit that the Distribution of Produce among the needy many and the powerful few has to be arranged, i.e., in a spirit of equity and fair play....

And, disagreeing with those advocating non-interference in agrarian relations, he concluded: "The orthodox Views of Finality in such matters must be reconsidered in all the relations of life." (343)

In discussing concrete tenancy legislation, for example, the Bengal Tenancy Bill, Ranade fully acknowledged the urgent need for remedial legislation and also justified the Government's right to undertake such legislation in spite of the

Regulations of 1793. In Bengal, he wrote in 1893, "the old customary rights of property have suffered a depression from long disuse", and the privileged zamindars "often press heavily, as in Behar, upon the Peasant majority of the population." Remedial legislation was, therefore, "urgently required to check these evils." But while favouring tenancy legislation as a short-term remedy to protect tenants, he opposed the Bengal Tenancy Bill because it would perpetuate the old pattern of agrarian relations, merely making it more complex and incapable of radical improvement, and act as a break on any real agricultural improvement. Under the Bill, he pointed out, both the landlord and the tenant would continue to live within the bonds of the old pattern of agrarian relations and the initiative of both the landlords and tenants would continue to be sapped. All that the Bill would succeed in doing was to increase their "mutual encumberances" and "the existing complexity of rights and interests", to reduce the landlords to "the class of Rent-receiving Pensioners" and teach the ryots "to look more and more to the State as their sole landlord, without acquiring the training necessary to raise them to a sense of their position." The Bill was no more than "tinkering with existing rights in the assumed interests of one class." The intended or unintended result of such tinkering would be that "the existing confusion will be still more confounded, class will be set against class" and, what was much worse, "the interests and ownership in land will still continue to be as divided as before between quarrelsome partners, and no real improvement will take place." Ranade made it clear that he did "not side with the optimist advocates of the existing condition of things" and that what was called for was "an urgent Reform, and a radical Reform." But, he added, the lines on which the Bill was framed were "radically mistaken." (224-30, 233-34) Before we discuss his model of 'radical reform', attention must be turned towards his attitude towards peasant's indebtedness and his relations with the moneylender.

x x x x x

Rural indebtedness increased during the last quarter of the 19th century and became an acute social problem, especially in ryotwari areas. High interest charges absorbed a large part of the peasant's income and his frequent inability to repay the debt led to the large-scale transfer of land to the non-cultivating moneylenders. The old peasant-proprietor was thus increasingly transformed into a tenant-at-will resulting in further depression of agriculture and the agriculturist. While the British Indian administrators looked upon the moneylender as the chief culprit, Ranade's approach was far more complex. Precariousness of weather, rack-renting by the Government and the rigidity of the revenue system compelled the peasant to go the moneylender, the only available source of rural credit, in order to avoid starvation and loss of land. The complicated and elaborate system of law accentuated the evil of usury for it helped the moneylender and encouraged him to seize possession of land. Thus the mass of ryots in the Deccan were "involved in heavy bonds of debt under circumstances beyond their control to a numerous mass of small creditors, largely foreign in their domicile, and not prepared to take up the cultivation of land on their own account." (20-5, 28-9, 160-3, 166, 176. The quotation is on p. 160)

While condemning "the sowcar's usurious dealings" and the increasing transfer of land to the moneylenders "who generally belonged to the mercantile and trading classes, and bought up the land for no other attraction than its character as a paying investment," (55) Ranade pointed out that the moneylender was, under the existing conditions and in the absence of alternative sources of credit, an economic necessity for he financed agricultural operations and enabled ryot to meet the land revenue demand. (27-8) It was, moreover, the British laws which had transformed him into an "unrelenting, and not infrequently, unscrupulous" person (102. Also 28-9, 107)

Again, as a short-term remedy, *Ranade gave unstinted support to judicial reform and control of the moneylender's activities.* This comes out clearly from his support to nearly all the provisions of the Deccan Agriculturists Bill, which the Government introduced in 1879 after the large-scale anti-moneylender riots of 1875, and other administrative measures undertaken to curb the moneylender's usurious practices. (See Article no. 2 and 80-1, 164-7) Justifying the Deccan Agriculturists' Relief Act, he wrote in 1881:

> The ordinary law assumes an equality of advantages and intelligence between the insolvent and uneducated Ryot and the thrifty and intelligent sowkar, which equality as a matter of fact does not exist. The assumption of equality was entirely a fiction of artificial legislation, and as it led to great abuses, it was time enough to correct the mischief by a return to the old conservative native traditions in favour of the protection of the weaker party. (165)

At the same time, *Ranade* qualified his full-throated support to the Act with the statement that it would bring relief to the ryot only if it was worked "in conjunction with a more liberal land revenue policy, and *on that condition alone.*" (Emphasis in original. 22-3. Also 164, 167-8) Otherwise, he asserted, the Act would do no lasting good, and might even "aggravate the present condition of things." (27) Since his need for credit remained, "as soon as a Ryot is white-washed, he is again driven into debt by his necessities, and the process has no end." (173.For detailed treatment, see 164, 167-8, 171-4. Also 79)

Apart from repeatedly recommending reform of the land revenue system and eradication of the ryot's poverty through the development of industry—through "a diminution of the pressure of the agricultural population on the land by opening out of new avenues for labour and industry and surplus capital" (164)—Ranade pressed for the provision of easier and cheaper credit facilities to the ryot. He argued that while it was necessary to save the ryot from the usurious moneylender, it was equally necessary to meet his necessary needs of credit for carrying on agricultural operations and for investment in improvements and, therefore, to provide him with facilities for borrowing funds at low rates of interest. To stop or curb the functioning of the moneylender without providing alternative sources of credit would mean to once again compel him to go to the moneylender but on much worse conditions than before. (Article no. 9, in particular 170-2; and Article no. 18) The answer lay in the organization of a network of agricultural banks in India. Ranade made an intensive study of the problem of rural credit in India in two essays "Land Law Reform and Agricultural Banks", published in 1881 and "Reorganization of Real Credit in India", published in 1891. (Articles nos. 9 and 18). He made an intensive and comparative study of credit organizations and their role in agricultural development in various countries of Europe where, he argued, conditions were comparable to those prevailing in India; and put forth a detailed plan for creating agricultural banks and other credit institutions so that capital flowed into agriculture. But this would require an active role by the Government; the work could not be left to private effort. This did not mean that it would have to spend its own funds. There was sufficient "capital ready to hand awaiting investment." The steady demand for Government loans at mere 4 per cent interest showed that there was "a considerable amount of floating capital available." In fact, "funds will be forthcoming to any amount, if only the Government would either organize credit agencies or support private effort and subsidise and guarantee it against risk, as had been done in the case of railways. Such state support to private effort had been given in Turkey, Egypt, Russia, Greece, Austria, Germany, France, Denmark, Sweden and the USA through banks, credit fonciers, credit agricole, Le Caissa Hypothecain, mortgage banks and mutual credit associations. In the absence of such support and because of land revenue policy, "it is not found convenient by the capitalist classes to risk their savings on investments in the improvement of land by advancing loans to the agricultural classes." Thus, state help in the form of State control and supervision was needed to inspire confidence among the lenders, and to bring "face to face" people "seeking secure investment" with those "who need their help". (Articles nos. 9 and 18) Putting forward a concrete proposal in 1891, Ranade asked the Government "to organize District or City committees of Indian capitalists, to empower them to receive deposits at fixed rates and lend them at slightly higher rates to the borrowers on the security of lands, or houses, etc." Furthermore, "the loans of these District Committees should be allowed priority over all other debts, and exempted from all duties, and certain and speedy execution should be permitted to them." He ended his 1891 paper with the exhortation: "The recuperative powers of Nature and Art are limited, and cannot stand the dead weight of prohibitive rates of interest, made necessary by disorganized Credit, and the uncertainties and delays and expenses of Civil Proceedings. Remove these difficulties and hinderances, and Credit will rise to its natural and healthy level." (321)

Interestingly Ranade also maintained that the old debts of the debt- ridden ryots had to be compounded and liquidated before they could stand on their own feet with the aid of agricultural banks. (171, 195)

Ranade was convinced that no breakthrough in agricultural development or peasant's welfare could occur within the existing structure of land relations. Basing himself upon the experience of the development of the agrarian structure in Britain, France, Russia and, above all, in Prussia, he came to the conclusion that in place of tinkering with the existing structure an entirely new structure based on capitalist relations of production should be evolved. Instead of a system where restrictions were placed on all agrarian classes, the new system should be based on "the principle of individual and independent property", that is, all land should be made "the absolute property of the owner" whether the landlord or the peasant-cultivator. (Article no. 13)

In 1883, after a detailed critique of the Bengal Tenancy Bill, he put forth his own proposals based on the pattern of Prussian land legislation:

> While the Bill would create an artificially defined class of subordinate Tenants tempted on all occasions to throw off their subjection, and a Landlord class hemmed in on all sides by inconvenient obligations, we would create an entirely independent Peasantry trained by thrift to prize its independence, and at the same time confer as absolute property in their lands on the Zamindars and Tenure-holders. (234)

Thus, Ranade's model of capitalist agriculture was two-pronged. The majority of the cultivators,—"the backbone of its (the country's) strength and prosperity"—would be free and independent peasants, who would be unencumbered in every way, who would enjoy their property in absolute possession, and who would therefore save and invest and work hard on their lands under the inspiration of 'the magic of property'. (232-5. Also 177-8, 195, 216-7) But this alone would not suffice. In Indian conditions, agriculture based entirely on small peasant-proprietors would neither be stable and progressive nor utilise the best energies of all classes of people nor make proper use of irrigation facilities, advanced techniques, etc. "A complete divorce from land of those who cultivate it is a national evil, and no less an evil is it to find one dead level of small Farmers all over the land," he wrote. (233. Also 16) Therefore, for a proper and balanced development of agriculture, it was necessary to have, he asserted, a large class of agrarian capitalists, who would be, unlike the Bengal zamindars, complete owners of their land on the model of British landlords or German junkers. "If this country sadly wants a proved and independent Yeomanry as the backbone of its strength and prosperity", he wrote in 1883, "it no less equally needs the leading and the light of Propertied men." (232-3) As early as 1879 he had written: "The monied classes, having no interest in the land, cannot occupy the position, nor enjoy the status, nor discharge the functions of landlords. The absence of such a class retards progress in all directions." And then expressed the hope that, once the land was free of artificial restrictions, "the provident and thrifty classes will succeed to the ownership of land, and a class of landlords will spring up all over the country, whose interest it will be to make the most of the resources of the soil, and of the great public works constructed by the Government." (16) And added the interesting remarks:

> In all old and backward countries like India, there is always only a minority of people who monopolise all the elements of strength. They are socially and religiously in the front ranks, they possess intelligence, wealth, thrifty habits, knowledge, and power of combination. The majority of the population are unlettered, improvident, ignorant, disunited, thriftless, and poor in means. No political manipulation can hold the balance between these two classes, power must gravitate where there is intelligence and wealth, and it is a hopeless struggle to keep up a poverty-stricken peasantry in possession of the soil, and divorce the natural union of capital and land. (17. Also 10, 12-3, 17-8, 78-9)

One of *Ranade's major criticism of the Bengal Tenancy Bill* of 1893 was that it tended to reduce Khamar land, or land in personal possession of the zamindars, and to increase land under the tenants. (225-6) In contrast, he praised the Prussian land legislation for permitting the old feudal lords to convert a part of their estates into large capitalist farms under their absolute unencumbered possession. (218-20, 222-4) Similarly, a major reason why he criticized the land revenue policy of the Government so stringently was because of his belief that it hampered the growth of large-scale capitalist agriculture.

It is, of course, to be carefully noted that Ranade's landlord was not a "rent receiving pensioner" or parasitie zamindar. He did not commit the mistake of seeing the Bengal zamindars as the capitalist landlords of his scheme. On the other hand, he reminded his readers that the situation in Bengal during the 19th century and in Prussia before the reforms of the first half of the 19th century was similar because there was "the closest resemblance between them (the Bengal zamindars) and the great Feudal aristocracy of Prussia." It was partially because of this resemblance that he advocated a careful study of the Prussian land question. (212-3) Nor was his new large landowner the traditional moneylender who gave loans or bought land to practice usury and not to assume the role of an agricultural entrepreneur. (160) Ranade's landlord was an improving landlord as in Britain or Prussia, "who will be interested equally with the Ryot in increasing the productive capacity of his land." Ranade was confident that impelled by "the magic of property" guaranteed by a permanent settlement of tenure and removal of all restrictions and encumberances, the landlords or zamindars would "apply themselves heart and soul to the improvement of the soil, 'supplying cultivators with superior seed and manures and machinery'." (96 and 83-4. Also 10)

To sum up this aspect: *Ranade* advocated that agrarian relations should be based on the creation of two new and basic agrarian classes which would live side by side: (a) a large petty land-owning peasantry which would be free of all encumberances, whether of the state or the landlords, and which would be bolstered by a permanent and low land tax and the provision of cheap credit through agricultural banks; and (b) a large class of capitalist farmers and landlords who, being unhampered by any tenancy rights or other restrictions, would be in complete possession of their land and in a position to invest capital, improve the soil, use fertilisers and better seeds, etc., and utilise the latest, advanced techniques.

In this respect he held up for approval and imitation the pattern of landownership, based on the growth of absolute property both in the landlord class and in the peasantry, that had been brought into existence in Prussia by the middle of the 19th century. (216-20, 225) In Prussia in 1860, he pointed out, 15 per cent of culturable land belonged to the state or the church, 44 per cent to large estate owners, 35 per cent to peasant proprietors, and 5 per cent to petty owners. Thus, he approvingly remarked, land had been divided equally between "the rich landlords and the poor Free men", and the feudal serf converted into a free proprietor and the feudal lord into an unencumbered owner of his property. (222-4) Applying the lessons of Prussia to India, Ranade advised: "High and petty farming, with an upper ten thousand of the holders of large landed estates, and a vast mass of peasant farmers, this mixed constitution of rural society is necessary to secure the stability and progress of the country." (233. Also 234-5) He also hoped that a proper class balance would be struck between the "upper ten thousand" and the "vast mass of peasant farmers", once the latter grow "in thrift, in knowledge and in power of combination." (233 and 17)

How were these two new productive agrarian classes to be brought into existence? Ranade had two sets of remedies to offer In the ryotwari areas, the permanent settlement of land revenue at low rates would transform the depressed 'state tenants' into sturdy peasant-proprietors, who would be able to borrow from agricultural banks and moneylenders for making improvements in land. (177-8) At the same time, in a regime of free competition and in the absence of any restrictions and encumberances on land, those among the moneyed classes who were willing and keen to perform the functions of capitalist landlords would buy the land of "the indifferent and lazy" ryots. (77-8. Also 15-6) He was also convinced that such a class of people who possessed "intelligence, wealth, thrifty habits, knowledge, and power of combination" did exist in India. (17) On the other hand, the thrifty, hard-working ryot would slowly "extend his operations and rise to a better position", i.e., become a capitalist farmer or what would be later called a kulak. Also, in course of time, he hoped, "the provident and thrifty classes will succeed to the ownership of land, and a class of landlords would spring up all over the country, whose interest it will be to make the most of the resources of the soil, and of the great public work constructed by the Government. (16) It was because of the fear that restrictions on peasant's right to alienate or transfer land with a view to saving him from expropriation by the moneylender would check the inevitable tendency towards "concentration of the landed capital of the country" in the hands of the more efficient and resourceful peasants and capitalists that Ranade opposed all such restrictions and argued for free transferability of land. (78)

For the zamindari areas of Bengal and Bihar, Ranade suggested a virtual copying of the Prussian precedent : both the zamindars and the tenants were to be raised to the status of independent proprietors of the soil, the zamindars to be transformed into capitalist landlords and the tenants to landowning peasants; but this was to be done through harmonizing the interests of the two without setting "class against class", (225.Also 230, 233) without "any violent disruption of the economic relations of different Classes of society, and without the shock of Revolution or internecine class struggles", (224) without any one-sided expropriation of the rights of the zamindars, and, therefore, with the zamindars being duly compensated for the abolition of any of their rights. (228) His own detailed proposal was as follows:

Full proprietary rights were to be conferred on the tenants but only over a part of the land under tenancy. As the price of purchase of these rights, they were to resign all rights over the remaining part of the land in favour of the zamindars. Thus one part of the presently tenanted land would be assigned in full ownership to the erstwhile tenant and the other part, also in full ownership, to the zamindar. If it was found that the zamindar needed to be further compensated, he might be paid money rent charges over a number of years. Thus, the zamindars would be paid some compensation for the loss of zamindari rights and permitted to resume a part of the land under tenancy for personal cultivation; they would be transformed from rent-receiving zamindars into entrepreneurial capitalist farmers and landlords.(230-1)

Ranade also tried to give a more concrete shape to this proposal. He proposed that in Bengal 2/3rds of the occupancy land and 1/2 of the non- occupancy land should be made over to the tenant in absolute right, and 1/3rd of the occupancy land and 1/2 of the non-occupancy land should be handed over as personal land to the zamindar. Since this division of land, he felt, would leave the zamindar partially uncompensated, the erstwhile tenant should continue to pay his old rent on the reduced holding under his possession for a period of thirty or forty years, "so as to repay balance of purchase money with interest." The Government might help hasten the process by advancing money to the tenants to purchase outright their zamindars' claims, which would amount to about 3,400 millions of rupees. Thus, Ranade hoped to "achieve the liberation of the Ryots in Bengal in a generation or two without any violence to vested rights."This plan would also "train and educate the people by a slow discipline of thrift to retain their newly acquired status."(231-2) It may be noted that, as was the case with the Prussian and Russian precedents he followed, Ranade's entire scheme was quite biased in favour of the zamindars. They would keep between 1/3rd to 1/2 of the land as personal possession in absolute right and get further compensated in the bargain. It was quite different from the later, more radical schemes of distributing zamindari lands to the actual tillers. It did, however, have the advantage of putting an end to the parantic non- developmental semi-feudal system and of opening up the path to agricultural development. Moreover, with the then existing man-land ratio, it would not have meant making millions of tenants landless as happened as a result of the implementation of the post-independence land reform legislation.

x x x x x

Although *Ranade* did not deal at length with the relationship between agriculture and industry, he did point out that industry alone could siphon off the excess agricultural population and create conditionsthe for agricultural development. In the wider context of Indian economy, he said, neither economic development could occur nor the agrarian problem solved unless the tendency towards the ruralization of the country was reversed and the pressure of the agricultural population on the land was reduced "by the opening out of new avenues for labour and industry and surplus capital." (164. Also 97) Similarly, pointing to the danger arising out of dependence "on extended cultivation, as the only resource for supplying the wants of our increasing population", he asserted that "the only escape from this danger lies in the direction of the gradual transformation of the chief means of our livelihood, and the growth of an Urban and Industrial Population." (376) As pointed out earlier, Ranade also argued that a country largely dependent on agriculture would be condemned to remain poor and grow poorer since agriculture operated "under the bane of the Law of Diminishing Returns" and, in India,"under the disadvantage of an uncertain rainfall." (339-40. Also 375-6) With his usual comprehensive grasp, Ranade also took note of the reverse relation between agriculture and industry: "There is no doubt, however, that the impetus given to agricultural pursuits will in the end communicate itself to other industries, and lead to a many-sided development of the country's resources in a way which cannot at present be anticipated." (174)

To relieve pressure of population on land, Ranade also advocated large- scale internal migration as well as external migration from congested regions and urged the Government to extend active support in this respect, though later he came to believe that there was not much scope for such migrations. (384 ff., 341, 375-6)

V

Ranade worked out elements of the concept of Indian Political Economy in several of his articles, but it took concrete and well-worked out form in his classic address on "Indian Political Economy" delivered at the Deccan College, Pune in 1892. (Article no. 19) His basic formulations have been discussed at length by several economists. Their influence was felt by most of Indian economic writers till the 1930s and even till the 1940s when the influence first of Alfred Marshall and the Neo-Classicists and then Keynes and Keynesians started becoming predominant. His formulations were also subscribed to on a wide scale by his contemporaries—and not only by economists like G.V. Joshi and G. Subramaniya Iyer but also others who commented on economic issues in the Press and on the platform. Just as in his economic policy formulations he had used the historical experience of other countries, in his theoretical framework he was deeply influenced by 19th century economists. In particular, he turned to those European and American economists who were dissenting in important aspects from many of the tenets of British Classical Political Economy—Fredrick List, Adam Miller, Hamilton and Henry Carey. He was highly critical of the position of English Classical economists like Adam Smith, Ricardo, Senior, Bastiat, James Mill, Torren, McCulloch, and Malthus, though he was influenced by John Stuart Mill and used him to support several of his own propositions.

Ranade denied the claim, quite popular among Indian administrators, that the assumptions of Classical political economy were universally and demonstrably true or valid for all times and places and for all stages of economic development. (For his brief summary of these assumptions, see pp. 327- 8 in the text.) These assumptions had been born out of the specific conditions of England and they furnished "valid explanations" of the economic condition of only those societies of which they were "approximately true." But, in fact, they "do not absolutely hold good of even the most advanced societies;" and they had hardly any validity in a backward, stagnant agricultural country like India where not competition and contract but status and custom and tradition ruled. (324-5, 328-9, 337, 306, 149-50) To quote him at length:

> It is obvious that in Societies like ours, they are chiefly conspicuous by their absence. With us an average Individual man is, to a large extent, the very antipodes of the Economical man. The family and the Caste are more powerful than the Individual in determining his position in life. Self interest in the shape of desire of Wealth is not absent, but it is not the only principal motor. The Pursuit of Wealth is not the only ideal aimed at. There is neither the desire nor the aptitude for free and unlimited Competition except within certain predetermined grooves or groups. Custom and State Regulation are far more powerful than Competition, and Status more decisive in its influence than Contract. Neither Capital nor Labour is mobile, and enterprising and intelligent enough to shift from place to place. Wages and Profit are fixed, and not elastic and responsive to change of circumstances. Population follows its own Law, being cut down by Disease and Famine, while production is almost stationary, the bumper harvest of one year being needed to provide against the uncertainties of alternate bad Seasons. In a Society so constituted, the tendencies, assumed as axiomatic, are not only not operative, but are actually deflected from their proper direction. You might as well talk of the tendency of mountains to be washed away into the sea, or of the valleys to fill up, or of the Sun to get cold, as reasons for our practical conduct within a measurable distance of time. (328)

Second, Ranade gave numerous instances to show that the past practice of British statesmen and the contemporary practice of other nations did not at all conform to the precepts or assumptions of Classical economics. (324-6, 331) There was, he wrote, "this conflict of practice with theory not in one, but all points, not in one place or country, but all over the world, which distinguishes contemporary History." (326) He also pointed out in another context, that Indian problems and conditions were "widely divergent" from those in Britain and were closer to those in Continental Europe and, therefore, "the lessons to be derived from the study of Continental Economy have a more practical bearing than the maxims contained in the usual textbooks of English Political Economy." (305-6. Also 345) Even in India, Ranade said, the British did not strictly adhere to these precepts in giving guarantees to railways and help to plantation industries or in trying to preserve through legislation *petit culture* by tenants. (341-2, 344-5, 296-7, 355 ff.) At the same time, he remarked sarcastically, "the absolute Truths of Political Economy, however, are appealed to as a justification for a curious change of front. Men who come from a Country where private property in land is most absolute, develop on their arrival here a taste for Socialistic Doctrines." (324)

Third, Ranade pointed out that the scientific claims of Classical economics had been seriously questioned by European and American economists and thinkers such as Hamilton, Carey, August Comte, Sismondi, Gioga, Ludovico, Muller and List, and were under attack even by several English thinkers and economists such as Cairns, Bagehot, Sidgwick, Cliffe Leslie, Jevons, Laing, and Maxwell Melvill. (326, 328-9, 333-6, 349) Moreover, some of the Classical economists themselves, for example, John Stuart Mill, and even Adam Smith had been at pains to avoid making claims of absoluteness and universality for their science. (326, 332-3)

Fourth, Classical economics might at the most explain static economic conditions of a society but could hardly cope with the processes of dynamic economic development. (328)

Keeping all these factors in view, the conclusion was inescapable, said Ranade, that the principles or laws of economics were not abstract and universal like those of physics or astronomy but relative and historically conditioned and derived; they differed in time and space. Hence, the specific stage of economic development of a people and not abstract economic theories should be the decisive factor in determining economic policies for a country. (323-5, 336-7) "If in Politics and Social Science," he wrote, "time and place and circumstances, the endowments and aptitudes of men, their habits and customs, their Laws and Institutions, and their previous History, have to be taken into account, it must be strange indeed, that in the Economical aspect of our life, one set of general principles should hold good everywhere for all time and place, and for all stages of civilization." (324-5) Arguing with those who urged non-interference by the state in the economy, on the authority of the Classical economists, he said that they "forget that Political Economy, as a hypothetical *a priori* Science, is one thing, while Practical Political Economy as applied to the particular conditions of backward Countries is a different thing altogether." And he added: "American, Australian and Continental Political Economy, as applied in practice, permits many departures from the *a priori* positions of the abstract Science."(297)

It is to be noted that Ranade did not deny the value of economic theory or the validity of economics as a science within specific conditions. (336) Like Carey and List, he assumed the premises of Classical economics but not their ahistoricity; he wanted economics to be adapted to specific historical conditions. At the same time, he specifically criticized the effort to reduce the "Economical Science" to "an Art", to "the position of a rule of Thumb." He only wanted to make economics more subtle and scientific by basing it on practice. He wrote: "Theory is only enlarged Practice, Practice is Theory studied in its relation to proximate Causes. The Practice is pre-determined by the Theory which tests its truth, and adapts it to different conditions by reason of its grasp of the deep- seated, permanent, and varied basal truth." (336) Ranade further suggested that economics being a social science its principles were to be derived historically through the study of specific economic activities of nations and not deductively so that they were closely linked with historical experience, practical observation, and social reality.

(336-7) Economics also, he said, should take into consideration social opinions, considerations, and interests. He quoted John Stuart Mill from his preface to make his point: "for practical purposes, Political Economy is inseparably intertwined with many other branches of Social Philosophy. Except in matters of mere detail, there are perhaps no practical questions, even among those which approach nearest to the character of purely Economical questions, which admit of being decided on Economical premises alone." (326) He also praised Adam Smith for never separating "Economical from Social considerations", and thus occupying "a position of advantage which his Successors gave up by their too absolute assertion of his doctrines." (333) Earlier, in 1880, Ranade had made the same point in the specific context of the abolition of cotton duties: "In considering questions of taxation nothing can be more unwise than to conclude that particular tax must be the best which is most in accord with the principles of economical science. The tastes, the habits and wishes of the tax-paying people must be consulted by practical statesmen. The cotton duties were not open to any objection on this ground as nobody in India complained of them". (49)

Here, Ranade differed from Classical economists on another ground: their "*a priori* conclusions" were "based on individual self-interest and unrestricted competition", whereas he wanted economics to take into consideration "the predominant claim of Collective welfare over Individual Interests." (337) Nor need collective welfare and individual interests necessarily coincide, as the Classical economists assumed. Instead, Ranade supported List's view that "the permanent interests of Nations were not always in harmony with the present benefit of individuals." (335) Consequently, he came to the conclusion that "the Individual and his Interests are not the centre round which the Theory should revolve, that the true centre is the Body Politic of which that Individual is a Member, and that Collective Defence and Well-being, Social Education and Discipline, and the Duties, and not merely the Interests of men, must be taken into account, if the Theory is not to be merely Utopian." (336)

Earlier too, in 1881, *Ranade had criticized English economists* for looking at the question of Free Trade "solely from the economical point of view" (and "this economy is itself of a very low and selfish type," he had added parenthetically) and ignoring "the political and social elements which enter into the question," and had averred that "the economical aspects ought to give way or at least be subordinated to the higher interests and aspirations (of a people) if political economy is to be anything more than schoolmen's metaphysics." In fact, he had pointed out, that was why one talked of "applied, i.e., political economy, where the practical and the so-called accidental elements have the greatest influence" and not of "pure economics." (149-50, 152) In this respect, Ranade remained for once true to the practice of the Classical economists and more often than not referred to economics as political economy. Moreover, in his own investigations into Indian economic problems, he constantly applied the historical method and kept in view considerations of social welfare and economic development.

x x x x x

The *laissez-faire* theory of the functions of the state was one of the tenets of Classical economics that was challenged vigorously and consistently by Ranade. On this, his break with the Classical economists was almost total. In his address on "Indian Political Economy," (Article no. 19) he rejected the idea that the state should confine its activities to the simple one of maintaining peace and order, and pleaded for the widening of the horizons of state activity so that it became "the National Organ for taking care of National needs in all matters in which individual and cooperative effort are not likely to be so effective and economic as National effort." (344) Earlier still, in 1883, he had argued that "the State, as representing the public, has a right, and is under corresponding obligation, to undertake all functions which it can best perform to public advantage." (296) And he was to remark in 1896 in his address to the Social Conference: "The State after all exists only to make individual members composing it nobler, happier, richer and more perfect in every attribute with which we are endowed."[14] In 1883, Ranade had maintained that in an economically backward country like India the obligation on the state to act as the guardian of national, and particularly industrial, interests was even greater than in advanced countries of Europe since it had to help the people overcome inherited weaknesses and their own inertia. (295, 298-9). In 1892, he supported Sismondi's declaration "that the State was not merely an agency for keeping peace, but that it was an organization for securing the progress of the people as widely as possible, and for extending the benefits of the Social Union to all." (333) Similarly, he cited Carey favourably for looking upon the state "as a coordinating power in Society, which checked the tendency of individuals to seek immediate gain at the sacrifice of permanent National interests." (335)

Ranade applied this doctrine of the state being the guardian of the entire community to fields where there was need for "protection of the weak against the strong." (343) Once again using Sismondi as his authority, Ranade also argued that the state must intervene for "protecting the masses against the classes and the weaker races against the pressure of the stronger and more advanced Nations under the *regime* of Competition." (333) For that reason, he justified the attempts of the state to protect agricultural labourers, tenants, factory workers and the indebted ryots against landlords, capitalists, and moneylenders, argued for more equitable distribution of national wealth, and asked for the reconsideration of "the Orthodox Views of Finality in such matters." (343) In 1883, even while disapproving of "the direction and spirit" of the Bengal Rent Bill, he had held that, since the zamindars pressed heavily upon the peasant majority, remedial legislation was "urgently required to check these evils" and that "the Government, in its capacity as Sovereign, has every right to undertake Legislation intended to remove admitted and general grievances." (224) Similarly, in 1880, while arguing for permanent ryotwari settlement and against any restrictions on the right to transfer land and asking the Government to let property gravitate to those who had knowledge and capital to invest, he had proposed that "if differences subsequently spring up between class and class, as they have on occasions sprung up in Bengal, the Government can interfere as a mediator, and right matters by protecting the weak against the strong." (78-9)

Ranade opposed the setting of any theoretical limits on the role of the state and said that the national needs should be the only criterion. "The question is that of time, fitness and expediency, not one of liberty and rights," (344. Also 296) More specifically, as we have shown earlier in Sections III and IV, *Ranade demanded a policy of direct and systematic promotion of industrial and agricultural development* and of India's transformation into a modern capitalist economy. This last aspect has to be seen in another context. Ranade's strong defence of state interference in economic affairs and his demand for state aid to industry did not amount to state capitalism not to speak of socialism. He basically favoured capitalism in both industry and agriculture and had an immense faith in the developmental and therefore welfare possibilities of capitalist system of production of goods. The state was asked only to make up the economic deficiencies of private enterprise in a backward country. This is clearly brought out in nearly all of his essays, particularly those on "Netherlands India and the Culture System","Iron Industry—Pioneer Attempts," "Industrial Conference", and "Prussian Land Legislation and the Bengal Tenancy Bill." (Articles nos. 13, 16, 17, 20. See in particular, 230 ff., 276, 278-9, 297-8, 358) A little known episode in 1886 sheds further light on his basic attitude towards the relation between state enterprise and private enterprise in industry. While he talked in general of producing "in State Factories all products of skill which the State Departments require in the way of Stores," (345) in the course of his minute of dissent to the Report of the Finance Committee of 1886, he strongly objected to the Committee's proposal for removal of restrictions on jail manufacture. This proposal, he said, "encourages the state officials with the help of public funds to bear down all private competition." In particular, he criticised the utilisation of jails "to drive steam machinery and work presses" and to produce "tents, and paper, and carpets with the help of State funds."[15] In other words, he objected to jails being used to manufacture goods which the Indian private enterprise also produced. His plea for production of government stores in state factories was designed to replace imported stores in cases where Indian producers could not supply them. We may add here that his co-worker in the field of economics, G.V. Joshi made this point even more explicitly as also more forcefully in two essays published in the *Journal of the Poona Sarvajanik Sabha.* The only objective of state action, he wrote, was to redress the balance in the unequal struggle of the resourceless Indian entrepreneur with the "powerful and go-ahead foreigner" so that the former was not "nipped in the bud". The state's role should, in fact, be temporary and limited to that of preparing the private entrepreneur to assume independent responsibility. Apprehending that state's role might "degenerate into aggressive State action, supplanting private effort", Joshi proposed surrounding it with strict "limitations of scope, direction, and time."[16]

x x x x x

Ranade also questioned the theoretical framework of the Indian officials regarding land revenue administration. Ranade's attack centred on two issues: the ultimate ownership of agricultural land and the nature of land revenue, and Ricardian basis of the Indian land revenue system. On the first question the dominant view among the administrators was that the state in India was, since time immemorial, the ultimate owner of the soil, and that the cultivators or other landholders were in essence its tenants and that, in consequence, the land revenue was in the nature of rent and not a tax. In his paper, "A Protest and A Warning Against the New Departure in the Land Assessment Policy", written in 1884 (Article no. 15 in this volume. Unfortunately, the full transcript of the article was not available and therefore only a part of it is reproduced here), Ranade firmly repudiated the "fallacious supposition" that "the Government was the lord of the soil." "As long as this erroneous conception of state rights in the soil finds favour with Government," he said, "so long there will be little chance of any fair settlement of this land controversy." The Indian landholder was as much a private owner of his land as a landholder in any other part of the world, and the "state has no proprietary rights in cultivated or waste lands." State's interest was "confined to a claim for a share of the produce, which may be more or less onerous, but is not of the nature of a monopoly or differential rent." (265) Ranade argued that the Government's own regulations from 1795 onwards accepted this fact and were based on it. (265 ff.) The ancient Hindu laws, as also those of the Maratha rulers, also made it clear that the ruler had no property in land and was only entitled to a tax on it or to a share in the produce. (266 ff.) The British officials, in their claim of state ownership of land, said Ranade, were basing themselves on the theory and practice of the medieval Muslim rulers. But these were an aberration from the ancient and truer theory and practice in India. (265) What the Government therefore levied in India as land revenue was a tax and not a rent. (265 ff.) In an article, "Proposed Reforms in the Resettlement of Land Assessment," (Article no. 14) published a few months earlier, he had already made all these assertions and asked the Government to "retrace its steps, forget its Mahomedan antecedents of absolutism, and return to the old Hindu traditions, where the King's power was restrained in all directions by the rights of the people, among whom the king was more of a father and a manager than a conqueror or a sovereign lord, and cultivated land belonged in absolute right to private owners who paid as tax a fixed share of the produce to the King like any of his other subjects for the expenses of protection." (255-6)

Ranade also attacked the Ricardian basis of the Indian system of land revenue. Underlying the official ideas and practice was the assumption that the ryot as the tenant of the state or the zamindar was a capitalist farmer who paid economic rent, that is the price differential between the produce of superior land and the produce of the poorest land at the margin of cultivation on which the cost of production was just covered by its produce. The cost of cultivation under this definition covered the cultivator's labour costs as well as his capital costs at the prevailing rate of profit. "In classical political economy the rent of a capitalist farmer was determined by the competition of capital, the size of the population, and the varying fertility of the soil." It was clear that according to this theory of rent the state as the landlord in India could absorb the whole of this economic rent as land revenue without raising the cost of production and without affecting prices or wages which were determined by the cost of production on the marginal land.[17] Ranade did not question the Ricardian theory of rent as such; but, relying on the argument of Richard Jones, Malthus's successor as Professor of Political Economy at Haileybury College, where members of the Indian Civil Service were trained, he denied that it was at all valid for India. The Indian agrarian system was, he said, quite different from the British system. In India, "the Ricardian Theroy that Economic Rent does not enter as an element of price, admittedly does not apply when all occupied land has to pay Monopoly Rent to the State Landlord"; there was no competition among landlords in India, for the state had become the "only one true Landlord" and was in a position to pitch the monopoly rent as high as possible. The result was that "the so-called Land Tax is not a tax on Rents proper but frequently encroaches upon the Profits and Wages of the poor Peasant, who has to submit perforce to a loss of Status and accommodate himself to a lower standard of life as pressure increases." (342-3. Also 175)

Ranade also criticized the theory of the unearned increment that was a natural corollary of Ricardo's theory of rent. According to this theory, if the rent of a piece of land increased by more than the prevailing rate of profit on capital that might have been invested in it, then the difference between the two formed an unearned increment to rent, which would be the product of the general fall in the rate of profit and the general progress of the community and the consequent increase in productivity. This unearned increment would, therefore, legitimately belong to society rather than to the owner of the land. Rather than let the landowner appropriate it parasitically, the society had a right to take it in the form of a tax, which should therefore increase with every increase in unearned increment of rent. It was on this basis that the Government of India enhanced rents at every resettlement at twenty or thirty year intervals.[18] Ranade argued that the application of this theory assumed a static situation in landownership, but that there was no warrant for this assumption. "The English conditions of Land-lordism, where the land under a complicated system of entails and settlements and primogeniture, continues in the same family for generations, allow free play to the law of the Unearned Increment." But in India land was constantly changing hands almost in every generation with the result that each incoming owner paid for its full current value "for the differential advantages of superior productivity and vicinity" and the unearned income of the past totally disappeared so far as he was concerned. (341-2)

x x x x x

Ranade's views on Free Trade and Protection were expressed vigorously in 1881 in the little known "Review of 'Free Trade and English Commerce' by Augustus Mongredien". (Article no. 8) Mongredien's was a Cobden Club publication. They were reiterated in a more sober tone in 1892 in his paper on "Indian Political Economy". His theoretical position was taken in the context of his general critique of Classical economics and his commitment to industrialization.

In general, Ranade too, along with other nationalists, demanded protection for India's nascent industries. (339. Article no. 8) By the Government not doing so and by its applying the doctrine of Free Trade, said, Ranade, India's best interests were being "sacrificed at the altar of this idol of English political economists." (149) This was one reason why he felt it necessary to criticise the Classical economists. He initiated the discussion of Free Trade in 1881 with the major point he was to repeat at length in 1892 that economical aspects of the problem should be subordinated to the higher aspects "if political economy is to be anything more than schoolmen's metaphysics." The English economists' failure to do so was, he said, one of their "cardinal errors in this matter." (149-50)

Ranade questioned the major premise of the Classical economists that free trade led, through the working of comparative costs, to the most efficient geographical division of labour. He refused to accept any division of labour that would consign India forever to be a producer of raw materials and assign Europe the work of transport and manufactures. If all nations had reached the same level of civilization and "peace and goodwill" prevailed among nations as the Cobden Club desired, then "the question would be one of pure economics." But the reality was that at the moment, "each country has a vital interest in securing a variety of industrial pursuits for its population." This "vital interest" was of such significance that in "all free countries" people have reconciled themselves to heavy taxation in the form of tariffs "rather than see life taken out of them by being confined to one or more precarious and universal means of livelihood such as agriculture or sheep farming." (152-3. Also 338-40) It was at this stage that Ranade gave all the arguments in favour of industrialization and against dependence on agriculture that we have discussed in section III above. Referring to the efforts of France, Germany and Russia to encourage their manufactures, he commented: "To talk to them about the advantages of the division of labour is, to say the least, doubtful wisdom, which though it cries from the house tops will get none but fools to listen to it." (153)

Ranade asserted that India was by its history, size of population, geography, location, and resources eminently fitted to be a great manufacturing country. (153, 339) In any case, said Ranade, temporary protection was needed to test whether or not certain industries were suited to a country or not. "It may fairly be questioned", he wrote in 1881, "whether before trial any really large country can be condemned off hand as being providentially intended for one or a limited set of industries only." (153. Also 339) To have universal free trade just at the moment, said Ranade, would stereotype the existing pattern of international division of labour and would mean that those countries which had developed earlier would forever remain industrially advanced while others like India would be further reduced to an agrarian status pure and simple. "To condemn this vast continent to the slavery of growing raw produce for ever will be to realize the parable that to him who hath much shall be given, while from him that hath little, his little shall be taken away," he wrote in 1881. (153) He repeated this argument as well as the parable in 1892. (339)

Ranade cited the authority of John Stuart Mill for having approved of an exception to the general rule of free trade in the type of situation prevailing in India. He praised Adam Smith for being "a Fair Trader". He also appealed to the practice of nations and pointed out that nearly all of the free nations of Europe and America and Britain's own independent colonies like Canada and Australia had given protection to their industries against foreign competitors. (148-9, 152-3, 339) He also took note of the strong sentiments in England itself in favour of reciprocity and therefore "a more or less modified form of protection of native industry". And he commented on this phenomenon with a sense of bitterness:

> There is a strange irony of fate in the fact that Conservative statesmen, with Lord Salisbury at their head, who during their term of office sacrificed the interests of India in the name of free trade, and partially repealed the duties on English cotton goods, thereby surrendering £250,000 of Indian revenue to gratify Manchester to be only replaced by more obnoxious forms of taxation, we say, it is a strange irony of fate that these very statesmen should now come forward as the champions of the rival theory, and feel the pulse of the nation in favour of reciprocity. (149)

Despite his criticism of free trade and demand for protection of Indian industries, he did not adopt a doctrinaire attitude towards protection. As in the case of his stand on other aspects of economic theory, his thinking on this issue was also linked to concrete economic policy issues. He gave open expression to this eclecticism in 1881: "We have no quarrel with the theory of free trade as such. Our only contention is that its practical application must be subordinated to the varying conditions of different countries, and that a hard and fast line of policy dictated by the experience of Great Britain cannot commend itself to the nations of the world." (154)

x x x x x

We may summarise Ranade's general economic thought in the form of four broad formulations: (i) the same propositions of economics or economic doctrines cannot be applied to countries at different stages of economic development; (ii) these propositions should be formulated in the context of the general social conditions and economic needs of the country; (iii) economic ideas and policies should serve and be subjected to socially derived and socially integrated goals and perspectives; and (iv) since India's economic conditions and interests differed from England's, the principles of economics applicable to it must also be different or at least should be differently applied. All these formulations have been very significant in the development of economic thinking and policy perspectives in India. Certainly, hardly any economist or political leader has questioned them. At the same time, it would not be correct to suggest, as some have, that Ranade initiated any specifically 'Indian economics' or 'Indian system of economic ideas or theories'. Ranade did not discover or put forward any new economic laws which would be specifically applicable to Indian conditions. His economic thought was really an effort to adjust the assumptions and theories of the Classical economists and their later-day European, American and British critics to the Indian economic reality. It might almost be said that the 'Indian Political Economy' which Ranade tried to bring into being and which got the support of his contemporaries as well as the next two generations of economists in India was more an attitude of mind, an approach towards Indian economic problems, and a method of economic reasoning than a system of economic thought.

This was largely due to the fact that despite his vast learning, razor- sharp intellect and a theoretical, reflective frame of mind, Ranade's interest in economic theory was secondary or derivative. He made no attempt to grapple with theory *per se*, and concentrated on concrete economic problems within the general framework of removing obstacles to economic development. His comments on economic theories arose out of his effort to change specific colonial policies and to reverse the ongoing colonial pattern of economic under-development. Because the British administrators in India as well as in Britain invoked the authority of Classical economics to bolster their policies and to oppose Indian nationalist demands, Ranade felt it necessary to challenge the universality of Classical economics and its applicability to India under all circumstances. Thus, as we have shown above, he took on the doctrine of *laissez-faire* because it was coming in the way of state assistance to industries and agriculture, the Ricardian theory of rent because it was used to justify the high pitch of land revenue and to deny the permanent settlement of land revenue, and the doctrine of free trade because it was used to justify the refusal to grant protection to Indian industries and the repeal of cotton import duties. Explaining his intervention in the controversy between Cobdenite free traders and the advocates of reciprocity, Ranade had written in 1881: "India, though administered as a trust, finds its best interests sacrificed at the altar of English political economists, and it cannot therefore afford with safety to stand aloof in this controversy." (149)

At the same time, it has to be said that, though there was nothing new in the economic thought of Ranade in terms of theory, the very act of choosing between different theoretical positions from the Indian point of view was an act of theorising and, therefore, even of theoretical significance. Moreover, Ranade did succeed in initiating the tradition of trying to look upon Indian economic problems in a consistent, integrated and interrelated manner and in an Indian setting. In fact, it would not be wrong to say that he tried to evolve some sort of political economy of growth in which developments in industry, agriculture, foreign trade and the role of the state were intertwined with modern industry playing the lead role. He also, along with Dadabhai Naoroji and G.V. Joshi, created the initial public opinion among the intelligentsia on problems of political economy and issues of economic development. Moreover, his considerable talent as an economist and publicist and his promotion of an 'Indian political economy' and the idea of relativity of economic doctrines were used by Ranade not to justify the so-called indigenous or pre-modern pattern of Indian economy but to struggle for its development along the most modern industrial capitalist lines. He subjected Classical political economy to considerable criticism not because it was leading to the disruption of the age-old pattern of Indian social life but because its rigid and indiscriminate application was tending to perpetuate the "old legacies and inherited weaknesses" and the "ancient bondage of Feudalism and status".

VI

Ranade was milder and less vociferous on foreign trade, railways, finance and currency and exchange than other nationalists though he was in basic agreement with them. On the other hand, with rare exceptions, he tended in later life to ignore the questions of tariffs and the Drain.

His relative neglect of these subjects is to be explained not by a lack of interest but by several other intervening factors. For one, because of his preoccupation with official duties as a judge and his deep involvement with social reform, he made a certain division of labour in research, writing and propagation with his co-worker in the field of the study of Indian economy, G.V. Joshi, and his pupil and 'heir' in political and economic agitation, G.K. Gokhale. These two covered foreign trade, railways, finance and currency and exchange at great length. G.V. Joshi's massive essays on these subjects were published in the *Journal of the Poona Sarvajanik Sabha* after being fully whetted by Ranade. Similarly, not only had he trained Gokhale in general on economic questions, but extensively coached and prepared him for his evidence before the Welby Commission in 1897 on questions of finance, currency and exchange. Another important aspect was his personality structure. He preferred, especially in the later part of his life, to take up for himself constructive and not critical aspects of economic policy and to make what he believed to be concrete and realizable proposals. Nor did he see himself, after early 1880s, as an agitator or polemicist in the mould of Dadabhai Naoroji, R.C. Dutt, G.V. Joshi or G.

Subramaniya Iyer. He did not write structured and comprehensive books as did R.C. Dutt and G. Subramaniya Iyer. He did not have to comment on current economic issues in the manner of editors like B.G. Tilak, G. Subramaniya Iyer, Surendranath Banerjea or the Ghosh brothers of the *Amrita Bazar Patrika* or of members of legislatures like G.K. Gokhale or Pherozeshah Mehta. He did not even have to survey the current economic and political national scene as did a President of, or even an active participant in, the Indian National Congress, for as a Government official his role in the Congress was confined to back-stage advice. After his detailed intervention in current agrarian issues and legislation in the late 1870s and early 1880s, he kept himself aloof from current issues and agitations, except for comments on Indian Sugar Duties Bill in 1899 in the form of the letters to the *Times of India*. It is, of course, very difficult to say to what extent his being first a senior sub-judge and then a high court judge was responsible for this reticence. It should, of course, be kept in view that many of the memoranda of the Poona Sarvajanik Sabha and resolutions passed at its public meetings dealt with financial and other current economic issues; and Ranade would have had a hand in their drafting or finalization. We have, however, not used them for this introduction or reproduced them in this volume because of lack of authenticity regarding the extent and nature of Ranade's role in their preparation. So far as the Drain and tariffs are concerned, there were perhaps one or two other considerations which we will discuss in the next section.

x x x x x

There was a rapid growth in India's foreign trade during the 19th century. The officials pointed to this growth as a visible proof of India's economic development and rising prosperity of the people. Ranade disagreed. He argued that foreign trade should be viewed in the context of its character and its impact on the basic question of industrial development of the country.

Seen in that light and comparing at length the nature of goods exchanged, Ranade came to the conclusion that the increase in foreign trade had not been an "unmixed good" and that, on the whole, its impact had been harmful. The increase in foreign trade, he commented, "shows that we are only perfecting ourselves in the faculty of growing Raw Produce, and are forgetting by disuse the skill and the wealth of resources which manufacturing and industrial activity brings in its train." His conclusion was: "when the whole situation is thus taken in at one view, we feel that we are standing on the edge of a precipice, and the slightest push down will drive us into the abyss below of unmixed and absolute helplessness." (272-3. Also 411 ff.)

At the same time, in 1893 Ranade took note of the reverse tendency, visible in the last quarter of the 19th century, of the export of the products of modern industry and the import of machinery, iron and steel and raw materials. (412 ff.) He also pointed out that, while this tendency was yet meagre, the rates of growth of manufactured exports and raw material imports were higher than the rates of growth of raw material exports and manufactured imports. (413 ff.) This recent tendency showed, wrote Ranade with his usual optimism, that "the tide has turned, and India has shown signs of a revival which marks its first step in the transition from a purely agricultural into a partly manufacturing and trading country." (413)

Ranade also complained of another abnormal feature of India's foreign trade. Its control was in foreign hands and so was that of the entire machinery of foreign and coastal trade, so that virtually the entire profits of the trade were appropriated by the foreigners:

> Our shipping is not ours; not even the Coasting Trade is carried on in our Bottoms. The proportion of Native Craft to the total tonnage is two and a third per cent; and it is stationary percentage. Our Banking is not ours, though to a large extent we find the money which finances the Exchange Banks. The Insurance and the Freight and the Commission Business are all Foreign Monopolies and the

> Foreign Merchant's hand is seen trafficking direct with our producers in the remotest and smallest villages. (273)

In conclusion it may be again pointed out that Ranade was not opposed to the growth of foreign trade as such but was critical of its impact on industry and the economy as a whole. As just noted, he welcomed the growth of exports of manufactured goods and import of machinery and industrial raw materials. As he put it:

> What we have to do in each case is to learn by organized cooperation to compete with the Foreigner, and take in as much Raw Produce from abroad as we need, and work it up here, and to send in place of our Exports of Raw Produce, the same quantities in less bulky, but more valuable, forms, after they have undergone the Operation of Art manipulation, and afforded occupation to our Industrial Classes. (425)

Ranade's too few comments on the railways were also made in the wider context of economic development. While not denying the general success of the railways, he noted in 1890 that their development had not "cured the particular weakness (i.e., lack of modern industries) which has crippled the growth of the Nation." (303. Also 295) Instead by facilitating the penetration of the Indian market by foreign goods, the railways had tended to perpetuate and extend India's economic backwardness. (295, 298) In any case, keeping in view the paucity of financial resources, investment in industry represented far better utilization of the existing resources than their use in constructing railways whose development, in any case, should be coordinated with the broader needs of Indian economy. "Facilities of communication are certainly desirable advantages, but more desirable still is the capacity to grow higher kinds of produce and develop manufacturing and industrial activities." (296) Nor was the broader impact of the railways anywhere equal to that of modern industries:

> The construction of Railways can never be compared in their educating influence, to the setting up of Mills or Steam or Water

> Power Machinery for the production of Manufactured Produce in all parts of the Country. A Railway runs from the one end of the Country to the other, and leaves no permanent impression on the face of the Country, at least none so durable and penetrating as that which surrounds a great Manufactory. (296)

In any case, felt Ranade, the needed network of railways had already been completed and the Government should, therefore, now shift the resources hitherto utilized for railway development to industrial development. (296- 7)

Ranade made three points in the context of the railways. First, in 1881, he criticized the high, in fact extravagant, cost of railway construction in India. To quote him: "The fixed guaranteed rate of interest being high (much higher than the average return on capital in England), it was found that the companies were not sufficiently economical in the construction of their works or in their management when constructed. It was their interest to keep their expenditure at as high a figure as practicable, in order to secure the guaranteed interest on the maximum amount that could be laid out." (126) Consequently, the Indian treasury had to bear the heavy burden of making up the guaranteed interest. Second, Ranade advocated that the expenditure on the railways and irrigation should be carried out as far as possible from surplus revenues and not from loans. But if loans became necessary they should be raised in India from Indian creditors. (52, 134, 145) Third, though unlike other nationalists he did not counterpose irrigation works to the railways, (135-6) he did favour faster development of irrigation works which he believed would be quite profitable, but which should be constructed "even though they may not be paying financially." (144) He also pointed out that in India in many areas irrigation canals could also be used as a means of cheap transport. (143, 145)

x x x x x

Ranade commented very little on finance and currency; and even his very few comments were made mainly in an essay in 1880. (Article no. 3) Possibly, he may have felt that no broader developmental issues were involved or that any major demand in these areas would lead to political confrontation. He agreed with other nationalist writers in holding that taxation in India was excessive and that, limits of taxation having been reached, "further increase of taxation must be adjured as political insanity." (51-2) In particular, he favoured reduction of salt tax, abolition of the Licence Tax (a tax on commercial and trading classes and artisans), and discouragement of liquor consumption irrespective of any loss in excise revenue. (52-3. Also 97)

Ranade criticized the Indian administration as being too costly and not within the capacity of India to bear it. Consequently, he supported the widespread demand for retrenchment of Government expenditure. "Indian economists," he wrote, "must not rest till the annual expenditure is reduced by another three or four millions." (51-3. Also 97) Military expenditure was one area where expenditure could be curtailed. Moreover, war with Afghanistan should be ended and all ideas of annexing it abandoned "on grounds of economy, if nct of justice and policy." (52) Civil expenditure could be brought down, said Ranade, by gradually replacing Europeans in the administration by Indians who could be employed for less. Since the ICS and other higher administrators were paid more than their counterparts in Britain or in the White Colonies, the cost of civil administration, said Ranade, could also be reduced by cutting down the salaries of "the higher officers to the English or colonial scale." (52) On the other hand, Ranade opposed any reduction of expenditure on education in general or on higher education and advocated, instead, its enhancement and allocation of "an adequate proportion of the revenues raised to such an important purpose as education."[19]

The currency question was one of the most debated in India,

especially in the 1890s. Since 1873, *gold price of silver* began to decline steadily, and consequently, since India was on silver standard, the rupee began to depreciate in relation to currencies based on gold. While this tended to give a certain indirect protection to Indian manufactures by making imports costlier, diverse British interests, from those of import merchants and British manufacturers to British civil servants whose remittances to Britain fell in terms of pound sterling to British-Indian Government which had to remit more rupees both for Home Charges in Britain and for servicing its gold-currency foreign debt, demanded steps to raise the value of the rupee in terms of the pound sterling. Indians opposed such a step. Ranade made only one comment on the subject and he took the same stand as Dadabhai Naoroji, G.K. Gokhale and others were to take.[20] He too advocated a policy of letting the rupee fall and wrote in 1881: "The temptation of manipulating the currency must be resisted as involving a breach of faith, and tending to depress silver, and raise the rate of exchange." (52)

VII

It is widely believed that on two economic issues—those of tariffs and the Drain—*Ranade differed widely from his contemporary nationalist economists.* This is grossly misleading.

We have already seen in Section V above that Ranade took up during the 1880s as well as the 1890s a strong theoretical position in favour of tariff protection in a backward country. We hope to show below that he upto the end asked for tariff protection whenever he felt it feasible and also supported and not opposed the Drain Theory.

In 1881, he criticized Lord Salisbury and other Conservative statesmen for having during their term of office "sacrificed the interests of India in the name of free trade" by repealing import duties on English cotton goods and thereby surrendering

£25,000 of Indian revenue to gratify Manchester. (149) More important, as late as 1899, he wrote three articles, under a pseudonym, arguing for strong protection for Indian sugar industry against the import of bounty-fed sugar from Europe. He cited facts and figures to show that sugar refineries were being closed down everywhere in the country, that unrefined sugar was also suffering, and that a serious decline had taken place in the area under cane cultivation and date trees. This result, he pointed out, was the result not of famine but of "the unprofitableness of industry due to foreign competition." It was true, he said, that there was not much of sugar refining industry in India at the time. But to take this view was to be extremely shortsighted. The real danger was that the entire future of this industry was being jeopardised. What Indian sugar industry needed was "breathing time."[21]

x x x x x

A great deal of nationalist agitation throughout the period of the national movement was based on the Drain theory according to which a part of India's national product and social capital was being exported to Britain for which India got no economic or material return; that is, India was being compelled to pay an indirect tribute to its rulers. The Drain theory began to epitomize as well as concentrate the entire nationalist critique of colonial economic domination. The high priest, the great theorizer and populariser of the Drain theory was Dadabhai Naoroji.

It has been widely believed that the opposite, anti-Drain school of thought was led by Ranade who "did not lay the blame for India's poverty upon what has come to be called 'the drain'."[22] The passage from Ranade's writings from which this inference is drawn is to be found in his address to the Industrial Conference at Poona in 1890. In this address Ranade declared: "There are some people who think that, as long as we have a heavy tribute to pay to England, which takes away nearly twenty Crores of our surplus Exports, we are doomed and can do nothing to help ourselves. This is, however, hardly a fair or manly position to take up." He pointed out that a portion of this drain represented interest on foreign capital loaned to or invested in India, "and so far from complaining, we have reason to be thankful that we have a Creditor who supplies our needs at such a low rate of interest." Another portion represented the value of stores supplied to India, "the like of which we cannot produce here." The remaining consisted of expenditure on administration, defence, and payment of pensions, "though there is good cause for complaint that it is not all necessary." "We shall not forget the fact," he added, "that we are enabled by reason of this British connection to levy an equivalent tribute from China by our Opium Monopoly." Ranade, therefore, advised his audience not to "divert and waste your energies in the fruitless discussion of tribute, which had better be left to our Politicians." (273-4)

In our opinion this passage does not really prove that Ranade was not aware of, or a believer in, the Drain of wealth from India and its injurious economic consequences. He was making a plea for underplaying the Drain question for reasons we will discuss a little later.

In fact, Ranade was one of the first persons in India to propagate the Drain theory. He had done so almost simultaneously with Dadabhai Naoroji with whom he had maintained close contact since the 1860s. In his Poona lectures in 1872, the burden of his criticism of British rule had been the Drain of capital and resources from India; and he had asserted that "of the national income of India more than one-third was taken away by the British in some form or the other."[23] In an essay published in the *Journal of Poona Sarvajanik Sabha* in January 1881, he had laid down that one of the basic conditions for the economic development and prosperity of India was the diminution of "the ever-expanding tribute which she pays to England in the shape of Home-Charges." (97) Later in that year, he discussed the question of India's unrequited export surplus at greater length in his review of Augustus Mongredien's pamphlet, "Free trade and English commerce." (Article no. 8) The very basic proposition of Mongredien that "exports necessitate imports to the same amount, and that it is perfectly futile to export much and import little" was wrong. It would be true, said Ranade, "if exports and imports were governed by the law of free exchange." But it was not so: Out of 64 trading countries, the exports exceeded the imports permanently in 32 and, on the contrary, the imports exceeded exports in the other 32. If the whole world constituted one community, "the propositions of the English economists would be correct both in theory and practice." But in real life the fact was that in the United Kingdom the imports exceeded exports while in India exports always exceeded imports by 15 to 20 millions. Instead of asserting that exports and imports balanced each other, the economists should explain this discrepancy. Instead of doing so, the English economists "make light of it by ignoring the disturbing causes as being merely accidental." "Political economy, however," he said, "cannot and should not, disregard these startling differences, for these accidents as they are called, form the very elements of the question which politicians and statesmen have chiefly to attend to." And he concluded: "The English imports exceed the exports because English capital and English rule levies a tribute from all backward countries like India, which have to pay enormous odds for their backwardness in this race of competition." (151-2)

In 1882, Ranade reviewed Dadabhai Naoroji's work on the *Poverty of India* (Article no. 10) and, expressing his agreement with him in his controversy with Juland Danvers, an India Office official, who had criticised Dadabhai for not including the income of the service sector in his calculations of India's national income and the proportion that the Drain bore to it, wrote: "Even if Mr. Danvers' objection be allowed, it is to be noted that in the general account which the adoption of his principle will necessitate, the drain of Indian wealth in respect of the home charges and remittances and interest representing at the lowest average 25 to 30 crores of rupees represented by the annual deficiency of our imports over exports will swallow all the surplus he can imagine, and leave still a wide chasm gaping at his feet." Ranade then took up the counter claim that "India gets in return the highest talent and integrity, and the cheapest capital for this sacrifice, and that the balance is restored in her favour." Here, again, he cited Dadabhai in reply: "Professor Dadabhai notices this aspect of the case in a short but very suggestive paper on the moral drain of India represented by the fact that all the talent, organization, and integrity is withdrawn from it just when it is qualified by experience to prove the most helpful." He ended his review praising Dadabhai's "exposition of the present system against which we have ourselves contended so long through good and evil report, and so hopelessly." (184-5)

And, barely two years after his address to the Industrial Conference, in an even more significant pioneering address on "Indian Political Economy" in 1892, Ranade remarked that to "old legacies and inherited weaknesses" which acted as depressing influences on economic development "must be added the economic drain of wealth and talents, which Foreign subjection has entailed on the country." (337)

x x x x x

There is, however, no doubt that in his later life, in the 1890s, Ranade did not stress or rather underplayed the tariff and Drain questions. He did not so much change his earlier views as decided not to press them at the time. This change in emphasis was because of several reasons, some of which we have discussed in Section VI above; but there was one other major and particular reason which applied to these two cases. Though he saw their significance and, as we have seen above, had written about them in the same vein as other nationalists, he increasingly came to believe that the acceptance of the nationalist demands for tariff protection and the ending of the Drain, especially in the form of the Home Charges, were beyond the realm of possibility. These demands were so basic and affected the springs of colonial rule, colonial interests and colonial ideology so directly that the colonial administration would not accept them, at least in the foreseeable future. Only an independent Government could adopt them; but the struggle for independence, believed Ranade, was not yet on the agenda. Hence it was futile and inexpedient to waste precious and scarce resources of time and energy in concentrating or harping upon them. It was useless to charge after the impossible. Thus he told the Industrial Conference:

> We cannot, as with the Governments of these Countries (of Europe and America), rely upon Differential Tariffs to protect Home Industries during their experimental trial. We cannot expect the Government here, to do what France or Germany does for their Shipping Trade, and their Sugar Industry, and ask Government Bounties, and subsidies to be paid out of general Taxes. These are heresies according to English Political Economy, such as is taught to us, and whether they be really so or not, it is useless to divert our energies in fruitless discussion, and seek to achieve victory over Free Trade. (275)

In the same address, in the long quotation we have given above in the beginning of our discussion of Ranade and the Drain, he had warned his audience not "to divert and waste your energies in the futile discussion of this question of tribute." (274) Similarly, he had ended by asking the Conference to keep in mind certain axiomatic truths, one of which was:

> What we have chiefly to avoid is the pursuit of impracticable objects. We should husband our little resources to the best of our power, and not exhaust them by vain complaints against the drain of the Indian Tribute, or by giving battle with Free Trade. (277)

We should also keep in view that, as his stand on social reforms also indicated, one of the basic tenets of Ranade's approach was his belief in piecemeal reforms and in attempting what was possible and nearest at hand. Thus, defining the moderate political outlook, he had written in 1896: "Moderation imposes the conditions of never vainly aspiring after the impossible or after too remote ideals, but striving each day to take the next step in order of natural growth by doing the work that lies nearest to our hands in a spirit of compromise and fairness."[24] That is why, when he felt that the Government of India was willing to extend protection to Indian sugar industry from bountyfed sugar imports from Germany and Austria since no British interests were involved directly and indirectly and because Mauritian and West-Indian sugar industries were also suffering in competition with Austrian and German sugar, he vociferously demanded protection for Indian sugar. Similarly, he supported wider employment of Indians in the Government as a way of reducing civil expenditure and the Drain since he believed that the Government was willing to take some steps in the direction.

In any case, he believed that other urgent economic issues such as industrial development could not wait till self-government was achieved or British outlook was changed. These issues could be isolated or delinked from politics. On them it was possible to influence Government policy. (269-70, 276) It was hence better to concentrate on them. Moreover in case of many of them Indians could take action on their own instead of asking for Government action which would not be forthcoming. As we have seen, Ranade put great emphasis on self-reliance and the possibility of success on that basis. In 1893, he ended his paper on the "Present State of Indian Manufactures," with the comment: "My object in reading this paper before you is chiefly to show you that, notwithstanding these disadvantages and Free-Trade Policy of the Government, we may win, if we will only persevere in our efforts." (426) Despite his sharp and many-sided critique of Government policies, Ranade believed that a part of the blame for industrial backwardness lay with

Indians themselves for not properly harnessing the existing resources of capital, men, enterprise and technique. (274-5, 278-9) Indians must, therefore, not fritter away their energy in blaming the Government and should, instead, adopt a constructive approach; they should depend on self-effort, using whatever help the Government gave them. (426, 274, 276-9) In his 1890 address to the Industrial Conference he warned against the Drain theory leading to the paralysis of Indians' own efforts for economic development; he was wary of people "who think that as long as we have a heavy tribute to pay to England... we are doomed and can do nothing to help ourselves." (274) This was one reason why he was opposed to making the Drain a central question of Indian politics or of nationalist propaganda. It was more worthwhile and productive of positive results, he felt, to educate Indians themselves into right thinking and action on economic issues. This he set out to do in his essays and addresses of the 1890s. It should also be noted that in the much-quoted passage of 1890, (274) Ranade advised against a conference like the Industrial Conference, convened for the particular purpose of encouraging Indians themselves to promote modern industry, taking up the question of the Drain and not against 'the politicians' doing so. (In parenthesis, we may also point out that Ranade was one of the founders of the National Congress and was constantly trying to arouse public opinion on political questions and to make every personal effort to create a cadre of public political workers; he did not therefore use the word 'politicians' in a pejorative sense as is the wont of many today). He was also keen to unite persons from all shades of political opinion in the work of the Industrial Conference and to inspire them with an optimistic outlook; all those issues which produced dissension or a sense of helplessness, leading to inaction, had therefore to be excluded or underplayed. Regarding the first, he said in the very beginning of his address to the Industrial Conference: "We are met here today, for a purpose which is acceptable to all. The programme of the Congress gatherings is avowedly Political. Here we eschew

Politics altogether, for there is really no conflict of interest between the Rulers and the Ruled, who all alike desire to promote the Industrial and Economic Progress of this Country. The object of the Social Conference, similarly, sets the Reformers and the Orthodox majority in apparent opposition. Here, on the Economical platform, all shades of opinion, all differences of views on Social, Political and Religious subjects may unite and cooperate." (269. Also 277) Regarding the second aspect, he had argued: "Of course, the situation is not hopeless, for no situation is ever hopeless to those who master its real significance, and resolve to do their best to improve it." (273)

Ranade also felt that harping day in and day out on demands which the colonial regime would not accept created a political impasse and led to premature political militancy. Dadabhai Naoroji and others like him were aware of this aspect of the two questions, i.e., of the close linkage of the Drain and tariff questions with militant politics, but they were willing to 'play with fire' and let political consequences follow, at least at the level of ideas and ideology.[25] Ranade's politics, however, were more, far more, moderate than theirs. His personal politics did not permit such a shift. He shied away from all issues which would lead to a confrontation with the colonial regime. He would rather in his personal role and for some time to come underplay or even ignore such politically explosive issues or at least keep them separate from economic issues just as he was doing in the case of social issues.

That expediency or a 'tactical decision' arising out of expediency and not a basic change in economic analysis or thinking was responsible for Ranade's later stand on and neglect of the Drain and tariff questions can also be inferred from the fact that his close collaborator on economic matters, G.V. Joshi, and his disciple and heir, G.K.Gokhale, took up a strong position on both the questions and carried on around them a vigorous intellectual critique and popular agitation.[26] It can, of course, not be said that we can substitute Joshi's and Gokhale's views for those of Ranade; at the same time it is difficult to believe that they could have adopted a stand, particularly on the Drain, that was fundamentally opposed to that of their preceptor. Moreover, Gokhale took a strong stand on the Drain in his evidence before the Welby Commission in 1897, and he had been prepared for his evidence by Ranade along with G.V. Joshi.[27] It is unimaginable that Gokhale could have taken this pro-Drain theory stand without Ranade's approval.

VIII

There were certain aspects of Ranade's thought which may be described as areas of darkness. One such area was that of class and class structure. Even though, as we have seen in Section V above, he expressed a general sympathy for the deprived and the oppressed, argued that the state had the right as well as a duty to protect "the weak against the strong" and "the masses against the classes", and wanted that "the Distribution of Produce among the needy many and the powerful few" should be arranged "in a spirit of equity and fair play", (91, 224, 343) he did not show much awareness of the class dimension of, or the class division and exploitation within, Indian society. He did, of course, as we have seen earlier in Section IV, favour drastic changes in the 'feudal' agrarian structure, but the alternate agrarian structure he recommended was weighted heavily in favour of the zamindars and the well-off ryots who were to be transformed into improving capitalist landlords and farmers. He supported legislation to protect the tenants and to regulate moneylending. He also took up the cause of the ryots against the heavy state burden in the form of land revenues. He adopted a very strong position regarding the social position of women and caste oppression in Indian society.[28]

In general, however, Ranade believed that inequality was inherent in any developing society and only extremes of inequity and inequality needed to be righted. In particular, he had very little to say about the problems and sufferings of factory and plantation labour which was being subjected to as ruthless and revolting an exploitation as known to the modern world. Though he justified legislation for the protection of factory workers and miners in Europe because their "combination is not so effective as that of the Employers of Labour", he used the argument to favour government measures to protect "the poor disunited indebted classes" from the moneylenders. (343) He did not comment on the factory legislation discussions initiated by the Government in 1875 and after or on the legislation mooted and passed in 1881 and 1891. In 1881, he permitted an article totally critical of factory legislation in India to appear in the *Journal of the Poona Sarvajanik Sabha.*[29] The only comment from his own pen came in 1891 when he described Indian factory legislation as "reasonable in its way". In the same comment he provided a partial explanation for his indifference by further describing factory labour as "a drop in the ocean of Humanity in India." (318) In other words, the contribution of modern industry to India's regeneration was seen as massive while the price for it was seen as being paid by a very insignificant part of the Indian people. Ranade also, along with his contemporaries, saw the Indian capitalists as the only available carriers of his project of industrial development. Their interests had therefore to be guarded at all costs.

x x x x x

Ranade differed from other economists regarding the role of foreign capital in India's economic development. In 1872 he had denied that foreign capital was of much use to India, for Indian workers were paid a subsistence wage while the profits of enterprise were pocketed and exported by the British capitalists. But later he reversed his position. In 1893, he argued that British capital and enterprise were assisting the recent phase of industrial growth. (415) Earlier, in 1890, he had praised foreign enterprises in India for acting as helpful teachers to the Indian entrepreneurs. (273) In contrast, other nationalist economists including Dadabhai Naoroji and G.V. Joshi opposed the intrusion of foreign capital in Indian economy.[30]

x x x x x

The main area of darkness was *Ranade's failure to understand the character of the colonial state.* In this respect, Ranade's public position was the weakest of all, especially when compared with that of Dadabhai Naoroji, G.V. Joshi and G. Subramaniya Iyer or even R.C. Dutt. He did, of course, point in general to the link between economic and political dependence, "Commercial and Manufacturing predominance naturally transfers Political ascendancy", he said in 1890. (273) The younger Ranade had also pointed out that political subordination prevented Indian people from undertaking measures that would promote industries and thus avoiding the fate of becoming "drawers of water and hewers of wood to the civilized nations of the world." (152)

But he failed to follow or make explicit the political logic of his own economic position. He was undoubtedly demanding fundamental changes in the existing economic relations between India and Britain. He was opposing the subordination of Indian economy to British economy and challenging the very basis of British rule. Yet he failed to draw the requisite political lesson that British economic policies in India were not the result of ignorance or failure to understand Indian society and reality or of dogmatic adherence to Classical Political Economy, but were rooted in the basic structure of the colonial relationship—they were the concomitants of foreign rule; they were closely related to the very nature and character of foreign rule; in other words, the fundamental purpose of British rule was to enable the economic exploitation of India. He did not reach the point of grasping, or at least stating, as other nationalist economists like Dadabhai Naoroji, G.V. Joshi and G.S. Subramaniya Iyer did, that it was in its political condition and the resulting foreign control of Indian economy that India differed most not only from Britain but also from other free nations[31] and that the economic development of India required a political system conducive to it, that it demanded self-government in some form or another.

The weakness in Ranade's understanding of the colonial state emerges clearly in his treatment of the role of the state in Indian economy. As brought out in Section VII above, while he did not regard the demands for tariff protection and the ending of the Drain as feasible, he regarded active support to industrial development by the colonial state as entirely within the realm of the achievable or the practical. Thus, as we have pointed out earlier, while arguing in 1890 that it was "useless to divert our energies in fruitless discussion, and seek to achieve victory over Free Trade," he asserted that "we may, however, fairly expect Government to try as an experiment the policy of the Culture System" (275), i.e., the policy of direct state aid to and participation in industrial development. Similarly, he said in 1892: "Even if political considerations forbid independent action in the matter of differential duties, the pioneering of new enterprizes is a duty which the Government might more systematically undertake with advantage." (344-5) He also argued that there was "really no conflict of interests between the Rulers and the Ruled" on the question of the promotion of industrial and economic development (269) and that "the Government of India is anxious to help us." (276)

Ranade repeatedly said that Indians should not chase after the unattainable but confine their efforts to the achievement of the possible or of what the rulers would agree to grant. By saying so, he was of course raising a tactical issue. But a basic question was involved in his understanding of what was attainable and what was not. Tariff protection was not feasible because deep-seated belief in Classical Political Economy was involved along with "Political considerations", but state policy of direct and systematic promotion of industrial development was quite feasible within the existing political structure. Missing here was the linkage between colonial economic structure and the colonial state, between colonial interests and what was possible or feasible as colonial policy, and therefore an understanding of the basic character of the state in India as a colonial state. Others among nationalist economists and leaders did make this connection.

Ranade saw the state as the representative of the public, of the collective will of society, and as the national organ of the national will for development or as the guardian of the community. But he failed to see, or at least articulate, that the Indian state was a colonial state and not a national state and that a colonial state was as incapable of promoting development in any basic manner as of ending the Drain or of providing meaningful or effective tariff protection against imports from Britain.

NOTES AND REFERENCES

1. Bipan Chandra, *Nationalism and Colonialism in Modern India*, p. 84.

2. George Hamilton, Secretary of State for India, declared in the House of Commons on 16 August 1901: "I admit at once that if it could be shown that India has retrograded in material prosperity under our rule we stand self-condemned, and we ought no longer to be trusted with the control of the country". Quoted in Bipan Chandra, *The Rise and Growth of Economic Nationalism in Modern India*, p. 27. He again declared on 3 February 1902: "I have more than once stated my opinion that our main claim, our only claim to rule India is the belief that we can improve the material prosperity of those who live within its borders". Quoted in *ibid.*, p. 27 n.

3. Even in Britain and the United States, he wrote in 1892, "the questions at issue are more Economical than Political in their character". In Ireland, too, he wrote, "the Political is really at its base an Economical Dispute...." (325) Nor was Ranade alone here. Bipin

Chandra Pal, the emerging Extremist leader, wrote in the very first issue of his militant weekly *New India*: "Of all the perplexing problems that confront New India, the economic problem seems to our mind, the most pressing and important". 12 August 1901.

4. For this view among officials, see Bipan Chandra, *The Rise and Growth of Economic Nationalism in India*, p. 72 f.n. 81

5. "An appeal by the Executive Committee of the Poona Sarvajanik Sabha", *Journal of Poona Sarvajanik Sabha*, January 1882, Vol.IV, No.3, pp.30-1. Also Parvate, *Mahadev Govind Ranade*, pp.280-3.

6. *Rise of the Maratha Power*. Also his addresses in *Miscellaneous Writings*.

7. *Miscellaneous Writings*, p.231.

8. *Ibid.*, pp.116-7.

9. Mankar, *M.G. Ranade*, Vol.I, pp.82-3.

10. Gokhale, *Speeches*, p.927.

11. T.V. Parvate, op.cit., pp.77-8.

12. Richard P. Tucker, *Ranade and the Roots of Indian Nationalism*, p.104.

13. Also Parvate, pp.130-1, since original pages 49 ff. in Article no.15 are missing from the article as reproduced in this volume.

14. Ranade, *Miscellaneous Writings*, p.172.

15. *Report of the Finance Committee*, 1886, Vol.I, p.407.

16. G.V. Joshi, *Writings and Speeches*, pp.746-50, 808, 820, 822-3, 826

17. Eric Stokes, *The English Utilitarians and India*, Chapter II, in

particular pp.77, 88-9, 93, 108-09, 114, 127-8, 131-5, 137; David Ricardo, The Principles of Political Economy and Taxation, Everyman Library Edition, 1943, Chapters II and XXXII; Eric Roll, *A History of Economic Thought*, pp.195-6.

18. Stokes, *op. cit.*, pp.89-90; Ricardo, *op.cit.*, Chapters II and XXXII. The theory of unearned increment found open expression in Curzon's *Land Resolution*, dated 16 January 1902. See paras 18, 22.

19. *Miscellaneous Writings*, p.276, Ranade's 'Memorandum of Dissent', *Report of the Finance Committee*, 1886, Vol.I, p.441.

20. For detailed treatment of the British and Indian points of view, see Bipan Chandra, *The Rise and Growth of Economic Nationalism in India*, Chapter VII.

21. *Plea for Protection—Indian Sugar Industry*—Three articles contributed by M.G. Ranade in May and June 1899 to the *Times of India*—with an introduction by V.G. Kale.

22. James Kellock, *Mahadev Govind Ranade*, 1926, p. 127; also see J.C. Coyajee, "Ranade's work as an Economist", *Indian Journal of Economics*, Jan. 1942, Vol.XXII, No.3, p.308.

23. Pradhan and Bhagwat, *Lokamanya Tilak*, p.8; Richard P. Tucker, *Ranade and the Roots of Indian Nationalism*, p.103; T.V.Parvate, *Mahadev Govind Ranade*, p.76.

24. Quoted in Tucker, *op.cit.*, p.270.

25. See Bipan Chandra, *The Rise and Growth of Economic Nationalism in India*, pp.228-31, 234-6, 245-51 (for tariffs), 689-708 (for the Drain).

26. G.V. Joshi, *Writings and Speeches*, pp.640, 683, 793-4; Gokhale, Speeches, pp.15, 87-8, 833, 908-10, and *Report of Royal Commission on the Administration of the Expenditure of India*, Vol.III, Parliamentary Paper (House of Commons), 190, Vol.29, C 130, Questions 18169-84

(Welby Commission).

27. Parvate, *op.cit.*, pp.230, 235; Tucker, op.cit., p.281.

28. See his *Miscellaneous Writings* and Tucker, *op.cit.*, pp.295-7.

29. "Factory Legislation in India", *Journal of Poona Sarvajanik Sabha (JPSS)*, July 1981, Vol.IV, No.1.

30. See Bipan Chandra, *The Rise and Growth of Economic Nationalism in India*, pp.95ff.

31. The younger Ranade did state this. See p.153 of this volume.

1

THE AGRARIAN PROBLEM AND ITS SOLUTION*

It seems very necessary in these times of excitement to whisper into the ears of the authorities that, notwithstanding the troubles and anxieties of the last few months, nothing has happened that we should lose our heads about, the hills are not on fire, the earth has not lost its balance, nor has the sea overstepped its limits. A few misguided hair-brained spirits have gone out into the wilds, and, taking advantage of the utterly defenceless and disarmed condition of the civil population, have stirred up the professional robbers to join them, and committed a few outrages, which the Police, being weak in efficiency and numbers, have not been able to anticipate or quell. A few incendiary and disastrous fires have indeed thrown a lurid glare upon these outrages, but they cannot be rightly understood as significant tokens of sinister combination and widespread conspiracy. Incendiary fires and *farwatia* outrages have occurred, and do still occur, elsewhere than in British India, and they are certainly not sufficient to bring down the heavens upon us or justify resort to extreme and reactionary measures. It is most unfortunate that these events should have happened just at a time when public attention was being concentrated upon

---

**JPSS*, July 1879, Vol.II, No.1.

the consideration of the most pressing question of the day, on the right solution of which depends all our hopes for the permanent material and moral prosperity of the country. These dacoities would never have been possible but for 'the rebellion of the belly', which is the one permanent menace to the tranquillity and progress of the people. If there had been no succession of famines in the land, if the ordinary channels by which labour was absorbed and regulated had not dried up, if poverty and starvation had not stared in the face of many thousands of the people from one end of the country to the other, the dacoits could never have seduced men from their homes. Again, if the country had not been disarmed, if the whole population had not lost all its old habits of watchfulness, if the ruin of the Inamdar classes had not denuded the country of its natural leaders, and reduced all classes to one dead level of helpless dependence, the dacoities would never have assumed any importance, and the police would not have been left single-handed to cope with the criminal classes, and their outlawed leaders. We are thus forcibly thrown back to the consideration of what may be called the statical and normal conditions of the diseased state of the body politic, we must probe the disease where its roots lie deep in the national heart, if we wish to remove the disgusting surface symptoms which strike our view.

There is, however, little danger that these unfortunate dacoities and incendiary fires will be allowed to divert attention from the great agrarian problem. The discussions and commissions of the last ten years have now established a sufficient basis of admitted facts and well-supported conclusions, which have carried conviction to the minds of the most adversely inclined authorities, both in India and England. The struggle was long and arduous ere the official conscience could be disabused of its long cherished illusions. We, who have borne the brunt of the strife, have certainly every reason to be satisfied with the ground that has been gained. The Deccan Riots Commission's report first opened the eyes of the Government of India and in England to the unwelcome truth that the Revenue Settlement had been a great failure and that the more recent operations of the Department had pauperized the country and brought the state vessel to the very brink of ruin. A majority of the Commissioners condemned both the principles and the practice of the Bombay settlement, and that Department has not yet recovered from the effects of the staggering blows it then received. Like another famous Department which was blown off by the first whiff of the Mutiny troubles, the Survey and Settlement Department has not mustered courage to vindicate its position and justify its existence, and we may soon expect to find that its days are numbered, and that sooner or later it becomes a relic of the past.

We shall here briefly summarize the charges which have been brought against this Department by the official Commission, in respect of which charges it has allowed judgement to go against it by reason of its confessed inability to offer any decent reply. It has been proved by the inquiries of the Riots Commission that the assessments, especially those made in the revised settlements, were made haphazard and without reference to any principle, that the old assessments have been too suddenly raised, and that the enhancements have been out of all proportion to any rise of rents, or of the letting value of land, and have thereby destroyed all private property in land. The enhancements were unforeseen, uncertain, capricious, unequal, full of mistakes so gross and so general as to show that the system was itself defective; they were based upon a fallacious assumption of the permanent continuance of the artificial prosperity which the country enjoyed between 1860 and 1870, and upon supposed encroachments and extensions of the cultivated area. The principle of classification followed by the Department furnishes no guarantee against error, and does not allow a sufficiently wide interval between the different classes of doubtful and inferior soils. The Survey Officers disregard the provision of the law which exempts private improvements from being taken into account in fixing their enhancements, and they make no allowance for the higher standard of life and the wants of an increased population, with diminished resources of waste lands to fall back upon. These and many other defects and faults, which were brought by the labours of the Riots Commission, have fully established to the satisfaction of the Government the necessity of an early and sweeping reform in the working of the Settlement Department. This exposure has for ever sealed the mouths and silenced the paeans of triumph which were till then dinned into the public ear, and which lulled to rest the official conscience. It is only the strong tie of official comradeship, at once both the strength and the bane of all bureaucratic oligarchies, which keeps up this costly and mischievous Department of the service. But such facticious support cannot last long, and there are already signs that it will have to succumb to its.fate.

If the lines of policy initiated by the Bombay Government in its famous Resolution of the 29th October 1874 had been followed out in full fidelity to its original conception, it would have been possible to stay the alarm in time, and put off the necessity for radical reform for a few years more. Unfortunately the interference of the Supreme Government nullified the beneficial action of the Local authorities, and thereby intensified the distress. His Excellency Sir Philip Wodehouse, the late Governor, proposed to cancel all increases of the assessments made by the Department on the fallacious assumption that the Ryots had encroached upon the state lands. He gave his sanction to a scheme by which all *kharab* (unarable) lands, included in the area but excluded from the assessment at the first settlement of a Ryot's holding, were to be exempted from all additional taxation for the express reason that the conversion of the unarable into arable land was due to labour of the Ryot, and should therefore be regarded as an improvement caused by the owner, and as such exempted by law from additional assessment. On this point, the action of the local authorities was overruled by the Government of India, then under the influence of Sir B.H.Ellis and other staunch supporters of the Bombay system of settlement. Sir Philip Wodehouse also insisted upon laying down fixed limitations to the discretion of the survey officers in the enhancements made by that Department. These limitations were fixed at the maximum figures varying from 33 to 50 and 100 per cent of the previous assessments of the Talooka, village, and individual holdings respectively. These fixed limits were justified by the Bombay Government on the express ground that the Survey Department had erred in calculating on the continuance of the high speculative prices which prevailed between 1860 and 1870. The settlements made by the Survey Department were accordingly revised by Mr. Pedder who was then Revenue Secretary to Government.

In consequence of the interference of the Government of India noticed above, Sir Philip Wodehouse's reform was emasculated of its chief strength, and the detailed revisions undertaken by Mr. Pedder, being entrusted to the Department, were thus rendered nugatory and ineffective so far as any practical relief to the Ryots was intended to be secured thereby. For instance, in the Madhe Taluka, where the old assessment of Rs.1,00,631 had been raised to Rs.1,74,448, that is, 74 per cent, by the Department, Mr. Pedder reduced it to Rs.1,42,208, that is to an increase of 41 per cent. In the Indapoor Talooka, where the old assessment was Rs.81,184, and the Department had raised it to Rs.1,25,845, or 55 per cent, Mr. Pedder reduced it to Rs.1,13,142, that is, about 39 per cent increase upon the old assessment. In the Bhimathadi Talooka, the old assessment was Rs.81,475 and was raised by the Survey Department to Rs.1,33,131, or 63 per cent; Mr. Pedder lowered it to Rs.1,22,571, that is, to a 50 per cent increase upon the old assessment. In the Sholapoor Talooka, the old assessment had been Rs.1,74,101, and was raised by the Department to Rs.3,07,972; Mr. Pedder reduced it by Rs.42,538, being a reduction from 77 to 44 per cent. In the Haveli Talooka of the Poona Collectorate, the old assessment of Rs.89,475 had been raised by the Department to Rs.1,33,174, or 65 per cent; Mr. Pedder's second revision reduced it to 41 per cent increase on the old assessment. In the Karmale Talooka, the revised assessment made by the department showed an increase of only 35 per cent, upon the old figures. Government accordingly declined to interfere, oblivious of the fact that the limitations laid down by its Resolution of the 29th October 1874, were intended to be effective not only where the aggregate Talooka assessment was excessive, but also to give equal relief to particular villages, and to individual holdings overassessed. In the Pabal Talooka, the old assessment was Rs.92,359, and had been raised by the Department to Rs.1,39,315, that is 50 per cent. Mr. Pedder contended himself with a reduction to Rs.1,27,334, of 39 per cent increase upon the first assessment.

These details will serve to show how the action of the Bombay Government was cramped, and its original intentions distorted by the interference of the Government of India, and the action of the Survey Department. The relief promised by the Resolution was not secured for the very sufficient reason, that the Departmental revisions had been pitched so high, that no mere tinkering with them could have done any good. The reductions in all cases still left the increase of assessments from 40 to 50 per cent, of the original figures for the Talooka, and as for the villages and individual holdings, Mr. Pedder's revision took no account of them, but left them at the mercy of the Department. It is no wonder that a scheme so maimed in all essential features failed to give relief. The Government at the same time were so frightened at their own goodness that they did their best to cancel their Resolution of October 1874, by another resolution dated 17th December 1874, which laid down the principle that the limitations to increase were not to apply to revision Settlements sanctioned for other Collectorates than Poona and Sholapoor.

The usual consequences of high pitched assessments followed with unexpected regularity, and the old evils of annual remissions and suspensions, which had ceased to disfigure the revenue statements for nearly thirty years, were reproduced in all the revised Talookas. In the Bhimathadi Talooka Rs.65,000 had to be remitted in 1873-74, Rs.16,572 in 1874-75, Rs.19,141 in 1875-76. In the same Talooka Rs.30,977 had to be suspended as outstandings in 1871-72, Rs.36,623 in 1872-73, Rs.75,036 in 1873-74, and Rs.2,11,937 in 1876-77. In the Indapoor Talooka Rs.73,160 had to be suspended as outstandings in 1871-72, Rs.11,907 in 1873-74, Rs.1,08,693 in 1876-77; while in the same Talooka Rs.14,229 had to be written off as remissions in 1875-76. In the Kheda Talooka Rs.21,589 had to be remitted in 1873-74. In the Sholapoor Talooka Rs.44,921 had to be remitted in 1874-75; and Rs.15,843 represented the outstandings in 1873-74, Rs.2,19,915 in 1876-77, Rs.41,925 in 1877-78. In the Madhe Talooka Rs.19,429 had to be remitted in 1871-72, and Rs.23,906 in 1874-75; while Rs.35,930 were allowed to remain as outstandings in 1871-72; Rs.1,14,384 in 1876-77, and Rs.17,604 in 1877-78. In the Pandherpoor Talooka Rs.21,750 had to be remitted in 1871-72, and Rs.9,169 in 1874-75; while the outstandings were Rs.22,058 in 1871-72, and Rs.90,356 in 1876-77. In the Sangole Talooka, Rs.21,072 had to be remitted in 1871-72, and the outstandings were in the same year Rs.9,608, and Rs.58,963 in 1876-77. Notwithstanding these remissions and suspensions, the Ryots found it difficult to pay up the assessment, and hundreds of Survey numbers were sold for arrears of land revenue, and realized only nominal prices, or came back upon the hands of Government unsold. In the Bhimathadi Talooka alone, the number of defaulting Ryots in 1873-74 was 4341, the amount due from whom was Rs.82,421. To realize this sum two lacs of acres of land assessed at Rs.1,35,000 were sold, and realized Rs.15,010 in the sale. As many as 21,252 acres were bought in by Government in 1874-75, and 14,174 acres in 1875-76, for nominal prices. Many hundreds of acres were thrown out of cultivation in all the districts, so that after 30 years of trial, the condition of these unfortunate districts was no better than what it was when Captain Wingate and Mr. Goldsmid, the founders of the Bombay system of settlement, entered upon their inquiries in 1834-35.

With falling prices, with diminished expenditure upon Public Works, with diminished employment of English capital on Railway and other works, with a great increase in population, with no resource of wastelands to fall back upon, with the encroachments of public forests, with increased salt duties, and a new License Tax, with three years of successive famines, in which the agricultural Ryots were allowed no remissions worth the name, with the depredations of locusts and rats their present condition can more easily be imagined than described. The Supa riots, and the recent dacoities can never be understood in their right significance till the history of the fiscal administration for the last 10 years is studied with a serious interest, and with a proper sense of responsibility for the welfare of the many millions of persons who are affected by the action of the Settlement Department, and all the sophistries about the advancing prosperity of the country are discarded as impertinent trifling with the most absorbing problem of the day. It is a hopeful feature of the times that the Ryots' position is now realised in the nakedness of its unmitigated helplessness by the highest authorities of the land. Even the Government of India, which hitherto refused to be persuaded to the contrary, has now deliberately given expression to its view that the latest revisions were based on an unduly high estimate of the normal value of field produce in the Deccan, and that it is desirable, in view of the great fall of prices and the vicissitudes of the seasons, to order further reduction of the assessment. On another point also the Government of India has now been pleased to admit that the rigidity of the assessment of a grievance which must be remedied by introducing a varying scale of Revenue demand, whereby in the event of a failure of the rains, or other cause of serious damage to the crops, the normal assessment might be reduced by a certain percentage over a whole district, or portion of a district. The recognition of the two facts that the assessments are excessive, and that their rigidity is unsuited to this part of the country, are both most important concessions on the part of the Government of India to the demands of public opinion in regard to this long disputed question.

The only point that now remains to be considered relates to the question as to what steps should be taken to give effect to the liberal counsels which have found acceptance of late with the Government of India. The most experienced officers of Government are now anxiously engaged in the deliberation of this great fiscal reform. We have ourselves come across two schemes of reform, propounded by two of the most philanthropic and experienced District Judges in this Presidency. One of these schemes takes it as proved by the admission of the revenue officers themselves that the revenue rules of Government have contributed to the Ryot's difficulties. In the words of Mr. Pedder, the assessments, moderate in average years, are found burdensome in bad years, when the land does not yield even the peasant's wage, and the necessity of maintaining themselves is one, though not the sole, cause of the peasants' incurring debts. Further as on all inferior lands the cost of cultivation and of the Ryots' subsistence approaches very nearly the whole value of the crop, no profits are earned by him, as he subsists only because he works on his field. There can be, therefore, no economic rent, and the Ryot pays the Government land-tax, either with borrowed money, or else from income derived otherwise than from his land. On the basis of these proved and admitted facts, it is suggested that in the districts liable to famine, the assessment should be on the crop rather than on the land. Instead of settling the revenue in cash, it should be ascertained what share of the crops should form the assessment, and option should be allowed to the occupant to pay it at commutation rates a little below the market value of the grain. The Government assessment should be one half of the true rent. This fraction of the true rent can be easily converted into a fraction of the gross produce, and thus converted should remain constant. The Settlement in this sense would be a permanent one, though the revenue actually received would vary with the amount of the crops and their market value. Such in brief are the more important features of this scheme of reform.

The other scheme follows the lines of the one we noticed in all the features above noted except that it is much less complex in its details. The proposal is to give the Ryot the option of paying, instead of the existing cash assessment, one anna share of the gross produce. As the Revenue officers contend that the cash assessments in the Poona District represent only 1/14th of the gross crops, in Sholapoor 1/35th, in Nagar 1/12th, there could be no loss to Government by the adoption of a general tithe of one anna in the rupee. This scheme provides a special machinery for the collection of the tithes which is wanting in the other proposal. The tithes are to be collected by capitalist farmers who will take leases from government for a fixed period, and pay in cash the amounts contracted for by them into the government treasury. This would enable government to dispense with the services of its costly Survey Department, and also to reduce to a considerable extent its revenue collecting agency. The rigidity of the present settlement rules would be obviated, because the levy of tithes would operate as a sort of a sliding scale of remissions in bad years, and it would be acceptable to the Ryots as a welcome return to the old native custom. It would also encourage the growth of a capitalist class of land farmers, who will be able to save Government from the risks at present incurred in unfavourable seasons, and who, as assignees of Government share, will be directly interested in the prosperity of the Ryots. These two schemes have been put forth by their authors for the consideration of Government, and they propose that they should be introduced experimentally in a few selected Talookas of the Deccan Districts, and their action carefully watched for a number of years to see what improvements may be desirable in their details.

Before such an experiment is made and its results are carefully ascertained, it may be to some extent presumptuous to judge the merits of either of these schemes, yet with all deference due to the experience of the officers who have proposed these solutions of the agrarian problem, we may be permitted to hazard a few remarks with a view more to stimulate discussion than to lay down any positive theory of our own. Our first impression about both these schemes is that they are too good, and too benevolently conceived in the interests of the

Ryots to secure any chance of acceptance from the practical administrators of this country, which is bordering on bankruptcy, and of which the land revenue is the chief resource. If the state is to receive only a half share of the economic rent of the national lands, the land assessments in this Presidency must be at once reduced from three crores to less than two crores. In the N. W. Provinces the settlement is made on the principle of taking from 55 to 60 per cent of the net or owner's economic rent. This proportion is felt to be very heavy in those Provinces, which are blessed with a richer soil and more abundant water supply than the parched districts of the Deccan can boast of. The population of those provinces is nearly double of that of this Presidency, while their land revenue is only one third more. On the principle therefore of following the N. W. P. system of taking 1/2 share of the economic rent, the land revenue, instead of being about Rs.2 per head as it is now, will have to be reduced by at least one crore of rupees. The Government is certainly not prepared to make such a sacrifice in its present straits. Another way of arriving at the same conclusion is to ascertain the total value of the produce of land, taking of course an average of several years. From the figures published by Professor Dadabhoy Nowrojee and endorsed by Mr. Hyndman, it would appear that the proportion of the gross produce of India estimated at 300 crores of Rupees, which falls to the share of this Presidency with its population of 1 crore and 60 lacs, is 40 crores, out of which if the Government land tax is to represent 1/16 share, the land revenue of this Presidency would be Rs.2½ crores or about 30 per cent of its present figure. The sacrifice would be too great for the Government to make in its present bankrupt condition.

The Poona Sarvajanik Sabha has taken the trouble of ascertaining the views of both the Ryots and the Sowcars in regard to both these two schemes. About 70 of the Ryots and Sowcars of Shinar in the Nasik District have expressed their readiness to pay 1/16 share of the gross produce. About 40 Ryots of Mandavagad, Pimpulsooti, and Shindee in the Shiroor Talooka have expressed their consent to pay 1/16 of the gross produce, and

1/6 of the net produce to Government. About 400 Ryots in the villages of Indapoor, Pimpri, Shegaum Mandangaum, Radesinge, Rajawadi, Kolthan, Varkoote, Takrarwadi, Kate and Shetpal &c. of the Indapoor Talooka, have expressed their willingness to pay 1/16 of the gross produce. About 50 Ryots of Gosewan, Agati, Chadgaum, Warkoote, in the same Talooka consent to pay 1/16 of the gross, or 1/6 of the net produce. About 100 Ryots from the villages of Kargam, Warwand, Koosegaum, Korolee, Wagone and Supe have expressed their consent to pay 1/16 of the gross, or 1/6 of the net produce. About 20 of the Sowkars and Ryots of the Tasgaum Talooka in the Satara Collectorate have expressed their willingness to pay 1/16 of the gross produce of the Jeerait land, and 1/20 of the Bagayet land. It may be gathered from these details that there is a sort of consensus of opinion on the part of both the Ryots and the Sowkars that there would be no ground left for complaint if the Government demand were confined to the levy of 1/16 of the gross, and 1/6 of the net produce; which latter amount comes as nearly as possible to one half of the economic rent, or the letting value of the land. The opposition to both the schemes would therefore come entirely from the Government, and we do not see our way to ensure their acceptance by the authorities under the present circumstances.

Independently of this consideration, we should feel no hesitation in giving our preference to the latter of the two schemes, which would fix 1/16th of the gross produce as the limit of the assessment. It is much the simpler of the two. It would involve no nice inquiries into the rent rolls of the country, it would commend itself to the people as a return to the old order of things, and it would secure the interests of Government in bad seasons much better by interposing between the Ryot and the Revenue official a capitalist middle-man who would be in a position to pay the Government dues without fail, if only his position were properly assured and guaranteed. Our only objection to the scheme is that it would be too wide a departure from the established order of things to be properly appreciated by the persons in responsible charge of the government of the country. In all matters of reform it is essential to bear this consideration in view, namely, that the departure from the established order of things shall be minimised as far as may be possible. The present tax gathering machinery is so completely developed in all its parts from the Revenue Commissioner and the Collector down to the village Patel and the Koolkarnee, so many vested interests have grown up in the long course of years that the substitution of an entirely novel machinery, such as that of the farmers of the 1/16th tithes, would introduce elements of trouble and disturbance which would of themselves be deemed by Government to be sufficient to withhold their sanction to any such experiment. Moreover the farmer of revenue will most certainly not be able to maintain himself in his new position without making encroachments upon the rights of the occupants of Government land. In fact, the scheme as proposed contemplates their eventual elevation to the status of Zamindars. The Bengal Zamindars are not in high favour with the Government of India, and several authorities on that side have not hesitated to condemn Lord Cornwallis' settlement as a great mistake, which the Government cannot too soon rectify, and it has been the steady policy of the last few years to nullify, as far as the solemn engagements of Government admit of it, the guarantees given by the settlement. All these considerations weigh heavily against the scheme, and preclude all chance of its being ever adopted with that earnestness of purpose which alone can ensure its success.

Having thus expressed our views about the merits of the two schemes noticed above, it will be expected from us that we should be prepared to suggest a scheme of our own, which will be free from all the objections which have been urged above. It is with great diffidence that we submit such a scheme. We take, however, our stand not upon economic theories or ancient custom, but we found our own scheme upon the basis of the despatches of the Secretary of State, *viz.*, Sir Charles Wood's despatch of 1862, supplemented by Sir Stafford Northcote's

Despatch of 1865. These despatches represented the outcome of the deliberations of 30 years, and were intended to be operative throughout all the old and settled districts of British India. Had it not been for the fact that Sir John Lawrence, the then Governor-General of India, was opposed to these measures, full effect would have been given to these views of the India Office long ago. The Despatches directed the extension of the permanent settlement of land upon the cash rates then in force to all provinces, where 80 per cent of the arable land was under cultivation, and where there was no likelihood of any Irrigation or Railway Works being extended. Both these conditions, it will be at once admitted, apply in the fullest measure to this Presidency, for it appears from an official statement published by the Bombay Government that out of 24,220,022 acres of culturable Government land the occupied area is 21,599,597 acres, or nearly 90 per cent. Since the completion of the great Railway lines, there is not much room left for any extension of the Railway system, and as for irrigation works, the circumstances of this Presidency afford little scope for any profitable development in that direction. There is thus no excuse left for refusing to extend the benefit of those Despatches to this Presidency. The cash rates, which at present obtain in all the unrevised settlements, have been found by 30 years' experience to be practically beneficial to the Ryots, and by no means injurious to the interests of Government. In those Talookas where the revised rates have been introduced, they have proved to be utter failures by the experience of the last 10 years. All that the Government has therefore to do under the circumstances is to take the unrevised rates as a basis, and make them permanent all over the Presidency. This would involve no loss of actual revenue, for the loss involved in the return to the old rates in the revised Talookas would be only nominal, because, as we have shown above, the increased assessment has never yet been collected without recourse to oppressive measures, and frequent remissions, and suspensions. The saving effected by the abolition of the Settlement Department, which would have no work left for it, would be clear gain in these hard times, when Government is at its wit's ends to find out sufficient scope for retrenchments. The existing arrangements for the collection of revenue will remain undisturbed, no nice calculations of economic rent will have to be made from year to year, nor will there be any necessity left for substituting grain in place of cash payments, no new class of farmers or middle-men will be artificially created to cause annoyance to the Ryots, and suspicion to the officials. These advantages will we hope commend the scheme to the favourable consideration of Government.

We are quite aware that it may be objected to the proposal we have made, that it will work no immediate change in the position of the Ryot, and in his relations to the Sowcar. We regard this more as a recommendation than as a draw-back. There can, however, be no doubt that the conversion of the cash rates, of the old settlement into a permanent land tax would effect a most desirable change in the course of time, and would remedy all existing evils in a smooth, natural and imperceptible manner. These rates having been proved to be moderate by the experience of 30 years, will most certainly encourage private capitalists to invest their earnings in the land to an extent which, under the present arrangements, is found impossible. As all the old settlements are now rapidly approaching the completion of their 30 years' term, there is not an estate in the country which can be said to be secure from the most arbitrary enhancement at the resettlement. The painful experience of the last 10 years in the revised Talookas has shaken general confidence in the pledges given by government that they will not tax improvements. The present race of capitalists have no inducements to invest their savings in the improvement of land. Their advances are all made for the Ryots's personal and unproductive expenditure, and mostly at usurious rates of interest. The new legislation intended for the protection of the Ryots, has absolutely increased the risks, of lending and with it the rates of interest, and rendered cooperation between the labouring and capitalist classes all but impossible. With the extension of the permanent settlement, a better confidence will be engendered, and the friction between the two classes will be much less than it is felt to be at present. Under the present arrangements the land tax is paid really by the Sowcar, but not on his own account. He pays it as an advance to the Ryot along with his other advances for seeds and subsistence; when the settlement is permanent, his position would be legalised, and insured against all risks. The thrifty Ryot will of course maintain his own place, and will extend his operations, and rise to a better position. The indifferent and lazy Ryot will make way for better people, who will take his place with great advantage to the general interest. The change will not be sudden, but a slow and organic growth, and the new order of things will develop the best energies of all classes without any shock to vested interests. Of course in course of time the provident and thrifty classes will succeed to the ownership of land, and a class of land-lords would spring up all over the country, whose interest it will be to make the most of the resources of the soil, and of the great public works constructed by Government. At present the enormous expenditure of Government on Railways and Irrigation works is all but thrown away on account of the all-pervading poverty of the so-called peasant proprietors. The political and social advantages of such a change would be even more important than the economical ones. The monied classes, having at present no interest in the land, cannot occupy the position, nor enjoy the status, nor discharge the functions of land-lords. The absence of such a class retards progress in all directions. The Presidency of Bengal enjoys this advantage over the rest of India, and this circumstance alone accounts for its prosperous and progressive condition. The change, we have proposed, will secure the same, if not better, benefits to the other Presidencies of India.

We are aware that the spirit in which the measures of protective legislation at present in favour with Government are conceived, will not dispose the authorities to extend their support to any scheme of the sort we have sketched above. We have, however, no misgivings on the point that, sooner or later, the Government of India will be forced to retrace its steps, and give in its adhesion to our proposal. The resources of the British Government are indeed great, and its power overwhelming, but great as are these resources and powers, they cannot fight against the elements without being discomfited. In all old and backward countries like India, there is always only a minority of people who monopolise all the elements of strength. They are socially and religiously in the front ranks, they possess intelligence, wealth, thrifty habits, knowledge, and power of combination. The majority of the population are unlettered, improvident, ignorant, disunited, thriftless, and poor in means. No political manipulation can hold the balance between these two classes, power must gravitate where there is intelligence and wealth, and it is a hopeless struggle to keep up a poverty-stricken peasantry in possession of the soil, and divorce the natural union of capital and land. The Ryots must grow in thrift, in knowledge, and in power of combination, before such a position can be realised. All the countries of Europe have passed through this stage, England even not excepted. Peasant-proprietors thrive well in France, because the difference between the French peasantry and the other classes of the population in all the elements of power is not so marked as in India. The French peasant knows thrift, is prudent enough not to marry till he has means, works day and night on his farm, knows to read and write, he is the lord of the soil, and not a tenant of the state, and his political education has qualified him to realise his equality with the best blue blood of the country. There can therefore be no comparison between such a class and the rack-rented Indian peasantry. Democracy cannot be transplanted into the Indian soil at a start, it will take many generations of patient education and the discipline of freedom to raise the Indian peasant to a sense of his equality with the Brahmin and the Bania. There is only one way out of the difficulty. Government must retrace its steps, and allow this country to grow and progress on the same lines which every other country in the world has followed with such ultimate success.

The prospective loss to government of what economical

writers call 'the unearned increment' has been advanced in some quarters as an objection to the scheme we have suggested. It is a public misfortune that theorists, who find no scope for their hobbies in England, are allowed to inflict their mischievous fallacies upon this country with unrestricted freedom. The unearned increment theory is one of those hobbies which has been ridden to death in this country, involving the Government and the people in common confusion and ruin. We do not see, however, why there should be any such loss of the unearned increment. On the other hand, we firmly believe that with the ever increasing poverty of the agricultural classes, there is little scope left for the unearned increment. The present revenue policy effectively diminishes the surplus of production by rendering impossible all improvements in the land. Moreover, there can be no doubt, that with the extension of the permanent settlement, and the development of the resources of the country, the increment, earned or unearned, will be so great that the direct and indirect taxes will yield a sure and certain increase of income from all sources, which will go to make up more than all the deficiency arising from the loss of this unearned increment. This is our solution of the agrarian problem; the only one which we feel sure will set at rest the present troubles, and quell 'the rebellion of the belly,' which now disturbs the sense of security of the people, and the equanimity of the ruling authorities.*

**N.B.*—In connection with the solution of the agrarian problem as proposed above we may be permitted to produce the following extract from a letter which we received a few months back from one of our esteemed English friends. Our friend who has had long experience about the Zemindari Settlement in Bengal, having passed the best years of his life in the Bengal Presidency, and who from the position he occupied there is entitled to speak with authority on the subject, is of the same opinion, that unless the benefits of the permanent settlement system be extended to the Bombay Presidency, the position of the Ryot will never be improved. The letter is dated London 20th December 1877, and we leave our correspondent to speak for himself:-

Your excellent article on Sir Erskine Perry's "Notes on the Deccan Riots Report" deserves the attention of all who have the welfare of India at heart. Improving the administration of justice and rendering legal justice accessible to the masses are doubtless two questions most intimately connected with the happiness of the people. At the same time it is an error, I believe, on the part of Sir E. Perry, whatever unfair advantages Sowcars may have taken of the law, to ascribe chiefly to their action, the evil from which the Deccan riots arose. There is ample evidence to show that the rigorous demands of the revenue officers compel the cultivators to have recourse to the money-lenders, and that the evil originates in demands being made, which the people cannot satisfy without recourse to the demoralising practice of constant borrowing. If this be so, the remedy to the evil must lie in the permanent settlement of the land tax on terms consistent with justice and moderation, which, by increasing the value of land as a security, would enable the cultivator to borrow on less onerous terms than those he has to submit to now, and would afford him the chance of ultimately freeing himself from debt. Regularity in the collection of the revenue as well as the prosperity of the agricultural classes would be promoted by such a measure; and as its tendency would be to render the cultivators less dependent on the Sowcars, the animosity, which was the ultimate and immediate cause of the Deccan riots, would not attain the same degree of virulence. Such has been the course of events in Bengal under the Permanent Settlement, whenever a cultivator was able to purchase *Putnee* or perpetual lease of his field as he could then take a correct account of his liabilities and safely incur expense in improving his farm.

If you agree with me in what I have stated, I shall be glad to see the Sarvajanik Sabha take up the question of impressing the Government with the facts, 1st that agriculture cannot flourish as long as cultivators are subjected to arbitrary demands on the part of the Government, and 2nd that the interests of the revenue as well as those of the people would be promoted by a *permanent* settlement of the Government demand on a just basis; as not only would the land revenue be then collected with regularity, but wealth would be created which would, under the general taxation of country, afford additional revenue to the State.

Comments on the above are quite superfluous. It will be seen from the foregoing extract that the proposal of our English correspondent exactly tallies in its main features with the one contained in the above contribution. That the Government of India will sooner or later be compelled to retrace its steps and extend the benefits of the Zemindari system of Bengal to all the other parts of India, we firmly believe. Now that the attention of the British public has been conspicuously drawn to the deplorable condition of the Indian Ryot, the requisite pressure will, we hope, be brought to bear at no distant date upon the Government of India to solve the agrarian problem in the only way in which it can be effectually and definitively solved.—*By the Editor.*

2

THE DECCAN AGRICULTURISTS BILL*

For the first time in the social history of rural Deccan under British rule, the law abiding Kunbi was found in 1875 to take the law into his own hands, assail the Sowcar, his creditor, and destroy the bonds, books, and papers on which the latter relied for proof of his claim. The agrarian disturbances in the districts of Poona, Sholapore, Ahmednagar and Satara were organized on a plan and after a method which at once proclaimed the seriousness of their causes, and the gravity of the issues involved. They would have spread far and wide but for the assurances conveyed to the Ryots by the Civil authorities that their grievances would be listened to, and remedied. But these pledges and promises remained long unfulfilled. A Commission was indeed appointed, and that Commission made a most searching inquiry into the causes of the disturbances and of the present condition of the Ryots, and submitted an elaborate and exhaustive Report on the subject. But the Government of India slumbered over this report for several years. Meanwhile successive famines and unfavourable seasons exhausted the slender resources of an already impoverished community. Matters, however, did not reach their climax in the Deccan until March

*JPSS, October 1879, Vol.II, No.2.

and April last, when the crimes of dacoity and house-breaking shook the peaceful population to its inmost depths. Lord Lytton, on the authority of Sir Richard Temple, endeavoured in the Council to assure the public that the recent disturbances and dacoities were not caused by the indebtedness of the Ryots. We are not disposed to enter into the discussion of this question at present, though our own view of the matter has been enunciated at length in the last number of our *Quarterly Journal*. We are glad to find that those views have met with welcome support from the highest authorities. Mr. Hope's able and exhaustive speech, when introducing the Deccan Agriculturists Relief Bill, contains a masterly analysis of the causes which have depressed the ryots in the Deccan, and of the remedies which it is in the power of the Legislature and of the Executive Government to adopt with a view to better their condition. Mr. Hope's untiring industry and marvellous capacity for work are well-known. Although a revenue officer who has spent most of his time in Gujarat, he has, in connection with the present Bill, as his speech throughout shows, spared no efforts to inform himself of the past history and present state of the Deccan Ryots. In fact he appears to have exhausted all the known sources of information on the subject. His whole measure undoubtedly proceeds upon the lines of the Deccan Riots Commission's Report. This Commission's investigations and recorded evidence probably left little to desire on the subject. Mr. Hope has also been a diligent student of the discussions in India and England on the condition of the Deccan peasantry. Not content with this, he had a personal conference in April last at Bombay with Sir Richard Temple and the Members of the Bombay Government. The Bill, therefore, is not a haphazard measure. It is the outcome of deep, steady, and diligent research into the condition and requirements of the Deccan peasantry.

It is in this spirit that we welcome the Bill, and although, in reviewing its principles as unfolded in Mr. Hope's speech and in the detailed provisions of the measure, we may have occasion to differ from Mr. Hope, we cannot help thinking that upon the whole, it is a measure, which working in conjunction with a more liberal land revenue policy, and *on that condition alone,* is calculated to afford that relief to the Ryot which he has so long needed, and which his most ardent well-wishers have so long desired.

To us amongst the most salient points in which the chief interest of Mr. Hope's speech centres, not the least remarkable are the passages in which the Hon'ble Mover calmly but effectively explodes the doctrinaire views of optimist officials in regard to the causes of the Deccan Ryot's indebtedness. It had until of late become a fashion with a certain class of Revenue and Survey officials in this Presidency to account for the Ryot's miseries by running the Kunbi down as a thriftless fellow, living beyond his means, spending his savings extravagantly in marriage expenses, improvident to a degree, and never thinking of the "morrow." The Deccan Riots Commission's Report most effectually exploded this theory. It showed conclusively that undue prominence had been given to the expenditure on marriage and other festivals as a cause of the Ryot's indebtedness. Mr. Hope's experience as a revenue officer and his deliberate opinion founded upon that experience ought to set at rest the notion that the improvident and thriftless nature of the Kunbi has been the cause of his depressed condition. Nothing can be more just and truthful than his noble, though a little forensic, vindication of the national character of the Maratha Kunbi. He says:—

"The Maratha Kunbi, is not the defective and useless creature postulated. No such material composed the armies of Sivaji and his successors, which defeated the Moguls, over-ran half India and founded an empire of which the remnants still flourish around us. As a soldier, the Maratha in older days was as enterprising as he was hardy equally able to bide a buffet and to strike a blow. At present he furnishes material, perhaps, second to none in India for the purposes of modern war. All representations of him as *thriftless, enervated, and puny* are incorrect. As a peasant proprietor he is no unfavorable specimen of the class. Mr. Chaplin and our other early authorities give him credit for many sterling qualities. He is still represented by the Commission as a simple, well disposed peasant, contented with the scantiest clothing and hardest fare, not without masculine qualities, and a stubborn endurance, though still mostly uneducated, and consequently without broad range of intelligence. Of course improvidence and slovenly cultivation may be detected in individuals or particular localities. But we must not expect too much. Under British rule, the Kunbi has undoubtedly progressed as fast as adverse circumstances allowed. He works his fields to the best of his lights, and in the dry season travels far in search of day labour, or with his cart on hire. During the late famine he displayed resources equally creditable to his thrift and his good feeling. His embarrassed condition seems to be rather his misfortune than his fault, induced by the obligation of ancestral debt, *the burden of the land revenue demand,* and the facilities for extortion conferred by our laws upon the creditors."

The Italics are ours. They emphasize another point on which Mr. Hope corrects official optimism, and establishes the connection of the ryot's indebtedness with the rack-renting revenue policy of Government. After admitting that *"to our revenue system, must in candour be ascribed some share in the indebtedness of the raiyat,"* and that "it seems likely that indebtedness arising mainly from other causes, normal, or special, may have been aggravated by our rigid system," he proceeds to say:—

"If the recovery of Instalments were more co-incident with the time when the Ryot realizes his produce instead of falling sometimes too early and sometimes too late, and so the land revenue were more in practice, (what it is in law), a first charge on the latter, much temporary borrowing, fraud in crediting produce, and eventual Government process for recovery might be avoided. Some debt, too, may be caused, by the fear of *eviction, a mode of recovering the revenue for which a substitute is much needed."*

Now mild as this expression of opinion is, (and perhaps, considering the official position of Mr. Hope, we think he could not put it stronger), it contains in so many words a silent, but not the less emphatic, protest against the rigidity of the revenue system and the enhanced rates of assessments. The exhaustive exposure of the unsoundness of the Bombay revenue system contained in the minutes of the Deccan Riots Commissioners could not fail to carry conviction home to any unbiased mind that the rack-renting policy of Government has been to a large extent responsible for the Ryot's indebtedness. But perhaps a stronger condemnation of the system can scarcely be found than in the words of His Excellency the Viceroy Lord Lytton. In the course of the debate which followed Mr. Hope's speech, the Hon'ble Sir Robert Egerton, the Lieutenant Governor of Punjab, pointed out that too little attention was paid to the fact of the stringency of our revenue laws having contributed to, if it did not entirely originate, the indebtedness and difficulties of the Deccan Ryot. His Honour considered it was clearly desirable that while steps were taken to protect the Ryot from the private creditor, adequate measures should be adopted at the same time to afford him some relief from the pressure of its own demand, in a way which would not throw upon the Ryot entirely the burden of meeting all the risks of a scanty rainfall and a precarious crop, but would leave those risks on the Government itself, and relieve the ryot who had been found to be incapable of meeting them. His Excellency, in noticing this objection, remarked that what "My Honourable friend the Lieutenant Governor pointed out to us yesterday is what I am afraid only too true, that this state of things exists, not indeed in the same degree of intensity, yet more or less potentially as it were, throughout the greater part of India, where a comparatively slight aggravation of existing circumstances might not impossibly produce results scarcely less distressing than those which it is our present object to mitigate in some parts of the Deccan." This confession on the part of Lord Lytton has a significance in the fact that the depression of Ryots is general over the greater part of India, and that the causes of depression are the same all over the country. What follows is still more reassuring, for His Excellency says:—

"I am personally disposed to believe that the question of relieving the Ryot from the unvarying pressure of claims on the part of the state itself has been urged by us on the attention of the Government of Bombay in special reference to those districts of the Deccan for which we are now legislating, and that it has engaged our own attention in reference to other parts of India. The indifference of the Government to this aspect of the question must not, therefore, be assumed from the absence of all allusion to it in the terms of the present measure. I am personally disposed to believe that the rigidity of our present land system might in various directions be relaxed with great benefit to the cultivator, unaccompanied by any serious inconvenience to the state. As the alterations in the *modus operandi* of our land revenue system, whether as *regards the collection or assessment of revenue*, can be effected without legislation, the provisions of the Bill now before us are properly confined to those remedial measures which absolutely require not only legislation, but legislation of a special and novel character."

These words of the Viceroy, while admitting the rigidity and undue pressure of the present land revenue system, sufficiently explain why the question of the land policy has been kept apart from the consideration of this Bill. In fact the Government of India have already drawn the attention of Sir Richard Temple's Government to it, both in their letter, dated the 26th February 1879, and in the covering letter of the 26th July, forwarding this Bill for the consideration of the Bombay Government. Judging, however, from the Bombay Government's reply in the last para of their letter dated the 18th April, Sir Richard Temple seems to show a certain lukewarmness in entertaining proposals having for their object the alteration of the present system. We are told that:—

"The Governor in Council has given his best consideration to the question of the possibility of superseding the fixed rates of land revenue assessment at present in force in the four districts in question by a scale of rates varying, as suggested by the Government of India, with the favourableness of the seasons. The proposal is one which, it is anticipated, there would be very great difficulty in adopting, but the Government have the matter still under their consideration, and should it be found feasible to recommend any alterations in the existing system of settlement of the nature suggested, a separate communication will be addressed to the Government of India on the subject."

We trust Sir Richard Temple's Government will see their way to comply with the wishes of the Government of India, and propose changes in the existing system, either by re-adopting the proposals made by the Government of Sir Philip Wodehouse, or by introducing a permanent grain settlement in lieu of cash payments. Of all the proposals this appears to us to be the only one that is likely to commend itself to the attention of the Government of India as solving the agrarian difficulty. Any remedy in the direction of an assessment fluctuating with the variations of the seasons is sorely needed. It must not for a moment be supposed that the difficulties of Government in regard to the collection of revenue would be over with one or two favourable seasons. If the question is shelved because the next season will probably find the Ryot able to meet the revenue from the sale of his crops, it may land the authorities in greater difficulties in the following year. And the difficulty of realizing the revenue will, we fear, be found overwhelming when, with the present Bill passed into law, the Ryot shall have lost all credit with the money-lender. We think with Mr. Hope that any relief intended in this direction should be given promptly and simultaneously with the working of the Act, as otherwise the Act alone will do no real, tangible, or lasting good, and might even aggravate the present condition of things.

The third official misconception which the debate on Mr. Hope's speech has cleared up is in regard to the Sowears, their character, and their relations with the Ryot. As a rule our district officials have painted the money-lender in the blackest of colours. He has been denounced for his greed, and his rapacity, and held up to ridicule as the village 'Shylock', and the sole cause of all the Ryot's miseries. The Deccan Riots Commissioners, however, showed satisfactorily that the money- lender is not only the curse of the Ryot as he is supposed to be, but that he plays a most useful part in the rural economy of the Deccan. But for him, the state would have found it extremely difficult to ensure the punctual realization of its revenue. A great portion of revenue, although paid directly by, and in the name of, the Ryot, is actually advanced by the Sowear. His trade is supposed to be unduly profitable, but when his risks are taken into account, the Commissioners found that his profits are not greater than those warranted by the precarious and risky character of his business

On this subject there was a pretty general agreement in the Council, as is shown by the observations of the Hon'bles Sir Alexander Arbuthnot, Mr. Rivers Thomson, Sir John Strachey, His Excellency the Viceroy, and of Mr. Hope in his second speech. It was admitted by all of them that the Sowcar was as necessary to the Ryot as the seed he sows, or the rain from the heavens that irrigates his field, and that without him Indian agriculture would probably be not possible, and we may add, the government revenue would not be realized except in kind.

While Mr. Hope showed some reserve in denouncing as strongly, as was desirable, the land revenue system, he felt no such compunction in condemning the evil effects of the other agency of government which has aggravated the Ryot's embarrassments by making the administration of justice a prolific source of revenue through the Limitation, Stamp, and Court Fees Acts. From 1827 to 1859 the Elphinstone Code eminently answered all the requirements of the law of debtors and creditors. It combined the outward forms of the native system of procedure, with European common sense and equity in practice. It provided for arbitration or Panchayat Courts, a usury law, and a long limitation of suits. In 1859, the old law of limitation gave place to a new one, in which the period for suits was reduced. In the same year also was passed the first Civil Procedure Act, followed by the Stamp Act in 1860. The procedure thus became complicated and expensive. The quick- witted money-lender, however, managed to accommodate himself to the new judicial system. The Courts chiefly look to bonds and their genuine execution for proofs of claim. They decline to go behind the bond. Suits are heard in the absence of the defendants and *ex parte* decisions are given in a great majority of cases. Of all the recent laws, however, those which have had a most disastrous effect on the condition of the poor peasantry, not only in the Deccan, but in other parts of this Presidency, —we might well say throughout India—are the Limitation, the Stamp and the Court Fees Acts. By the Limitation Act, the creditor was bound to obtain a renewal of the bond, or file a suit every third year, and get a decree. In either case, it was the debtor who suffered. The renewal of bonds added not only fresh costs in the shape of Stamps, Vakil's fees and Court Fees and batta &c., but increased the principal by the amount of interest accrued and the law costs. Well may therefore Mr. Hope say:—

"The condition then (1859-60) consummated has lasted with but slight variations for about twenty years. The procedure is highly elaborate and technical, the penalties of contravention of it severe; and litigation, dangerous without the guidance of a pleader, whose services are costly, and interests often at variance with those of his client. The procedure is the same for a debt of Rs.5 and 5000, except in the rare instances where Small Causes Courts are established. *Stamp and Court expenses have nearly doubled. Arbitration has been gradually shouldered out*, partly by the superior prestige of the Courts, partly by the Stamp duties, partly by its disadvantages for the money-lender. Thus owing to the penalties of contravention of procedure being severe, the law *compels the creditor, whether willing or not, to put the debtor into an embarrassing position.*"

We think, therefore, that the extension of the period of limitation for suits is one of the most valuable amongst the many new and important concessions which the Bill will secure in the interests of the Ryots. We give our most hearty support to it. We are firmly persuaded that this extension will operate most beneficially in the interests of the debtor, without in the least compromising the claims of the creditor. Seeing that his claim is not barred by limitation, the creditor will gladly give more time to the debtor for payment. Compound interest, even if not otherwise provided for in the Bill, would, in the great majority of accounts, be eliminated. The extended limitation will breed greater confidence between the Sowcar and the Ryot. There will also be a considerable saving of stamp expenses as the renewal of bond will be deferred. We are glad to find that the weight of authority in favour of this change has been overwhelming. It is one of those seven principles on which the Government of India is not prepared to entertain any compromise at any stage of the

Bill.* We find that the Government of Bombay, though not supporting it themselves, have expressed no strong opinion against it. It has accordingly been provisionally adopted in the Bill. Probably Sir Richard Temple was not aware that that question was one of those on which the Government of India was not prepared to entertain any compromise. If His Excellency had known this previously, he would probably have not only given his own adhesion to it, but would have got even his colleagues in the Government to support it. But it is not even too late now for His Excellency to convert his government over to the views of the Government of India. We grant that the extension of the Limitation Law will probably operate to diminish the stamp revenue at present realizable from the districts. But this diminution will be as nothing compared to the immense relief that it will give to the Ryots. This consideration so much outweighs that of revenue that we should rejoice to see the extended limitation applied to the whole of India.

Another concession that, in our opinion, must be made in the same direction is in regard to Stamps and Court Fees. This may be done in the four districts at once, seeing that real relief to the Ryot is the main object of the Bill. In a Memorandum by Mr. W.M.Coghlan, the District Judge of Tanna, on the cost of the Courts in this Presidency, it was shown by the learned Judge, by a reference to figures of receipts and costs, that,

"excluding the Original Side of the High Court in which the Moffusil inhabitants of the Presidency have no more interest than in the Supreme Court at Hongkong, there would have been a clear profit on litigation of no less than Rs.4,60,106-7-6. Deducting from this amount the item of loss on account of the working of the Original Side of the High Court, there is a reduction of the profits on litigation to Rs.2,48,025-3-9. There-

* The seven principles that are to be strictly adhered to are :—(1) The power to go behind the bond, (2) the necessity for simplifying the procedure, (3) the augmentation of the number of tribunals, (4) village registration to which great importance is attached, (5) the establishment of courts of conciliation, (6) the extension of the period of limitation, and (7) the abolition of imprisonment for debt.

fore, the learned Judge says, 'the 1941000 sets of litigants in the Mofusil in 1873 paid amongst them Rs.2,48,025-3- 9, or Rs.1-4-5 per case to the general Treasury in excess of the cost of their litigation, and Rs.2,12,081-3-9 or Rs.1-1-6 per case to keep up the Original Side of the High Court for the inhabitants of the Island of Bombay, and notably for the benefit of lawyers and placemen."

Now, we can easily understand laws made for the purpose of bringing revenue to support the charge of judicial establishments for dealing out justice between man and man; but to make these laws operate in a way that should bring not only revenue enough to maintain them but leave a surplus or profit to go to the General Treasury, is we maintain utterly indefensible on any principle of justice. It must be remembered that such laws are not intended to secure revenue. And yet what is more common of late than to find attempts made to fill up the void in general revenues by increased stamp duties and Court fees, whenever an occasion is offered for revising these laws ?

Bringing these principles to bear upon the condition of the Ryots in the Deccan, we strongly urge on the attention of the Select Committee on Mr. Hope's Bill to see its way to a reduction of stamp duties and Court Fees in the four Deccan districts. Mere simplification of Court procedure, unaccompanied by any reduction of its costs, will scarcely afford a tangible relief. Doubtless, the extension of limitation will be some relief, but to make the relief real and thorough, it is of first importance, we think, for Government to make this additional concession even at the sacrifice of a few thousand rupees of its surplus revenue of 4 lakhs. This is no new suggestion that we offer. Experienced district Judges, in reply to enquiries made by the Deccan Riots Commission, recommended these very concessions. For instance Baron De H. Larpent, District Judge of Poona, Mr. Coghlan, District Judge of Tanna, and Mr. Birdwood, District Judge of Surat, in reply to the circular questions addressed to them by the Commission recommended that the only way whereby trials of suits between Sowcars and Ryots may be cheapened, would be to reduce the Court Fees which at present are scandalously high, and keep hundreds of defendants from going into Court. Probably there is hardly a district in which the working of the Civil Courts does not show a surplus every year. In the Deccan districts Government might well rest satisfied with a smaller surplus. It may perhaps be urged that the establishment of twelve additional Courts as proposed for the districts will absorb this surplus. We are not sure whether it will have any such effect. We think that, even after defraying the cost of the proposed establishment, there will still be left a surplus which, instead of being applied to the purposes of the general Treasury, may well go to afford a much desired and needed relief to the Deccan peasantry.

Another valuable concession to popular demands which the Bill makes, is in the direction of giving a wide scope to the principle of conciliation. To afford facilities for a friendly settlement of disputes, the Bill provides that no litigation shall commence until the conciliator appointed by Government certifies that all his attempts at an amicable termination of the dispute have failed. The office of a Conciliation-Judge will be entirely distinct from that of the Civil Judge. In the selection of a Conciliator, regard will be had chiefly to his local standing and personal influence over the people. It will be an honorary, but at the same time a most honorable, post. Since much will depend on the selection made, it is to be hoped that amongst the numerous class of old pensioners, non-practising Vakils, and respectable bankers or traders there will be found men who, by their position, character, and influence, will prove themselves fit to discharge the duties of this honorary office. At all events, the experiment deserves a fair trial before any opinion is hazarded in favour of, or against, its success. It should be remembered that the Village Panchayat is one of the oldest institutions known to this contending country, simple in its character, and least costly to the parties. These Panchayats have of late ceased to be useful to the community, owing to the establishment of regular courts of justice, and also to the discouragement they have received at the hands of the Government. But the institution has not died out altogether; for, under the form of Arbitration Courts, it has been, since the last few years, revived at Poona, Surat, and elsewhere. We think the time has come when its traditionary status may be restored and recognized with benefit to the people, by giving it a certain position in our judicial system. Nothing, in our opinion, will better popularize the principle of conciliation and amicable arbitration, or more effectually discourage useless and expensive litigation, or more successfully educate the people in self-government, than a due recognition by law of such of the Lawad or Arbitration Courts as exist in the country with advantage. Out of these bodies, conciliators might be selected. If necessary, their decisions may be made subject to review by the revision Judge, but it is desirable in the interests of the community, for whom special legislation has been deemed necessary, that such institutions should receive a legal status even under certain control, if such control be deemed necessary.

The appointment of Village Munsiffs to try suits of less than 10 Rs. in value is also another concession made to popularize the administration of justice. The Government of India appears to be of opinion that the appointment of Village Munsiffs should be restricted to village headmen, and that as these will, in many instances, be illiterate persons, whose judgments can not be expected to stand the scrutiny of our courts of revision, it is proposed that their decrees should be made final. We are sorry we cannot approve of the reasons assigned for the provision regarding finality which is proposed to be given to the decisions of these Munsiffs. It should be remembered, that in taking our model from the Madras system, our end will be best gained by incorporating the spirit of the system and not its letter. For instance, we do not see why, in the first place a good district hereditary officer, or an Inamdar, or a pensioned government servant, who has retired after faithfully serving the Government, should not be appointed to the post. When it becomes generally known that such village headmen and other leaders of the rural community, as can show themselves qualified by their education and character to exercise judicial functions, shall be invested with these responsible duties, the sons of the present village Patels and other Vatandar gentry will be induced to fit themselves by good education for such honours. It will not do to say that because there are no Village Patels at present in whom this trust can be reposed, the plan should be abandoned. A new institution like this deserves to be tried before any opinion is pronounced as to its suitability or otherwise. If the system has succeeded in Madras, there is good reason to believe that it will equally succeed in Bombay also.

It is especially in connection with suits coming for disposal before Conciliators, Arbitrators, and Village Munsiffs, that we think relief should be given to the Ryots by providing that the stamp duties on awards and court fees on applications to file such awards are altogether abolished or considerably reduced. Unless this is done, no tangible relief will be given to the Ryots. Of late years the legislature has positively discouraged conciliation and arbitration by imposing a prohibitory tax in the shape of stamps on awards. We hope this mistake will be corrected in time, and that in so far as the Deccan districts are concerned, stamps and court fees on awards and applications will be abolished.

We now come to the substantive principles and provisions of the Bill. They have a threefold object namely, (1) the protection of the Ryot from the frauds of the money-lender, (2) simplification of law procedure, and (3) the granting of relief to the Deccan Kunbi from the weight of indebtedness under which he is at present being crushed. The inquiries of the Deccan Riots Commission have established that creditors have often been found either forging bonds, or withholding the consideration mentioned in a bond, or obtaining new bonds in satisfaction of old bonds and decrees, while at the same time trying to enforce the latter. It is not a rare occurrence to find them neglecting to give credit for payments made and to refuse to satisfy their debtors, nay, misrepresent their accounts to the Kunbis. On the other hand, debtors have often been charged with tendering false receipts in evidence, making false statements in regard to payments, and not unfrequently pleading that the bonds are false when, as a matter of fact, they are genuine. The Bill seeks to provide against these frauds by requiring that every bond to which a Kunbi is a party, shall be written by, or under the supervision of, the village registrar, appointed for the purpose and shall be executed in his presence and attested by him. The village registrar shall endorse on the bond whether the consideration money was or was not paid before him, and where a bond is renewed, shall put his mark upon the document which the bond supersedes. All this is, we think, very reasonable and fair to both parties. The Ryot will know what he is about. He will have no ground to complain of the failure or non-receipt of consideration. It has been urged that the payment of consideration before the registrar will after all be only nominal, and that the debtor will pay back to the creditor the consideration money after he left the Registration office. But in that case the ryot has himself to blame for his folly. The law can obviously lend no further help. The creditor also is, by this registration system, so far secured. The instrument he gets will be one the validity of which can never be impugned, executed as it will be in the presence of the registrar. The Government of India seems to entertain doubts as to whether village Registrars will be found who can be safely trusted to discharge these duties satisfactorily. For our part we have no misgiving on the subject. We think persons fit for this office will be found without difficulty. And as the village officers will be responsible to General Registration Department, which will exercise a strict watch over their work, the success of this part of the scheme seems to us to be beyond question. Other safe-guards against frauds provided for in the Bill are, that every agriculturist shall be entitled to obtain a written receipt of the payments made by him, as also a statement of his accounts at the end of every year. He will also receive from the money-lender on application a pass book containing entries of all payments made and received. These will be duly attested by the creditor. Entries made in the pass book will be deemed equivalent to the granting of receipts. Failure to comply with this requisition will render the Sowkar liable to a fine up to Rs.100. Considering that agriculturists are already acquainted with the practice of obtaining receipts and pass books from Government for revenue instalments paid by them, we do not apprehend the least difficulty in the carrying out of these provisions.

The simplification of procedure aimed at by the Bill consists (1) in the diminution of the local jurisdiction of the present Subordinate Courts by the enlargement of their number from 24 to 36, so as to bring them as near to the Ryots' homes as possible; (2) in the enlargement of the powers of these Courts by investing them not only with the powers of the Small Cause Courts, but with these powers enlarged so as to include mortgage-suits and insolvency proceedings. The question of giving summary jurisdiction to the Civil Courts was warmly debated in the Council. The Honourable Mr. Stokes and the Hon. Mr. Cockerell questioned the propriety of conferring the extended powers without the right of appeal and maintained that such extensive powers will leave the Judges in fear of nobody, and mistakes will often arise from incapacity, corruption, laziness, haste, ignorance, and the love of arbitrary power. In simple suits, it is urged, there will be little fear of such mistakes occurring, but mortgage cases involve difficult questions of title, priorities, and the taking of accounts. The investigation of these questions demands considerable experience on the part of the Judges, and no right decision can be arrived at in regard to them without the Courts having the aid of a criticising bar, which the Bill proposes to do away with. A special revising agency will, they say, be no adequate substitute for a Court of Appeal. The special officer will be so much over-whelmed with work that he will simply scamp his duties. The Honourable Mr. Hope replied to these objections that the suggestion of conferring summary jurisdiction had been recommended by the Secretary of State, that the revision scheme combined all the advantage of an Appeal Court and something more, in the fact that, whereas the Appeal Court tried such cases only which came before it in appeal, the revising agency would supervise the work done in a large proportion of suits brought before it. Again, as to the expediency suggested of placing mortgage-cases beyond the pale of the revising agency, on account of their intricate character, Mr. Hope contends that as a matter of fact mortgage-cases are not very intricate. But granting that they are, the revision Judge and assistants, being members of the regular Judicial Department in subordination to the High Court, may be expected to do full justice to them. In the course of the examination and revision proceedings, most of the serious abuses and irregularities of law will come to be perceived. 'After all,' says Mr. Hope, 'the would-be appellant is deprived of nothing by the proposed substitution of inspection and revision; for he can draw attention to his case by petition, when it will be dealt with just as he can have it now on appeal. If the Appellate Courts are supposed to be less harsh than the courts of first instance, there is nothing to prevent the revising Judge from showing leniency too. If Appellate Courts often confirm decisions on a mere perusal of the record, the special Judge's inspection may have the same effect.' On a balance of arguments *pro* and *con*, and having regard to the consideration that the main object of the Bill is to dispense cheap, and speedy justice, and discourage costly and useless litigation, we are of the opinion that the procedure contemplated in Mr. Hope's Bill, which displaces the system of appeals by a revising agency, is calculated to carry out the objects which the legislature has in view far more satisfactorily than the cumbrous machinery of the Appeal Courts, and that the provision regarding the finality of the decisions even in mortgage cases will not be attended with any failure of justice, or loss to the creditor, seeing that the decisions of the Courts of first instance, who try mortgage suits, have in the great majority of cases been hitherto found to be upheld, and that they are far better situated to deal with facts elicited in evidence than the superior Courts.

The power of making a searching inquiry, and of going behind the bond, and examining item by item, the mode of taking separate accounts of principal and interest, of allowing payments made by the debtor to go first towards payment of the interest charge; of disallowing all compound interest, and giving a wider scope to the principle of Hindoo law of *dam-dupat*, by which the aggregate amount of interest payable by the debtor shall not exceed the principal—all these provisions have our approval, with this exception, however, that where the claim is admitted by the defendant and the court sees no reason to doubt the truth of such admissions, it would be a simple waste of the time of the Court as well as of the suitors to go further into the inquiries. As to payment of ancestral debts, where there are assets left, we concur with the Honourable Mr. Sayyad Ahmed in thinking that the obligation to pay is a matter of natural equity common to the English, Hindoo and Mahomedan law -one with the solemnity of which the people of this country are thoroughly impressed, and a sense of which is one of the best traits in their character. We would accordingly recommend that the provisions relating to ancestral debt be omitted, as suggested by the Government of India in their letter of the 26th July last. In the execution of decrees passed by the Court, the Civil Procedure has already provided for the exemption of such of the moveables from sale as are absolutely necessary for the debtor and his family. The abolition of arrest and imprisonment for debt is one of those wise provisions of the Bill which we trust the Legislature will, in course of time, extend to other parts of the Presidency, nay, to the whole country. Repudiation of debt will be the last thing a native of India will be generally found guilty of, unless he is driven to it by sheer destitution. The provision restricting the sale of immovable property under Court decrees seems to us to be the result of the conviction growing on the official mind that it is desirable to prevent the transfer of landed property from the peasantry to the wealthier classes. As a matter of fact such transfers of property to the capitalist class have taken place and will go on in spite of the restrictive provisions of the law. In the North-West Provinces we have the best proof of this. There it is certain the law has not been able to prevent them. But this is a very large question into which we cannot enter here, since much may be said on both sides of it. We shall be content with the simple statement that if the State, in solicitude for the welfare of the agriculturist classes, is jealous of the capitalist classes becoming occupants of the soil, it behoves it to give up the right claimed by it of eviction for default in the payment of land revenue so far as such eviction is due to the rigidity of its own land system. The Bill provides that no land shall be attached or sold under the decrees of the Courts unless specifically pledged as security for payment of the debt. In ordinary cases the Court, when passing a decree, shall direct the Collector to take possession of the land and manage it for seven years, for the benefit of the decree-holder. After seven years the land will pass to the agriculturist.

The bill goes beyond the Civil Procedure Code in respect of its insolvency provisions. In case of debts amounting to less than Rs. 50, it gives the Court powers to direct, if satisfied that there is no other claim against the debtor and that the debtor is unable to pay the whole of that sum, that only a portion of it may be paid and that he be discharged from all further liability in respect of the balance. Where there are more claims than one, the procedure in the Bill is much simplified by empowering the Court to appoint a receiver in the person of the Nazir who shall take inventory of the debtor's movable assets. He shall not, however, sell them by auction but shall get the aid of the two assessors to appraise their value, and direct the transfer of them to such of the scheduled creditors as shall be entitled to share in the distribution of the property. The Collector will have to take possession of the immovable property and manage it for seven years for the benefit of the general body of the creditors. In case of lands specifically pledged, the Collector will either let it rent-free for a premium for a term not exceeding 20 years or sell it as he thinks fit. How far these provisions will work practically remains to be seen. That the insolvency procedure is much simpler than is to be found even in the amended Civil Procedure Code admits of little doubt. We are not, however, surprised at the Hon'ble Messrs Stokes, Cockerell and Sayyad

Ahmed expressing their disapproval of the clauses relating to the punitive provisions which obtain in the Civil Procedure Code or the Presidency Insolvency Acts. There is doubtless some force in the objections put forward by them—the principle involved in them being that under the present provisions of the Bill even a dishonest debtor will find it easy to indulge himself in the luxury of white-washing—a process well known to traders in the Presidency towns. Mr. Hope, however, makes a distinction between the fact of a debtor's insolvency and his conduct as an insolvent. If he should be found dishonest, the Court may hand him over to the Magistrate to deal with that part of the question, but that should not, according to Mr. Hope, prevent the Court from declaring him insolvent so soon as the Court finds that the debtor has not assets to meet all the claims in full. Anyhow there is a state of insolvency, which admits of no dispute. There is considerable force in this argument, and we think from what we know of the Deccan Ryots generally, that cases will be found to be very rare where the debtors will be shown to have been guilty of concealment of property. Knowing this to be the case, we are inclined to support Mr. Hope. At the same time it must be admitted that where acts of dishonesty are proved, some provision, whereby the protection of the Court may be withheld from them is absolutely called for.

No doubt one direct and immediate effect of these provisions will be to put a stop to the Ryots' credit, at all events, on a mere note of hand or a bond. Nor will much credit be given him on the security of land specially pledged, seeing the many obstacles thrown by the Bill in the way of realizing this security. If credit is at all given to the Ryot, it will be on some valuable security. Simple credit he will have none whatever. The Bill destroys this altogether. Remembering that "necessity has no law," we think that mortgages, in spite of legal restrictions and legal diffculties, will be on the increase as they have been in the N. W. Provinces. In this respect the Bill will produce results entirely opposed to its express intentions. The Ryot, we say, *will* need money. He *must* pay his assessment to the state punctually. It is this which will drive him to the Sowcar. Finding that he cannot raise money on simple credit, he will have no other recourse left him but to pledge his land. It is the only security that he *can* offer. There is one way of preventing the transfer of land from the Ryot to the capitalist and, in our opinion, *only one way*, that is, for Government *to reduce its rates of assessments* in the revised Districts *to the level of the old rates*. Mr. Hope clearly sees this when, at the end of his long and exhaustive speech, he observes:—"If I am asked what I think will probably be the effects of the measure, and how far I expect it to be successful, I must reply, that although I cannot undertake to answer for all the detailed provisions of a Bill which is the outcome of revision at more hands and authorities than one, I think that it cannot but be most beneficial, and that it will, to a great extent, meet the needs of the Deccan, *provided it be supplemented by executive action in the directions already indicated.*" Clearly the executive action indicated here is in the direction of moderating the admitted rigidity and pressure of the revenue system. In the discussions in the Council, too, the unsuitability of the present system and the need of modifying it in a way, which may afford scope for the present legislative measure to work beneficially, was admitted on all hands. We have already alluded to the opinions of the Honourable Sir Robert Egerton, the Lieutenant Governor of the Punjab, and of His Excellency the Viceroy. Sir Alexander Arbuthnot referred the Council to an extract from the letter addressed by the Government of India to the Government of Bombay, urging that "in view of the very great fall of prices and the vicissitudes of the season in the Deccan during the last few years, it would be desirable that the present Government of Bombay should consider whether the recent (1873-75) revisions of the revenue have given sufficient relief from an assessment which was based, in part, on an unduly high estimate of the normal value of field produce in the Deccan." And further, the Governor-General in Council wished the Government of Bombay to consider whether in these districts, or in parts of them, it would not be wise to have a *varying scale of revenue demand* to be applied in unfavourable seasons, whereby the normal assessment might be reduced by a certain percentage over an entire district, or division of a district, in the event of a failure of rain or other course of serious damage to the crops.* Mr. Rivers Thomson felt satisfied that "the caution necessary at the revision of settlements in the one matter of the enhancement of the land revenue will receive the consideration which the great importance of the subject demands at the hands of the Bombay Government." Even Sir John Strachey, who, while Lieutenant Governor of the North-West Provinces, is known to have shown an unbending attitude in respect of the revenue policy of the State, admitted the necessity of modifying this rigidity. "I cannot doubt," said he, 'that means will be found—although they unfortunately have not been found up to the present—to combine complete and proper security for the recovery of the demand upon the land with some greater leniency to the peasant-proprietors, who, from no fault of their own, but from misfortune of season, cannot meet their engagements to the State. Bombay has now for its Governor a great administrator : If he can initiate measures in the direction to which I have now been referring, he will do a greater service to the country than any which this Council can accomplish by this Bill." Thus while the Government of India have, both by the views of their individual members as well as by their united voice echoed in their letter, pressed on the attention of Sir Richard Temple's Government the paramount necessity of considering this question, it is clear that, if through want of action on the part of the local Executive in the directions pointed out, the Bill fails to accomplish its objects, the onus of responsibility of its failure is thrown on

*Since this article was in type, we have seen a scheme put forward by the Hon'ble Mr. H. S. Cunningham in a draft bill to be called "the Fluctuating Assessment Bill," and intended to provide for variations in the collection of land revenue during unfavourable seasons. We say nothing at present in regard to the merits of this scheme, but the fact of such a Bill having been brought forward shows how greatly an arrangement of a fluctuating assessment is needed in the general interests of the state and the Ryot.

the local government. We trust, therefore, that Sir Richard Temple's government will duly respond to the call made upon it. As yet, however, no indications appear of any steps having been proposed to be taken in the directions pointed out. On the contrary, if the letter of April last be any guide, it would seem that no serious plan has yet been matured by the local government whereby relief may be given to the Ryots suffering from this cause. Are we to suppose that Sir Richard Temple is temporising? Does the government expect to find that, with the return of favourable seasons, all will be forgotten, and that the Ryot will have no cause of complaint left in regard to the pressure of the assessment? In the Deccan matters have really gone too far, and it will require a succession of good harvests before the peasantry is able to recover from the depth of its present misery. The normal condition of the country is this. The rainfall is precarious and the yield of soil poor. Mere suspension of government demand will afford no tangible relief. Complete or partial remission of revenue in a year of famine or deficient rainfall and moderate rates of assessment in ordinary years are the remedies that are most needed to avert the dire effects of the scourges. Doubtless the Sowcar and the Civil Courts have had some share in contributing to the Ryot's miseries, but the State has been no less a relentless offender in this respect. The rigidity with which revenue has been collected in these districts during the present year may well excite the commiseration of the most hard-hearted. The government ordered the District Collectors, and the District Collectors ordered the Mamlatdars or native revenue Collectors to collect the revenue as fast as they could, and that if they failed to bring the collections up to the full amount, their conduct would be viewed by government with displeasure. Under such orders even the cooking utensils and the grain-grinding mill stones of the half starving and miserable Ryots were sold off by the collecting officers to realize the government demand! When nothing remained in the shape of assets for these officials to collect, the survey holdings of the Ryots were put up to auction, and, no bids being found, were bought in on behalf of government for almost nominal sums, such as an anna or two for each number! Unless such a system underwent thorough modifications, one or two good seasons will assuredly do no good.

We have thus given our opinion of the Bill. Its objects are good; but it is not free from the charge of one-sidedness. It discourages private contracts by relieving the peasantry from obligations incurred under those contracts, while it leaves the action of the State as free and rigid as ever before. It will perhaps relieve the peasantry from its present indebtedness, and prevent it from running headlong into debts hereafter. But as to bettering its condition, much will depend on the nature of the alterations in the land system which may be brought about by those who have the destinies of the people committed to their charge.

3

REVIEW OF FAWCETT'S "THREE ESSAYS ON INDIAN FINANCE"

Mr. Fawcett's "Three Essays on Indian Finance republished from the Nineteenth Century," in which journal they first appeared during the last year, travel over the whole of the ground covered by the great financial problems of the day, and though the present volume was published in January last some months before the elections took place, the success of the Liberals in the new Parliament and the fact that the illustrious author of these essays occupies an important position in the New Liberal Ministry have lent all the importance of a political manifesto to the views set forth therein. The lines of thought suggested and the conclusions laid down in these essays will certainly shake the counsels and regulate the dealings of the new administration for many years to come, and as the chief difficulty of the Indian Government resolves itself into the question of its finances, the value of avoiding erroneous and exaggerated views in regard to our present condition and future prospects can hardly be overrated. Mr. Fawcett may well claim to have made Indian finances his speciality, and to him belongs the rare credit of having converted statesmen of both parties and the authorities in India to his views as affording the only reasonable prospect of re-establishing the solvency and prosperity of the country. We can only hope to lay down briefly the more important of the positions elaborated at length throughout these essays.

1. The first fundamental position regarding Indian finance is the recognition of the fact that India is an extremely poor country, and that the great mass of the people are in such a state of impoverishment that the Government will have to contend with exceptional difficulties if it becomes necessary to procure increased revenue by additional taxation. Relatively to population and extent England is 70 times richer than India.

2. The real net revenue of India is derived from six sources, *viz.* land, opium, salt, excise, customs and stamps; excluding collection charges, the net revenue amounts to 38 millions a year. The other items of revenue, which swell up the gross total to 63 millions, are either nominal ones, or are counterbalanced by corresponding items of expenditure.

3. The real net revenue of India is inelastic, and has been stationary for the last 12 years, and represents year after year a diminishing value. The land revenue is for the most part permanently or temporarily settled, and in the latter case at such a pitch that the agricultural classes are not in a condition to bear heavier assessment at the time of the resettlement. The opium revenue is uncertain, and depends for its continuance on the variable temper of the Chinese Government. The salt duty is already 2000 per cent on the prime cost of the article, and cannot bear any increase without checking consumption. The revenue from excise and customs can never be great in a poor population like that of India, and admits of no increase in the face of the English agitation for the abolition of the duties.

4. As the whole of the revenue is obtained in silver, while nearly one half of the revenue is absorbed by the payments in gold made in England, the fall of the value of silver relativel[illegible] gold decreases the money value of the revenues of Ind[illegible]

considerable percentage.

5. While the revenue is stationary, inelastic, and diminishing in money value, the expenditure under all heads has a tendency to increase, and this upward tendency has been intensified of late by the effects of a foreign war, famine, and loss by exchange, and the interest on increased national debt.

6. The military expenditure is excessive, being 45 per cent of the net revenue. Even before the Afghan War, the military expenditure had in consequence of the amalgamation increased from 12½ millions, fixed as the reasonable maximum charge by Lord Canning after the mutinies, to 17 millions and the forward policy of the war would require a permanent addition of three millions more per year. The general cost of administration, exclusive of the Army and Public Works, has increased during a period of 15 years (1856 to 1871) from 15 millions to 23⅓ millions, partly by reason of enhanced prices, and partly owing to the absence of adequate economy.

7. The loss by exchange was scarcely regarded as a considerable item on the expenditure side before 1870. During the last ten years it has increased from a few thousand pounds to three millions by reason of the depreciation of silver, and disproportionate increase in the Home Charges.

8. The annual payment of interest on the national debt has doubled in twenty years, having increased from 2 millions of pre-mutiny times (1856) to 4⅓ millions in 1876, under the influence of the policy of borrowing a large sum every year for so-called reproductive works on which the returns are but nominal. During the last few years 16 millions were borrowed for famine relief purposes, and the Afghan War charges and the cost of the frontier Railway will mount up to another 20 millions.

9. Over and above the increased imperial taxation, there has been an increase of nearly 3 millions in what is called Provincial taxation since 1870.

10. A comparatively stationary revenue having to meet an ever- increasing expenditure, it will be necessary unless a policy of retrenchment is carried out earnestly, sooner or later, to add to the taxation of India. Constant borrowing will, so far from remedying the ever-recurring deficit, only lead to additional indebtedness, and necessitate additional taxation.

11. It is not possible to suggest, not politically safe to effect, any sensible addition to the taxation. Direct taxes like the Licence and Income taxes, succession duties, and a tobacco tax have been condemned on all hands as likely to foment discontent by their inquisitorial character and in consequence of the general poverty of the people, will after all yield an insignificant sum. Indirect taxes also cannot be imposed without defeating their own object, because the people consume no luxuries, and the only necessary of life salt is already taxed most heavily.

12. It therefore follows that retrenchment and substitution of Native for European agency are the only remedies open to the Government. The cardinal error has been that India has been governed on too costly a scale, and the Indian Government has been living beyond its means on borrowed capital for years together, and of late it has sacrificed Indian finance to the exigencies of English estimates. It must retrace its steps, reduce its army charges, and the cost of its Civil administration and its public works expenditure, and govern India in her own interests.

13. Finance is the key of England's position in India. The checks on extravagance which used to obtain under the rule of the E. I. Company from the wholesome fear of Parliamentary inquisition, were removed with the extinction of the Company's power and the checks substituted by the Act of 1858 have been found insufficient, as the Secretary of State, himself has on diverse occasions overruled his Council even in matters which directly affected the finances of India.

These thirteen propositions, represent the substance of Mr. Fawcett's first essay, and must be laid to heart by every impartial student of Indian Finance, as they bring out all the weak points of the existing arrangements with singular clearness and force. In his second essay, Mr. Fawcett has attempted to illustrate his several propositions by a review of the Indian Budget of 1879. We shall only touch upon those portions of his observations which touch upon the abolition of the cotton duties. Mr. Fawcett most unmistakably condemns the surrender of the cotton duties at a time, when the Government of India, having no surplus of its own, had, notwithstanding the increased famine taxation, to take power to raise $15^1/_2$ millions for current expenditure.

(a) In the first place he questions if the duties are really protective.

(b) Further that even if they were protective, they should not have been surrendered as long as India had no real surplus, and could not pay its way without borrowing or imposing additional taxation, and there were other taxes to be abolished which should have been given the preference in Indian interests.

(c) In considering questions of taxation nothing can be more unwise than to conclude that that particular tax must be the best which is most in accord with the principles of economical science. The tastes, the habits and wishes of the tax-paying people must be consulted by practical statesmen. The cotton duties were not open to any objection on this ground as nobody in India complained of them.

(d) The cotton duties on the finer stuff of English manufacture were to some extent a tax on the wealthy, and the only tax which reached the subjects of Native States. Their abolition tends to aggravate the inequality of the existing taxation.

(e) Even if India could afford to give up an existing source of revenue, the export duties on rice should have been the first to go as they sin more flagrantly against economic maxims, and their abolition, by increasing the export trade would lessen the loss by exchange, while the abolition of the Import Duties would affect the exchange unfavourably.

(f) Another objection to the policy of this surrender is comprised in the fact that the famine taxation was diverted from its own proper purposes for defraying the cost of the Afghan War, to create an artificial surplus with a view to meet the letter, though in utter violation of the spirit, of the Parliamentary Resolution of 10th July, 1877 on the subject of these duties.

(g) The surrender moreover was dictated by the exigencies of English party politics to which the interests of India were sacrificed against the express protest of the Supreme Council by an extraordinary straining of the powers confirmed by the Sea Customs Act of 1878 on the Viceroy. Mr. Fawcett concludes his second essay by a forcible exposition of the injustice involved in the arrangement by which England threw nearly the whole burden of an imperial war, on the Indian Treasury, and contented itself with advancing two millions free of interest though the war was waged beyond the frontiers of India to maintain the influence of England in Europe. By a narrow majority of 12, the late ministry secured the sanction of Parliament to this adjustment, but as the war charges have now mounted to 15 millions, the question will have to be reopened again in the present Parliament when Mr. Fawcett's well-known views cannot fail to secure final justice to India. The general review of the Budget statement of 1879 was thus full of despondency. In every important respect, there was a violation of the principles of sound finance, while beyond reducing the extraordinary Public Works grant by a crore of Rupees, no effort at retrenchment was made or promised. As might have been expected, this unnatural condition of things broke down, and the Government of India soon found it necessary to retrace their steps, and admit their mistake. This change of attitude was effected in the interval of a few months which elapsed from the publication of the Budget in

India and its discussion in Parliament. Mr. Fawcett's third essay is devoted to this new departure in Indian Finance, when statesmen of both parties for the first time admitted that the financial condition of India was gloomy enough to justify the worst apprehensions and that the rosy coloured accounts of Indian prosperity and its deficits turned into surpluses were all a delusion which no manipulation of items should have blinded men from mistaking for a reality.

It may be of use to specify more particularly the delusions which for so long held sway, and had to be abandoned at last under the stress of a great calamity. The first of these delusions was that India possessed a normal surplus of revenue. The second delusion was that the Public Works became reproductive simply because they were paid for out of the extraordinary grant from year to year. The third delusion was that India was rich in its actual and possible resources, and could bear easily the burden of the most costly administration. The fourth delusion was that a policy of aggression represented by the Afghan War could be carried out without any strain on the finances. The fifth delusion was that the limit of taxation had not been reached in India, and that persons with Rs.100 of annual income were fairly competent and able to pay two per cent direct taxes on their incomes. Another delusion was that things would get right of themselves, that there would be no accidents and no mishaps, no famines and no wars. And lastly that retrenchment on any large scale was impossible. All these delusions were dispelled by the stern reality of the situation as it developed itself in the latter half of 1879. Under the pressure of a costly war, heavy loss by exchange, and the necessity of providing against famine, the Government of India admitted its readiness to effect a saving of one million in the Civil departments, of 1½ millions in the Public Works grant, and another million in the military charges. Such a recognition of the true situation of affairs was a great fact in itself, and a considerable portion of the credit of having effected this conversion belongs to Mr. Fawcett's persistent agitation and advocacy of Indian interests in and out of

Parliament. The only danger now is that this change of mind may be only temporary in its effects, and that under the influence of better seasons, and peace abroad and a more favourable exchange, the lesson learned in adversity might be forgotten, and the old speculative buoyancy of spirits might return. (1) The alternative of retrenchment as against additional taxation is always disagreeable to a bureaucracy, and every effort must, therefore, be made to enforce it at all risks and annoyance. (2) The cost of the civil administration must be reduced by cutting down the salaries of the higher officers to the English or colonial scale. (3) Further increase of taxation must be adjured as political insanity. (4) The ever increasing home charges which so heavily tell upon the exchange must be kept down. (5) The Military charges must be reduced by doing away with the short service and Staff Corps systems, and by establishing a local Indian army under a centralised command on the scale recommended by Lord Canning. (6) The temptation of manipulating the currency must be resisted as involving a breach of faith, and tending to depress silver, and raise the rate of exchange. (7) Public Works should be carried out as far as possible from surplus revenue, and not from loans. (8) If loans have to be raised they should not exceed 2½ millions as recommended by the Parliamentary Committee, and they should be raised in India rather than in England, in silver and not in gold. (9) England's contribution to the cost of the Afghan War must be raised proportionately to the imperial interests involved in its successful conclusion. (10) And the war brought to an early close, and all idea of annexing Afghanistan abandoned on grounds of economy, if not of justice and policy. (11) The gradual substitution of Native for equally efficient, but more costly, European agency must be carried out wherever practicable and safe. These are the directions in which those who have at heart the protection of Indian interests must persevere before the recent conversion of Government can be expected to produce lasting good. Indian economists must not rest till the annual expenditure is reduced by another three or four millions, which reduction will enable government to do away with the

Licence Tax, lower the salt duties, abolish the export duty on rice, and resume many useful Public Works intended to insure the country against famine out of surplus revenue in place of foreign loans. This is the ideal condition of Indian Finance which Mr. Fawcett sets forth as the goal which Indian administrators must reach, if India is to be permanently rescued from its present normal confusion, and ever increasing indebtedness, and its resources developed healthily and progressively. A Parliamentary Commission of Inquiry can alone ensure such a happy result, and secure that control of the Council over the Secretary of State which is so urgently needed in the interests of economy and good rule. We cordially endorse this suggestion. Our summary of Mr. Fawcett's work cannot more fitly close than with an expression of his main position that India can never be well governed unless she is governed in her own interest, and that above all sound Finance is the chief of Indian interest.

4

THE LAW OF LAND SALE IN BRITISH INDIA*

The question of the Law of Land Sale in British India has been the subject of a standing controversy for the last twenty-five years and more, and the new Act for the Relief of the Deccan Agriculturists has raised the subject from one of speculation into a matter-of-fact reality in its relation to this Presidency. Prior to this period, the tendency of British Indian Legislation and Administration had been generally to assimilate the Laws and Institutions of India with the latest innovations in Europe. Usury Laws were abolished in 1855, because Mr. Bentham and others had denounced them in England, and the English Legislature had removed those restrictions on the universal freedom of Contracts. Local Cesses and Octroi Duties were abolished not only in British India, but also throughout the Native States, because they interfered with the freedom of Trade. Inám Commissions were set up, and so-called Settlement operations were carried on with a view to equalise taxation on all classes without distinction. It was a part of this same system that led Government to abolish the old Mirasi Tenure, to abolish the Joint Liability of the village, and substitute in its place the Survey Occupant's Tenure, and when the first settlements were introduced, much credit was taken for conferring on the Ryots the most unrestricted power of transferring their interests in

*Published in *JPSS*, October 1880, Vol.III, No.2, and in *Essays*.

land. This tendency to innovation and the levelling up of Oriental Institutions to the requirements of the most radical theorists in Europe was in its full swing before the Mutinies, and the Annexation Policy and the Denial of Adoptions were only the Political phases of this same spirit. The fearful blaze of that period of troubles opened the eyes of the ruling Authorities to the great mistake that had been committed, when the Conservative traditions of the first conquests, the policy associated with the memories of Elphinstone, Munro, Malcolm, and Metcalfe, was given up for new- fangled ways of thought and revolutionary action, recommended by men like Bird and Thomason in the North-Western Provinces, and in our Presidency by Goldsmid, Hart, Cowper, and Willoughby.

With the reversal of the Political Maxims which had till then obtained sway in regard to Native States, a similar reaction was for the first time, seen to influence what may be called the Home Administration of the Empire. In consequence of the law which made land, both ancestral and acquired, freely alienable for the debts of its owner, a great change was slowly but steadily taking place in the status and position of the Proprietory Classes. All over India, lands were sold for arrears of Revenue by the Revenue Officers, and for decreed Debts, both secured and unsecured, by the Civil Courts, through the coercive process of Sales, and this change was visibly tending to the impoverishment of the old Proprietors, and transferring the lands into the hands of strangers and non-residents, who generally belonged to the mercantile and trading classes, and bought up the land for no other attraction than its character as a paying investment. This change of possession had excited some attention even before the Mutinies began, especially in the North-Western Provinces, but at that time the Government of that Province expressed its inability to do anything more than to watch the natural and unrestricted course of the free transfer of property. During the height of the Mutinies, it was, however, noticed that in many cases the ousted proprietors had re- entered into possession, and that the old Tenantry had sympathized with them, and sided with them against the new purchasers. In August, 1858, this matter attracted the notice of the Court of Directors. They observed that the rapid transfer of lands from the hands of the old proprietors to those of persons with no local influence was a source of weakness to the Government, and without suggesting immediate measures of relief, they recommended the subject to the attention of the Government of India. The Government of India, in forwarding the Home Despatch to the Government of the North-Western Provinces, suggested the advisability of restricting coercive Sales of Land to mortgage decrees, and the Sadar Court of the North-Western Provinces was also in favour of a similar restriction. No further steps, however, appear to have been taken at the time with reference to this suggestion. Early in the next year, Lord Stanley (afterwards Lord Derby), sent out a Despatch which may be said to be the starting point of this controversy regarding the policy of permitting land to be freely sold for all secured and unsecured debts of the owner by coercive process of the Civil Courts, or of his own will and choice. After noticing that the freedom of transfer had been a source of weakness to the Government, inasmuch as the new purchasers had no hold on the Tenantry who sided with the ousted proprietors, the Despatch suggested that in respect of past transactions, efforts should, if possible, be made to bring about compromises, and in regard to the future, it was recommended that the powers of the Judges of the lowest Courts should be restricted to suits for money and movable property, that no execution against land should be permitted for decrees below a certain amount, and that lands should not be sold without the sanction of the District Judge, as had in fact been the practice in the case in those Provinces before 1834.

This Dispatch was forwarded by the Government of India to the Local Authorities, who in due course elicited the views of their Chief Revenue Officers, and, through the Sadar Court, of the District Judges, with reference to the questions raised in it. As might be expected, the Revenue Officers gave their opinions in favour, more or less, of Restrictive Legislation, while the Judicial Officers for the most part maintained the wisdom of masterly inactivity in this matter. The minutes recorded by Mr. Reade, Mr. Muir, and Mr. Strachey (since Sir W. Muir and Sir J. Strachey), on one side of the question, and by Sir G. Edmondstone, the then Lieutenant-Governor, and Mr. Pearson (since the Hon'ble Justice Pearson), on the other, may be said to exhaust all that can be said for and against the measure of allowing land to be freely sold in execution of decrees. The most noticeable feature of this correspondence is, that while the chief Judicial authority of the Province, the Local Sadar Court, sided with the views of the Revenue Officers to a great extent, the Chief Executive Officer, the Lieutenant-Governor of the Province, minuted strongly against all the proposals made by the Revenue Board, and suggested only slight improvements in procedure as a sufficient palliative for the disease. We can only present a short summary of the views held by the several officers who took part in this discussion.

Mr. Muir suggested that there should be no restriction on voluntary mortgage or sale, or on the action of the Courts in enforcing such contracts. In the case of simple debts, he was of opinion that the person and movable property of a debtor, and his houses and town gardens, might be attached and sold, but not his lands. In the execution of decrees on mortgage bonds, it was suggested that the Collector should try to secure satisfaction by transferring the property for a term of years, on the payment by the transferee of a sum equal to the decree, or by making over the land to the mortgagee creditor for a term of years to pay himself out of its usufruct, and have his claims discharged. If neither of these alternatives was possible, the land should be sold, or the debtor and his estate should pass through the Insolvency Court, which should be allowed to count the usufruct of the land for fifteen years among the assets of the estate. Mr. Reade, who was then Senior Member of the Revenue Board, suggested that Sales might take place in execution of even money decrees after all attempts had failed to secure payment by selling the movable property of the debtor, and by letting his lands on farm for a period of years, but that such sales should not be ordered without the sanction of the District Judge. The creditor should be required to pay ten per cent upon the value of the decrees to reimburse the Government for the trouble of realizing his debts. Mr. Thornhill, Commissioner of Allahabad, disapproved of the sale process, and suggested that the best way to ensure a check was to tax extravagance in marriage expenditure. Mr. Cocks, Commissioner of Jabalpur, suggested in addition to the prohibition of Sales by Civil Process of the Lower Courts, that no alienation by a Proprietor should be held valid, which had not the consent of his next two generation of heirs. Mr. Pinkney, Commissioner of Jhansi, thought that the transfer of land from the old Proprietors to the mercantile classes was not capable of being remedied. Mr. Williams, Commissioner First Division, approved of the proposed prohibition of transfers of Land by decrees of Courts on the ground that it would check extravagance, and in the meanwhile, suggested that the Civil Courts should be directed to try first the effects of temporary attachment of the profits of Land by way of satisfying the Decree. Mr. Harvey, Commissioner of Agra, suggested that under strict Hindu Law it was only the usufruct that was liable to be sold in payment of the debts of each Hereditary Holder in possession and that no larger interest should be sold. Mr. Batten, Commissioner of Rohilkhand, was of opinion that the political evil of such transfers was much exaggerated, and that any restrictive Legislation would be a confession of error and weakness, and opposed to the teachings of Political Economy. If a change were to be made, he would only restrict the exemption to Decrees below three hundred Rupees, and in suits above that amount the Execution against Land should be in the hands of the European Judge, who should refer the adjustment to the Collector. Mr. Gubbins, Commissioner of Benares, proposed to extend the exemption to Sales for arrears of Revenue along with those under decrees of Court. In the first case, the Sales should hold good for twenty years at the most, after which the property should return to the owner. In the case of Sales under Decrees, including simple and mortgage debts, only the life interest of the debtor should be transferable. If he and his heirs join, the alienation might hold good for two lives, but beyond that period, it should not be binding. Even private alienations should be void beyond the period of two generations. Mr. Currie, Collector of Boolandshar, suggested the necessity of the introduction of a Law of Entail to take up the place of the obsolete provisions of the Hindu Mitakshara Law of Joint Property as the only effective remedy. Mr. Mayne, Collector of Banda, disapproved of the proposal regarding Entail as being opposed to Native feeling, and maintained that the necessity of borrowing was forced upon the Ryots by the pressure of the Revenue Assessment. He, accordingly, suggested that the Assessment should be lightened. He was of opinion that the political consequences of free transfer were exaggerated, and that there were benefits arising from the infusion of stranger blood. At the same time, he considered that the change, as far as it had gone, had been sufficient, and that, if possible, the further destruction of the old proprietors should be prevented, and while upholding private contracts, he suggested that Decrees for simple debts should be satisfied by a temporary transfer, or farm, and not by the sale of land. The Collector of Cawnpore, Mr. Sherer, was of opinion that the evil complained of was due to the direct engagement of the Government with proprietors of small estates, and that no prohibition of Sale could remedy it. Mr. Strachey, Collector of Moradabad, in a very suggestive minute, urged that the evils complained of, were owing to the novel and rigid Revenue System that had been introduced, substituting individual rights and liability, in place of the old joint responsibility and the absence of the power of Alienation. The change was not in all cases from bad to worse, for stagnation would mean impoverished Proprietors, and the curse of Landlords, impotent for good, would be doubly heavy in a country which was almost entirely an agricultural one. The evil, in Mr. Strachey's opinion, could not be remedied by merely Legislative changes, or the reform of the Procedure of Courts. The Government must take upon itself all the functions of a wealthy Landlord. He, accordingly, advocated the plan of

Government Agricultural Banks on the model of the French *Crédit Foncier*. As far as Legislative relief could legitimately be extended, he thought that the Government had done enough by enacting Sections 194, 243 and 244 in the new Code of Civil Procedure.

The North-Western Provinces Government, after eliciting the views of its Revenue Officers, referred the question to the Sadar Court, who consulted the District Judges upon the matter. Mr. Pearson, Judge of the Sagar and Narbada Territories, in an exhaustive minute, discussed both sides of the question, and gave his opinion against the proposed restrictions upon Sale, and the proposed substitute for Sale, namely—temporary transfer or farm of the profits. Mr. Wynyard, Judge of Shahjehanpore, suggested that Sales in execution of decrees could not well be abolished, as long as the Government retained that process to recover its arrears of Revenue, and that all that could be done by way of remedy was to take steps to secure the attendance of both parties when the suit was tried, and to make the District Judge's sanction necessary in cases of sale for decrees exceeding three hundred Rupees. Mr. Lean, Judge of Mirzapore, expressed his doubts about the validity of the Political argument urged for a change of the Law, and he concurred in all essential points with Mr. Pearson. Mr. Vansittart, Judge of Bareilly, maintained that although the mischief was chiefly owing to the Revenue System with which the Civil Courts had no concern, yet, as political expediency required it, he would vote for the change, and exempt all Revenue paying lands from liability to any Process of the Courts. Mr. Plowden, Judge of Ghazeepore, also suggested that the remedy for the evil complained of was to be sought in a reform of the Revenue System. The Revenue System broke up the Talukdaries, and violated the principle of the joint liability of Village Communities, and substituted individual ownership in its place under the *Pattedari* and *Halkabandi* system. Mr. Ross, Judge of Farrakabad, urged that under a settled and strong Government, the evil complained of was unavoidable under the operations of a Law of equal succession. While, therefore, a complete check was impossible, he suggested, as palliative measures, the necessity of registering all bond affecting land, of increasing the powers of pre-emption, and exempting lands from Sale for debts below one hundred Rupees, and lastly, he advised that a preliminary inquiry should precede the Sale with a view to ascertain and define the interest sold.

The Sadar Court of the North-Western Provinces expressed themselves in favour of compelling the creditor first, to exhaust the Personal Property of the debtor, and then of limiting Sales of Land to decrees in which the property to be sold had been distinctly hypothecated, and to cases of fraud on creditors. They were also in favour of declaring the exemption land from liability to sale in respect of decrees for small amounts, and requiring the Munsiffs to secure the sanction of the District Judge, before proceeding to sell the land. The Lieutenant-Governor of the North-Western Provinces, in reporting his views upon the whole correspondence, expressed himself strongly against all the heroic remedies, and thought that the provisions of Sections 194, 243, and 244 of Act VIII of 1859 were sufficient for the present, with a slight amendment of Section 244, so as to dispense with the necessity of finding sufficient security, and he suggested that it was desirable to watch their effects for some years, and to be content till then with a direction to require that, in all executions of decrees for money, process shall in the first instance issue against the movable property, and that the interests to be sold should be carefully ascertained by the Collector, so as to secure to the purchaser a carefully defined title.

This summary of the views of the Revenue and Judicial Officers in the North-Western Provinces will show the wide diversity of opinion that prevails on the subject among persons in every way competent to judge about the issues involved in the dispute. All varieties and shades of opinion are represented in it, from the extreme conservatism which would abolish entirely the powers of even voluntary transfer, and make the Ryot a Serf of Government lands, or revive the system of Entail, to the extremely radical principles of a *laissez faire* policy of doing nothing by way of interference between man and man. A strong consensus of views appears, however, to be in favour of a middle course, which, while restricting the enforced Sale of Land to decrees, which by their express terms affected it, would uphold the power of private transfer by way of sale or mortgage, but would, even in cases where sales might be necessary and proper, first try the effects of a temporary attachment and farm of the profits. This view, it will be seen, was first suggested by Sir W. Muir, and coincides in all essential details with that which has received the sanction of the Legislature in the Deccan Agriculturists' Relief Act.

To proceed however, with the history of the Land Sale controversy, the Government of India appears to have taken no further action in the matter, on the conflicting views of the North-Western Provinces Officers, and to have contented itself with watching the effects of the new Code of Civil Procedure for some years as recommended by the Lieutenant-Governor. It must be remembered, however, that the revulsion of feeling caused by the Mutinies suggested the introduction of Sections 194, 243, and 244 in the Code, and these Sections may well be reckoned as the first acknowledgment of a change of policy on the part of Government in this connection, and a recognition of its obligation to respect the national sentiment regarding Ancestral Land, and its duty to preserve the old Hereditary Proprietors of the same in their possession. It was hoped at the time that by making the decreed amount payable by instalments, and by permitting temporary attachments of the lands either through a Receiver appointed by the Courts or through the Collector of the District, sufficient time and consideration would be secured to help the involved Proprietor to redeem his lands and retain his status.

In its newly acquired Provinces, the Government of India proceeded a step further in the declaration of this new Policy.

In the Punjab, a Circular Order, having the effect of law, was issued as early as October 1858, directing that no hereditary or jointly acquired property in land should be sold in liquidation of a sum decreed in the Civil Courts without the sanction of the Judicial Commissioner. In 1866, when the Code of Civil Procedure was extended to the Punjab Provinces, a proviso was ordered to Section 208 (which declares all rights in lands as liable to attachment and Sale)—to the effect "that no immovable property should be attached or sold without the sanction of the Commissioner of the Division, and no Hereditary or Jointly- acquired Property in land should be attached or Sold without the sanction of the Chief Court." Similar provisions were introduced by the Government of India in its Proclamations, extending the Code of Civil Procedure to the other Non-Regulation Districts. In the Central Provinces and in Oudh it was added that no ancestral property in land should be sold in satisfaction of a decree without the sanction of the Judicial Commissioner, and no self-acquired property in land should be sold without the previous permission of the Divisional Commissioner. In the Chota Nagpur District of the Bengal Provinces, under orders of the Government of India issued as far back as 1833, Immovable Property was not sold in liquidation of debts, but under the order of the Political Agent of the Province the estate of the debtor was sequestrated, and the assets were appropriated to the payment of the creditor after allowing a small maintenance to the indebted Proprietor. When the Code of Civil Procedure was extended to this Province, these powers of the Commissioner or Political Agent were expressly reserved, and without his sanction no sale could take place. In the Berar Districts, the sanction of the Divisional Commissioner and of the Resident respectively, was required before ancestral or self-acquired land could be sold. It was only in the so-called Regulation Provinces of Bengal, Bombay, Madras and the North-West, that no legal restriction was placed upon the freedom of Sale. In all the other Provinces, the power of allowing Sale was left to the discretion of the Chief Revenue and Judicial Authorities. The necessity of such sanction acts as a deterrent upon Money Lenders, who seldom, if ever, succeed in making out a case sufficiently strong to satisfy the higher Authorities. As the introduction of Sections 194, 243, and 244 was the first step in the way of securing the restriction of complete freedom of transfer in land, this requisition of superior sanction might well be regarded as the second decisive step taken by the Government with a view to protect the old Proprietary Classes from being deprived of their lands by the superior enterprise and intelligence of the Money Lenders.

In course of time, it was, however, discovered that the checks sought to be imposed in both the ways above mentioned proved comparatively ineffective in operation, and this led to what may well be called the next phase of this Land Sale controversy. The subject was first broached by the Judges of the Chief Court in the Punjab, who complained that the discretion vested in them by law required some definite rules to guide it in a spirit of uniformity throughout the Territories, and they asked for a legislative measure which would define more particularly the circumstances in which the sanction should be given or refused, independently of the question, whether the other assets of the land-owning classes were sufficient or not, which was the only point inquired into in practice. This reference reopened the larger question of the desirability of such restrictions upon the freedom of Sale. Mr. Justice Boulouis expressed himself strongly in favour of absolutely refusing permission for the Sale of Land in a Zemindari or Bhayachari Village, in respect of money debts, unless the land was mortgaged to the decree holder. Mr. Justice Simpson went further, and desired that there should be no exception even in cases of mortgage bonds. The Divisional Officers who were consulted on the point, reported their views with the same diversity which has been already noticed in respect of the North-West Provinces. The Commissioner of Delhi was of opinion that the Sale of Land should be prohibited in all cases except under decrees for arrears of Revenue, in which cases, as the Government claimed the right to oust owners for such arrears, there could be no hardship in selling the land at the instance of the private suitor. The Commissioner was not inclined to make any exception in favour of mortgage. The Deputy Commissioner of the same Division expressed himself in favour of reserving the mortgagee's right, and would only extend the prohibition to sales for money decrees. The Deputy Commissioner of Goorgaon was inclined to object to the restriction proposed, but would allow one year of grace to the involved debtor to stave off the Sale. The Deputy Commissioner of Karnal would dispense with all restrictions, as also with the necessity of sanction, and was of opinion that the provisions of Sections 243 and 244 were quite sufficient restrictions in all cases. The Commissioner of Hissar was also inclined to take an equally favourable view of the Zamindar's position, and was content to watch the effect of the provisions of Sections 243 and 244. He was, however, opposed to the policy of allowing Forced Sales in cases of decrees for arrears of Revenue, and for money borrowed for improvements. The Commissioner of Jallandar, on the other hand, would prohibit all Sales of Hereditary and jointly acquired land under all circumstances. The Commissioner of Amritsar thought that Mr. Boulouis's proposal to forbid Sales in respect of money decrees, and to allow them in case of mortgage debts, would simply prove futile, and lead only to an increase of mortgage transactions. The Commissioner of Lahore was in favour of the total prohibition of Sale under all circumstances. Mr. Griffin, Deputy Commissioner of Lahore, would restrict the prohibition to Ancestral Property only, leaving jointly acquired property to take care of itself. The Commissioner of Rawal-Pindi was in favour of Mr. Boulouis's proposal. The Commissioner of Derajat was opposed to prohibitory Legislation, and thought that the restrictions under Sections 243 and 244 were sufficient. Mr. Brandreth, Commissioner of Multan, thought that our Revenue arrangements were chiefly responsible for the indebtedness of the Zamindar classes, and that as long as these arrangements continued, ancestral lands should not be liable to coercive Sale on account of simple debts and mortgage transactions. Mr. Barnes, officiating Commissioner of Multan, thought that there was no need of amending the Law, and that the present restrictions were sufficient.

The Financial Commissioner of the Punjab, Mr. P.S. Melvill, reporting his own views upon the reference, urged that the Punjab had passed through its stage of pupilage, and had entered upon vigorous manhood, and that the people were growing in intelligence and wealth; he was of opinion, therefore, that it was not necessary to have recourse to retrograde Legislation, and that the security of land should continue to exist for all debts for which no special security was provided, but that it should not be sold in execution till all other arrangements to pay the decree within a reasonable period of about fifteen years had failed. He, accordingly, suggested that the existing Law should remain unchanged except that the requisition about adequate security in Section 244 should be done away with. The Lieutenant-Governor of the Punjab, however, in reporting upon the whole correspondence his own views, expressed himself strongly in favour of an absolute prohibition of the Sale of all hereditary and jointly acquired lands in execution of decrees and suggested that the term for temporary Alienation under Section 244 should never exceed twenty years. The Judges of the Chief Court were requested accordingly, to submit a draft of the proposed amending Law. These Judges, however, differed among themselves. While Mr. Justice Boulouis and Mr. Justice Simpson were in favour of further express prohibitory Legislation, Mr. Justice Lindsay was strongly disinclined to move in the matter, and took his stand upon the Financial Commissioner's dissent, and the Report made by the High Court of the North-West Provinces, in regard to the satisfactory working of Sections 243 and 244 in those Provinces, as palliative measures. In consequence of this conflict, no further action was taken in this connection. This closed what may be called the Second stage of this Land Controversy.

The Third stage of this Controversy began in 1870, with a

reference from the Government of India to all the Subordinate Governments, requesting an expression of their views, in regard to the success which had attended the working of Sections 243 and 244, since the new Code became Law. These Sections, it will be easily seen, were in the first instance suggested by the land systems of the Northern and Eastern portions of India, where individual Zamindars, as in Bengal, Behar and Benares, or Zamindaris held by Village Communities, as in the North-West Provinces and the Punjab, were sufficiently large in extent to allow a prospect of their being profitably managed by means of Receivers and Collector's agents under Attachment. This state of things did not exist in the Ryotwari Districts of Bombay and Madras, where the system obtains of small holdings and individual responsibility, and in their case it was to be expected that the Sections would prove inoperative and obsolete. The Reports of the two Governments and of the Judicial Officers subordinate to them confirmed this anticipation. The Madras Authorities reported that Section 244 had never been extended to their Provinces, and that Section 243 also, was not much resorted to. The Bombay Authorities also made a similar report. In the Non-Regulation Districts of the Punjab, Oudh, the Central Provinces, and the Berars, the Sections were inoperative on another account. These provisions presupposed a division of authority between the Judicial and Revenue Services. In these Provinces, however, both these functions were combined in one and the same Official, and while the check of superior sanction was in operation, Section 244 was found to be unworkable in its practical application. In the North-West Provinces and Bengal also, Section 244 was proved to have been either not worked at all, or to have been abused. As regards Section 243, however, the Authorities in both the Provinces reported that it had secured on the whole beneficial results, by way of mitigating in a considerable percentage of cases the extreme severity of the Law implied in the final resort to the Sale Process; yet, even in these Districts it was observed that the Sections worked less satisfactorily in the case of small than in large estates.

It was in the course of this inquiry into the working of Sections 243 and 244 that the Authorities of the Central Provinces ventured on their own account to re-open the Land Sale Controversy, and the views of Colonel Keatinge, Chief Commissioner, Mr. P.S. Melvill, Judicial Commissioner, Mr. (now Sir Charles) Bernard, Commissioner of Nagpur, and Mr. Brooks and Mr. Nicholls, Deputy Commissioners, were elicited upon the general merits of the Policy of restricting the Freedom of Sales in execution of decrees. In view of the fact, that the Settlement had been recently introduced in these Provinces, and that property in land had been a new creation of the Settlement, Mr. Melvill saw reason to change the views he had expressed as Financial Commissioner of the Punjab, and urged the necessity of a Restrictive Measure by which lands would be exempted from Sale for debts contracted prior to the Settlement. He, further, proposed that after due notification during which all debts contracted since the Settlement might be cleared off, all Sales of Land in execution of decrees, should be prohibited without any distinction of ancestral or self-acquired lands. Colonel Keatinge, the Chief Commissioner, was not prepared to go so far as Mr. Melvill. He would confine the exemption to estates yielding more than three hundred Rupees as annual rental. All smaller estates should be left to be dealt with under the existing Law which requires sanction before Sale. The two Systems of Freedom and Restriction of Sale would, he thought, be thus working side by side, and serve to educate the people out of their tutelage. The Chief Commissioner also differed from the Judicial Commissioner on another point. He proposed to make a distinction between Ancestral and Self- Acquired Lands, and to regard all lands, howsoever acquired, as ancestral after fifty years' possession or two successions of heirs, and to exempt only the Ancestral Lands so defined from Sale. In the case of large ancestral properties preserved from sale, the Chief Commissioner proposed that the debts of the owners should be paid off by an attachment of their profits, or by handing them over to the creditors for a term of twenty-five years at the most, to be in the end restored back to the owner free of all claims. In these several ways the inevitable change would, he thought, be sufficiently retarded to avoid all political inconvenience and any sudden Social Revolution. Of the minor authorities consulted, the Deputy Commissioners of Jabalpur, Chindwara, Nimar, and Narbada Division, were of opinion that no change in the existing Law was called for. Mr. Bernard, Commissioner of Nagpur, however, proposed to exempt all lands, whether ancestral or acquired, from compulsory Sale by process of Civil Courts. Mr. Brooks, the Commissioner, and Mr. Nicholls, Assistant Commissioner, Seoni, were inclined to make a distinction between ancestral and Self-Acquired property, and while exempting the one from Sale, when there were heirs living, and subjecting it, instead, to temporary alienations, they did not think any protection should be extended to the other, whether it was joint or divided, and they would extend the same law to Mahomedans as well as Hindus.

Here, this Fourth stage of the Controversy ended for the present without leading to any practical result, so far as the Central Provinces were concerned. In 1872, Sir William Muir became Lieutenant-Governor of the North-West Provinces, and in connection with the new Rent and Revenue Bills, re-opened the whole discussion. The Honourable Mr. J.D. Inglis, Mr. C.A. Elliott, and Mr. Reade wrote strongly in favour of Restrictive Legislation. Mr. Inglis suggested that, after a certain time, Personal Property alone should be held liable for unsecured debts, as also for arrears of Revenue, that Ancestral Property should be exempted from Sale, on account of unregistered mortgage debts; and that decrees founded on registered mortgage bonds should be satisfied as far as possible, by a temporary transfer of the property, which should be only sold when such an arrangement was impossible. Mr. Reade was of opinion that mortgage transactions should be respected, and that in regard to the past, simple debts also had a claim to be satisfied out of land. He, therefore, proposed that a term of two years should be fixed for the realization of all previous unsecured debts, and that, after that term, simple debts should be only realized from the person and out of the movable property of the debtor. In regard to mortgage debts, he proposed that there should be no interference when the property mortgaged was Self-Acquired. Where it was Ancestral, the claim should be paid off by a farm or attachment of profits for a term not exceeding thirty years. Mr. Elliott urged that the Zamindar should be regarded as a person holding land burdened with a public duty, and that while all claims in respect of old debts should be respected, it should be declared for the future that the Civil Courts would not lend their help to realize new debts by the Sale of the Land, or by any process severer than a thirty years' farm, the Zamindar holding during the farm as a privileged tenant.

In the meanwhile, Sir William Muir had learned to moderate his old extreme views, and he contented himself with the proposal that lands should be exempted from sale for unsecured debts, that there should be in every District a Court for the relief of encumbered estates, like the Court of Wards, and that *'Seer'* Lands should be inalienable beyond the lifetime of the holder. These views were referred to the Judges of the High Court, Allahabad, two of whom, Mr. Justice Turner and Mr. Justice Pearson, strongly condemned retrograde measures, while the third Judge, Mr. Justice Spankie, gave a very doubtful support. Sir William Muir afterwards toned down his proposals still further, and contented himself with recommending that the execution work in the case of Land Sales should be transferred to the Collectors, who, if they found the Lands hopelessly involved, should proceed with the Sale. If there was a hope of rescuing the estate by good management within twenty-five years, the Collector should assume such management. Eventually, Sir William Muir withdrew all his chief proposals, so far as the North-West Provinces were concerned, on the ground that it was now too late to think of prohibiting the Sales of Land for unsecured debts, and expressed himself satisfied that a better execution of the powers conferred under Sections 243, and 244, or an enlargement of these powers, was all that was required under the circumstances. The effect of this unconditional surrender on the part of the Lieutenant-Governor was that in the North-West Provinces Rent and Revenue Acts of 1873, the only new provision that was inserted was in Section 7, relating to ex-Proprietary Tenants, by which Proprietors who lost or parted with their Lands were recognized to have the status of Privileged Tenants in Seer Land, holding at a rent of four annas in the Rupee less than that paid by Tenants-at-Will, and this rent could not be enhanced except for specific reasons laid down in the Law. This was the only outcome at the time, so far as the North-West Provinces were concerned, of all this lengthy controversy. Subsequently, as suggested by Sir William Muir, in amending the Code of Civil Procedure, the Legislature took care to enlarge the Collector's powers, and to lay down Specific Rules of Procedure for his guidance, in the matter of the execution of Decrees against Land, the absence of which rules was so much complained of by the various Subordinate Governments who were consulted about the working of the Sections 243 and 244 of Act VIII of 1859. In Oudh, however, a Relief Act in favour of the Talukdars was passed in 1870, by which special provision was made as to the way in which Revenue Officers were to assume the management of encumbered estates, and to arrange for the liquidation of the estates. The Broach Talukdars' Act, passed in the next year, was modelled on the same principles, and later on, we have had several Acts in the same spirit for the benefit of paticular classes, notably the Zamindars of Sind and Chota Nagpur. Before the Deccan Agriculturists' Relief Act was passed, the Acts named above were the only outcome of this long discussion.

The Land Sale Controversy, however, did not end with the enactment of these measures. It was re-opened in the Central Provinces in 1874 under the Chief Commissioner, Mr. (since Sir John) Morris, when the subject was started in connection with a new Revenue and Tenancy Bill for those Provinces. The Minutes recorded by Mr. Morris, Mr. Grant and Mr. Carpenter, Commissioners of Jabalpur, Mr. Jones, Commissioner of Nagpur, and Mr. Low, Commissioner of the Narbada Division, go over the whole ground of this most controversial subject, and might be said in some degree to complete the literature of the Restrictive School of Thinkers and Statesmen. As the Government of India was not prepared to prohibit all involuntary transfer of landed properties, the discussion at this time was confined chiefly to the devising of means by which the evils of a too rapid transfer might be obviated. Mr. Grant, for instance, proposed that the best way to protect the Ryots' interests, and deter Bania purchasers from investing their spare cash in land, was to hold that no absolute proprietary title to land could be recognized in India, and to enforce upon the purchasers the full responsibilities of the holders of land by placing a check upon the choice of managers, and in the last resort by cancelling the Settlement, if necessary, and pensioning off the dispossessed holder by a part payment of the Jamma. These drastic remedies alone could, in his opinion, check the evil; all the other measures only touched the surface symptoms of the disease in the body Politic. The necessity of sanction, for instance, enforced in the Non-Regulation Provinces, had become, in the course of time, impotent of effect. Mr. Jones also proceeded on the same track, when he laid down as one of his postulates that the mere exemption of lands from Sale for money debts would be an insufficient remedy. He, however, thought that Mr. Grant's Scheme would effect too sweeping a change and it would be impossible to work it. The land might be protected, but the produce of it from year to year would be sequestrated. He, accordingly, proposed his own Scheme which would allow private transactions of Sale, but put a stop to involuntary transfer by Civil Process, except in the case of debts expressly secured on the land, and with a view to secure a check upon extravagant loans, he would require that all loans, for which ancestral property was to be mortgaged, should be contracted only under the Collector's supervision, and should be held to be void and of no obligatory force without such consent. Further, he would leave parties to exercise their rights freely, in respect of self-acquired land, except that he would encourage Family Entails and Settlements. In respect of past transactions, he would constitute each Deputy Commissioner's

Court into an Encumbered Estates Court, and help the speedy release of estates by loans from Government. Mr. Grant thought that Mr. Jones's Scheme about investing Collectors with the power of certifying good and legitimate loans would be found impossible to work, though he thought better of the Encumbered Estates Scheme. Mr. Low thought that the old Proprietors, were ruined not by the Banias so much as by the excessive temptations to borrowing placed in their way by the Settlement. He agreed with Mr. Grant in thinking that the best way to reduce these temptations was to enforce the responsibilities of proprietary possession. After this was done, the next step was to limit the power of alienating Ancestral Land to one quarter of the estate at the owner's pleasure, and to declare the remaining three-quarters inalienable. The only form of alienation that Mr.Low would permit under his Scheme was a lease for ten years only. Involuntary alienation of ancestral estate by Civil Process would only be allowed in cases when the original bond had been certified by the Collector as having been passed for sufficient consideration, and the property charged did not exceed one-fourth of the owner's possessions. Mr. Carpenter, Commissioner of the Jabalpur Division, contented himself with a more modest and certainly less involved Scheme of Reform. He thought that the evil would be best checked by insisting upon the creditor the necessity of filing a written statement of his account with his debtors in the Registrar's Office, and he would also have a register of all properties, showing how far they were encumbered or free. He disapproved of all strong remedies, but, if further Legislation was desired, he expressed a strong opinion in favour of exempting Lands from Sale, but leaving them liable to the attachment of their profits for eight or ten years. Finally, Mr. Morris, the Chief Commissioner, discussed all the views of his subordinates, and found more or less fault with them all, as being either unworkable, or undesirable, but at the same time he refused to take upon himself the responsibility of suggesting any particular measures for adoption. He, however, made alternative suggestions to the effect that all property in land should be declared exempt from sale in execution of civil decrees, and that the only alienation which should be allowed to the owner was a lease for a term of less than ten years, which lease might be transferred to the creditor in satisfaction of his claim. If the latter measure seemed to be too radical, he suggested the establishment of Encumbered Estates Courts, and was of opinion that the Civil Courts should refuse to recognize all alienations save those certified by the said Courts. This concludes the Sixth phase of these Land Sale Controversies.

None of these discussions of 1859, and 1873, in the North-West Provinces, of 1869, in the Punjab, of 1871 and 1874 in the Central Provinces, seem to have produced much effect upon the Legislature, except in measures of partial operation for the relief of particular classes, which were never recognized to be anything but temporary expedients. The general law for the Presidencies of Bengal, Bombay and Madras continued to be one of unfettered freedom. Sir A. Hobhouse very justly characterized the extreme proposals of the Officers of the North-West and the Central Provinces as violating the spirit of all sound Legislation, and advised more cautious proceedings. The subject was, however, not to be laid at rest by the dictum of the Law Member, and the Government of India was soon after forced to take action in the last stage of this controversy which had its rise this time in the Bombay Presidency. The immediate occasion which attracted public attention to the subject in this Presidency was the outbreak of the riots in the Deccan Districts in 1875. The inquiries undertaken by the Commission included this among other topics, and they raked up the whole of the past literature on the subject as far as this Presidency was concerned. It appeared from this research into past records that as early as 1844, Captain Anderson of the Revenue Survey had complained of the mechanical action of the Courts, and urged the necessity of getting a valuation of landed property made by independent assessors, prior to the issue of the order of Sale and compelling judgement creditors to accept it at that price. Mr. Frere and Mr. Rose recommended the establishment of Usury Laws, and the opening of licensed Government Pawnbroker's Shops. Mr. Rose further urged the justice of exempting Houses and Mirasi Rights from being sold in execution of money decrees. Usury Laws had obtained in the Madras and Bengal Presidencies and in the North-West Provinces, but they had found no place in the Bombay Code of 1827. Accordingly the Enactment of a Usury Law limiting interest to a maximum rate of twelve per cent., also the introduction of some provision requiring all bonds to be registered, and transferring houses and lands into the creditor's possession, to pay himself out of the usufruct thereof, in a term of years,-these measures were suggested as palliative remedies in 1844, in the interests of the Ryots. The Government of Bombay, however, negatived all these proposals. In 1852, Captain Wingate took up the subject of the Compulsory Sale of the Ryots' lands in execution of decrees, and urged a change of the law on the ground that such Sales were unknown in the times of the old Rulers, were further opposed to Native feeling, and were but rarely resorted to till the land Settlements were made. He advocated the policy of declaring that lands should not be sold on account of unsecured debts, though they might be freely mortgaged and sold voluntarily, and in such cases, decrees might be specifically enforced in regard to them. Captain Wingate also recommended a Usury Law and proposed to invest the Courts with a discretionary power to allow proper interest. He suggested the advisability of reviving the Institution of Panchayats to try Summary Suits valued at less than thirty Rupees and the extension of a general Insolvency Law. These recommendations remained unnoticed for nearly thirty years, but it is strange that almost every one of the proposals then made by Captain Wingate has of late received the sanction of the Legislature. The Usury Law, the Exemption of Lands from Civil Process for Unsecured Debts, the Panchayat Courts, a liberal Insolvency Law—these are the leading features of the new Deccan Agriculturists' Relief Act. To proceed, however, with the history of the subject, in 1859, Mr. Tytler recommended the establishment of a Registry of the Ryots' debts in the Mamlatdar's Office, with a view to check fraud, and show all payments made by the Ryots. In 1860 Mr. Jacomb submitted a plan of Government savings and Town Banks to help needy Ryots with easy interest. The Government of Bombay did not support either of these proposals. For the next twelve years, Bombay Officers seemed not to have thought much of this subject as the prosperity brought on the Country by high prices secured a sensible advance in the comfort of the people. In 1872-73, however, hard times returned, and Mr. (now Sir Raymond) West published his pamphlet "The Land and the Law of India," which gave birth to a long discussion, both in and out of the Presidency. Mr. West proposed that the power of alienating land should be limited. He urged upon the Government that it should declare all assessed land to be expressly inalienable except with its assent, or reassessable to a rack rent on such alienation for the benefit of the public. If this might be deemed to be too strong a measure, he proposed to confine the power of alienation with the Collector's consent to the surplus land, *i.e.* land exceeding a certain fixed necessary minimum for comfortable subsistence, and it was this excess land alone which was to be liable to Attachment and Sale. The Dwellings, and the Crops, and the cattle of the Agriculturists should also be exempt. His next proposal was that mortgages and leases for more than one year be subjected to the same rules as Sales. Mr. West further proposed to limit the right of enforcing a Specific Partition of Property. The necessary minimum requisite for the support of a family should not be partitioned, but the separating sharers should be paid off in money. A system of Family Settlements for large estates, and a liberal Law of Insolvency, crowned the edifice of these proposed sweeping reforms. Mr. Pedder also contributed his mite to the literature on this subject. He argued for a reformed procedure, a Law of Bankruptcy, and finally the exemption of Land from Sale in execution of decrees. This exemption, however, was not to apply to the crops or profits of land. We next have the inquiries conducted by the Deccan Riots Commission, of which the immediate outcome has been the Deccan Agriculturists' Relief Act of 1879. As far as the subject of Land Sale is concerned, it is to be noted that the Commission reported in favour of abolishing Sales of Land in execution of money decrees. They further suggested the necessity of a liberal Insolvency Law, of the abolition of Civil Imprisonment, and the establishment of Public Notaries and registration of all payments in Pass Books. The Bombay Government, under Sir Phillip Wodehouse, however, negatived the recommendation in regard to the exemption of Land from Sale, as also the proposal to abolish imprisonment for debt. When Sir Richard Temple, however, became Governor, he took up the subject again, with his usual energy, and urged the necessity of giving effect to the recommendations of the Commission in the matter of a law exempting Lands from Sale in execution of money decrees except when they had been specifically pledged. He also pressed for a more liberal Insolvency Law, and a Law for Limiting the Rate of Interest. These suggestions were approved by the Government of India, and the Deccan Agriculturists' Relief Act was passed into Law.

We have thus reviewed the whole history of this lengthy discussion for the past twenty-five years in the North-West Provinces, in the Punjab, in the Central Provinces, and finally in the Bombay Presidency. There can be no question that the relief so tardily given is in accordance with the conservative instincts and traditions of the people. A thorough review of the whole discussion like the one we have now summarized can alone bring out all the bearings of this most important question. The government of India has shown great practical wisdom in refusing to lend its support to the more extreme proposals of its Revenue Officers. Mr. Justice West, Mr. Elliott, Mr. Grant, Mr. Jones and the other authorities appear to us to have ignored the main conditions of the problem. The Country is in a transition stage, passing from semi-Feudal and Patriarchal conditions of existence into a more settled and commercial order of things, from a period of disturbance and wars into one of peace and tranquillity, from payments in kind to cash payments, from the laws of custom to the rule of competition, from a simple to a more complicated Social Organization. No Economical Legislation can succeed under such circumstances, which seeks to run against the current, or stem the torrent. In all countries property, whether in land or other goods, must gravitate towards that class which has more intelligence, and greater foresight, and practices abstinence, and must slip from the hands of those who are ignorant, improvident, and hopeless to stand on their own resources. This is a law of Providence, and can never be wisely or safely ignored by practical Statesmen for any fancied political or sentimental considerations. As long as the difference in the habits and education of the saving few represented by the Bania and Brahmin classes, and the spending many who count by millions among the Military and the Cultivating classes remains good, property will gravitate from the one class to the other, notwithstanding all prohibitory Legislation. The utmost that Government can safely venture to do is to regulate this inevitable transfer, to temper the change so as to avoid all immediate hardships. An Insolvency Law cannot benefit anybody, where none but the castaways and waifs of Society wish to degrade themselves to seek its advantage. A Law of Forced Entails cannot be expected to work when the notion of equal inheritance by birth-right is so thoroughly ingrained in the national mind. A minimum sufficient for subsistence cannot be fixed when the natural conditions of soil and climate permit of the lowering of the standard of necessary comfort to any conceivable limit. The force of resistance must well forth from within, and cannot possibly be super-imposed. The forcible prohibition of all transfer of real property, voluntary and involuntary, can never mend matters—it can only stereotype existing poverty and aggravate existing helplessness. The Government of such a large Empire cannot afford means to be the Banker of its millions of Insolvent Tenants, and cannot equalize the changing conditions of bad harvests and scanty or irregular rainfall. As we have said above, it can only adopt temporary expedients, and watch anxiously the effects of its experiments. It must accept as inevitable the tendency to concentration of the landed capital of the Country, and only limit its agency to the minor work of smoothing the gradual change. The only settlement of the Problem that is possible is not to its taste. It should withdraw from its position as Landlord, and look upon the land tax as a tax like any other monopoly taxes. A permanent Ryotwari Settlement fixed in grain which the land produces, and commuted into money values every twenty or thirty years, can alone furnish a solution of this Agricultural Problem. If differences subsequently spring up between class and class, as they have on occasions sprung up in Bengal, the Government can interfere as a mediator, and right matters by protecting the weak against the strong. It will not, however, for fancied Political considerations accept this position or allow Middlemen to come between itself and its Pauper Tenants, and its attempts to undo the legitimate influence of the saving classes can only end in a great disaster. The Deccan Agriculturists' Relief Act can hardly bring any permanent real relief, while the standing cause of all the embarrassments of the Ryots continues at work with untempered rigidity. It is hoped that the new Régime, from which all hope so much, will turn its attention to this aspect of the question, and devise a remedy which will establish an accord between the Economical, Social and Intellectual conditions of the population, and secure the real advancement of the Country on a permanent foundation.

5

Mr. WEDDERBURN AND HIS CRITICS ON A PERMANENT SETTLEMENT FOR THE DECCAN*

Mr. Wedderburn's scheme of a modified permanent settlement for the Deccan Provinces has, we are glad to see, attracted notice both in India and England in the highest quarters, and now that the much- abused Sowcar has been well nigh suppressed, it may be hoped that the unprecedented fall of prices, which has occurred in the course of the last few months, will suggest and secure an equally liberal modification of the rigidity and onerous character of the land settlement which has been admitted by the highest authorities to be, with the Sowcar's usurious dealings, the principal cause of the Ryot's wretchedness and misery. The compulsory resort to the conciliators, the necessity of Plaintiff's personal presence in the Civil Courts during all the protracted stages of the hearing of the case, the absence of Vakils, the provision enforcing Defendant's presence before the hearing can come on, the provision permitting the Courts to go behind the bond, and interfere with, and cut down, usurious rates of interest and set aside one-sided contracts in taking the account, the

JPSS, January 1881, Vol.III, No.3.

exemption of the debtor's person from arrest, and his land and house and cattle from attachment, the liberal provisions regarding insolvency, the longer period of limitation —all these beneficial concessions have been enforced in the interest of the Ryots as against the Sowcar. It is now time, therefore, that some similar concessions were made by the State landlord to its pauper tenantry to supplement this work of relief. The spirit, however, of the measures, recently adopted by the local government, gives no indications of a conciliatory spirit, and it requires no great powers of prophecy to foresee that, with the fall of prices, the Ryot's miseries will be multiplied a hundred-fold by the very measures intended for his relief. The proposal, or rather order, directing the forfeiture of Inam and Khalsa lands on default to pay the fixed instalments within ten days is a sad irony of fate which the Sowcar and the Ryot will find it hard to reconcile with the declared intentions of Government, and cannot fail to drive the Ryot into the hands of the Sowcar more helplessly than ever. No wonder that under such circumstances a correspondent of the *Bombay Gazette* who signs himself C.S., and is to all appearances a member of the executive service, condemns the Relief Act in no measured terms as a costly failure, "an illustration of the vanity of all legislation in restraint of the freedom of contracts. Such legislation generally fails because it does not go far enough, and it does not go far enough because it cannot." However that be, it is plain, now that the Sowcar has been disarmed, the responsibility for the Ryot's miseries, if they remain in *statu quoante* or are aggravated, will be at the door of his sovereign landlord.

Even the Honourable Mr.Hope who is one of our ablest revenue officers acknowledged with a frankness which does him infinite credit that "to the revenue system must in candour be ascribed some share in the indebtedness of the Ryot," and that "the burden of the land revenue demand is one of the causes of the Ryot's embarrassed condition." The Lieutenant Governor of the Punjab was perhaps more out-spoken and thorough-going in his condemnation of the revenue-system when he observed, "that too little attention had been paid to this cause which must in a great degree have contributed to, if it did not entirely originate, the difficulties of the Deccan Ryot," and "thought it desirable that at the same time as measures of relief were afforded to the Ryot from his private creditor, the Government, which appeared as a public creditor of the Ryot, should also take measures to lighten in some way the pressure of its own demand." Lord Lytton also, unlike Sir Richard Temple and some of the Bombay Revenue officers, was far from being a believer in the divine perfection of the Bombay revenue system. For he was "personally disposed to believe that the rigidity of our present local system might in various directions be relaxed with great benefit to the cultivator, unaccompanied by any serious inconvenience to the state." A majority of the Deccan Riots Commissioners were also of the same opinion as that expressed in the extracts already quoted above regarding the defects and imperfections of our local system, and the necessity of amending it. It also appears from one of the speeches of the late Viceroy "that the question of relieving the Ryot from the embarrassing pressure of claims on the part of the state has been urged by us on the attention of the Government of Bombay with special reference to those districts of the Deccan for which we are now legislating."

More than a year has elapsed since the attention of the Bombay Government was earnestly drawn by the Supreme Government to this pressing question and yet there are no indications on the surface of any change of policy. The hot haste with which the Relief Act was ushered into existence contrasts sadly with the immovability of Government in redeeming its own most solemn pledges. It is in this connection chiefly that we welcome the appearance and publicity of Mr. Wedderburn's pamphlet, as it cannot fail, among other purposes, to remind the authorities in India and England of their unfulfilled promises of last year. Besides this service, the scheme propounded by Mr. Wedderburn as the result of twenty years' study of the Ryot's condition deserves the most patient consideration at the hands of the authorities. He occupies, a standpoint which permits him to feel equal sympathy for the Ryot and the Sowcar, a rare advantage in these days, whose value is heightened by his personal character as a pains-taking and a conscientious officer. Mr. Wedderburn commends his scheme to the notice of Government as securing for the cultivator reduced responsibility, complete security of tenure and a stimulus to improvement,—for the capitalist a lucrative and honourable employment for his money,—and for the state a secure and increasing revenue. To attain this desirable end, he proposes to revive the ancient *batai* system by which the assessment, forming a definite portion of the gross produce of each field, was levied in kind, for he says—"The old is better." With a view to avoid the abuses of the old native system and secure its unquestioned benefits, the scheme limits the demand of the state to 1-16th (one anna in the rupee) part of the gross produce, and also gives the cultivator the option of a quit-rent, amounting to 3-16ths of an average dry crop. If the Ryot wishes to be free from the annual vexation of an appraisement of his crops, he can choose to pay 3-16th (three annas in the rupee) share of an average produce as quit- rent in kind. For collecting the assessment in kind, the agency of middlemen like the zamindars of Bengal is to be employed. These middlemen will enter into an engagement with Government, either permanent or for a number of years, for annually paying to it its fixed share in money, which they will receive in kind from the villages committed to their charge, and they are expected to reimburse themselves for the losses of bad years with the gains of plentiful harvests. The existing landholders, pensioners, professional men, and Sowcars are to be drawn upon for forming this new class of Zemindars, who will relieve the Ryot from the unvarying and trying difficulty of paying assessment in cash, and also will ensure to the state a prompt and punctual payment of its dues in money without let or hindrance, be the harvest good or bad, and thus do away with the painful necessity of remissions and suspensions in years of drought or famine. The Ryot, it may be added, will be further secured from the demoralizing effect of remissions and suspensions, the apprehension of which, it is said, influenced not a little the inconceivably hard and stringent policy followed in exacting the arrears of land revenue during the late famine in this Presidency. Impelled by the magic of property which a permanent settlement of tenure is affirmed to ensure, the Zemindars *in posse* are expected to apply themselves heart and soul to the improvement of the soil, "supplying the cultivators with superior seed and manures and machinery."

With a view to illustrate the elastic advantages of the *Batai* system as opposed to the existing rigid and unequal system of cash assessment, Mr. Wedderburn has framed what he calls a financial statement of Bapu bin Rama. It is necessary to study this statement closely, as it appears evident to us that much of the misunderstanding disclosed in the criticisms upon the scheme which have appeared in the Bombay dailies is owing to the absence of such study as much as, if not more than, to the imperfections, and even errors, which, as we shall show further on, vitiate it to some extent. We may observe *en passant* that Mr. Wedderburn's estimate of 4 maunds of produce per acre in an average year, and 2 maunds in a bad year appears to us to be rather too high, at least for the four Deccan Districts which may be fairly estimated to yield 5 maunds of corn in a good year, 2 maunds in a medium year, and only a maund or under in a bad year. We see in the excellent treatise on agriculture and horticulture in Western India by Rao Saheb Ramchandra Sakharam Gupte, an experienced pensioned Mamledar, that only a bumper harvest is credited with yielding 4 maunds of Jwari or Bajri per acre. Mr. Fardunji Jamshetji's estimate of a favourable season at 6 maunds per acre may be true of Aurungabad, but it is hardly applicable to the Districts of the Deccan which we have in view. However any correct estimate of an average produce per acre is not essential to Mr. Wedderburn's scheme, though it may have its value in practice when the average yield of an acre will have to be appraised for determining the amount and value of 1-16th share thereof.

With regard to the financial statement of Bapu bin Rama Mr. Wedderburn observes :—"From this table it will be seen at a glance (cols. 4 and 5) that although the present demand of Government is nominally fixed, the pressure of this demand varies greatly according to the season and market. Rs.20 are levied whether the crop is worth Rs.960, Rs.320, or Rs.80; so that in an exceptionally good year when the Ryot can well afford to pay a handsome bonus, he only contributes 1-48th part of his crop; in an average year 1-16th is taken; while 1/4th of the total crop is taken in a bad year, when he has not even enough to feed himself and his family." The accuracy of this view has been energetically questioned by Mr. Wedderburn's critics in the public

Financial Statement of Bapu bin Rama.

Ryot's crop.				Government demand			
				Modern System (a.)		Ancient System (b.)	
Season	Total Crop.	Market rate per Rupee	Total value of crop.	Cash.	Equivalent share of crop.	1-16 share of crop.	Equivalent in cash.
1	2	3	4	5	6	7	8
Good (6 maunds per acre.)	12,000 seers	Seers.	Rs.	Rs.	Seers.	Seers.	Rs.
		12½	960	20	250	750	60
		25	480	20	500	750	30
		50	240	20	1,000	750	15
Medium (4 maunds per acre.)	8,000 seers	12½	640	20	250	500	40
		25	320	20	500	500	20
		50	160	20	1,000	500	10
Bad (2 maunds per acre.)	4,000 seers	12½	320	20	250	250	20
		25	160	20	500	250	10
		50	80	20	1,000	250	5

Press who seem to imagine that by demolishing the table they could also demolish the unsavoury scheme of a permanent settlement. One critic remarks:—"Mr. Wedderburn says that under the old system in good times the Ryot would pay the equivalent of Rs.60, and in hard times he would pay only the equivalent of Rs.5. In other words, he supposes that in the best season when the yield of the crops is the highest, prices would be at famine rates, *i.e.* 12½ seers the rupee, and in hard times when the land yields only two maunds an acre, the price of grain will be fifty seers the rupee; in fact the very lowest supposed price that can be obtained in the market, when the supply must be abundant. This certainly appears to be fallacious." Another critic exclaims:—"It is inconceivable how an official of Mr. Wedderburn's experience could have made this mistake." It should, however, be observed that the validity of Mr. Wedderburn's conclusion, viz., that under the modern system, the pressure of the land tax varies inversely with the Ryot's ability to pay, in other words, that the demand is light when the harvest is good, and is heavy when the latter is bad, is nowhere impeached. At first sight it certainly appears paradoxical that the prices are high and low when the crops are respectively good and bad; the reverse of this strange phenomenon is what generally happens. It should, however, be remembered that though prices vary inversely with the harvest, the variation is far from being regulated with any mathematical exactness or precision. Were the variation to follow any such exact law, there would certainly remain very little to choose between the ancient and modern systems of land assessment. For in that case it will appear evident from the table that when prices are invariably at 12½ and 25 seers respectively in bad and medium years, the Ryot will be paying the same fixed proportion of his crops, that is, 250 and 500 seers when the crops yield 4000 and 8000 seers, whether he pays the assessment in kind or cash. And the same would happen were we to further suppose that in good years when the harvest yields 12000 seers, prices will be at 37½ seers the rupee, according to the mathematical calculation, instead of 50 seers. For there is no reason why prices which are supposed to follow an invariable law in bad and medium years should not observe the same regularity in good years. So that in good years when a field of 50 acres yields 12000 seers, and corn is at $37^1/_2$ seers the rupee, whether the ryot pays Rs.20 or its equivalent share of crop, *i.e.* 750 seers, he will have to pay the same proportion of the produce of his land. But in spite of these mathematical assurances to the ryot of his happy or at least unchanged lot, the shoe nevertheless pinches under the modern system of cash payments. What is the cause of this apparent anomaly? How is it that though mathematical deductions fail to show the superiority of the ancient over the modern system, yet it is acknowledged even by the advocates of the latter "that the present system does not work well, and that the Ryot would only too gladly return to the former system." An explanation of this strange anomaly will be found, we think, in the unsoundness of the theory that supposes that prices vary exactly, with the harvest. They would no doubt do so, were it necessary for them to depend solely and wholly upon the quantity of corn grown in a particular district or province. But facilities of communication and the free, unrestricted interchange of commerce supply the deficiency of one province or country with the sufficiency or superabundance of another, so as to prevent prices from being enhanced to a degree that would otherwise be warranted by the scanty yield of the local harvest, and present the strange and striking phenomenon of wheat being cheaper in England in a year when the crops may fail than it ever was even in a season of plenty, but foreign supplies were checked by the Cornlaws. Under a system of free-trade and easy intercourse, the Ryot finds that the importation of corn, though benefiting the general community and him too as a consumer, inconveniences him as a producer, for these large imports prevent or retard the rise of prices, and thus deprive him of the benefit which otherwise would have consoled him for the scanty produce of his field, and enabled him to easily bear the burden of assessment. This can be best illustrated by means of an example. Suppose that free importations of corn, facilitated by railways, canals and good roads, prevent the upward tendency of prices to rise to $12^1/_2$

seers per rupee in a bad year, and keep them stationary at 25 seers per rupee, (which supposition is not absurd or chimerical when we bear in mind what has recently occurred in England, and is more and more likely to be realized with every improvement in the means of communication in India), then the value of the produce (4000 seers) of 50 acres at 2 maunds per acre would only be Rupees 160, and the assessment (Rs.20) representing 500 seers would be an eighth share of the gross produce. If we estimate the prices in a bad year at any other figure below 25, but above 12½, say 20 or 15 seers, the difficulties of the ryot would be so much the smaller. But they cannot altogether disappear unless the prices rise to 12½ seers, which foreign supplies even under the present condition of imperfect communications tend to prevent. And even the rise of prices would be of no use to him when the crops altogether fail. We hope we shall not be understood as laying down the absurd proposition that free trade and facilities of communication are among the causes of the Ryot's embarrassment. We only mean to say that, in years of drought and famine, the system of cash assessments heavily weighs upon the Ryot in his present deplorable circumstances and that he would obtain a certain measure of the desired relief if the base of the system was payment in kind commuted into money before it reached the Treasury. Perhaps Mr. Wedderburn had in his view the beneficial effect of free trade in arresting the upward tendency of prices in bad years when he framed the table, though this cannot be gathered from the explanation which follows it. If this be so, it may be safely said that it is not that Homer nods, but the critics that dream. It may also be added that even if the figures of this statement be discarded the value of Mr. Wedderburn's scheme will not be impaired in the least. For it does not form a part of its essence, but is simply an illustration of what is generally acknowledged to be true, that the Ryot finds it extremely difficult to pay the assessment in cash, and would certainly prefer to pay it if fixed at a moderate proportion in kind.

Let us now turn to some other objections that have been urged against the scheme. One critic from his Khandesh Camp bursts out in the following strains:—

"Do I sleep ? Do I dream ?
Do I wander and doubt ?
Are things what they seem ?
Or is vision about ?
Is our civilization a failure ?
Or is the Caucasian played out ?"

and asks Mr. Wedderburn whether he really believes "that our civilization is a failure," necessitating the abolition of "the simple settlement," planned by such great heads as Mountstuart Elphinstone, Munro, Wingate and others, and a return to "the old confusion" of the batai system. Perhaps the critic would have done well to cool down his agitation, with the reflection that one's belief in the general success of Western civilization is not inconsistent with a thorough disbelief in the infallibility of the Bombay revenue system. Our Judicial organization and procedure are as much the offspring of Western civilization as the revenue Survey and settlement, and can be fathered upon as wise heads as the latter can boast of; so that if the former can be safely condemned without losing one's faith in modern enlightenment (for the critic characterizes it as the bane alike of the Ryot and the revenue system) it will hardly seem logical to inveigh in this exaggerated manner against those who find fault with the latter and not without reason. This critic besides while accusing (unreasonably in our opinion) Mr. Wedderburn of hankering after the old confusion, is really himself guilty of the same offence. His panacea for the Ryot's woes appears to be a revival of the old exploded combination of the revenue and judicial authorities, as may be gathered from the following wild declamation. "Instead of multiplying Munsifs, make Munsifs Mamledars-Combine the Revenue and the Judicial functions in the same hands, and the result, at any rate, will be an increase of common sense. Take a lesson from the Central Provinces, and O thou proposer of a permanent settlement for Bombay, forget not the wretched condition of the Ryot under the Zemindari system of Bengal." The critic has evidently forgotten that the played out Caucasian civilization inculcates the political and economical advantages of the division of power as well as labour, and that it is any thing but common sense to confound Mr. Wedderburn's scheme of a modified permanent settlement, based on fixed, and proportioned payment in kind, with the Bengal Zemindari system of large holdings with fixed assessment. Had there been an intelligent unfettered press in the Central Provinces, we feel sure it would have told a different tale regarding the working of the heterogeneous combination of the revenue and the Judicial offices in the Central Provinces. And the so-called wretched condition of the peasantry under the Zemindari system, is as much mythical as the wild narratives of our Purans. For, compared with their brethren of the Deccan, the Ryots of Bengal certainly enjoy a happier lot. Our latest authority for this statement is the present Lieutenant Governor of Bengal, whose fine picture of prosperity and plenty smiling upon the quiet industrious peasantry entrusted to his care may be within the recollection of our readers, and Sir Ashley Eden, we believe, cannot be reproached with possessing any superabundant friendly feelings towards the Bengal Zemindars.

It is also objected to Mr. Wedderburn's scheme that, though it may look perfect on paper yet it will be found to be attendant with demoralizing effects in practice. It will expose the Ryot's to the irresistible temptation of clandestinely removing the grain from the threshing floor, and subject them to the further evil of oppression and corruption on the part of low paid officials, who will either harass the Ryots by practising all sorts of zulum upon them or cause loss to the Government revenue by extorting bribes from them for their forbearance and connivance. It should, however, be borne in mind that Mr. Wedderburn's scheme altogether dispenses with the agency of the state or its officials in the collection of the land-revenue in kind from the Ryot, and assigns the duty to an intermediate class of Zemindars. It may be replied that the latter worthies will be guilty of the same practices that can be laid to the charge of government officials. It may well be asked what guarantee is there that the middle-men will be less oppressive, tyrannical, and unscrupulous in their dealings with the Ryot than the government officials. How, moreover, will the proposed scheme be free from the well-known evils of annual appraisements? Will not the task be attended with worry and harassment alike to the Zemindar and the Ryot? But in these discussions, we should not lose sight of the fact that the scheme is not essentially much different from what actually occurs in practice every year For as things stand at present, in ninety cases out of a hundred, if not more, the Sowcar makes advances to the Ryot for seed and subsistence and Government assessment, on the condition of the latter's giving the former the whole or half the produce of his field, till the advances are paid off, which happy event seldom occurs. The Sowcar is not infrequently obliged to keep watch and ward upon the growing crops for preventing any clandestine attempt in the way of removal of any part thereof by the Ryot. When the harvest is gathered in, an equal division of the produce is effected between the two on the threshing floor in some rough sort of way. If the sharp Sowcar sometimes drives the Ryot into giving him more than his proper share the latter often takes care that the whole of the produce shall not appear in the grain yard. It may, however, be mentioned alike to the credit of the Sowcar and the Ryot that this matter is generally satisfactorily settled between them. So that Mr. Wedderburn's scheme, if adopted, will simply legalize the prevailing practice with regard to assessment, with this additional benefit that it will no longer be necessary to the Ryot to sell a portion of his crops at a price ruinously below the market rate to secure the much needed Rupees for paying the Government dues. Any objection to the scheme that it will involve an annual inspection and appraisement of the crops, and thus cause misunderstanding or friction between the Zemindar and the Sowcar, is, therefore, hardly tenable, when it is remembered that the Ryot now voluntarily submits to something like it every year for satisfying the claims of the Sowcar and the Sirkar. For his field does not produce the rare Rupees, but only their value, and the process of converting the crop into cash at an inequitable under-value is highly disadvantageous to him.

It is also urged against the scheme that it initiates a retrograde or backward movement incompatible with the people's progress in civilization, and makes such a distinct departure from the prevailing system that it can never be adopted by Government, tending, as it does, to disturb the existing arrangements of the revenue survey which have existed so long, and have cost so much expense and labour, more especially when the change involves a considerable loss of revenue. The present assessment is far from representing only 1-16th share of the gross produce of land. On the contrary according to the admissions of some of the survey and revenue officers, the assessment averages to 1-10th or 1-11th of a good crop. To adopt a change of system on the plan proposed would thus make it necessary to sacrifice 25 per cents of the revenue collected at present. This objection will not appear unanswerable if it is borne in mind that exceptional circumstances (as observed above) may necessitate exceptional measures. Can it be maintained that the Deccan Ryot's Relief Act is perfectly compatible with the progress the 19th Century has made in legislative wisdom ? Does Bentham's or any other theory of legislation justify the retrospective provisions of the Act which prevent the recovery of the debts, contracted before it came into force, by the sale of the debtor's immovable property, not specifically mortgaged, and by his imprisonment, when the Sowcar must have made loans to the Ryot in the belief that the whole of the latter's property would be available for the satisfaction of his claims and that the fear of imprisonment would deter him from concealing his movables ? Had the Act made these provisions applicable to debts that might be contracted after its enactment, they could not have been found fault with on the ground of equity. For the Sowcar then would have been at liberty to choose to lend or not under the changed legislation of which he was made well aware. But at present by the fiat of the legislative authority of Government, all old loans for the recovery of which the creditors had not brought their suits before the commencement of the Act, are almost cancelled. Nevertheless the Act has been gladly welcomed by the general public, on account of the exceptional circumstances of the Deccan temporarily requiring such a measure. But should not the same circumstances induce the state, which is reputed to be full of paternal instincts towards its subjects in general, and the cultivating portion thereof in particular, and which squandered away about twenty crores on a scientific frontier, to forgo a part of its gains and revert to an arrangement which may appear retrograde, and cause some loss to the revenue, and some disturbance of the existing order of things but which nevertheless may be necessary for the relief of the Ryot ? Does not consistency require that the Sirkar should treat itself somewhat in the same self-sacrificing manner in which it has freely dealt with the Sowcar in its legislative capacity?

Had space permitted, we should have noticed some other objections which have been advanced against Mr. Wedderburn's scheme, but which in our opinion are not calculated to upset it, and strike us as being suggested more from the fact of its author's being without the sacred pale of the Revenue branch of the Civil Service, though he is a member of it, than by any inherent defects in the scheme. We believe the tiresome talk of his want of experience, and of his ignorance of the Ryot and his necessities, which is found in the vigorous protests of the Revenue objectors against it calls for no comments. Mr. Caird's reply to the Government of India is fully in point on this alleged absence of experience. It is one thing to possess experience, and another to interpret it aright, and to generalize from it. What is the use of that experience which does not enable its possessors to suggest anything at once practical and desirable for the correct solution of the agrarian problem ? Perhaps Mr. Wedderburn's critics, at least some of them, are not incapable of suggesting a scheme of their own, if they will only relax their faith in the divine perfection of the Revenue system they have been administering, and cease to inveigh against the Sowcar, when he is already satisfactorily disposed of by the Ryot's Relief

Act, and the Civil Courts which are no longer open to the charge of unduly favouring the Sowcar against the Ryot.

It will appear from the considerations urged above that Mr. Wedderburn's scheme has been well thought out, and if worked out sympathetically, it will go a great way to mitigate the rigidity of the present revenue system by adopting the assessment of the land revenue to the variations of the seasons, and thus afford an appreciable relief to the Ryot in his present embarrassing condition. If permanency of tenure is allowed on all hands to work the miracle of converting a desert into a garden, it will not fail to be attended at least with some of its beneficent effects in the Deccan by "stimulating the energy of the rural classes," as observed by Mr. Wedderburn. He also hopes that "as Zemindar, the capitalist will have scope for his enterprise in developing the resources of the land, and working a safe and profitable partnership with the Ryot." But if the proposed Zemindar be simply required to hand over in cash one sixteenth share of the produce which he will levy in kind from the Ryot, there will remain, we fear, very little inducement for him to undergo the labour and trouble of collection, and devote his capital and energy to the improvement of the land, unless he is allowed for his benefit to collect a little more than the State's 16th share of the produce, say a 12th part thereof, which will still be less than the officially estimated assessment, said to amount only to a 10th or 11th of an average good crop, especially when it is remembered that his gains of plentiful harvests are likely to be absorbed by his losses during years of scarcity and drought. The realization of the bright future prospects which Mr. Wedderburn holds out for the Deccan by the adoption of his scheme will considerably depend upon the character of the new class of Zemindars that is to be created. If they prove to be enlightened, wealthy, public spirited, enterprising and alive to their sense of duty, they will be an unmixed good. Mr. Wedderburn thinks that land-holders, pensioners, professional men, and Sowcars, will supply admirable material for making the new class of middle men. There are no doubt sufficient materials available at hand to justify an experiment on the tentative and small scale which Mr. Wedderburn advocates. Property in land never changes hand except in a slow and gradual manner, and it may be safely expected that with the growth of a leisurely and affluent class interested in the agricultural prosperity of the country, other liberal influences, represented by higher education and scientific cultivation, will spread abroad, and ensure the success of the scheme in the long run. Even as it is, the change from the present Sowcars, who have but a distant and stealthy interest in land, to the new race of tenant farmers will work wonders in reconciling hostile interests, and inducing them to work for the improvement of their common property. Mr. Wedderburn, it is true, suggests that when no suitable person can be found as a permanent Zemindar, the Government share might be realized from year to year by sale to the highest bidder in the way provided for in chapter 6 of Regulation XVII of 1827. We strongly protest against any such alternative, for if anything of this kind be adopted, the scheme will be divested of most of the benefits expected from a permanent settlement, and the middlemen will have very little encouragement to lend the helping hand of capital of enterprising labour. We, therefore, hope that permanency of settlement will be extended alike to the Ryots and to those who will come forward as Zemindars farming the collectings of large amounts of revenue. Even under the present circumstances of society, we have every reason to hope that the new Zemindars will be found not totally unworthy of occupying the honourable position of middlemen land-lords under strict conditions of tenure which will prevent them from rack-renting the Ryots, or abusing the trust that will be reposed in them. The task of compelling the Zemindars to the strict observance of their engagements with the Sirkar will not be impossible to a Government that has undertaken to regulate the monetary dealings between the Sowcar and the Ryot.

Mr. Wedderburn assures the state that this scheme will bring in a secure and increasing revenue. The scheme will certainly benefit the state in obviating the necessity of periodical remissions and suspensions of land revenue as stated above. But it is not so evident to us that it will lead to any increase of revenue. For with regard to the state demand, the very foundation of the scheme rests in the concession that the land tax is to be permanently settled at 1-16th of an average common crop of bajri or jwari, commuted into money on an average of prices (periodically if necessary), and rendered payable by the Zemindar from year to year. Mr. Wedderburn thinks that an enterprising cultivator will so much increase the quantity or value of produce by means of improvements that he will find it more profitable to pay the quit-rent of 3-16ths of an average crop than the 1-16th part of an increased or more valuable produce, and thus the revenue will receive an increment. But these large improvements can be only effected by means of money which the cultivators as a class are lamentably too poor to spend freely. And we have to suppose that the requisite funds for improvements will be supplied by the Zemindars, who will be interested equally with the Ryot in increasing the productive capacity of his land. But if the Ryots will not allow the Zemindar to share in the increased produce, but will simply pay him 3-16th of an average dry, crop, it is questionable whether money will be readily forthcoming from himself for making these improvements. And it is also highly problematical whether any really large sum spent in improvements will not take a number of years for its realization, and whether the work will not be extremely slow, considering the general apathy of both the agricultural and lending classes in such matters. We are not then very hopeful about the increase of revenue. And we think the Government, for once and all should give up any hope of increasing its land revenue in the arid or dry Deccan districts, consisting of lands, rendered unfertile by want of irrigation and manure, and by a scanty and precarious rain-fall. The Government should in these districts trust to only indirect sources for the increase of its revenue, after the general prosperity of the people is assured induced partly by a permanent settlement of a light assessment. We advisedly say partly for such a settlement as the one proposed will be found to be only one of the causes, though a powerful one, whose combined action is necessary for ameliorating the condition of not only the Deccan peasantry, but of the Indian Empire generally. For without the spread of education, not simply elementary but, higher or liberal, which is necessary for lessening the inequality of the contest between the shrewd Sowcar and the ignorant and helpless Ryot, and for improving the general intelligence of the community to understand wherein lie their true and real interests; without the revival of the manufacturing industries of the country that are now totally extinguished in the struggle for existence with European and American rivals, and the diversion into new profitable channels of some of the labour that is now exclusively concentrated upon a single industry without any diminution of the taxes that press heavily upon the labouring classes, and of the extravagant cost of Government for such a poor country as India, as also of the ever-expanding tribute which she pays to England in the shape of Home-charges, the Utopian plenty and prosperity fore-shadowed by Mr. Wedderburn will hardly leave the dream land of vain wishes and become an objective reality. We have already given our own solution of the Agrarian Problem in a previous number* and we were glad to see it has found favour with the well known correspondent of the Bombay Gazette who signs his name W.R.H. If it be deemed too radical, we earnestly hope that the same disregard will not be shown to Mr. Wedderburn's excellent scheme, which, though it is not capable of bringing about all the happy results attributed to it, if not aided by other agencies alluded to above, still upon the whole promises to be a decided improvement upon the present Revenue System, and therefore, deserves the serious attention of both the Government and the Public.

*Vide *JPSS*, Vol.II, No.1. (Article no.1 in this volume)

6

THE CENTRAL PROVINCES LAND REVENUE AND TENANCY BILLS*

If there is one point more than another which strikes every student of British Indian administration in this country, it is its incapacity to realize to itself the fact that the institutions of a country can never be permanently, or even for a long time, out of harmony with its intelligence, social advance, and economic conditions, without producing demoralizing consequences. The differing conditions of national development in the various provinces of India are too often ignored and set aside to make room for a uniform administration. One code, one law, one measure, the same taxation, the same routine forms, a fondness for uniformity as an end in itself—this is the besetting sin of the administration. The mischief is aggravated by alternations of policy which alike err in exaggerating the action of Government out of accord with the contemporary wants and aspirations of the people. The change when it comes is so late, and has such a violent swing, that, far from curing the mischief already accomplished, it breeds fresh and great troubles, and further demoralization, setting class against class, destroying the best

*JPSS, April 1881, Vol.III, No.4.

elements of national life and growth, and stimulating the worst instincts. These vicissitudes of policy make themselves most felt in the dealings of Government with the settlement of land in the different provinces of the empire. At times the prevailing sentiment is more democratic and radical than the latest patents of American or French political prophets, and at other times the reactionary feeling is more conservative and superstitious than in the most backward of Asiatic countries, and the worst of it is, that the change of feeling always comes too late for securing any beneficial reform. From one end of India to the other, it is the same sad tale of old institutions decayed, old ties broken up, old associations severed by the hand of violent innovation, and just when people are seeking to reconcile themselves to the new order of things an equally violent reaction takes place, unsettling all, and completing the destruction by its untimely effort to repair the mischief too thoughtlessly encouraged in the first instance.

The latest instance of this tinkering policy on our side of the country is furnished by the Deccan Agriculturists Relief Act. The same influences which recommended that measure as a panacea for the misery of the agricultural classes in this Presidency have suggested a similar experiment with the land settlement of the Central Provinces. The Central Provinces Land Revenue and Tenancy Bills are by far the most important measures which are now awaiting the consideration of the Supreme Legislative Council. Unfortunately, the Central Provinces have no recognized exponent of the views of their native population, who are too backward, or too much blessed with comfort, to feel the want of a Free Press and free associations. The changes which these Bills seek to introduce are, however, so questionable and sweeping that they seem to have waked up the very dead to life, and stirred up the Malguzar Zemindars of the Nagpore and Damoh divisions to thought and action. In the Central Provinces as in the Bengal Presidency and to some extent in the Konkan Districts on our own side, the Government officers are anxious to pose as the friends of the Ryots, and enforce in their interests concessions from the intermediate Zemindar classes which, in its own direct relations with the Ryots of the Deccan, the same Government is not disposed to respect. While coolly laying down the law that there shall be no enhancement beyond certain limits of the rents of so-called occupancy tenants at the instance of the Zemindars, it refuses to circumscribe any such limit to its own exactions; and while eviction for non-payment of rent in these Provinces is sought to be surrounded with all manner of restrictions as to compensation for unexhausted improvements, in our own Presidency it has been only recently ruled that non-payment of rent or assessment shall lead to the absolute *forfeiture* of the land, whether alienated, Vatan, or the Ryot's miras. The Central Provinces Zemindar or Malguzar is not a new creation; he is moreover not an absentee land-lord, nor a mere rent receiver. He is a cultivator himself, and after the solemn pledge given to him when the settlement was first introduced in 1860, it is very hard lines to break the pledge in spirit, and run him down as though he was an Irish land-lord settled by force of conquest in a foreign country.

With a view to understand correctly the bearings of the proposed measures, it will be necessary to treat the subject historically. Sir R. Jenkins is the great contemporary authority for the condition of the country under native rule, and the official minutes of Sir Richard Temple, the first Chief Commissioner, and of the Honourable Mr. C. Grant, who compiled the C.P. Gazetteer, and is at present in charge of these Bills, furnish most valuable materials for such a historical survey. Under the rule of the Bhoslas of Nagpore, every village had its *Patel*. He was generally the recognised head of the community. He was the agent of the Government for apportioning and collecting the village assessment. He also possessed in an undefined way judicial authority, both civil and criminal. His office was not strictly speaking hereditary, but as a matter of fact he was frequently succeeded by his son, or in the absence of sons, by some other capable member of his family. This took place more by sufferance than by virtue of what would now-a-days pass muster as a legally enforceable right. But the Patelship could not be taken away from the members of a family which had enjoyed it for generations without doing violence to the feeling of the community, and, except where a Patel had made himself unpopular or proved incompetent, he was seldom removed. He paid his *kist* to the kamavisdar—as the Perganna revenue officer was called. If a Patel of good character happened to be badly off, and unable to meet the government demand, the kamavisdar not unfrequently became his security, and a sowcar paid the amount due on this security. Otherwise the Patel made over the rents of his village, or those of as many of the ryots as covered the amount of defaulted revenue, to the sowcar. If the village was large, the Sowcar sent an agent of his own to keep the accounts. Generally, however, the Sowcars were satisfied with the accounts of the Pandia or the village accountant, which were compared and investigated in the presence of Ryots at the end of the agricultural year. Though the arrangement had not the sanction of "law", yet it always worked well, and to the satisfaction of the parties concerned. Mutual good faith did then what the "law" of the present day fails to accomplish. The cultivators held the land on yearly leases granted them by the Patel. Only the area under actual cultivation was liable to Government assessment. The Government demand was on the village as a whole, and not upon particular fields. It was the Patel's duty to apportion the assessment field by field. And generally before the commencement of the agricultural year, he settled the proportionate part of the whole assessment, which each individual Ryot was ultimately to contribute. The *Bida* or betel, which was considered as the pledge of mutual good faith, was then distributed by the *Patel* to the Ryots. The year's engagement being thus completed, the agricultural operations commenced. Any special enactment to protect the rights of Ryots was then unknown. But the general sense of the community in those days did what the scientific legislation of these days attempts to do, but seldom succeeds. Sir Richard Jenkins, for a long time Resident at the court of the Nagpore Raja, endorses the opinion of Captain Comerson who says, "he has always found the Patels ready to do their Ryots justice, and their proceedings are seldom vexatious, unless with a view of getting rid of a bad or intriguing character out of the village." The Patel, where necessary, gave *tuccavee* advances to those of his Ryots, who were in bad circumstances, or who had been particularly unfortunate during the past year. The *tuccavee* consisted of cash for the purpose of purchasing cattle or implements of husbandry, or these were furnished at a fixed valuation. Seed grain *(Bij)*, and grain for the subsistence of the Ryots and their families *(Potga)* were also advanced by the *Patel*, or his banker. All this was done as a matter of course; and the transactions, unlike similar transactions of the present day, did both the Patel and the Ryot good. The accounts of the Ryot were generally settled before the first of *chaitra* (April). Patels, to whom their Ryots were thus in debt, were allowed to place the property of the defaulter—including the produce of his field—under restraint, but not to sell it without the previous sanction of the Perganna Revenue officer. The spectacle, however, of a rich and powerful *Patel* taking advantage of the social inferiority, ignorance, or inexperience of his dependent Ryot for the purpose of driving a hard bargain was an occurrence then very rare, if not almost entirely unknown. The Patel never sold up his ryot unless forced to do so by the circumstances of the case. At the present day, the Marwadis form the bulk of the money-lenders. All the miseries of the people are laid at their doors. They have come to be looked upon as worms eating into the vitals of society; and taken all in all, they are perhaps the best abused people of the community. But here is what Sir Richard Jenkins says of them before the "laws" of the present day transformed them into what we find them now—unrelenting, and not unfrequently, unscrupulous. "The Marwadis are the principal shroffs or bankers in the city. They are extremely intelligent, quick in the despatch of business, and correct and fair in their dealings. In their general conduct and demeanour, they are sedate and respectable, and they bear, perhaps, the highest character of any class in the community for integrity and fair dealings". What a falling off is here? And how great must be the responsibility and accountability of those who have brought about such a sad change!

Justice was administered in an equally simple fashion. There were no separate officers of rank connected with the administration of justice. The people generally settled their disputes by their village panchayats. In each village there was an arbitrator—or as he was called "the Mahajan," chosen by the Patel and the Ryots, jointly. His office was not strictly hereditary, but in accordance with the usual practice of the country, it often descended from the father to the son. Sir Richard Jenkins says, the Mahajan settled all disputes between the Patels, and the Ryots as far as was in his power. The aid of the regular panchayats was invoked in all cases of a civil nature arising amongst the villagers. The Panch were assembled by the Patel. They had no fixed place of meeting, but the platform of the village God was generally selected as attaching the sanctity of religion to whatever might transpire before the panchayat. The most respectable men in the village were chosen members of the panchayat, irrespective of caste or profession. The Patel generally named the members, but the parties had the right to challenge his selection. Sometimes the parties chose their own panch, and an umpire or Sir-panch was chosen with mutual consent. The agreement of the parties to abide by the award was usually verbal, but in cases of importances, or where the parties were known to be litigious, it was reduced to writing. Their proceedings were rarely recorded. Even in cases coming before the Government officers, the panchayats were extensively resorted to. With them fraud was next to impossible. Nothing is easier now than for an unscrupulous litigant to palm off upon a judge of the present day, who knows nothing of the antecedents of the parties and their witnesses, a false claim supported by false evidence. But before the village Panch, with their local experience as derived from personal knowledge of the past history of each litigant and witness, it was not an easy thing to sustain a fraudulent claim. Moreover, a man might swear anything at a strange place and before a strange judge, removed from the control of the public opinion of his villagers, but he would think twice before he would so commit himself in the presence of the headmen of his village and in the hearing of all his neighbours.

Under this system which suited their genius and tradition, the people were in a state of peace with one another, and of general contentment with their condition. So long as the government demand was moderate and equitable, and it was generally so under the Nagpore rulers, and there was no interference with the natural working of the above system, the Ryots prospered. The contrary only happened when, owing to misrule and oppressive assessment, they were not allowed to shape their conduct towards one another in accordance with their time-honoured customs and institutions. Sir Richard Jenkins's report affords abundant evidence of this fact. From the first commencement of the Marhatta rule down to the year 1792 the country was uniformally prosperous. But from this time the inhabitants began to date the period of misrule and oppressive assessment. Things returned to their old course during the Regency (1818-1827), and there was no break when, on the late Raja attaining his majority, the kingdom was made over to him.

The late Raja died on the 11th of December 1853, and his territory then passed into the hands of the British Government. At that time the old native system under which the people had lived in comfort for so many centuries had lost none of its vitality. Though grey with the dust of ages, the accumulated weight of many centuries had failed to crush down its life-giving power. It was as potent as ever to conduce to the happiness of the people, and it was certainly most desirable that with the change of government, there should be no change in the constitution of the village communities, and that their internal economies should be left untouched in all their essential particulars. The Government of the day was fully alive to this fact. The Governor General, in his instructions to the Resident dated 7th March 1854, laid down that the guiding principle which should pervade the new administration was "to establish plain, simple and efficient regulations on the basis of the ancient usages and laws of the country." This looked well upon paper. But nowhere throughout India has the British Government been able to adhere to this principle. The past history of British administration of India would rather lead one to conclude that the continued existence of native institutions is against the spirit of British Rule. Certain it is the indigenous institutions of the land have never long survived its introduction in any part of India. No sooner did the new Government settle down, than the Governor General in Council thought that the rules in force in the Punjab on the subject of the administration of civil justice "might be introduced with great advantage" into the newly acquired provinces. They were accordingly very soon introduced. The Nagpore Commission was then formed to administer the new law. A code of procedure framed by the Judicial Commissioner of the Punjab was also introduced for the guidance of the officers. All this took place within four years of the change of government. In 1859 it was ordered that the Civil Procedure Code (Act VIII of 1859) should be partially introduced as an authoritative guide, supplementing where necessary the existing rules, the object to be kept in view being "the eventual adoption of the Code as law." In the same year a number of rules and principles, sanctioned originally for the Panjab, and regulating the limitation of suits, the registration of deeds, the law of evidence, the cost of litigation and other kindred matters, were introduced. The reason assigned for this was that it was "convenient, and on many grounds advisable that, so far as practicable the system of administration pursued in the provinces under the Government of India should be the same." This was a complete departure from the declaration with which the new administration had opened namely, that the people were to be secured in their own laws and customs. In attempting to give effect to this principle of uniformity the declaration of 1854 was soon lost sight of, and but scant respect was shown to the feelings of the people, and to their own laws and customs. In less than six years of the change in the Government, the country underwent a complete transformation, and to crown the edifice, the Patels were turned into malguzar farmers by the settlement of 1860-61, and the Ryots were taken under protection by the extension of the Bengal Act 10 of 1859 to the Central Provinces. It is not necessary that we should trace step by step the development of the principle laid down by the Governor-General in Council when introducing the Panjab Rules. Suffice it to say that the introduction of new laws and regulations on the basis of those obtaining in the older provinces of the Empire went on at a vigorous pace; and by the time the several districts now forming the Central Provinces were consolidated under one central jurisdiction, the territory which had lapsed on the death of the late Nagpore Raja had become assimilated to the other parts of India in its possession of an equally costly, elaborate, and intricate system of law and procedure.

Sufficient time has now elapsed to judge of the effects of the introduction of the new system upon the economic condition of the people. Though only 27 years have now gone by since the Native raj ceased to exist, the supplanting of the old Native system by the new foreign system has been so complete and thorough, that one may travel far and wide before he comes across any trace of the old institutions of the land. And except perhaps in some hilly, out of the way, and inaccessible places, where the influence of British civilization has not yet been able to penetrate, or make itself felt, the whole thing has been swept clean out of the country; so much so that even the very materials wherewith to reconstruct society on the old lines are now hard to be met with. The people have now lost all relish for their own old institutions. The Panchayat system is at a discount. Very seldom it is that the parties now think of invoking its aid. There is amongst them an unhealthy hankering after litigation for litigation's sake, which every new law that is introduced tends to foster. They have lost all faith in one another, and not perhaps altogether without reason. Nothing is more difficult now than to secure a body of Panch who will be above all suspicion, and fighting in courts with all its evils has almost become a necessity.

Thus, while justice has become dear and difficult of attainment, the system under which it is administered has served to bring about a complete disintegration of the old happy social relations between the several classes. Here, as elsewhere in India, there is the same war of class against class, capital against labour, labour against capital. The money-lender, perhaps forced by the very necessity of the case, has become hard, unrelenting, and very often unscrupulous. The land lord has lost his old love and good feeling towards his tenants; and the latter in their turn have ceased to look upon the former as their indulgent master and kind friend in their difficulties. The bestowal of proprietary right upon the Patels of the Maharata raj at the settlement, and the almost simultaneous introduction of Act X of 1859 for the protection of the ryots—both of which measures proceeded from the purest motives of benevolence towards the people—have only served to accelerate their ruin. The relations between the several classes having become embittered, and there being no longer any readiness on the part of one class to make the smallest sacrifice in supporting the others, the proprietary right has proved a most tempting bait to the Marwadi moneylender to bring about the ruin of the Malguzar, by means fair or foul. A war to the knife is being carried on between the two. The Marwadi fights the Malguzar by taking the Ryot under his protection, and ends by ruining both the Ryot and the Malguzar.

As for the Ryots, Act X of 1859 has proved the veritable apple of discord. In the days of the Bhoslays, there was no such enactment to protect the Ryots in their rights, yet so considerate had been the Patels of those days in their relations with their *kirsans* (cultivators), that at the time of the settlement when the Patels were turned into Malguzars *i.e.* farmers of revenue and transferees of the Government interest in the lands, it was found practicable to confer upon numbers of Ryots substantial possessary rights over the lands they held. Some were made *Malik*

Makbuzas, or absolute proprietors of their holdings, others were turned into what are called in these Provinces absolute occupancy tenants. They hold at fixed rates, and their tenures are heritable, and, subject to the land-lords' right of pre-emption in case of sale, also transferable. Those that could not show longer possession than twelve years, were declared simple occupancy tenants. Even if all other evidence had been wanting, this is a proof pretty conclusive that the relations between the landlord and the tenant in those olden days were healthy, for it was only the previous forbearance of the Patels that made such a result possible. But whether this can be predicated of the present state of things is more than doubtful. Sixteen years have now elapsed since the introduction of Act X, and it is yet to be seen whether the expectations of the Government in introducing it have been realized. An enquiry has lately been ordered to ascertain the number of occupancy tenants existing at the present day. Even if the result of the enquiry be to show that their number has, since the settlement, received as much increment as could reasonably be expected under the circumstances, yet, looking at the status of the ryots and their relations with their Malguzars and Sowcars, it is a question whether too high a price has not been paid for a right which after all does not benefit those on whose behalf provision was made for its growth. At the beginning when the law was but little understood and appreciated, the landlord and the tenant shaped their conduct towards one another as if it had no existence. But with the diffusion of legal knowledge, the old state of things, which depended for its continued existence on the ignorance of the people, has fairly given way, and is rapidly disappearing. The landlord now is wide awake to the fact that an occupancy tenant, with his special rights and privileges, is too dangerous a person to be tolerated and shown any favour. Naturally, when you set up a tenant against his landlord, the latter tries his best to put such a person out of his way. As the close of the eleventh year draws near, the struggle between the two commences. The landlord uses his best endeavours to prevent the growth of the tenant right by ejecting the occupant before the twelfth year commences, while the latter in his turn clings to his land with all his might. The Courts, with their doors wide open, invite them both, and they rush to them with all the feverish recklessness of a set of gamblers. Forged documents and tutored witnesses are the weapons with which they generally fight. It is seldom that a tenant dares fight with his landlord single-handed; and seldom it is that he is left to do so. He has always at his elbow the money lender, with his purse wide open to lure him on to his ruin. The war once begun is carried on to the bitter end; and the poor deluded man seldom looks behind and casts up the cost. That task he leaves to his friend the money-lender, who slowly but surely draws his meshes tight round his victim. If he loses, he is ruined; if he wins, he is equally ruined. That little account of his friend the moneylender has a tendency to grow out of all proportion to its original dimensions. His field and agricultural resources are his only property, and his friend very soon relieves him of them. But as a money-lender has no relish for agriculture—his own profession being much more paying—he generally takes the ruined tenant into his service, and gets the field cultivated by him. When the holding is not transferable according to law or custom, the name of the tenant is allowed to remain in the village papers, but to virtual serfdom he is reduced all the same. He gives the sweat of his brow, but others enjoy the fruits of his labour. If the landlord loses the ejectment suit, he generally follows it up next year by a counter-suit to enhance the rent. If the ruin is only half accomplished by the first suit, the second leaves nothing to be desired. Henceforth reconciliation between the two becomes next to impossible, and how best to revenge themselves upon one another becomes one of the chief pastime of their lives. And they find in fresh litigation, for which the law affords so many facilities, the surest means to accomplish their object. The law is always accommodating enough, and they are never at a loss for an opportunity. The picture we have drawn above is saddening enough in all conscience, but it is drawn from nature. It may not apply to every case that is presented to our courts here, but that substantially, and in the majority of cases, the picture given above accurately describes what is actually happening every day, will be borne out by the experience of all who have had anything to do with the Courts here, and had his attention drawn to the matter. And it would serve no useful purpose to cry out peace when there is no peace. Matters have reached a crisis, and the truth, however unpleasant, must now be faced and not shirked.

If the experience of the past is to be our guide for the future, it is clear as the noon-day sun to us that all future legislation ought to have for its keystone the great principle of reconciliation, which was the talisman that worked such wonders in days gone by. We have had enough of class legislation, and never before than now has it become more necessary to bring about a renewal of the old fellow-feeling by removing all causes of needless irritation. The *raison d'etre* for which fresh legislation is considered desirable may be thus stated; the creation of proprietary right at the settlement, and the simultaneous introduction of Act X. of 1859 with its inevitable tendency to drive out the old unwritten customary law of the land, has been "absolutely to curtail the ancient privileges of the cultivators." The Bill attempts to make reparation for the wrong thus done to this class of people, but in spite of the excellent intention with which it has been brought forward, we are forced to say that, instead of acting as a balm, it will, by creating new sources of litigation, defeat its own end, and by widening the gulf between landlord and tenant, aggravate the evil for which it proposes to find a remedy. If the existing law is irritating and peace disturbing, and the existing procedure wearisome and intricate, those proposed to take their place will, we are afraid, be equally injurious, if not more so, to the best interests of the country. This admittedly incomplete review of the past history of the economical relations between the Zamindars and their tenants under Native and British rule will enable the reader to understand our detailed criticism upon the new Bills. We shall first address a few brief observations on the Land Revenue Bill before adverting more in detail to the provisions of the Tenancy Bill.

In regard to the Land Revenue Bill, one general remark which occurs to us on the most superficial view of it is, that the Bill is framed on the outlines of the Ryotwari system which obtains in this Presidency, than which nothing can well be more unsuited to the settlement made with the Malguzars in 1861-62. The jealousy of all alienations, and of the action of Civil Courts, which characterize the Bombay system, has suggested the provisions contained in sections 73, 78, 83 and 131 of the C.P. Revenue Bill. The Malguzar system bears no analogy whatever to the Bombay settlement, and we think this jealousy of alienations is out of place. The principles of the Bengal Regulations of 1793 should influence the action of Government in regard to disputes which may arise in respect of the extent and title to exemption of lands for which the Malguzar holds a sanad, and many of which he has acquired under the waste land rules in full property in perpetuity, or the revenue of which has been redeemed by him under the rules for redemption laid down by Lord Canning. The adjudication of such matters should be left to the higher grade of the Civil Courts, who alone can deal out effective justice, fix the character of the alienation, and settle whether the grantee has broken his conditions. The vesting of such powers in settlement officers twenty years ago might have been expedient in the then circumstances of the country, but all such justification has now ceased, and there is a general consensus of views that these powers should be transferred to the Civil Courts. As early as 1793, Bengal Regulation 11 of that year laid down "that the proprietors can never consider the privileges which have been conferred on them as secure while Revenue officers are vested with judicial powers. * * * The revenue officers must be deprived of these powers. All financial claims of the public, when disputed under the Regulations, must be subjected to the cognizance of the Civil Courts, superintended by Judges, wholly disinterested in the result of their decisions, and bound to decide impartially between the public and the proprietors of land." Not only does the Bill seek to perpetuate and enlarge the judicial powers of these so-called settlement officers in the matter of disputes between land lords and tenants, but it sanctions the retrograde step of divesting the Judicial Commissioner of his existing powers of appeal, and transfers them to the chief executive officer, the Chief Commissioner of the Province. As this latter officer is overburdened with an infinite variety of duties, this transfer will force him to entrust this essentially judicial work to one of his secretaries. The Central Provinces are now sufficiently advanced above the non-regulation stage to justify greater confidence on the part of government in the Chief Judicial authority of the Province. In this Presidency, the non-Regulation rule lasted only nine years (1818-1827), while in the Central Provinces it has now lasted more than 25 years. So far from investing larger powers of review and appeal in the Chief Commissioner, we believe the time has now come when all judicial authority should be vested in an independent tribunal. The work of the settlement officers has been finished, and full registers of all existing customary rights of tenants have been prepared. There is thus no occasion left for re-opening this closed controversy, and stirring the waters of strife.

The next important innovation relates to the creation of the office of Mokadam. The reasons assigned for the creation of such an office are mostly of a speculative nature, as it is feared that the Zemindaries will be broken up, and bought by absentee landlords, in consequence of which there will be no responsible head left in the village with whom Government can deal. We think the Honourable Mr. Grant has been too much influenced by his own observations in the discussion of the effects of free alienation in 1874. The burden of the new office will it is thought lead to a check upon the grasping monied classes of the town who now buy land as an investment, and not for the social status it confers. The Mokadam is to be a nominee of Government. The sharers in the proprietary rights will have no voice in his nomination, though he is to be paid by them. He may be a stranger to the family, and need not be even a resident lambardar. He will be thus both the thin and the thick end of the wedge—a perpetual source of discord and trouble to the proprietors, who will be reduced in status and power. The substitution of stipendiary in place of hereditary unpaid officers is one of the worst agencies that can be devised for breaking up the integrity of a village community. We fear this innovation will be the last straw to break the camel's back. The Government might fairly leave this power without profit in the hands of the Malguzar proprietary classes, confer as in this Presidency the right of electing a head or agent or officiating Patel on the members of the family, and enforce the residence of such nominee.

The question of the limits within which the Malguzar's power to enhance rent should be limited has been very summarily dealt with in sections 87-89 of the Revenue Bill. The settlement officer is in the first instance to fix rents, after taking into his consideration the Government assessment, and the customary rents paid by the same classes of tenants for similar lands, and allowing for change of prices. The Government, however, refuses to lay down any principles by which it agrees to limit its own demands for enhancement of land revenue on revision, and we think so long as there is no principle laid down on this head, it is not open to it to interfere between the private land-lord and his tenant. Custom is now rapidly giving way to competition, and the settlement officer will find it hard to fix what the customary rate is if he does not accept the prevailing rate as the customary rate. As if these inequalities were not enough, power is left to the Chief Commissioner to fix what changes of price shall be taken into account in fixing the enhancement. We fear all this complex effort to regulate by outside agency relations, which must be left to private competition, will fail. The rule of proportion fixed by the Calcutta High Court in the great Rent Case, though not far from doubt and difficulty, has at least a power to adopt itself to the circumstances of each case. The Government may well lay down that in its own exactions at the revision settlements, as well as between the Malguzar and the occupancy tenants, no enhancement shall take place unless it is proved to the satisfaction of a Civil Court that there has been a general rise of prices, or improvement of the land at the landlord's or state's expense, and that this enhancement shall be so proportioned that at each recurring thirty years' period, the increased assessment shall be equally divided between the Government, the Malguzars, and the tenants. This will be the most satisfactory termination of this never-ending difficulty. Any attempt to bolster up the class of mere tenants-at-will, which appears chiefly to have influenced the executive government in framing the new provisions, will lead to fresh endeavours to defeat it and make confusion worse confounded by reason of these tinkering efforts. These few observations will serve to show that the new Revenue Bill is not accurately described when it is stated to be a measure of consolidation only. We must content ourselves with this brief notice of its more important features; we have no room to refer to the sections in detail, which we doubt not will receive due attention from the Legislature.

To turn next to the Tenancy Bill, we think objection may fairly be taken to the ambiguous definition of 'tenant' in this Bill. It is wide enough to include by implication the farmer of less than half of any village as also usufructuary mortgagees. Both these classes of persons, as holding the land of another under a liability to pay rent, would under section 75 be entitled to claim occupancy rights, which certainly it was never intended to confer on them. This is, however, a mere mistake due perhaps to inadvertent drafting. No such excuse, however, can be urged for the interference of the state in the private contracts of parties legalized by the subsequent sections 6, 11, 13-16, and 17-22.

Section 6 empowers the Chief Commissioner to fix the dates for the payment of the instalments, not of the Government assessment only, but of the rent due by the tenants to the Malguzars. These last payments are now regulated by contract or custom. The Government is no way directly interested in the matter, and this new power will derogate greatly from the independent status of the Malguzar. This innovation is, however, a mere trifle by the side of the direction contained in section 11, which lays down that all private contracts fixing the rent payable on land at a lower figure than the Government assessment levied therefrom shall be null and void. This stretch of power is sought to be justified by the philanthrophic motive of protecting improvident proprietors from injuring their own resources. There is no precedent for thus inflicting a new discipline of thrift upon a whole Province whose tutelage it will perpetuate. The government will not allow itself to be bound down to any rules in fixing the assessment, and it is, to say the least, preposterous to require that no Malguzar shall charge less rent for his land than the government assessment as fixed by the Survey Department which works in the dark and often without any guiding principle and whose settlement is so liable to err both ways. In the reclamation of waste lands, great relaxation has to be allowed for the first few years to induce people to break them up, and this innovation will seriously interfere with the progress of improved cultivation.

Sections 13-16 carry still further the interference of the revenue officer to a practically most mischievous extremity, for which no shadow of a precedent can be shown in the existing law. Whenever there is a dispute between a land-lord and his tenant as regards the appraisement of a crop, or the division of the produce, the revenue officer is authorized on application to appoint a commission for the settlement of the dispute, and if the parties are dissatisfied with such settlement, they are then allowed three months to refer the matter to a Civil Court. This provision appears to us to be the surest way of fomenting open discord between the opposing interests, and enlarging the interference of the revenue officials in every man's private affairs. While the revenue officer is thus to have his hand in every man's pie throughout the country, the independent powers enjoyed by the Malguzars to this day for the protection of their rights are sought to be narrowed in all directions. His power to levy distress for rent is to be taken away from him, the right of first charge which his rent has hitherto enjoyed in respect of the crops is also to be done away with, and in place of this simple and self-acting remedy, he is to be permitted to bring a suit and obtain a decree for rent which may be executed preferentially over other and prior attachments. While the Malguzar is thus disabled, and may not collect his rents except under the shelter of a decree, his responsibility to the demands of government is retained with the full penalty of forfeiture on failure to make the payment punctually. Such a change in the law of distress might have been justified if it were proved that the land-lords had abused their existing powers. It has been officially admitted, however, in the last administration Report of the Central Provinces that the land-lords there do not give their Ryots any cause for complaint and that the Ryots are alive to their own interests and are prepared to assert all the rights they can claim. This power of distress is moreover not a creature of British law. It existed under native rule, the Patel was permitted to place the standing crops of defaulting Ryots under distraint, and no prior assignment by the Ryots was allowed to prevail. The force of this tradition is so strong that even when out-and-out sales take place, the Sowcar never questions the Malguzar's lien and pays up the rent without contest. The proposed alterations will teach the Ryots and their Sowcars to set the Malguzar at arm's length, and lead to deception and fraud, multiplication of suits, and vexation and general demoralization.

This same tendency to increase the occasions of official interference, and make matters which are simple enough if left to be settled at the convenience of parties, complex beyond all conception by reason of such interference, shows itself in sections 27 and 28 which relate to evictions. All evictions by land-lords of tenants must under the new law be made through a process of the Civil Courts. In the majority of these eviction cases, there is really no contest, and the necessity of bringing a suit is a mere costly impertinence and a temptation to dishonesty. In the few cases where a contest may be expected, the present law, which allows a tenant unjustly evicted to be put in summary possession, is a sufficient protection. The whole of the complex process laid down by the new Bill will only benefit the stamp revenue. As if these sources of trouble and litigation were not ample enough, the Bill empowers even a non-occupancy tenant to spend, at his own pleasure, money in what are called the improvements of land, after first giving the choice of a refusal to the land-lord to effect the same at his own expense, and no such improving tenant can be ousted unless he is recompensed fully for his expenses. Every bit of land manured, every pit dug in the soil, every little repair made to the well hedge or farm house, will thus be a perpetual source of conflict between the two classes. The whole tenantry of a village may thus combine and ruin a poor Malguzar out of his property and hold his land free of rent, for he has no power to evict them till the so-called improvements are paid up. The Civil Courts do not encourage even a mortgagee who improves the mortgager out of his estate. Here we find the legislature deliberately holding the apple of discord right in the face of the tenants, and in the name of improvement teaching them the ways of strife and deceit. The truth appears to us to be that these matters are so delicate and complex that they must be left to be settled by individual contract, and that any officious interference can only end in failure and demoralisation.

The next innovation which the Bill seeks to legalise is the creation of a new class of occupancy tenants. Under the existing law direct occupation of 12 years is necessary to confer the status of occupancy tenants on a cultivating Ryot. Under the provision of section 58 of the new Bill a resident Ryot, cultivating land in a village for five years, who has received no help from the landlord, may not be ousted by the land-lord except under certain conditions which it will be difficult for him to establish, even if he fails to pay the higher rent demanded from him. These tenants are called protected tenants, and their status is intermediate between the Malikmakbuza or old proprietors and occupancy tenants, and the yearly tenants-at-will. This provision of the Bill is entirely a creation of the new craze for limiting the Malguzar's power. When the settlement was first introduced, the rights of all the old Kadim Ryots were separately registered. It is, therefore, not open to the Government which gave proprietary sanads to the Malguzars to sanction this new encroachment so alien to the old traditions, without awarding compensation to the Malguzars for the loss of their rights. The Ryots in the early days were mostly annual lessees, and the Patels exercised freely the right of distributing the village lands among the resident cultivators. Mr. Morris the Chief Commissioner was, when he acted as Settlement Commissioner, so impressed with this fact that he proposed a sixty years' term as necessary to constitute occupancy right, and Sir R. Temple, then Chief Commissioner, himself thought that twelve years' term was too short, and advocated a term of 20 to 25 years. The Supreme Government fixed 12 years as a medium term upon the analogy of Act 10 of 1859, and suggested that the question of enlarging the term might be taken up at the settlement. The proposal to lower the term from twelve to five is thus opposed to all the old pledges and traditions, and will virtually lead to the extinction of all Malguzar or land-lord rights, which seems to be the only consummation to which these and other changes noticed above will lead. The Ryot will be driven by the stress of this new rule to borrow from a stranger in preference to his Malguzar, and thus the elements of strife will be multiplied beyond all precedent. The so-called protected Ryot will thus become the victims of the Marwadi lender, who as a rule has not half the interest to see him thrive and be happy which the Malguzar feels.

While the Government seeks on one hand thus to extend its protection to a new class of occupancy tenants, it proposes at the same time to deprive the old occupancy tenant of his independence in respect of the power of free alienation (sections 82-83). This is sought to be done in the teeth of the emphatic declaration in the record of rights that the position of these Ryots was independent of any future modification of the law and the only ground urged for this reactionary step is the thrice refuted allegation that Ryots voluntarily ruin themselves by getting needlessly into debt, and cannot be trusted with the power of free alienation. The oscillation of views represented by this ultra- conservative measure, contrasted with the no less extreme radicalism which abolished usury laws in India at one sweep because they had been denounced in England, appears to us to be the most serious danger of the times. Even the Deccan Relief Act stops short of this revolutionary proposal of abolishing the power of free alienation. In the Central Provinces there is really no occasion for such restriction, because without the sanction of the Revenue officers no sale of land can take place, and even without such a sanction the tenant has at present no power to charge his land with a claim for a sum exceeding five years' rental, for if the charge exceeds this amount, the Malguzar has a right of preemption. Compulsory sale of such interests by the process of Civil Courts may be usefully restricted, but there appears to be no justification for this wild attempt to lay the axe at the root of all free hold rights of the very class whom the Government is so anxious to protect.

We have thus reviewed all the more important alterations embodied in these two Bills. We trust many of the anomalies and objections we have pointed out above will be removed during the discussion of the Bill in the Select Committee, but the opposition to be effective must take a stand on the broadest grounds of the rights of property, and the sacredness of pledges, so solemnly given only twenty years ago.

The whole subject of the law of land sale in British India has been discussed thread-bare for more than a quarter of a century, and the panic which seems chiefly to suggest these measure so destructive of all independence of individual or national character, and perpetuating tutelage, and encouraging official interference in every affair of life, seems to us to be a most disastrous reaction from the indifference of the last two decades. We can only hope that this craze will soon run out its short term, and cease to haunt official conscience, and that government will resign itself to the only safe policy for an alien race of rulers, and remain masterly inactive, and allow the reign of impersonal law and free competition now that they have been in operation for so many years to assert their ascendancy over patriarchal custom and officious tutelage.

7

PARLIAMENTARY COMMITTEE ON INDIAN PUBLIC WORKS*

It may be in the recollection of many of our readers, that a Committee of the British Parliament was sitting sometime ago with the object of discussing the advisability of constructing Public Works in India out of borrowed money, and that the suggestions made by this Committee have been to some extent carried out by the Government of India. The sittings of this Committee commenced at the beginning of March 1878, and were brought to a close in April 1879. Among the members of the Committee were many statesmen and politicians who have all along taken the most active interest in Indian affairs, and possess an intimate acquaintance with the system of British administration in this country, such as Lord George Hamilton, Mr. Fawcett, Mr. Ayrton, Mr. Grant Duff, and Sir George Campbell. The evidence collected by the Committee is of a very important nature —especially at a time like the present, when there is a great financial pressure in India, and when Government, both in England and in this country, is turning its attention to all practicable sources of reduction with the object of lightening the burdens of the Indian tax-payer. The question, therefore, of adding to the already heavy public debt of India for constructing what are called

---

**JPSS*, July 1881, Vol.IV, No.1.

Productive Public Works requires the special attention of every well-wisher of this country, and it is with the object of ventilating the subject, and bringing it prominently to the notice of our readers, that we propose to give a short summary, in this issue, of the information collected by this Parliamentary Committee. The interest on the present public debt is a heavy charge against the Indian exchequer, and any additions to it must be made with great caution. The Anglo-Indian statesmen and professional Engineers examined before the Committee were all officially connected with India. Many of them occupied high positions in the general administration of this country, and were intimately acquainted with the management of the Public Works Department of the Government of India. Their opinions are, therefore, entitled to great consideration, and the information they have given is of high value.

The following witnesses were examined by the Committee:—Major General Dickens, Secretary to the Government of India in the Public Works Department during the administrations of Lord Dalhousie and Lord Lawrence, Lord Northbrook, late Viceroy of India, Sir George Campbell, the late Lieutenant Governor of Bengal, General Sir Arthur Cotton, the celebrated Irrigation Engineer, employed on the Ganges Canal, Godawary scheme, and other Irrigation projects, Colonel Fifo, Chief Engineer for Irrigation in Bombay, Sir Thomas Seecombe, and Messers Sowerby and Juland Danvers, the former a Local Fund Engineer in Bombay, and the latter, the Government Director for guaranteed and state Railways.

Before the year 1854, there was no separate Department of Public Works in India. All works were executed and designed by Military Engineers working under the orders of a Military Board at each Presidency. The Ganges Canal and other important works were projected and commenced under this system. In progress of time, however, the number and importance of Public Works increased to such an extent, that it was deemed desirable by the Government of Lord Dalhousie to create a separate branch of civil administration for the management of Public Works. Accordingly in 1854, a Public Works Secretariate was attached to the Government of India, and its connection with the Military Department was severed entirely. Departments of Public Works were similarly organised in Bombay and Madras in the following year. Subsequently on a further expansion of the Department, it was thought desirable to separate it into different branches—each branch having its own especially qualified Engineers for executing and supervising its works. Thus the Department came to be divided into the following four branches;—

1st Military Works.

2nd General, or Roads and Civil Buildings.

3rd Irrigation.

4th Railways.

The first branch comprises the works that relate to the accommodation of troops, fortifications, and other works of defence, and the manufacture of ammunition and materials of war; the second comprises Civil Buildings, and such lines of communication as do not possess any military importance; the third comprises works relating to drainage, reclamation of ground, water supply of towns and the storage and distribution of water for Irrigational purposes; and the fourth comprises works in connection with guaranteed and state railways.

Under the decentralisation scheme brought into operation since 1872, the works comprised in the second branch, that is roads and civil buildings, were made over by the Government of India to the local Governments and administrations, reserving to themselves, however, the power of vetoing works costing more than 2 lacs of Rupees in Madras and Bombay, and 50,000 Rs. in Bengal, North West Provinces and Oudh, and the Punjab. Within the above limits, the local Governments were given the power of constructing any works they chose from the Provincial funds placed at their disposal, without the previous sanction or approval of the Government of India. All works thus constructed are submitted for general review annually to the Government of India and the Secretary of State, but superior authorities never interfere with their management and construction, which are wholly placed in the hands of the local Governments.

The works appertaining to the remaining three branches are kept by the Government of India solely under their direction and control, and no local Government possesses the power of incurring any expenditure in connection therewith on their own responsibility. For works costing above ten lacs of Rupees, the projects have to be submitted to the Secretary of State for India for his approval and sanction before the works are commenced.

The system by which Public Works are carried on in this country is as follows:—Each Presidency or Province is divided into a certain number of circles or divisions which are placed in the charge of officers called Superintending or Chief Engineers, who correspond with, and work under the orders of, the Public Works Department of the Secretariat. Each Superintending or Chief Engineer supervises the work of a certain number of Executive or District Engineers employed under him. The scheme for a work is in the first instance framed by the Executive Engineer of the District to which it relates, and is submitted for the sanction of Government through the Superintending Engineer of the circle in which the District is situated. The estimates and designs are scrutinised by the last named officer before submission to government. They then go through the usual official channel for final scrutiny and sanction to the proper authority, that is the local Government, the Government of India or the Secretary of State, as the case may be. All Public Works in India were before 1875 under the general control of a department of the Governor-General's Council. It sometimes happened that the department was under the personal supervision of the Governor-General himself, as in the case of Lord Mayo, and for sometime, of Lord Northbrook. The last named Viceroy, however, found the work too heavy for him, as he had to look after the foreign and political Departments in addition.

He, therefore, delegated the management of Public Works to a separate member of his executive Council. It was long thought desirable to appoint a special professional minister for Public Works, and attach him to the Council of the Governor-General for professional advice and control. The appointment was at last sanctioned, and Sir Andrew Clarke was the first Public Works Minister appointed in 1873. The special work of this officer was to watch and guide the Public Works policy of the Government of India, and to exercise a close and careful supervision over the schemes submitted for sanction, both as regards professional points, and as regards their ultimate remunerative character.

When Lord Dalhousie was Governor-General of India, he thought it desirable to import foreign capital into this country, if practicable, and have it invested in the construction of railways, Irrigation schemes, and other remunerative works. To encourage foreign capitalists to start these enterprises, he guaranteed from the Indian revenue a certain fixed rate of interest for all money sunk in this country. The rate was fixed at 5 per cent in the case of railways, and it was stipulated that when the profits on any line after paying off its working expenses exceeded 5 per cent, half of them were to be made over to Government in repayment of the amount advanced by them to make up the full guaranteed rate of interest. A good deal of capital was obtained on these conditions, and several companies started work in the different provinces of India. The principal of these guaranteed Railway companies are the East India Railway, the Great Indian Peninsula Railway, the Bombay, Baroda and Central India Railway, the Sind, Punjab and Delhi Railway, and the South India Railway. The construction of railways on the guarantee principle was commenced in 1851, and is still in progress to a greater or lesser extent in many parts of India. The total traffic receipts of the guaranteed railway companies in 1878 were Rs.3,92,08,770, and the total expenditure Rs.4,97,95,000, thus showing a loss for the year of Rs.1,05,86,230. Since then, on account of the heavy pressure of the famine traffic, the great Railways have earned interest at 7, and in some cases even at 9 per cent which they shared with the Government.

All expenditure on guaranteed Railways is under the control of Government officers. In actual practice it was found, however, that this check was simply nominal, and that the control was not effective in preventing unnecessary and extravagant expenditure. The fixed guaranteed rate of interest being high, (much higher than the average return on capital in England), it was found that the companies were not sufficiently economical in the construction of their works or in their management when constructed. It was their interest to keep their expenditure at as high a figure as practicable, in order to secure the guaranteed interest on the maximum amount that could be laid out. The capital expenditure thus, by reason of this want of economy, largely exceeded the estimated figures, and the profits fell far short of what they were anticipated to be, when the works were first taken in hand. Payments from Indian treasuries for making up the guaranteed rate of interest became, therefore, very heavy, and were found to be a constantly increasing charge on the Imperial revenue, though the lines chosen in the first instance were highly advantageous, and calculated to return a high rate of interest, had the expenditure been kept within proper bounds. The Government of India in consequence of this state of things thought it expedient to modify their conditions of guarantee for future railways, so as to keep under effective check the propensities of guaranteed companies to go in for extravagant expenditure. They tried to form companies with a guarantee of less than 5 per cent for such additional lines of railway as were found to be necessary. No capital was, however, found to be forth-coming for the projected works on these modified conditions. Government were, therefore, compelled at last in 1869 to resolve upon constructing their own railways by employing their own Engineers, or as an alternative accept the old guarantee of 5 per cent. They chose the former course, and commenced making their own railways, the requisite funds being derived from money raised by loans both in England and in India.

The system of constructing Railway Works out of borrowed money was afterwards extended to Irrigation schemes. All works constructed out of loans were called Extraordinary Public Works. Separate accounts were kept of the expenditure upon them, and of the revenues realised from them. It was generally understood that no work was to be undertaken from money obtained by loans, unless its remunerative character was fully established. This principle does not appear to have been uniformly acted upon, as we find that the Government of India undertook to lay out their borrowed funds over such works as the canals of the East India Irrigation Company, and the Indus Valley State railway. The former of these works were abandoned by the company on account of their unremunerative character, and were subsequently bought over by government, not at their market value, but at their cost price. With reference to the other work, *viz.* the Indus Valley State Railway, it was never anticipated that it would commercially be a paying line, as it runs through a sandy and sparsely populated portion of the country, with a cheap line of water carriage like the Indus running close by. The work was, however, taken in hand as one of military and political importance, and its construction sanctioned out of borrowed money. For the construction of these Extraordinary Public Works, it was found necessary to borrow a certain sum of money annually, extending sometimes to 5 crores of Rupees. It was anticipated that the works undertaken would soon be remunerative, and enable the Government of India to go on in its course of borrowing and constructing fresh Public Works, thus covering the country, after a certain period, with a close and thickly woven network of Railways and Irrigation Canals, affording complete security from famines and droughts in future. When large and extensive Public Works are undertaken, it is necessary to provide for a steady annual expenditure upon them. The annual cash balance out of the Indian revenue, after paying for ordinary Public Works and other expenditure, was so small, and that too so fluctuating in its character on account of the varying nature of our annual expenditure, that no dependance could be placed on it for the prosecution of large and heavy works. Hence arose the necessity of certain fixed annual loans for covering this extraordinary outlay. It was found, however, that the schemes chosen for construction out of borrowed money did not yield as early and as satisfactory a return as was anticipated. The amount of loans continued to increase annually without a corresponding return from the works on which they were laid out. The interest-charges, therefore, rose to a high figure, and became a heavy charge against the Indian Exchequer, entailing additional taxation upon the people in one shape or other. Thus the policy of constructing any more works out of borrowed money came to be seriously questioned, and this led to the appointment of a Parliamentary Committee to enquire into the matter.

The principal classes of works constructed from borrowed money are :—

(1st) Harbour works such as those of Calcutta, Madras and Bombay.

(2nd) State railways.

(3rd) Irrigation Works.

The harbour works of Bombay and Calcutta were originally constructed or purchased by Government, and made over for management to a local committee called the Port Trust, who realise the revenue from them by the imposition of Bunder and wharfage fees. It is expected that each Port Trust will return to Government suitable interest on the amount that has been expended in the construction of the works made over to them for management. These expectations are being partially fulfilled in the case of Calcutta, but in Bombay the amount expended in the purchase of the Elphinstone states &c. was so heavy, that there is little likelihood of its ever yielding an adequate return. The harbour works of Madras have been only recently commenced. It is said that the success of the scheme is doubtful, several Engineers of great standing and experience like Sir Andrew Clarke having pronounced opinions unfavourable to it. There is no Port Trust at Madras formed as yet, but on the completion of the works in progress a similar institution to that in Bombay will be organised, and entrusted with the management of the undertaking. Harbour works of a special character are in progress at Karachi, on the completion of which it is expected that that town will take the place of Bombay as regards European traffic with the Punjab, Sind and other provinces of North India. These schemes are all useful and will do good generally to the country, though their commercial remunerative character may be rather doubtful.

The next class of Public Works constructed out of borrowed money are State Railways. As has been said before, the Government of India were highly dissatisfied with the system of guaranteed railways, and inaugurated in 1869 the policy of constructing further railway works by means of government agency. The first state railway was commenced in 1870, and completed in 1871. Other lines were subsequently constructed, and in 1876 the total mileage of State Railways completed was 934. Since then, State Railways have progressed rapidly, till now the total mileage of completed State Railways is 1500, with 1000 more under prospective construction. In 1876 the interest and working expenses of state railways amounted to Rs.80,84,850 and the traffic receipts amounted to Rs. 28,95,120, showing a loss of Rs. 51,89,730. The loss on this head has been diminishing every year with the extension of system. The state railway works are yet in their infancy and the traffic receipts compared with the capital invested in them have been very meagre. Most of the lines have not yet paid their working expenses, and there is little likelihood of their doing so for sometime to come. A few of the lines constructed are of strategical and political importance, and will never return adequate interest on their capital amount. As stated before, the Indus Valley State Railway belongs to this class. When government fixed upon the policy of constructing railway works themselves, most of the paying lines of traffic, such as those between the great commercial centres of the Presidency towns, had already been made over for construction to guaranteed companies. They had, therefore, to take up less remunerative schemes, and it will take sometime before even a few of them become paying as commercial undertakings. Ultimately, however, most of the lines will earn an interest of about 5 per cent.

The principal guaranteed Railways in India are the Bombay, Baroda and Central India Railway, the Great Indian Peninsula Railway (South-east and North-east branches), the South Indian Railway (Beypore Vellore lines), the East India Railway (South-west and North-west branches), the Oudh and Rohilcund Railway, and the Karachi and Kotri railway. The principal state railway lines are Durbhanga state railway, the Northern India state railway, the Tirboot state railway, the Indus Valley state railway, the Rajpootana state railway, the Neemuch state railway, the Dhond and Manmad state railway, the Khamgaon and Umraoti state railways, and the Holkar state railway. Of the guaranteed railway companies, the only ones that have commenced paying commercially are the Great Indian Peninsula and the East India railway companies. Other guaranteed lines and the state railway lines generally, with the exception of a few such as the Rajpootana railway, are paying a very indifferent return, and it will be sometime before they commence yielding a return of from 4 to 5 per cent. It is the opinion of experts that in the long run all these lines, with the exception of such of them as have been simply constructed on political and military considerations, will pay not less than 6 per cent on the capital expended upon them.

The third class of extraordinary Public Works are Irrigation schemes. It may be mentioned that these were in existence in large numbers in this country before the advent of the British in India. The people of India have been always fully alive to the benefits of Irrigation, as testified by the numerous canals and tank works scattered over the whole country from Cape Comorin to the Himalayas, wherever there are facilities for their construction, or where cultivation is impracticable without their aid on account of the scanty rainfall. The small *bandaras* and *pats* on the streams in North Deccan, some of the heavy works in the river deltas in the Madras Presidency such as that of the Cavery, the numerous old tanks which cover the Madras Presidency and the southern parts of Bombay, and lastly the large old Irrigation canals in the North West Provinces and in Sind, are all works which were constructed during the administrations of native Princes and rulers, long before the commencement of the British rule.

When the English rulers gained a firm footing in this country, they turned their attention to the improvement of these old native works, and the construction of new ones wherever suitable sites presented themselves. The first extensive Irrigation project undertaken by the British government was the Ganges canal, which was commenced in 1831, and brought into working in 1854. Subsequently, other schemes were undertaken from time to time, the requisite funds for their construction being provided for by loans. The principal Irrigation works in this country may be enumerated as follows; the Bari Doab canal, western Jumna canal, lower Sutlaj and Chenab Inundation canals, Sirhind canal, and Swat canal in the Punjab; Eastern Jamna canal, the Ganges canal, Agra canal, Rohilcund canal, Dun canal, Bijnor canal and Agra Irrigation works in the North Western Provinces; Orissa canal and the Midnapur canals in Bengal; the Godawary, Cavery and Krishna Delta works, and some tank projects in Madras; and the Hatmati canal, the Muta Lake and canal, Ojhar canal, Palkhed canal, Krishna canal, Ekrukh tank, Jamda canals, and Sind inundation canals in Bombay. Of these some of the works are yielding a large return on the capital invested in them. The most paying of them, however, are old native works that have been improved and extended by the British Government. In this class may be mentioned the Cavery works in Madras, the Sind Irrigation canals in Bombay, and the western and eastern Jamna canals in the Punjab and the North West Provinces. These works are yielding a very large return, in some cases as much as 85 per cent, if we accept as correct the figures given by English Engineers about the valuation of native portions of the works. Of the works which have been wholly constructed during the British administration of the country, those that are located in favourable situations, and have a perennial water supply in connection with them, such as the Ganges canal, the new Sind Inundation canals, and the Krishna Irrigation works, are paying from 5 to 6 per cent on the outlay upon them. Other schemes, however, where the water supply is precarious and unreliable, or where the people are not used to Irrigation, have, financially speaking, turned out to be failures. Their prospects may not unlikely improve in time. There are some works, however, like the Ekrukh tank, on which there has been proportionately a very large outlay, which is not likely to pay even after the lapse of a number of years. The total outlay on Irrigation works up to 1876 was about 15 crores of Rupees, and the excess of receipts over working expenses in 1876 was Rs.6,72,420 showing a very small return on the outlay incurred. Since 1876, five crores of Rupees have been invested by Government in its irrigation schemes. Colonel Fife, Chief Engineer for Irrigation Bombay, stated in his evidence that the Bombay Irrigation works, which are all of a recent growth, paid a return of ½ per cent of direct revenues realised mostly by the sale of water in 1876. He anticipates that the average percentage of return during the first 15 years after the construction of a work will be five per cent, and after 15 years it will be about ten per cent.

It should be mentioned here, that in calculating the returns from Irrigation works in Sind, the Punjab, the North West Provinces, and Madras, it has been the practice to include in Irrigation revenue, such share of the land revenue enhancement as can be ascertained to be due to improvements caused by the construction of Irrigation works. This is called indirect revenue and its amount in the case of each work is arrived at by the best practicable approximation after consultation between the Rev ue and Public Works officers of the District. If this indirect revenue be excluded from the returns of the Madras, Punjab, and Northern India works, the percentage of revenue will be much below what it is shown to be in official statements. For instance, the Ganges canal has been shown to have paid 4½ percent in 1876. If we expunge from this revenue the land improvement share, the return stands at 3¾ per cent.

The Government of India tried to form guaranteed Irrigation companies similar to the guaranteed railway companies. The East India Irrigation and Madras Irrigation companies were accordingly formed. They were found to work very unsatisfactorily, and Government had to buy up the works of the Orissa company at a great loss to the state, and a heavy annual burden to the Indian Exchequer. The Madras Irrigation company has likewise come to a stand-still. They have not been yet able to repay entirely an advance of 60 lacs of Rupees that was made to them by the Government of India for the prosecution of their works. Both companies have failed financially, the works constructed by them not paying their working expenses.

The mass of information collected by the Parliamentary Committee has satisfactorily proved that some of the so-called reproductive works have not proved to be so much remunerative as was anticipated. The reasons assigned are :—

1st The choice of works has been faulty in as much as several schemes have been undertaken in places where they are not likely to be utilised to a great extent, and cannot, therefore, be made to pay.

2nd Some projects were undertaken for Political and Military purposes, and charged to money raised by loans. These of course will never prove remunerative financially.

3rd It has often happened that works have been under-estimated, and shown to pay a handsome return on the basis of the estimates so framed. The actual cost in construction having far exceeded the estimated figure, the projects have proved to be unpaying, in some cases so much so as not to pay even their working expenses.

4th The establishment charges of the Public Works Department have always been very heavy in India, and they have added materially to the cost of works.

5th The data on which the calculated returns were based were necessarily meagre at the commencement, and they led to results which have proved to be erroneous.

As regards the desirability or otherwise of constructing future Public Works in India out of borrowed money, Lord Northbrook, General Dickens, Colonel Fife and other witnesses examined maintained that the course was desirable and should be pursued. Lord Northbrook was of opinion that the annual loans raised should not exceed 2½ crores of Rupees, which sum, he said, could be raised without difficulty in the local markets of India. It is a point of great importance to have all the requisite funds borrowed from Indian creditors, instead of going for them to foreign markets. The nationalization of the Indian debt is desirable both on political grounds, and on account of the increasing difficulty of loss by exchange. Lord Northbrook laid particular stress upon the principle, that the prosecution of productive Public Works should be so arranged as not to necessitate additional taxation upon the already heavily taxed Indian Ryot. General Dickens advocated the raising of 4 crores of Rupees annually for Public Works purposes, of which 1½ crores should be spent on Irrigation works and 2½ crores on State Railways. General Dickens and the other witnesses further stated that in order to know before hand what the Extraordinary Public Works expenditure for any year is to be, it was necessary to maintain the system of having forecasts prepared for such works, showing expenditure for the next five years. These forecasts will be highly useful for the guidance of the financial Department of the Government of India. It was suggested by the members of the Committee, that on the completion of many of the works that are in hand at present in India, it would be difficult to find other schemes that would be equally paying and remunerative. The witnesses examined stated in reply that the thing was not so difficult as might be imagined. There are still numerous schemes which the Government of India can take up as funds become available. There are many comparatively unopened districts where new lines of railway are urgently required, and where they would pay when constructed. Similarly there is a great number of Irrigation schemes at present pigeon-holed with the Government of India, which have had to be shelved pending the supply of funds required for their construction. It is possible like wise to find numerous and perhaps equally paying new schemes of Irrigation in all parts of the country if a careful examination is ordered for the purpose.

The question of the relative cost and usefulness of navigation canals and railways as means of carriage for traffic is one upon which a great deal has been written. The warmest advocate of canals in preference to railways is the celebrated General Sir Arthur Cotton, the great Engineer, who designed ana constructed the Ganges canal works. The average cost per mile of a navigating canal was stated by Sir Arthur Cotton as not likely to exceed Rs.30,000, while railway works cost as much as Rs.80,000, or even one lac-per mile. Railway works are besides expensive to work and maintain. The advantages in favour of navigating canals are that their first cost is smaller; that they are more inexpensively maintained; that their working cost is much smaller than that of railways; and that besides serving as means of carriage, the canals can be used for irrigating and water supply purposes. It must, however, be borne in mind that canal works are not possible in all places and localities, that water may fail and canals dry up, and lastly, that the speed of locomotion in canals cannot be equal to that of railways. Navigating canals should, therefore, be constructed in preference to railways only in such places as offer special facilities for them, as regards the constancy of water supply and the cheapness of construction. In other places, and for military considerations, wherever in fact speed of locomotion is a matter of great importance, railways must in preference be undertaken. In India both railways and canals are needed. Wherever practicable all irrigating canals should be capable of carrying light traffic by boats and rafts plying over them.

With reference to the question as to whether railways or irrigation works are more conducive to the protection of the country from famines, Sir George Campbell stated that under the peculiar circumstances of this country, preference must be given to the Railways. In years of drought and scanty rainfall, the water supply of irrigation works, with the exception of such of them as are supported by the perennial streams of the Himalayas or in the Madras Deltas, generally fails, and the works do not in consequence afford the anticipated relief in times of scarcity. Railways, on the other hand, are equally serviceable at all times for the transport of food grains to the afflicted districts from those which may invariably be expected to be blessed with plentiful harvests. The value of railways was abundantly proved during the last famine in Madras and Bombay, when the G.I.P. and E.I. Railways did great service to the country by importing grains from Bengal, Bihar and Northern India. Had it not been for this railway communication, and the abundant food supply that was poured daily into the heart of the afflicted country, the condition of the Southern Districts of the Madras Presidency would have been something too terrible to imagine. There would have been no grain to buy though there was plenty of money supplied from Government relief works for its purchase. Another noteworthy point with reference to the comparative merits of railways and Irrigation works, as regards their famine-protective character is that Irrigation works are impossible in some districts on account of the absence in them of perennial streams, or suitable sites for the storage of water. In such places, railways are the only means that can be resorted to for provision against famines and times of scarcity.

Regarding the possible further extension of Productive Irrigation works, and their distribution in the different provinces of India, it was mentioned that Irrigation, wherever it is carried out in connection with perennial streams such as the Indus and the Ganges, is most successful financially, as the expenditure to be incurred is comparatively light. The provinces of Sind and the Punjab, being watered by the Indus and the five Punjab rivers, are very advantageously situated in this respect. Their rainfall besides is so scanty and precarious, that they stand in absolute need of Irrigation for the maintenance of their cultivation. This want has been provided to a great extent where the districts are sufficiently populated, though a good deal yet remains to be done. The Ganges canal and the Western and Eastern Jamna canals have likewise provided for the protection by Irrigation of such portions of the North West Provinces as stand in need of it on account of their precarious rainfall. The districts beyond Benarès, and Oudh, Bengal and Behar, are moist tracts of country in which the rainfall is generally abundant, and water can be obtained by means of wells sunk to short depths below the ground level. No Irrigation on an extensive scale is, therefore, needed for the protection of these provinces. Some important works, however, have been already provided here. In the Madras Presidency, the most favourable situations for Irrigation works are the deltas of the great rivers like the Godavery, the Krishna, and the Kaveri. Irrigation has already been provided here. There are besides a large number of irrigating tanks constructed under the native rule, which have been improved and repaired by the British Government. In the Central Provinces, there are very few streams, and no suitable sites can, therefore, be obtained for the construction of large Irrigation works. To come now nearer home. The rivers in the Bombay Presidency, exclusive of Sind, are all small rivers. All of them, with the exception of those in Guzerat, take their origin in the Western ghats of the Sahyadri range, and run east and west to meet the Bay of Bengal and the Arabian sea respectively. Those that run to the west traverse the North and South Konkans. These portions of India have a plentiful monsoon rainfall almost every year. The crops that grow there are monsoon dry crops and rice. The soil is not capable of producing Rabi crops, and therefore, does not stand in need of irrigation and irrigating canals. There is garden cultivation all over the tract, but the people have provided their own wells which retain a perennial supply of water at no great depth. The depth at which water can be met within these wells is very small, seldom exceeding ten feet. The country between the ghaut range and the sea does not exceed 50 miles, and the whole of this narrow strip is traversed by a number of hill torrents. No large canals are, therefore, profitable in the Konkans, and their supply, if constructed, would prove insufficient, unless they are supplemented by large and expensive storage tanks. No irrigation works are under these circumstances required for the Konkans, nor will they be profitable, if constructed.

It is what is pre-eminently called the Desh portion of the Bombay Presidency that requires Irrigation. The Desh districts include Khandesh, the Deccan, and the Southern Maratha country. The rainfall here, except in the Mavals or near the ghauts, is very scanty and precarious; and it is by no means unusual in these parts to have one year of good harvest after every two or three of bad ones. Protection by means of Irrigation works is essentially needed here. Unfortunately it happens that the Desh rivers, which run east to meet the Bay of bengal, are too near their sources in the Bombay Presidency, and in consequence the volume of their water is very small. Most of them dry up in the hot weather, and the canals from them run dry in consequence. All the canals constructed in the Bombay Presidency are works of this description. They are taken off from rivers which run copiously for eight months in the year, but during the four hot weather months, the supply proves insufficient, and is sometimes completely stopped. It, therefore, becomes necessary in the case of these works to supplement their supply in the hot weather months from extraneous sources. To meet this difficulty, storage tanks have been provided in some instances, and are being provided in others. These are large artificial tanks, which store up monsoon waters. The stored water is let into the canal or the bed of the river feeding it, as soon as the natural supply commences to fail in the hot weather. After the first few falls of rain, when the river is replenished, the tank sluices are closed, and are not opened unless the river again dries up. The smaller rivers in Guzerath are also of the same character, and the canals from them likewise are incomplete without storage works.

The province of Sind which forms a portion of the Bombay Presidency is a tract of an altogether exceptional character. It has a very slight rainfall, and that too does not extend over a longer period than one or two fortnights. All cultivation in this province is carried on by means of Irrigation from the Indus, the great river which runs through it from North to South. The crops are principally rice, and cold weather crops. The river rises in the cold weather, and in the rains, and feeds a series of canals which are taken off at a high level. These canals are known as inundation canals. There is a large number of them scattered over the whole province. They are full and running, when the river is in floods, and empty when it is low. There are inundation canals of a like character in the Punjab and the North West Provinces.

As regards tank irrigation, these are constructed in favourable positions in such a manner that the greatest quantity of water can be stored at a minimum of expenditure. The most favourable site is generally a narrow gorge between two hills with a river running through it. The gorge is closed by a dam or embankment, and a lake is formed behind it, varying in extent and depth according to the configuration of the ground. Sometimes a natural hollow amongst the hills is formed into a lake by bringing into it water from a river or a running stream, by means of a canal taken off at a higher level. There are some favourable sites of this description. But almost all the tanks that have been constructed for Irrigation or water supply purposes have been formed by throwing dams or embankments across a running drainage course, at a place where its valley has been narrowed by hills closing in from both sides. The dams constructed for the formation of tanks are either of masonry or of earth. Every tank is furnished with a channel for the escape of surplus water, and with outlet works for letting out stored water when necessary.

The main considerations which have to be attended to in the selection of tank sites are good foundations for dam works, a low and favourable saddle for the waste weir, and above all adequate drainage or catchment area, capable of filling the tank in a year of ordinary rainfall. The catchment area or gathering ground of a large tank must also be large. In the Bombay Presidency, the best catchments are the Ghat districts, where the rainfall is unfailing and copious. A portion of the rainfall over the catchment basin of a tank is absorbed in the ground, another portion is taken up and assimilated by trees, some is lost by the evaporation and the remainder finds its way into the tank. It is found generally that about $^1/_4$th or $^1/_5$th of the rain-fall waters is under favourable circumstances available for tank filling.

We shall now briefly notice the chief irrigation works that have been hitherto constructed in India. We find a large number of canals and small tanks that were constructed in the times of the Mahomedan and Hindu rulers of the country. The province of Mysore, the Southern Maharata Country, the northern portion of Khandesh, and the western portion of the presidency of Madras, are full of irrigating tanks constructed in all likely places, each tank having a distinct irrigating area of its own. Rice is generally grown on the lands protected by these tanks. The great defect with the old works is that the waste water provision made in them proves too often insufficient, and results in the breaching and destruction of a great number of them. Many of these old tanks are very large, much larger than the tanks constructed by the British Government. The tank of Chumbrumbokum in Madras may be mentioned here. Its area, when full, is $9^1/_2$ square miles. The number of old canals, constructed by the Native and Mahomedan rulers in India, is also very great. Almost all the existing inundation canals in Sind, and the western Jumna, Bari Doab, and other canals in the North West Provinces, are indigenous works. They have only been improved and enlarged by the British Government. Similarly, the Cavery and Godavery Delta irrigation systems in the Madras Presidency, which are so successful financially at present, were originally native works, which have been improved by the British Government. Besides the larger canals mentioned above, there are several small ones known as Pats. These *pats* are especially numerous in Khandesh, where each important village on the banks of the principal ghaut rivers has got a weir and irrigating channel for itself. The Panjra, the Mosum, and the Girna rivers have a large number of these weirs and irrigating channels. In the Khandesh Bagayit villages, a certain area of the village lands is specially kept apart for irrigation, and all the principal villages are co-sharers in it. This area is called the *Thal*, and there is a regular system of triennial or quadrennial, rotation practised upon it. In the Konkan also, there are small *pats* of this description, but they are few and far between.

Of the principal Irrigation works undertaken and constructed by the British Government, the Ganges canal stands foremost. It is taken from the Ganges near Haridwar, is 654 miles in length, and has cost, over three crores of rupees. It is a navigable canal. Loaded steamers work upon it. Next in importance to the Ganges canal, are the eastern and western Jumna canals, the Bari Doab canal, the Sutlej canals, the Sone canals and the Orissa canals. This last work was constructed by the East India Irrigation Company, and was subsequently bought over by Government. The Bari Doab canal is 469 miles in length, the Eastern Jumna canal 130 miles, the Western Jumna 445 miles and the Sutlej 530 miles. These canals are the chief works in Bengal, the Punjab and the North West Provinces. The principal Irrigation works undertaken by the British Government in the Madras Presidency are the Delta Irrigation works of the Cavery, the Krishna, and the Godavery. These works are financially very successful. As has been said before, they were old works which have been improved upon and materially enlarged and extended by the British Government. Besides the above, there are the Buckingham canal lately completed as a famine work, and the numerous Irrigation tanks in the Presidency, many of which have been restored by the British rulers after their conquest of the country. In the Bombay Presidency, the works carried out under British rule are very few, and comparatively unimportant. As remarked before, the rivers in this Presidency are small, and no large canal schemes can, therefore, be undertaken in connection with them, without constructing very expensive and costly storage tanks to supplement the natural flow of the river when it falls short of irrigation requirements. The foremost irrigation work constructed in the Deccan is the Fife Lake and the Muta canals. This work is still in progress, and is estimated to cost about 90 lacs of Rupees, including direct and indirect charges, when complete. Next in importance to the Muta canals, are the Ekruck tank and canals in Sholapur, the Jamda canals, and the Mukti tank irrigation in Khandesh, the Krishna canal in Sattara, and the Hatmati canal in Guzerath. Besides these works, there are several smaller tanks and canals which it is not necessary to name here. In the Southern Maratha Country, many old tanks have been restored and improved by the British Government.

All the principal irrigation works in India have been constructed from loan funds, and they are expected to pay more than four and a half per cent on the capital invested in them. With reference to the question of their paying character, it may be remarked, that some of the Madras and Northern India works have commenced paying more than 5 per cent on their capital cost. Of the Bombay works, none, not even the Muta canals, have met with any financial success hitherto. The principal reason of this is the occasional failure of water supply which disheartens the Ryots, and keeps them from going in for perennial and costly irrigation. Another reason is the poverty of the Ryots. In the course of time, when the water supply is made permanent by means of storage tanks, and when people become more used to irrigation, the paying character of all these works will improve. Besides the above mentioned works many new irrigation schemes were commenced in the Bombay Presidency as famine works. Among others may be mentioned the Nira canal works in the Poona District, the Rajewadi tank in the Sattara District, the Pangaum and Asti tanks in the Sholapur District, the Don Project in the Kaladgi District, and the Gokak canals in the Belgaum and Dharwar District.

It may not be out of place here to enumerate the various advantages the country derives from the formation of new irrigation works :—

(1) The land commanded by them is rendered thoroughly independent as regards its productive power of the notoriously precarious and uncertain rain-fall of many parts of India. Efficient irrigation works, even though not paying financially, afford a complete protection against famine, for the area which they are capable of irrigating.

(2) Irrigation works raise the water level of the adjoining wells, and thus render lift irrigation easy and less costly.

(3) They secure a copious and unfailing water supply for drinking purposes in the villages and towns through or by the side of which they pass.

(4) They encourage the growth of vegetation, and being large masses of water themselves, attract rainfall, and render it less capricious and fluctuating.

(5) Irrigation canals, when large, serve the purposes of navigation, and secure the cheapest means of carriage as compared with roads and railways.

(6) They increase production from the soil by converting Jirait into Bagait lands.

On the other hand, the following may be set down as the disadvantages arising from irrigation works. (1) All these works tend to increase malaria on account of the great quantity of water that penetrates below the surface of the soil by percolation. This complaint can be removed to a very great extent by proper attention to drainage. (2) Again it is found that irrigation works in some cases render some of the adjacent soils unfit for cultivation, on account of their becoming marshy and saturated with water. This complaint also may be removed in some instances by drainage. Some soils may be deteriorated in this way, but this loss is quite insignificant, when compared with the immense good all irrigation works do to the country. Thirdly it is complained that irrigation brings to the surface of the soil salt efflorescence, which makes it sterile. This efflorescence is called *reh* in Bengal, and is said to have made its appearance on the Ganges canal. It has not appeared as yet in the case of any of the Bombay works, and at the worst it can do damage to a small area only. None of these disadvantages, therefore, can weigh against the many advantages that are derived from irrigation works.

In conclusion it may be said, that it is desirable to construct a number of efficient irrigation works in this country, even though they may not be paying financially, as they are one of the great means of warding off famines, and thus saving the enormous expenditure which the Public Treasury has to bear when famines occur. Let large works be carried out wherever they are possible, and in time we can afford to be independent of the aberrations of the annual rainfall. At present, where no irrigation works exist, the country is dependant upon the rain waters for our crops from the soil. When the rain-fall happens to be scanty, the whole of the agricultural population is put to great straits, and government has to remit its land tax and open relief works. All these difficulties will diminish, as irrigation works increase.

Sir Arthur Cotton in his evidence tried to show the cheapness of water carriage by navigation canals when compared with railways. This is no doubt a fact, but the cost of making Irrigation canals navigable is very heavy, and it is not possible to secure communication by means of them to any desired place. They therefore cannot be undertaken to the exclusion of railways as advocated by the enthusiastic Sir Arthur Cotton. The portion of the Godavery canal that has been constructed in the Madras Presidency is navigable, but as it does not pass by any great centres of trade, very little traffic has developed upon it. Navigable canals like that of the Ganges are no doubt desirable in places where they can be taken along the centres of traffic, and where there are no serious natural difficulties in the way of their construction. They would do a great deal of good by taking cheaply to the nearest market the agricultural produce of irrigation districts. In suitable situations, therefore, where they can be constructed cheaper than railways, their construction is greatly to be encouraged.

Almost all the witnesses examined before the Committee were in favour of raising the annual loans required for Public Works purposes in India instead of England. It was suggested that a higher rate of interest should be allowed to small bondholders, so as to induce many natives of moderate means to invest their monies in these loans. Another alternative suggested was as follows:—When the construction of a work is determined upon, the people to be directly benefited by it should be induced to contribute to the loan required for its construction. A small rate of interest should be guaranteed on these loans from the Indian revenues, and the contributors should be made co-sharers with government in the profits of the work according to the sums of money contributed by them. Seeing the numerous old native works in the country, and the manner in which they have been designed and executed, one is led to believe that the natives must have a great aptitude for the Engineering profession.

The Commission accordingly tried to elicit opinion as to the possibility of introducing the native element to a greater extent than at present in the higher branches of the Public Works Department. It was presumed that the measure would lead to greater economy by reducing the establishment charges in the construction of new works, the natives, if systematically admitted, being paid less than Engineers brought from England. Several witnesses examined stated that the natives would make very good intermediate Engineers, though there were doubts as to their capability of discharging the duties appertaining to the higher appointments of the Department. It was stated that they were wanting in energy and powers of endurance, and were inferior to European Engineers in both those respects.

The results of the evidence collected by the Committee may be summarised as follows :—

1st It is desirable to continue the course of constructing Public Works in India in future out of borrowed money.

2nd A forecast should be prepared for every five or a fixed number of years, showing the details of the works that are to be constructed out of borrowed funds, and the annual expenditure upon each of them.

3rd All cash balances from the ordinary Revenues of the country should be utilised in the construction of Extraordinary Public Works, and only such amount raised by loan as would be necessary to make up the amount previously fixed upon for expenditure during the year.

4th The amount of loan for each year should be so adjusted, that no additional taxation will ever become necessary for the payment of interest charges thereon. It should not exceed a certain maximum amount annually of from 2½ to 4 crores of Rupees.

5th The requisite annual loans should be raised in India and not in foreign markets, partly to obviate the serious charges of loss by exchange, and also from grounds of political importance. The amount of loan thus obtainable without difficulty in India should regulate the maximum referred to in the preceding paragraph. It was stated by Lord Northbrook to be about 2½ crores of Rupees.

6th No works should be constructed out of money raised by loans, except such as have their remunerative character fully established beyond all doubt.

7th Each project for a remunerative work, as it is submitted for sanction, should be most carefully scrutinised, and its capability of paying on its estimated outlay thoroughly sifted by responsible and qualified officers both in the Revenue and

Public Works Departments.

8th The estimates for all works should be most carefully scrutinised and investigated, so as to leave no chance for an excess occurring on the original estimate, on which the figures as to anticipated return of revenue have been based.

9th The establishment of the Public Works Department should be reduced to the requisite strength necessary for works to be constructed annually.

10th The works should be made cheaper by employing natives to a greater extent in the higher Branches of the Indian P.W. Department, whenever they are found qualified to occupy such positions.

The above is a general abstract noting the chief points of importance in the evidence before the Parliamentary Committee. We have tried to make it of general interest by divesting it of its multiplicity of figures, and of discussions with reference to professional matters which are not likely to be interesting to our readers. When the report of the deliberations of the Committee is out, we propose and hope to be able to review it at some length in these pages.

8

REVIEW OF "FREE TRADE AND ENGLISH COMMERCE" BY AUGUSTUS MONGREDIEN*

"FREE trade and English commerce" by Augustus Mongredien is one of the Cobden Club publications which has been extensively circulated throughout India by Babu Lal Mohan Ghose. It consists of two parts, the first of which enunciates the general doctrines of free trade, while the second part discusses the bearing of those doctrines on the practical development of English commerce. Our general attitude in regard to the theory of free trade, as elaborated by English writers on political economy, is so often misunderstood that we gladly seize this occasion to set forth our views more in detail than we should otherwise have felt inclined to do. The recent depression of trade and manufactures in England, due partly to foreign competition, and partly to the reaction of the excessive inflation of commercial and manufacturing activity in the early part of the last decade, as also the spread of protectionist doctrines all over Europe, America and the British colonies and the refusal of France to negotiate a favourable commercial treaty with England, all

*JPSS, July 1881, Vol.IV, No.1.

these facts have created a strong sentiment in England itself in favour of a more or less modified form of protection of native industry. There is a strange irony of fate in the fact that Conservative statesmen, with Lord Salisbury at their head, who during their term of office sacrificed the interests of India in the name of free trade, and partially repealed the duties on English cotton goods, thereby surrendering £250,000 of Indian revenue to gratify Manchester to be only replaced by more obnoxious forms of taxation, we say, it is a strange irony of fate that these very statesmen should now come forward as the champions of the rival theory, and feel the pulse of the nation in favour of reciprocity. In the great manufacturing towns there is a strong agitation gathering head against the extreme positions of free trade, which will not fail, sooner or later, if the present depression continues, to assume formidable proportions, and be the war cry of party strife. It is the consciousness of this change of public opinion, and the dangers attendant upon it, that has stirred the Cobden Club to issue this defence of free trade as the only safety anchor of English Commerce. India, though administered as a trust, finds its best interests sacrificed at the altar of this idol of English political economists, and it cannot therefore afford with safety to stand aloof in this controversy.

In our view, English writers commit the mistake of looking at this question solely from the economical point of view, and this economy is itself of a very low and selfish type. The political and social elements which enter into the question, when it descends from theory into practice, are absolutely put out of view, or are judged only from the English standpoint, which, as a matter of course, cannot suit the conditions of other communities not similarly circumstanced. If the whole civilised world were one integral political and social community, the economical aspects would be the only ones which need be considered. As a matter of fact, the millennium is far off, and the civilised world is split into a hundred different states with conflicting interests and aspirations, and perpetually in peace and war opposed to one another in a thousand ways. Under such circumstances, the economical aspects ought to give way, or at least be subordinated to these higher interests and aspirations, if political economy is to be anything more than schoolmen's metaphysics. The refusal of the English writers to recognize these differences, and their unwillingness to accord full importance to the higher interests involved, appear to us to be their cardinal errors in this matter.

To illustrate our meaning, we shall briefly touch upon the several axiomatic propositions laid down in the first part of the publication under review, and endeavour to point out the direction in which they need correction to fit them as guides in practice. The first proposition laid down is that exports necessitate imports to the same amount, and that it is perfectly futile to export much and import little. If exports and imports were only governed by the law of free exchange, this would be a true position. As a matter of fact, however, out of 64 countries which constitute the present civilised and trading world, the exports exceed the imports permanently in 32, and on the contrary the imports permanently exceed the exports in the same number. These permanent differences mutually eliminate each other in the total result, as they may even *a priori* be expected to do. The total of the exports of these 64 countries comes in round numbers to £1,316,000,000, and the total of the imports is £1,456,000,000. The excess of 10 per cent in the latter is accounted for by the freight and insurance charges and other profits. If the whole civilised world constituted one community, their exports would exactly balance their imports, and the proposition of the English economists would be correct both in theory and practice. When we come, however, to particular communities, the startling fact meets us in the face that in the United Kingdom the imports exceed the exports by 120 millions annually which is about one half the value of the exports, and one third of the imports, while in India the exports always exceed the imports by 15 to 20 millions. We take extreme instances to illustrate our position that, as a question of political economy, it is not true that exports and imports balance each other.

English writers themselves are aware of this discrepancy, but they make light of it by ignoring the disturbing causes as being merely accidental. Political economy, however, cannot, and should not, disregard these startling differences; for these accidents as they are called, form the very elements of the question which politicians and statesmen have chiefly to attend to. The English imports exceed the exports because English capital and English rule levies a tribute from all backward countries like India, which have to pay enormous odds for their backwardness in this race of competition.

The second position laid down is that if protection is beneficial as between country and country, it must be beneficial as between province and province in the same country. This position is also open to the same objection, *viz*, that the theory of economists is made to over-ride all the practical considerations which differenciate the wants and necessities of one province against another of the same country bound together by political and social ties, and the interests and aspirations of different countries with different polities and social economies. The *reductio ad absurdum* demonstration, sought to be attempted by this analogy, is thus as futile as if one were to argue that the motions of all the heavenly bodies should be straight, because the first law of motion enunciates that all bodies have a tendency to move in straight lines.

The cry against reciprocity is vitiated by the same defect. No body advocates reciprocity for its own sake, but there can be no doubt, judging from what is now transpiring in England, that if France and the other great European countries were to shut out English goods from European markets by heavy tariffs, English statesmen will think twice before resigning themselves to the situation. When Napoleon in his days of power formed the project of the armed neutrality of the great European states, the English statesmen of the day spared no efforts of war or peace to demolish the coalition against the supremacy of its mercantile navy. Just so English statesmen will resent any similar coalition of the European powers which, under the guise of commercial tariffs, shuts out English goods from the ports of Europe. The fact is, the question of reciprocity is not one of pure economics, but, to borrow a phrase from mathematics, is one of mixed or applied *i.e.* political economy, where the practical and the so-called accidental elements have the greatest influence.

The question of the division of labour, as influenced by free trade, comes also under the same category. If all nations were on a par in the matter of their civilisation, and the standard of the Cobden Club, "peace and good will among nations" was universally accepted, then the question would be one of pure economics. At present each country has a vital interest in securing a variety of industrial pursuits for its population. This vital interest is so paramount that in all free countries, the nations have reconciled themselves to heavy voluntary taxation rather than see life taken out of them by being confined to one or more precarious and universal means of livelihood such as agriculture or sheep-farming. In the words of an American writer, no country of modern times which is without manufactures, and we would add trade, and which exports raw produce for foreign made goods, and the inhabitants of which are almost wholly engaged in cultivating the soil, has succeeded in obtaining wealth, prosperity, and power as a nation. The present condition of India makes it a question of life and death to her millions to rescue themselves from this worst form of slavery, which would turn her people into drawers of water and hewers of wood to the civilised nations of the world. An adequate proportion in the town and country populations and in their coordinate and mutually self sufficing pursuits is a *sine qua non* of all real progress. The British colonists in Australia, New Zealand, Canada, and in Southern Africa, feel this necessity as much as we do here, with this difference only that they have the power, which we have not, of giving effect to their wishes. France, Germany and Russia feel the importance of encouraging their mercantile navy and their great manufacturing towns to serve as feeders for their agricultural products, and to sustain their position as first class powers. To talk to them about the advantages of the division of labour is, to say the least, doubtful wisdom, which though it cries from the house tops will get none but fools to listen to it.

The same observations apply with equal force to the positions laid down in regard to the alleged necessity of protection in young and old states. To take up the case of the young states first, it may fairly be questioned whether before trial any really large country can be condemned off hand as being providentially intended for one or a limited set of industries only. India for instance is a continent by itself, with vast natural and social elements of power and with a traditional instinct for all pursuits. To condemn this vast continent to the slavery of growing raw produce for ever will be to realize the parable that to him who hath much shall be given, while from him that hath little, his little shall be taken away. The instance of young states mentioned in the publication under review has no application to the oldest country in the world, inhabited by one fifth of the whole entire population of the world, with a central position and an extensive sea-board, with all varieties of climate and soil, and a limitless consumption. In the case of old states again, the necessity of giving preference to indirect over direct taxes is a factor which finds its due weight with European statesmen, though it is set down as a trifle by English writers. There is no reason in the world why Great Britain alone should have the largest mercantile navy, and France and Germany should not aspire to the same pre-eminence. Even England while it prides itself upon its advocacy of free trade, exempts with one hand what it takes freely with the other, for it makes no difference in the world whether duties on foreign goods are levied as customs duties or excise duties. England promotes its interests as a great mart of the world by levying light customs duties, but it makes up the difference by imposing heavy excise duties on the consumption of many of these foreign articles. Other countries cannot at present imitate her policy in this respect, but they can not be justly condemned for their inability under present circumstances to do so. We have thus briefly reviewed all the leading propositions of the first part of this publication. We have not much to say in regard to the positions laid down in the second part which have an exclusive bearing upon a transient phase of English commerce. We have no quarrel with the theory of free trade as such. Our only contention is that its practical application must be sub-ordinated to the varying conditions of different countries, and that a hard and fast line of policy dictated by the experience of Great Britain cannot commend itself to the nations of the world.

9

LAND LAW REFORM AND AGRICULTURAL BANKS*

The discussion in regard to the agrarian problem of the Deccan Districts has received a new impetus during the last few months from the judicial condemnation pronounced by the Honourable Mr. Justice West upon the special legislation which has commended itself to the counsels of Government. Like everything else which proceeds from such a high authority, this note of warning and alarm will not fail to excite general attention, and incline Government to pause before it reaffirms its faith in the principles which found favour with the Legislative Council two years ago. The conversion of Mr. Justice West, half-hearted as it is, to the views which we have all along entertained on this subject is a most agreeable surprise to us; for, if we mistake not, in his pamphlet on the "Rent and land of India," published a few years ago, he gave utterance to ultra-radical and communistic views which were rejected by Government because of their too sweeping and revolutionary character. Mr. West proposed as his solution of the agricultural problem to abolish entirely the power of free alienation by the Ryot of his lands, even to the extent of excluding temporary mortgages or leases without the sanction of the Revenue officers, who were expected to see that, in the exercise of this power under such limitations, the Ryot did not improvidently deprive himself of the minimum required

*JPSS, October 1881, Vol.IV, No.2.

for his subsistence. It was by way of practical compromise between this extreme suggestion and the absolute freedom till then enjoyed by the Ryot in the disposition of his land, that the Legislature sanctioned the middle course represented by the Deccan Agriculturists Relief Act in some of its most important provisions. The disappointment which has resulted from the working of this modified compromise in such a revulsion of feeling must have convinced. Mr. Justice West of the utter hopelessness of securing any relief to the Ryots by reducing them to the condition of land-serfs, with no other right of property except a license to work on the state domain from year to year, and pay the highest economic rent which could be screwed out under the absolute monopoly of land enjoyed by the Government, and the entire absence of all competing industrial resources. While giving full credit to Mr. Justice West for that rare virtue among Indian civilians, the courage of avowing his honest convictions, even when they belied the irresponsible ideals of his most cherished thoughts, we must at the same time frankly confess that his onslaught is only vigorous on its destructive side, and lacks the strength derived from a fertile and constructive suggestion by way of remedy for evils which are too real to be overlooked, and must be grappled with and not shirked. The misery and helplessness of the agricultural classes in the Deccan districts is not a problem of today, though until recent years the scandal was not publicly acknowledged to be a blot upon the otherwise fair fame of British Indian statesmanship. If there were no other way open, we could reconcile ourselves to accept thankfully the doubtful blessings of the Relief Act at present in force, as at least furnishing a visible index of the solicitude of Government to do its duty to this long neglected class of its subjects. It is our consciousness of the fact that a safer course is open to Government, which adds to our regret that Mr. Justice West has not lent his advocacy in recommending a positive remedy along-side with his negative criticism with the weight which his words will always command with the highest Indian authorities.

Fortunately there are other workers in the field, who are proceeding upon the right track, and leading the forlorn hope against great odds in the shape of Phillistine prejudices and self-satisfied confidence with the existing order of things. Among such workers we must allow Mr. Wedderburn the foremost place in the rank of practical philanthropists, who forget their service connections in the earnest solicitude to promote the welfare of the unfortunate Ryots over whom Providence has set them to rule. In his proposals for a modified permanent settlement for the Deccan Districts, as well as in his later suggestions about the feasibility of the establishment of agricultural banks in these Districts, he has worked under many disadvantages his way to a clearer perception of the causes which have reduced many millions of people in two generations to such a hopeless plight. In one of our earlier numbers, while discussing from our stand-point the true solution of the Agrarian Problem, we found occasion to express our opinion of the scheme of settlement proposed by Mr. Wedderburn, and we hope to review in the course of the following observations his proposals in regard to the land-banks scheme. Whatever differences of opinion we may be led to entertain in regard to these proposals, there can be no room to doubt that Mr. Wedderburn has fairly grappled with the difficulties of the question, and, while agreeing with Mr. Justice West in the expression of his disappointment with the methods of relief which have found favour with Government, his suggestions have the rare advantage of presenting a constructive alternative scheme, which cannot fail, with larger experience of the failure of all other plans, to find before long a hearing at the hands of Government and the public.

It will be necessary at the outset to present a few figures illustrative of the existing economical and social condition of the population in the four Deccan Districts more immediately under consideration. Without the basis of such detailed information, the best thought-out schemes have too often the appearance of visionary utopias which fail to carry any real conviction to the mind of the most earnest inquirer, and he is too often bewildered in the mazes of optimistic or pessimist views which are placed before him with such exaggeration, as to lead him to suspect that the arguments urged are shaped by forgone conclusions. The four Districts of Poona, Nagar, Sholapoor, and Satara form, so to speak, the very heart of the Deccan, and were once the home of the Maratha confederacy. Their total area is 21,029 square miles, and the population of these districts as ascertained by the Census of 1872 was 8,460,209 souls. Throughout this territory, there are only 37 towns with a population of more than 5,000 inhabitants each. The total of the urban population is 479,329. The number of inhabited villages on the other hand is 4,552 with an estimated population of 2,980,880 souls. The proportion of the urban to the rural population ranges from 80 per cent in the Poona District to 90 per cent in the Satara District. The importance of these figures will be better understood when they are compared with Gujerath, which is the most prosperous province of this Presidency, and with the Konkan which ranks lowest in material wealth. In Gujerath there is one town for every 288 square miles, the proportion in the Deccan is 1 for 502. Gujerath towns have between them a population of 6 lacs against a rural population of 22 lacs, which gives the proportion of 1 to 3¾. This same proportion sinks to 1 to 6 in the Deccan, and in the Konkan it is 1 to 11. Again the number of houses per square mile is 27 in the Deccan as against 76 in Gujerath, and of these houses the better sort, that is the tiled houses, are 1 to 20, while in Gujerath the proportion is 1 to 3. Of the thirty-four and half lacs of the population, 1,710,721 are males. The proportion of children to adults is 36 per cent. With this deduction, we find that the adult male population of these four Districts is between eleven and twelve lacs. The Brahmins and the Banias, the only intelligent and thrifty classes, are about 8 per cent of the whole population, and the percentage of the male population able to read and write ranges from 7 (Satara) to 10½ (Poona). The proportion again of the agricultural to the non-agricultural population is 57 to 43 in every 100, which deduction results in the fact that of the male adults estimated to be between 11 and 12 lacs, 7½ lacs are adult male agriculturists in these four Districts. Of this number, more than $6^1/_2$ lacs are what are called peasant proprietors, the rest, about a lac, are either tenants or labourers on the farms. These $6^1/_2$ lacs of agriculturists pay by way of land revenue to the state about 53 lacs of rupees a year. The total acreage of arable and unarable lands in these four Districts is $132^1/_3$ lacs, of which nearly 27 lacs are Inam, and the rest about $105^1/_2$ lacs belong to Government. Of this the occupied land is about 78 lacs of acres, the rest are either unoccupied or unassessed. It will thus appear that about $6^1/_2$ lacs of male adult agriculturists own between them about 78 lacs of Government lands, and pay by way of land revenue about 53 lacs of rupees every year. Adding to this figure the incidence of the salt tax, seven pence per head, and the Local Cesses we get a total of nearly 60 lacs of rupees as the limit of the Government demands from the agriculturist classes in these four districts. Each agricultural head of a family thus pays about 9 rupees per head for the privilege of cultivating about 10 acres of Government land. It is impossible in the absence of accurate statistics to state exactly the value of the agricultural produce raised in these four Districts. The Famine Commissioners, however, have furnished an approximate total of 350 millions sterling as the value of agricultural produce in British India, with a population of 190 millions. Seeing that most parts of India are better situated in respect of climatic and soil conditions than these arid districts of the Deccan, where the soil is poor, and the rain scanty and irregular, this estimate of the Famine Commissioners is more likely to be favourable than otherwise in regard to these districts. The estimated yield of agricultural produce on this basis of calculation for a population of 35 lacs is about 7 crores worth of produce, of which $^1/_6$th or more than one crore is taken up by the seeds, cattle fodder and wastage, leaving 6 crores worth of produce for consumption and export. Of this total produce, $^2/_3$ rds or 4 crores represent the consumption of the producing classes, at the very moderate figure of 20 rupees a head per year for 20 lacs of people, leaving about 2 crores of produce as the available store out of which the Government demand of 60 lacs has to be satisfied, and all other charges paid.

The Government demand absorbs thus nearly 1/3 rd of the net gains of cultivation, and under these circumstances it cannot be a matter of surprise that uncertain rain-fall and changes of price force the cultivating classes to borrow under great disadvantages. It has been estimated that there are some 22,000 persons engaged in the business of money-lending and retail sale of goods to the agricultural classes in these four Districts. This is a much larger proportion than what is found all over India. Throughout British India, with a population of 190 millions, the number of money-dealers, including Bankers, money-changers, and money-lenders, is 2½ lacs, or 1 in 700 of the population, while in these Districts the proportion is 1 in 150. Along with these facts, it is to be noted that there is an utter absence of all thriving commercial and manufacturing industries, and that the resource of available arable land is admittedly exhausted in these Districts. We have thus a poor soil afflicted with scanty and irregular rains, inhabited by a sparse population, for the most part agricultural and uneducated, with no openings for labour save an exhausted soil, with average holdings of less than 10 acres per each head of family, burdened with a payment of state demand which represents 1/3rd of their net gains, forced to be content with a hand-to-mouth subsistence represented by a maximum of 60 rupees for a family, and involved in heavy bonds of debt under circumstances beyond their control to a numerous mass of small creditors, largely foreign in their domicile, and not prepared to take up the cultivation of land on their own account. These are the salient features of the social and economical condition of the people which it is necessary to bear in mind, while discussing the question of the best method of relief.

It is no wonder that people so circumstanced have made little or no progress during the last 30 or 40 years that they have enjoyed peace under a settled Government. The best and most unfailing test of prosperity is that afforded by the increase of population, and their ability to bear up against bad years. The results of the recent census as compared with the census of 1872 afford a safe basis of comparison of such a character that no exception can be taken to it. If this test be applied, it will be seen that in the four Districts with which we are at present concerned, the loss of life and decrease of population during the last famine is something frightful to contemplate. The following statement of figures will convey this impression more adequately than it is in the power of words to express.

Name Of District	Population 1872	Population 1881	Decrease
Poona	907,235	859,088	48,147
Nagar	773,938	742,038	31,900
Sholapoor	662,986	578,155	84,831
Satara	1,116,050	1,010,385	105,665
Total	3,460,209	3,189,666	270,563

These figures show that there has been a loss in these four Districts of $2^1/_2$ lacs of souls, and if to these be added the loss represented by the absence of the normal growth in ten years which would be $^1/_2$ per cent, or nearly 80 thousand, we have a decrease of $3^1/_4$ lacs, or 10 per cent of the population in 10 years. The other Districts of the Deccan show equally sad results, as will be seen from the following statement.

Name of District	Population 1872	Population 1881	Decrease
Belgaum	938,760	834,705	104,055
Dharwar	988,037	926,680	61,357
Kaladgi	816,037	667,309	148,728
Total	2,712,834	2,428,694	314,140

These figures are for entire Zillas, and represent the average of the several Talukas. The proportion of the arrested growth will be best ascertained from the figures of those districts where the pressure of famine was not felt, as in the Konkan Districts of Ratnagiri, Kolaba, and Tanna, which had a total population of 2,216,965 in 1872, and are now found to have this number increased to 2,278,703, or an increase of 62,000, which represents an increase of $1/3$ per cent every year in the poorest of the Districts. Owing to the famine, there has been thus a loss or decrease of 7 lacs of souls in the whole Presidency, and including the Native States, the total loss to be set to the account of famine comes to about 10 lacs, on our side of India. This is not a pleasing picture to contemplate, at the same time there is nothing to be gained by hiding the truth.

The loss of cattle which represents the only tangible wealth of the agricultural classes has also to be taken into account. For some reasons not yet satisfactorily explained, the last census, unlike its predecessor, did not include the statistics of cattle. We have, however, the records of the Survey Department which furnish these figures for many Talookas, where the re-assessments were introduced after the famine. In the Dharwar Talooka, for instance, while the population showed a fall-off from 84,872 in 1848 to 79,414 in 1879, the loss of agricultural cattle and milch-cows was respectively 29 and 52 per cent in 30 years, the figures being 22,646 agricultural cattle and 42,333 cows and buffallows in 1847, as against 15,920 and 20,073 in 1879-80. In the old Nurgoonda Talooka, the fall-off in population was from 21,431 to 16,208, the loss in agricultural cattle was 33 per cent, and in non-agricultural cattle it was 66 per cent; the detailed figures being 3,775 of the former and 5,471 of the latter in 1859-60, as against 2,546 and 1,819 respectively in 1879-80. In Moolgund Peta, Dumbal Talooka, the loss of human lives in 18 years was 12 per cent, while the loss of agricultural and non-agricultural cattle was nearly 60 per cent. In the Mishricote or Kalghati Talooka, the loss of agricultural cattle was 33 percent in 30 years. These Talookas are selected from the Dharwar District, which is justly regarded as being the most prosperous portion of the Presidency, and the heart of cotton producing districts.

As regards the sheep, ponies, and horses, the fall-off has been, if possible, still more marked, being in many places tantamount to the total extinction of these forms of agricultural wealth. These figures for Dharwar, which happen to be the only ones available for purposes of comparison, justify the most gloomy anticipation for the much poorer districts of the Deccan proper, and the reluctance of Government to furnish statistics in regard to the loss of cattle, though injurious to its best interests, can be to some extent explained by reason of the frightful decrease which detailed statistics would have revealed.

No wonder that a peasantry so situated is inextricably involved in debt. In 12 villages of the Parner Talooka of the Ahmednagar District, it was found after detailed inquiry instituted by the Deccan Riots Commissioners on the spot, that while the revenue of these villages was about 25,000 Rs., the debts of the cultivating classes approximately reached the total of 2 lacs. In the villages of the Satara collectorate, with a total of 15,000 Rupees as annual revenue, the debts came up to Rs.180,000. These figures represent the state of things as it existed before the famine. The Riots Commissioners have unanimously stated that about 1/3rd of the agricultural population was hopelessly involved in debt, the average indebtedness being estimated at 18 times the assessment on the holdings. Since then, the land has been visited by three years' famine, and it can easily be anticipated that the miserable condition of the Ryots must have been greatly aggravated by the horrors of that time. We cannot be, therefore, far wrong in estimating the present situation to be fairly represented if we calculate that at the least from 50 to 60 per cent of the Ryots, or from 3 to 4 lacs of peasant proprietors are hopelessly involved in debt, which would, according to the Riots Commissioners' estimate, amount to a total of nearly 4 crores of Rupees, being considerably more than the total gross value of their agricultural produce for one year.

We hope thus to have shown, as far as official figures accessible to the public enabled us to do, what the exact economical condition of the country at the present moment is. From 50 to 60 per cent of the agriculturists are involved in debt to about 5 per cent of the Brahmin and Bania classes, the amount of the debt is four crores of rupees, and the assets, as represented by the net gains of agricultural industry, are about two crores, from which the Government assessment and other state demands, being about 30 per cent of the net gains, are to be paid. All other avenues for industry are closed under foreign competition, and even the resource of agriculture is, under present circumstances, exhausted by reason of the absorption of the waste lands, and the loss of cattle. Relief measures to be effective must take account of all these diverse conditions. During the debates on the Deccan Agriculturists Relief Bill in 1879, all these circumstances were fully brought out before the Legislature and the Executive Government, and the highest authorities held out a hope that along with the legislative remedy, confined chiefly to the action of the judicial courts, great administrative reforms would follow, and complete the remedial work. It is needless in this place to re-capitulate the solemn pledges and assurances held out by Lord Lytton's Government in the course of those debates. Our position in regard to the measures of judicial relief set in operation two years ago has always consistently been to the effect that, while judicial reform was welcome as far as it went, it would be practically ineffective for good if administrative relief on the lines sketched out in the discussions of the bill was not attempted. The malady in its worst forms lies deep in the heart of the political system, and no mere external alleviations or dressings of the surface skin will really prove of any avail. What the country wants, equally with or even more than, cheap and equitable justice, is a diminution of the state burden on the land in a form which will encourage the investment of capital on a large scale, an investment on more advantageous terms to the cultivators of the soil, and a diminution of the pressure of the agricultural population on the land by the opening out of new avenues for labour and industry and surplus capital. We shall examine more in detail what has been done by Government under each of these three heads, and shall point out what remains to be done if full relief is to be given to remedy the helplessness and the crying wants of the country.

First in regard to the reforms of judicial procedure, we do not agree with Mr. Justice West in condemning wholesale the principles and the practical results of the working of the new Act. The Act is admittedly a heroic experiment to be judged by the same standards of public policy which have found recognition in the enactment of a similar measure for the relief of the Irish tenantry this year. Its sole justification consists in the fact that the ordinary law assumes an equality of advantages and intelligence between the insolvent and uneducated Ryot and the thrifty and intelligent Sowcar, which equality as a matter of fact does not exist. The assumption of equality was entirely a fiction of artificial legislation, and as it led to great abuses, it was time enough to correct the mischief by a return to the old conservative native traditions in favour of the protection of the weaker party. Being intended as an experiment, and to some extent an admitted leap in the dark, it must be judged on its own merits after a sufficiently fair trial, which certainly it has not yet received. Judging from our recent sad experience, every one will acknowledge that the modified restrictions on alienation, implied in the abolition of the power to sell lands in the coercive execution of decrees on simple money bonds, is a step in the right direction, so also is the exemption of Ryot's houses and agricultural cattle from liability to sale, and of the Ryot's person from imprisonment for debts. These measures are in conformity with the old native traditions, and may be safely extended to the other provinces also. The requisition of the defendant's attendance in all cases, where formerly the dispensing of it was so scandalously abused in the form of *ex-parte* decrees is also a step in the right direction. The appointment of honorary Moonsiffs for small village areas and of intermediary Conciliators for Talookas is correct in principle, though there are serious defects in the practical working of the provisions relating to them which will be corrected in the course of time by the results of additional experience. There is one evident direction of improvement, already suggested to Government, by some of its most competent advisers, which seeks to raise the status of the Moonsiffs and Conciliators to that of the old Panchayats and Arbitrators of facts, leaving questions of law, which seldom arise in small disputes, to be dealt with by a special professional agency. The principle underlying these institutions is a sound one, as it seeks to associate the better classes of the population in the work of administering justice, and discourages recourse to law without an effort being made to bring parties amicably to face each other before a tribunal of their amicably to face each other before a tribunal of their neighbours. The powers of equitable interference in the matter of allowing instalments both before and after decrees, as well as of cutting down exorbitant rates of interest, will command approval of all who are alive to the actual wants and uncertain resources of the Ryots. The fact is the usury laws were abolished too soon in this country. These laws were out of date in England with its development of trades and manufactures, and yet it took nearly 50 years of agitation before Parliament could be brought to recognize its duties in the matter. Here with no similar preparation, usury laws were abolished under circumstances which were entirely different, and Government has had to retrace its steps with some violence, but without practical injustice, as the courts have ruled that from 12 to 24 per cent interest are reasonable rates. Even the peculiar mode of taking accounts by going behind the bonds to the first transaction is found in actual working to be not so revolutionary a step as one is led to think from first impressions. Properly worked, the provision is found to be practically not unfair to both parties, though it leaves too much discretionary power in the hands of judges for individual mischief in sundry cases. The substitution of revision for appeals, and the exclusion of Vakeels are both questionable reforms, but they are not by any means essential parts of the scheme, and after the first experimental years, the suitors in our Courts may safely be left to their old guarantees for final justice, if they so prefer it. The extension of limitation in agricultural suits is a return to the old law which may safely be made general in its scope all over the country. The provisions regarding insolvency, being unsuited to the habits and instincts of the people, are harmless because they are inoperative. The same may be said about the provision regarding the receipts of payment and periodical accounts. They will continue to be inoperative as long as the percentage of scholars attending schools is so low as one in one hundred of the population. The compulsory registration of all bonds has been so mismanaged that the provisions regarding it might safely be expunged without detracting from the benefits of the general law. We have thus noticed all the more important provisions of the Relief Act. The dislocation and disturbance of credit, attributed to it in anticipation, and to some extent realized in practice, must be admitted to be a serious draw-back, and it can only be hoped that it will be transitory in its operation. Although there is little evidence that this transitory effect has made itself manifest on a large scale, we can well suppose that in a country where credit was already so low, the worst will happen unless Government retraces its steps in respect of its land policy, and by a diminution of its burden and the encouragement of foreign capital, rehabilitates the Ryots with a fresh accession of credit. We have, therefore, no sympathy with those who decry the Act *in toto*, and deny that it is based on any sound principles. At the same time, the mistake that appears to us to have been made by the Government in its original inception is, that too much stress was laid upon its working. The country did sadly require a more elastic and less rigid and costly system of adjudication, but this was only one, and the least crying, of its wants, and it is a public misfortune that the whole energies of Government were devoted in this direction, and no room was left for the appreciation and proper management of the more pressing needs of the country, represented by the absence of capital seeking investment, not only in agriculture, but in other industrial pursuits, and the necessity of lightening the burden of the state demand on land.

That the country sadly needs an accession of capital is a fact admitted on all hands, and the need is so obvious that it strikes even the most superficial observer. Our chief complaint against the relief measures adopted by Government is, that it ignores either expressly, or by implication, this great want of the country, and attributes the mischief so patent exclusively to the improper dealings of the Sowcar. The Deccan Riots Commissioners' Report exhaustively discussed this question, and laid down finally that the profits of the money lender did not appear to them to be any way abnormal or disproportionate to the risks. Where 60 per cent of the population are inveterate borrowers, it can serve no purpose to pass a law against borrowing, which, in the main, is the attitude of Government as represented by its remedial Act. For every single transaction which comes into the civil courts, there are and will be a hundred transactions which will be kept out of court, not that the pressure on the debtor in those hundred cases is more bearable, or the conditions of the loans more equitable, but because the inevitable necessities of their position prevent the more sensible of the Ryots from questioning these dealings, which their good sense teaches them, must be borne with to escape greater evils. The beneficial interference of the Government must, to be useful, direct itself to the provision of facilities which will lighten the pressure of these hundreds of cases which never come into court. The statistics we have furnished above show that the great want of the country is more capital. Excluding the Presidency town, the returns of assessed taxes show that accumulations of surplus income from year to year are measured by lacs when they should be as many crores, under such a settled rule as that which the country now enjoys. One per cent income tax on the English scale is estimated to yield one crore of rupees for the whole of British India, which shows that the taxable income is about one hundred crores of rupees for the whole country. For the four districts of the Deccan, with no large towns and no manufactures or trades, and with a poor soil and uncertain rains, the taxable income cannot be more than a crore of rupees, and of this the portion available for wages must be still more insignificant. The four crores of debt referred to above are mostly of the nature of paper debts, which oppress the solvent Ryot while the insolvent goes scot-free. In this connection, the question will suggest itself what, under these circumstances, can the Government hope to do beyond what it is at present doing in the shape of its great public works and its free customs, and an appeal will be made to theoretical maxims of political economy which prohibit Government interference beyond its proper work of preserving the peace. Our answer to this suggestion is that the Government of India should do what every other Government, which is at the same time intelligent and national, and which does not burden itself with responsibilities which the Government of India has undertaken, is found to do all the world over. The Government, for instance, of England through its Board of Land Commissioners in Ireland has undertaken in its Irish legislation of 1870 and 1881, to advance state funds to enable Irish tenants to buy up on favourable terms waste lands, or the interests of their land-lords with a view to improve their status. Mr. Wedderburn has in his recent communications to the *Bombay Gazette* thrown a flood of light upon this question by summarising from the Blue-Books the results of the experiments made within the last 20 or 50 years in Turkey, Egypt, Russia, Greece, Austria, Prussia, Germany, France, Denmark, and Sweden, in fact in all the bigger and smaller states, by the national Governments to improve the status of their agricultural classes by extending their credit and countenance to private efforts in the shape of rent charge—banks, credit fonciers, credit- agricole, Caisse hypothecare, mortgage-banks, and mutual land credit associations. It cannot be said that in this country there is no capital available in private hands for such enterprises. The steady demand for Government loans at 4 per cent and the stock quotations show that there is a considerable amount of floating capital available, if only Government will lend its countenance to private efforts during their early and experimental existence. Throughout India there are between two and three crores of rupees in deposit in Government Savings

Banks, and at least twenty crores of Rupees of Government loans are held by natives. The Port- Trust bonds at 4 per cent have found a ready demand in Bombay. It cannot, therefore, be said with any justice that there is no available floating capital in the country. However, owing to the land policy of Government it is not found convenient by the capitalist classes to risk their savings on investments in the improvement of land by advancing loans to the agriculturist classes. In the words of Mr. Wedderburn, (we quote from memory) we have on the one hand a burnt-up soil panting for every drop of water, and side by side with it we have dark thick clouds eager to burst with their treasures. The state however, with its land policy sets up a huge mountain barrier preventing the clouds from reaching the lands lest per-adventure its monopoly of land might be endangered. This obstructiveness is in its own permanent interests a very suicidal policy. The scheme of establishing agricultural banks for the Moffusil has been before Government for more than 20 years. During that interval, the self-governed countries of Europe have worked wonders, although the condition of the agricultural classes there did not stand so sorely in need of such help as its poor tenantry in India require. The Public Works undertaken by Government are good of their sorts, but unless they are backed up by agencies which will increase the credit and status of the Ryots, the spectacle of canals running waste for the Ryot's inability to use them with advantage, which so astonishes the stranger in India, will be too common to excite surprise. Every industry is starved for want of capital which will enable Indian labour and Indian materials to organise themselves so as to compete on equal terms with more advanced countries. The working of the Relief Act in its exemption of agricultural suits wholly or partially from Court Fees, and the charges of its new Courts and additional establishments represents a net loss of between 3 or 4 lacs of rupees a year of Government Revenue in the four Deccan Districts. With the same money as a guarantee fund, the Government might safely calculate upon enabling private capitalists to advance between one or two crores of rupees at moderate interest, so as to extricate the Ryots from their present difficulties, and start them on their own feet. The usual rate of interest which obtains at present in the dealings between the petty Sowcars and the Ryots to whom they are accessible, is abnormally high chiefly because the wages fund is so low, while the demands upon it are so numerous. If this capital were doubled or trebled as it might well be, it would lead to a fall of interest, and if its repayment were spread over a long term of years, it would be easy to provide, besides a moderate interest, a sinking fund, and extricate the Ryots from their load of debts. The Government has, as a first step, sanctioned inquiries into the existing debts of the agricultural classes with a view to their amicable settlement on a wholesale scale before the parties go to law. The defect of the present Act is that it takes up the individual Ryot and the Sowcar when their disagreements drive them into the Courts. These are generally hopeless cases, where no amount of judicial adjustment on correct principles can prove of the least use, for the Ryot has not the money wherewith to pay the just amount due, and having quarrelled with his long-standing creditor, he finds no resource left to him between becoming insolvent to which he is disinclined, and throwing himself into the hands of a more unscrupulous dealer. This is a radical defect, and it cannot be remedied by any manipulation of the Act. The inquiries undertaken by Government must end in disappointment, because while the Sowcar is ready to accept a settlement if cash were offered to him, he is naturally unwilling to throw up his chances for no immediate advantage. In two villages where such inquiries were undertaken it was found that 178 Ryot families obtained from their land gross produce worth nearly 20,000 Rupees, and they had to pay out of this some 500 Rs. for the expenses of cultivation, thus leaving 15,000 Rupees as their net gain. Of this money, they had to pay Rs. 4,600 as government assessment or nearly one-third of their net gains and the rest was all swallowed by the interest charge on 50,000 Rupees of their secured and unsecured debts. What is wanted under these circumstances is, that Government should encourage, and even guarantee private effort wherever it is willing to undertake the loan business with agriculturists on less exacting terms so as to have a margin for the Ryots subsistence. Government cannot directly undertake this business for itself, as the experience of the failure of the Tagai system has abundantly demonstrated. The principle of guaranteeing private efforts for a time is recognised by the Indian Government in its dealings with railways and canals, and its subsidies to the great overland and coasting steamer companies. With three or four lacs spent for the first few years to ensure private loan companies against risk, a most wholesome change will be brought about. The business of money-lending will continue pretty much in the same hands as now. Small Sowcars would borrow from the Banks the funds they required on easier terms, and this would regulate their loans to the agriculturists. All that the Government need do is to ascertain in a rough way the existing debts of its tenantry. When the debts were so ascertained, the guaranteed private banks would advance the sums settled to the Ryots on terms varying from 6 to 12 per cent, and Government would thus be able for such a small consideration to provide easily loans to thousands of people who should thus be better enabled to pay off from year to year the instalments fixed over such a long term, as to ensure the discharge of the debt in most cases without fail out of the sinking-fund payments. The margin between existing and possible rates of interests is sufficient to allow of this operation. The advantages of substituting a wholesale settlement in the place of individual inquiries now undertaken by the courts, mostly in very bad cases, have been abundantly illustrated in the settlement of alienations and boundary disputes. For a long time, and hopelessly Government contented itself with the piece-meal system of inquiry into Inams and disputed boundaries. The work made no progress. The cost of establishments more than covered the gains, and the results were so unsatisfactory as to fill the whole land with heart-burning and discontent. A change of policy occurred after the mutinies, and Government found that the work of settlement, when it anticipated disputes by a moderate compromise, was much more thorough and effective. A debt settlement commission woking with full powers, and with due regard to fixed principles, will lead to a similar result by ascertaining the amount of existing indebtedness for whole Talookas and Districts, without waiting for the time when disputes arise, and demoralize both the Sowcar and the Ryot. In the absence of such an inquiry, the piece- meal method of working now in vogue may go on to the end of time without any body being the better for it; for as soon as a Ryot is white-washed, he is again driven into debt by his necessities, and the process has no end. With the results of such an inquiry to guide them, both Government and the lending and borrowing classes will know exactly how they stand, and this knowledge will encourage foreign capital to seek investment in land by advancing loans to the Ryots on more advantageous terms. Besides guaranteeing against risks and ascertaining the existing debts, the Government will only be called upon to facilitate the recovery of the instalments agreed upon by the same agency which collects its land revenue, and under the protection of the same processes to ensure punctual payments. These are not exorbitant concessions looking to the great interests at stake. The preset times especially are favourable for such an undertaking. Even if Indian capitalists prove unable to advance all that is needed, there is an abundance of capital in England which will come to our rescue if only the guarantees before mentioned were secured. The Government of India has become fully alive to its duty of encouraging home industries. Money is cheap beyond all former precedent, and the advisability of taking immediate action in this direction has commended itself to the highest authorities. We have the best authority to state that the matter has attrracted the attention of the Secretary of State, and it has been referred by him to the local Government for practical consideration. The history of what has been attempted with success in other countries has now been placed fully before us, and the bill to amend the Relief Act is before the Legislature. There are capitalists in Bombay who have expressed their willingness to advance one crore of rupees in the establishment of Agricultural Banks, if Government on its part is prepared to ascertain existing debts, to guarantee 4 per cent interest, and afford facilities for recovery. These favourable circumstances will never recur again. It is not only agriculture which stands in need of such help. Every other industry, especially in the moffusil, stands more or less in need of similar help. The difficulties, however, in the way of directing joint-stock private agencies in these channels, and at the same time ensuring them against all risks, are at present very great owing to the absence of skill and knowledge, and the fact that Government is the sole customer for stores, and its own departments carry on the great Public Works of the country. There is no doubt, however, that the impetus given to agricultural pursuits will in the end communicate itself to other industries, and lead to a many-sided development of the country's resources in a way which cannot at present be anticipated.

Just as mere judicial reform has been shown to be likely to end in disappointment, as long as the crying need for more capital is not recognised and attended to, it must be laid down that no action that Government might take in this latter direction will lead to any permanent beneficial result as long as the pressure of land revenue under the existing system of assessment continues unabated. Notwithstanding what political economists in their love of doctrinaire thoroughness may assert to the contrary, it has been found by bitter experience that no country has hitherto made the least progress in civilization where the land was not held in full proprietary right by the people to whom it belonged. Indian traditions under British rule have departed widely from old native customs in this respect with the results which we now deplore. The state monopoly of land and its right to increase the assessment at its own discretion are the two most prominent obstacles in the way of the growth of our material prosperity. Cultivated land everywhere owes all its advantages as much to human efforts as to natural resources, and the tendency everywhere is to increase the one and diminish the other. The Government of India, however, has for a long time resolutely set its face against all proposals which in the most distant way might loosen its hold upon the land. Between 1862 and 1865, the Secretary of State in Council had made up their minds that the time had come for the extension of the permanent settlement to all the more settled districts of this Presidency, where nearly the whole available land has been brought under cultivation. These Despatches of the Secretary of State were set at naught by the passive resistance of the Government of India, resting presumably on the ground that it would lead to a loss of prospective revenue, the temptation of which the Government could not forgo. Twenty years have elapsed since then, and the cry from all quarters of the country, from Oudh, from the N.W. Provinces, from Madras, and notably from this Presidency, has the same burden of lamentation and misery. We have for the last fifteen years, in good and in evil report, exposed the failure of the present system, and advocated a permanent settlement of land as the only alternative open to Government, by the side of which reform all other agencies sink into insignificance. The only guarantee against excessive enhancement, which is found effective where land is held in private right, is the competition of the land-lords among themselves. There is no place for this guarantee under the Indian system, because the land is the monopoly of the State, single and individual. The absence of such a check has resulted in wholesale enhancements all over the country to an extent of which the Government itself is now ashamed. All the prophecies about the permanent continuance of the country's agricultural prosperity have been falsified, and the sad fact has to be faced that the land has lost all value as an investment, except in a few favoured localities. The inconsistency of official advocacy in this matter was never better illustrated than by the fact, that the same Government which opposes the permanent settlement as regards lands held by its native subjects, is ever willing to afford every facility to the English settlers by allowing them to purchase the fee simple of their lands in

Assam and in other parts of India, and by bringing its pressure to bear upon the Maharaja of Mysore to grant a similar boon to the Mysore planters. Human nature is everywhere the same, and it cannot logically be maintained that the same incentives and guarantees, which the English planters require in their own interests, are out of place in the case of Native farmers. If possible, these latter, wanting as they do sadly in the spirit of pushing enterprise and cool forethought which distinguish the European, need to be more gently dealt with by a Government which seeks with paternal solicitude to elevate its subjects. We are sick of the cry so invariably raised on such occasions about the habitual improvidence, idleness, and thriftlessness of the Indian peasantry. The inquiries undertaken by the Deccan Riots Commission have established the fact beyond all doubt that the Ryot cannot be fairly charged with these defects of character. As long as the precariousness of the seasons and the rack-renting policy of the settlements continue to damp all their energies, what can be expected of a peasantry which finds, taking bad and good seasons together, that the revenue demand absorbs 1/3rd of their net gains. Although the good intentions of the Secretary of State were frustrated for the time by the passive opposition of the Government of India, yet the hard necessities of the case have at last prevailed and succeeded, in securing a recognition for the unwelcome fact that the revenue policy of the Government is responsible to a great extent for the present condition of the agrarian classes. Even before the Riots Commission made their report, the Government of Bombay were forced to admit their mistake, and reduce the enhanced assessments which they had sanctioned only a few years before. The effect of these reductions was minimised by the manipulation of the Survey Department, which persuaded the local Government against its own conviction to screw up the enhancements in the Southern Maratha Country in the same unconscionable manner, as though nothing had happened to disturb the success of their work. The Deccan Roits Commissioner's report at last opened the eyes of the Government of India to the enormity of the mistake which had been committed, and the latest correspondence on the subject between the Indian Governments, local and Imperial, and the Secretary of State contains distinct admissions that the survey system of assessment is radically defective, and that the enhanced assessments erred on the side of being over-excessive. During the debates on the Relief Bill, distinct pledges were given that, along with judicial reform, a great change of system in the Revenue arrangements would be inaugurated. Like too many pledges given by the same Government, this solemn assurance remains to this day unfulfilled. The only concession made in this direction is a promised reduction of the enhanced assessment to a maximum limit of 20 per cent for three years, and even this Resolution has not yet been acted upon. Coming as it does after the strict enforcement of famine arrears by the Government of Sir Richard Temple, this promised relief will not reach many thousands of poor Ryots who have been sold out of their lands and homes. No such half measures will suffice, however, under present circumstances. The Government must make up its mind to be generous for once, and by conceding the benefit of a permanent settlement make some amends for its past mistakes. The fear of losing its hold on prospective revenues need not fetter its hand; for by guaranteeing a permanent settlement fixed in kind, and commutable into money at long intervals according to permanent changes in prices, the Government will not have to forgo the smallest fraction of their just claim. If on account of general prosperity, there is a rise of prices, the money commutation of its grain assessment will also rise in the same proportion. If prices fall, the assessment in money will also fall in amount, and thus will not press very hard upon the Ryots. There will be no violent change of system and disturbance of existing institutions; at the same time, the Ryots and the middle classes will look upon their lands as their own property, which under present circumstances it is found impossible to induce them to do. All improvements in husbandry suggested by science and experience pre-suppose a great expenditure of capital to be invested in land. The magic of property can alone induce people to incur such expenditure. Neither private Sowcars,nor joint-stock land-banks, will venture to advance capital to sink wells, or use manures, and throw dams across streams, unless the Ryots to whom these advances are to be made possess full proprietary rights over their lands. If the land-banks have succeeded in other countries so well, most of this success must be undoubtedly laid to the credit of the fact that the peasants in those countries are not tenants of the State, but own the lands they cultivate in absolute right. Without such a guarantee of full property, all endeavours to ameliorate the condition of the Ryots must fail to produce any but a temporary benefit.

Judicial reform, increased banking and loan facilities, and the guarantee of a permanent settlement, these are the three-fold elements in that organic reconstitution of our agricultural economy which, as they hang upon each other, each receiving strength and coherence from the other, will alone rescue the country from its present sad plight. The Government has too long allowed itself to be blinded to the iniquity of an arrangement by which more than the full weight of its burdens is made to fall upon the least helpful and the most suffering of its subjects. The easy facilities of collecting a large revenue have lulled its conscience into oblivion, and persuaded it to regard that the millions who clamour for bread will be satisfied with the gift of stones in the shape of legislative enactments intended to patch up the surface rents without infusing new life blood and strength into the system which is gaping with its deep wounds. Now that the stern irony of fate has dashed its day-dreams aside, it may be hoped that the fresh insight Government has obtained into the real nature of the disease in the body politic, will induce it to make one great effort to remedy past wrongs, and restore contentment and prosperity to a part of the country which has such claims upon its consideration. For nearly two hundred years the Deccan Districts were the home of all that was great and hopeful in the decaying fabric of the old Empire. The spirit still remains intact, and though its outward symptoms are too often mistaken by superficial observers for restless ambition, its people have a great future before them in the coming times. All that they demand is freedom from the oppressive dead-weight of revenue settlements, which paralyse their energies, and dissipate their strength in the hopeless struggle to better themselves in the social scale. Let the weight of this heavy hand be lightened, and the inner springs, activity, and elastic power, will surge up in an upward movement of material well-being, which will heal all past sores, and bind the Deccan in the golden chain of gratitude to a power that helped it to accomplish a permanent liberation from its present sad condition.

10

REVIEW OF DADABHAI NAOROJI ON POVERTY OF INDIA*

Professor Dadabhai Naoroji has followed up his investigation into the subject of the Poverty of India by a letter addressed to the Secretary of State containing an analysis of the crop returns in weight and value of the Punjab Province, and has thus obtained an inductive confirmation of his well-reasoned deductive conclusions regarding the material condition of India on the strength of official figures. Those who are practically acquainted with the methods, or rather absence of method, in accordance with which these statistical crop returns are compiled from year to year, do not require to be told that they are always cooked up by the village authorities to suit the pleasures of the higher powers, and err generally on the side of being hopelessly in advance of actual facts. Such as they are, however, they have been made use of to support pet official theories, and Professor Dadabhai has done right yeoman's service in meeting the enemy on his own lists, and removing the veil from these mysteries of Indian administration. We wish Professor Dadabhai, as a Bombay citizen, had taken up the Bombay returns, but it may well be Professor Dadabhai judged better in grappling the bull by the horns, and demolishing the returns of the model Province, which

---

*JPSS, April 1882, Vol.IV, No.4.

also had the rare advantage of presenting most ambitiously complete information in regard not only to the agricultural, but the manufacturing and mining wealth of its inhabitants. The method observed by the Professor in this investigation may be briefly described as the method of averages. The acreage under each individual crop in the different districts of the Province is pretty accurately given in these returns. This acreage is multiplied by the average gross yield which varies from district to district and the total thus obtained is multiplied by an average of the prices which also differ from place to place. The final product gives the value of the crop. From this total the Professor deducts first the percentage of seeds which vary with the crops, and he makes a further deduction for middle values, as the prices given in the official tables are always the dearest prices and of the best quality of the produce. With these deductions, the final valuation for each crop is arrived at, and these valuations are then added up. In the case of inferior grains which are for the most part raised as much for human as for animal support a deduction of two-thirds of the acreage is made in anticipation to prevent all mistakes. The fodder of cattle represented by the stalks and kadbi are excluded from both sides of the account. Professor Dadabhai takes no account of them as sources of national wealth, nor does he deduct anything on account of food required by the cattle maintained therefrom. This elaborate calculation results in the following startling figures. The total value of the gross agricultural products of the Punjab with an extent of 100,000 square miles in the 32 districts included in it and inhabited by a total population of 17½ millions, and paying a land tax of 2 crores of rupees is thus seen to be about 27 crores, which means an average yield of 12½ per acre, the total being about 22 millions of acres under cultivation. The chief heads of the food crops or other agricultural produce of the Punjab with their acreage, quantities and values will be seen from the following summary.

PUNJAB 1876-77
Summary of Produce of all Districts.

Produce	Acres	Total Quantity. lbs.	Average Per Acre. lbs.	Total value Rs.	Average price per Re. 1. lbs.
Rice	708,688	541,492,369	796	2,25,35,693	20.12
Wheat	6,609,497	5,332,813,517	840.4	9,17,42,419	53.48
Makai (Indian Corn)	1,084,339	1,593,872,255	1500	2,33,01,266	60.4
Jow (Barley)	1,874,217	883,781,444	503	1,06,78,175	82.76
Gram	2,272,236	1,417,173,807	645	1,86,72,194	75.89
Inferior Grains	6,534,963	3,169,169,607	510.5	4,54,14,114	69.78
Poppy (Opium)	12,348	154,550	12.51	3,86,375	.4 { 2-1/2 Rs. perl lb Paid by Govt.
Tobacco	71,867	60,804,785	846	48,32,541	12.58
Turmeric	4,130	677,320	164 (dry)	67,732	10
Coriander Seed	6,934	2,288,220	330 (")	1,43,014	16
Ginger	286	58,630	205 (")	8,376	7
Chillies	23,518	3,800,700 (dry)	{ 808 (Green) 161.6 (dry)	4,75,100	8
Other kinds of drugs and spices	35,074	11,574,420	330	8,26,744	14
Oil seeds	846,679	325,730,071	392	1,20,64,076	27
Cotton	668,876	70,013,890	105	1,23,54,344	5.66
Hemp	51,260	18,770,866	366	9,38,543	20
Kassamba (Safflower)	24,708	988,320	40 (dry)	3,95,328	2.5
Indigo	129,465	4,070,941	31.44	30,53,205	1 1/3
Vegetables	256,800	{ 1,068,002,055	4753	1,06,80,020	100 Green Veget.
		78,966,000	2460	25,47,290	31 potato
Tea	8,884	832,864	96	2,84,288	3 { Average of 4
Sugar	391,680	237,831,405	646	1,78,55,427	15 { qualities
Total	21,616,420			27,72,56,963	

To this total of agricultural products Professor Dadabhai adds 4 crores of manufactured wealth, the valuation for which as given in the official statements is accepted by the Professor with the necessary deduction for the value of the material worked up in its natural condition, as this last is already included in the total of 27 crores. To avoid all risk of errors, the Professor adds 3½ crores to these totals and finds that Punjab annually yields in gross produce to its 17 millions of inhabitants 34 crores of Rupees, or 20 Rupees a head of the population. The minimum cost of maintenance in bare food and clothing, barring all contingencies and luxuries, is ascertained by a careful analysis to be 34 Rupees per head, and we are thus brought to face the fact that in the model Province the average produce per head is 40 per cent less than the minimum consumption. The two ends can only be met by the shift of enforced starvation, or living below the standard of necessary support, of a vast majority of the inhabitants.

We may as well notice in this place that the official calculations of gross value do not vary much from those elaborated by Professor Dadabhai. Including straw and grain used for the support of animals the total value of agricultural produce is put down at 35 crores, and the gross income of the agricultural classes is estimated to be 27 Rupees per head. The official statement, however, allows only 200 sheers of food as enough to maintain a native of Punjab throughout the year which comes sufficiently near the ½ lb ration of the famine regime. It is only on this calculation that it evolves a surplus profit of 15 crores as available in the hands of the agricultural population. Professor Dadabhai doubles the rate allowed by the official figures for necessary consumption and the result is that there is a heavy deficit instead of a fancied surplus. We shall extract in this place from the official return which is available to our hand a few illustrative figures regarding the agricultural wealth of this Presidency. The total quantity and value of food grain crops in this Presidency is put down at 45 million maunds valued at 12½ crores, of non-food crops 11½ crores, of straw 2½ crores, and of live stock $1\frac{1}{2}$ crores. This means a total of 28 crores for a population of 16 millions which gives a return of 17 Rupees per head of the population. Bombay has the unenviable distinction of not being able to produce food grains enough to maintain its own population at the comparatively low rate assumed by the officials of 225 lbs. per head per year or less than $\frac{3}{4}$ lb. per day. This is less even than the famine ration. At the rate of one pound per head the produce is barely sufficient even to maintain the agricultural population estimated at 60 per cent of the total inhabitants. It is true the returns take no account of the alienated lands, which come to about 6 million acres and yield possibly a return of 6 crores of rupees. Even if this addition were made, Bombay would still show a considerable deficiency of produce over necessary consumption. The average income per head is only $14\frac{1}{2}$ lbs in this Presidency, while the land tax is on an average 9 per cent of the value of the total agricultural produce. Deducting the cost of seed and labour, and the maintenance of live and dead stock, the land tax would represent a charge of 25 per cent upon the net yield. Excepting the last deduction we have been simply quoting our figures from the official tables, and the picture they present of the miserable condition of our agricultural classes is too frightful to contemplate. Need we wonder that it takes away Professor Dadabhai's spirits out of him to dwell on the misery of this desperate condition of the vast majority of our population. Professor Dadabhai's letter naturally filled the India Office authorities with alarm, and Mr. Juland Danvers undertook to dispel the gloom. After questioning the soundness of the principle of averages, Mr. Danvers objected to the Professor's calculations on two distinct grounds, firstly that he made no-allowance for straw and the annual increase of agricultural stock, and secondly that the Professor took no account of the income of the shopkeeping, mercantile, and propertied and unproductive classes. Professor Dadabhai retorted on the first head that he did make some allowance for straw and cattle fodder, and that if full allowance was to be made on this head, it would only swell both sides of the account. As to agricultural stock there is no increase, from year to year the stock is decreasing owing to various causes, notably the contraction of waste lands, and the substitution of natural agents for pack animals. As regards the second objection, Professor Dadabhai replied that in an investigation of the annual income derived from the land, the income of shop-keeping, propertied and unproductive classes can possibly find no place. These classes produce no wealth, they only distribute with more or less fairness the wealth already produced. We subscribe our adhesion to the soundness of the principle thus enunciated. Even if Mr. Danvers' objection be allowed, it is to be noted that in the general account which the adoption of his principle will necessitate, the drain of Indian wealth in respect of the home charges and remittances and interest representing at the lowest average 25 to 30 crores of rupees represented by the annual deficiency of our imports over exports will swallow all the surplus he can imagine, and leave still a wide chasm gaping at his feet. It is often urged that India gets in return the highest talent and integrity, and the cheapest capital for this sacrifice, and that the balance is restored in her favour. Professor Dadabhai notices this aspect of the case in a short but very suggestive paper on the moral drain of India represented by the fact that all the talent, organization, and integrity is withdrawn from it just when it is qualified by experience to prove most helpful. We trust these brief observations will suffice to recommend these papers to the thoughtful attention of our readers. It is a great relief to us that Professor Dadabhai who cannot be suspected of any interested or partisan motives and whose qualification to speak with authority on this subject is too well known, should have with evident grief and reluctance been forced by the enormity of the evils to emphasize his exposition of the present system against which we have ourselves contended so long through good and evil report, and so hopelessly. Sooner or later the glamour of conquest and selfish advancement will cease to dazzle and blind the conscience of the English nation, and we feel that when the day of reckoning comes, the tale of past negligence will startle even the most optimistic complacency.

11

EMANCIPATION OF SERFS IN RUSSIA*

Now that the Governments of England and India have seriously taken in hand the task of relieving the Agricultural Classes from their heavy depression, it cannot fail to be of use to note the progress of a similar Emancipation undertaken in European Russia about twenty years ago, and which, so far as one can judge from Official Reports, has been attended with great success. European Russia, including the Kingdom of Poland, the Grand Duchy of Finland, the Baltic Provinces, and the Trans-Caucasian Regions, covers an area of nearly 2,000,000 square miles of Territory, inhabited by a population of seventy-two millions, including the Cossacks and Kerghiz Hordes. The extent of Russia proper is about 100,000 square miles, and its population is sixty millions. Of this number, nearly eighty per cent. constitute the Rural population, and about ten per cent are Urban, including the Nobility and the Clergy. About seven per cent represent the Military element of the population, which gives to Russia its position as a First Class European Power. For administrative purposes, European Russia proper is divided into forty-five Districts. One-third of the whole cultivable area is Crown Land, one-fifth of the same area belongs to the great Landlords who number about a Hundred Thousand Families, one-fifth belongs to the Peasantry who number about forty-eight

*Published in *JPSS*, October 1882, Vol.V, No.2, and in *Essays*

millions in all, and the rest belongs to the Church, Mines, Military Colonists, Royal Appanage Lands, *etc.* Of the total of forty-eight millions of Peasants, nearly one half, or twenty-five millions, were attached as serfs in 1861 to Crown and Appanage Lands. The great Emancipation Act of 1861 was not directly intended to apply to this large number, but the scope of relief was extended from time to time, till there is now no Serf left on Russian soil. They are at present, like the Survey Occupants of this Presidency, Peasant tenants at fixed rents called *Obrok*, payable to the Government, and revisable every twenty years, and may alienate their Holdings subject to this liability, at a fixed price, which represents the capitalized value of the rent at five per cent. As long as this *Obrok* is paid, the State Tenant's land cannot revert to the State.

The Emancipation Act of 1861, sought chiefly to elevate the condition of the Peasants who cultivated the private lands of the Nobility and Gentry, and made up a total of nearly twenty-two millions of Serfs. Serfdom, like Caste and Slavery, was originally founded on the great fact of Foreign Conquest. Serfdom, as a recognized Institution, was introduced in Russia about the end of the Sixteenth Century, by a Law of 1592, which prevented the Peasants from migrating from one estate to another, without their Lord's permission, and attached them to the soil in a way to secure their transfer with the land. Peter the Great introduced the Poll-tax in Russia, and made the Lords responsible for the tax due from the Peasants on their lands. The abuse of powers, so natural under these circumstances, soon degraded the Land Serfs to the still lower depth of landless Bondsmen and life Convicts working at the Mines. The landed Gentry owned in all, in 1861, about three hundred million acres, of which one-third was in the occupation of the Serfs, and of the two-thirds in the occupation of the Landlords, one half was mortgaged with the State or private Creditors. In consideration of their free occupation of one hundred million acres, the Serfs were compelled to serve a fixed number of days, which was generally three days in the week, on the two-thirds in the occupation of their

Landlords, or paid them rents or services instead. The Serf could hold no property of his own, and although remedial measures were introduced from time to time, since the commencement of this Century, it was not till 1847, that the Serf could buy his personal freedom from his Landlord, or buy even Waste Lands from his private savings, except in his Landlord's name. The Serf had no Civil Rights against his master, the latter could flog him at his pleasure, or banish him to distant Plantations, or send him into the Army. When the noble Landlord required a loan, he mortgaged his Serfs with his land and cattle. The Serfs on Crown and Appanage Lands were in much the same condition as private Serfs, in respect of the incapacity of free locomotion and Civil Rights, only their rents were lower and less variable. Such was the condition of the unprivileged Rural Classes throughout Russia proper scarcely twenty years ago. Of the forty-eight millions of Serf population, representing ten millions adult males, attached to Crown, Appanage, and private lands, seven millions of Serfs were in pawn with mortgagees, 7,50,000 Serfs were domestic servants or land-less Bondsmen, and 5,00,000 were employed in the Mines in 1861. These ten million. serfs cultivated one hundred millions of acres of land. Each adult male Serf enjoyed thus the usufruct of ten acres of land, which agrees with the average holding of an Indian Ryot in this Presidency. It was in respect of this immense population that the late Emperor Alexander promulgated the great Charter of Russian Liberty, and completed their Emancipation between 1861 and 1869.

It will be interesting to note the chief features of this Reform, and to study the details of the method by which it was accomplished. The grant of Civil and Personal Liberty, and the assurance of this independence by securing to the free Peasant a minimum of property, represented by the allotment of a parcel of land in tenancy or free-hold purchased with Public Funds, and a recognized voice in the management of local affairs, these were the three-fold and principal features of this great Reform. Domestic Serfdom, the right of the master to the control of the person of the Serf, was first abolished without any reservation or compensation, except that the Poll-tax, which the master used to pay for his Serfs, was now transferred to the Emancipated Serf. Between 1861 and 1863, the Emancipated domestic Serf was required to pay to his master this Poll-tax of five shillings for each male, and four shillings for each female. After 1863, the freed Serf paid his own Poll-tax direct to the State.

In regard to the allotment of land held by the Serfs on their master's estates, and the right of the latter to receive Quit Rents and Services from them, the question was not so easy of solution. As a rule, the allotments were one-third of the whole estate, and never exceeded one half. For allowing the Serfs to enjoy the usufruct of this land, with the right of pasture on the commons, and of cutting timber and fuel for building and burning purposes, the masters either received rent on this allotment, or more generally required the Serfs to cultivate three days in the week the unallotted or reserved portion. They seldom paid Quit Rent in money. The personal labour which the Serfs gave on their master's land was the usual consideration received by the master from the Serfs attached to his land. In the Industrial Provinces, money rents were more common. It has been estimated that about twenty-five per cent. of the Land Serfs paid Quit Rent varying from 2s. 3d. to 2s. 9d. per acre; the rest rendered services instead.

The Emancipation Committee had first to settle the maximum allotment of the land which was to be made over to the Serf as his private Holding discharged from all burdens, and they had next to determine the amount of compensation which the Serfs, or on their behalf the State, should pay to their masters for the loss of their rents and services. The money rents which ranged from Rupees four to Rupees fifty according to the quality of the land, and the necessities of the master, could be easily ascertained and valued, but the valuation of personal services was not so easy, as these services were of a most miscellaneous variety, and subordinated the Serf to the most ordinary necessities of his master's every-day life. Another source of complication was due to the fact that many of the estates belonging to the Privileged Classes were mortgaged, together with the Serf population on them, to the State, which had advanced about fifty millions Sterling on their security. This condition of affairs furnished, however, the working lever for the action of the State. After much discussion, the final plan adopted by the late Emperor Alexander's Government was a compromise of several more extreme proposals. An average allotment of ten acres was fixed as the size of a Serf Holding. This Holding, together with the Homestead, was ceded in Perpetual Tenancy by the Master to the Serf on terms settled by mutual arrangement, or failing that, on conditions fixed by law, which, however, limited the compulsory occupation of the tenant to nine years. Over and above this right of tenancy, the Serf could compulsorily demand the sale of this allotment with the Homestead on it at a price fixed by mutual agreement, or failing that by the State Officials. The State undertook to provide the Serf with funds to enable him to buy off his master's rights over the allotment. The rights of Personal Service on his master's lands were commuted into a money payment equivalent to the Quit Rent which would have been received, if no service had been rendered, and this Quit Rent was capitalized at a fixed valuation. The Political Rights of the master, and his profits derived from the drudgery of the domestic Serfs, were abolished without compensation. While the Serf's interests were thus advanced, the master was absolved from all liability on account of Imperial and Rural Taxes due from the Serfs, and he had not to pay his Serf's fines, or defend his actions in Civil or Criminal Courts at his own cost as before. The State protected its own Finances by establishing, or rather reviving among the Serfs the Institution of Communal or Cantonal responsibility, *i.e.*, the joint liability of the *Mere* or Village Community. The Allotment and the Quit Rent were all fixed in a lump sum for the Communal units, and the individual Serf was made responsible to the Commune of which he formed part, and each local community of Serfs became in their turn jointly responsible to the State. To borrow an illustration from our Indian Revenue System, the Settlement was made with the collective body of Village Zemindars or Mirasdars, as in the Punjab and North-Western Provinces, and not with the individual Ryot as in this Presidency. The Russian word for Canton or Commune is *Mere*, which has an ethnical and lingual affinity with our Indian Miras.

At first, the change of condition in the Serf's lot was a transfer from the Yoke of a private alien master to that of the collective Commune. The Serf, though emancipated, was not allowed to leave his native Village, or to detach himself from the land without the permission of the heads of the *Mere*, who received the redemption price from the Serf as a condition of his release. In the old Social Polity of Russia, the father, or the head of the family, under whose protection all the subordinate members lived together, had very large powers, and as these Village *Meres* or Communities were most of them settled by the descendants of one family, next to the Lord's power, the Patriarch's authority was all-potent for good or for evil. As may be easily imagined, this power was greatly abused, even to the extent of degrading the purity of family life. The financial interests of the State, as the mortgagee of all the redeemed estates, and the receiver of the Poll-tax, compelled it to lend its countenance to the maintenance of this Patriarchal and Communal system. As a counterpoise to these drawbacks, the new organization set up by the Emancipation Committee greatly strengthened the hands of this Peasant population by the constitution of elective Communal and Canton Councils with the broadest suffrage, and with very extensive powers of Local Self-Government. The Serf, once freed from his Lord's control, and possessed of full Civil and Political Rights, was not likely to submit long and patiently to this Communal restraint, and the process of this second liberation may already be said to have commenced. The disintegration of the old Patriarchal System and domestic oppression may be safely regarded as by no means the least of the beneficial changes inaugurated by the great Emancipation. Between 1861 and

1869, the latest period for which information is available, it appears that about one-third of the adult male Serfs were converted into Perpetual Tenants of their ten acre allotments and Homesteads. The rental these free tenant Serfs pay for their land is fixed in the shape of a Poll-tax, which, when spread over the extent of their Holdings, represents a charge of two Shillings an acre. The State claims the right of reassessing the rentals after twenty years. As will have been seen from the summary given above, the Scheme of Emancipation presented two alternatives, compulsory Perpetual Tenancy, or compulsory Purchase of Free-Hold, as a qualification for elevating the Serf to the condition of a Freeman. A third alternative was also left open to the Serf by which he might accept a quarter of the maximum allotment from his master as a settlement, in compromise of all compulsory relationships. About six hundred thousand Peasants have accepted this alternative, which enables them to dispense with the aid of Government Funds, and the necessity of submitting to the restraints of Communal life upon free locomotion and residence. Out of a total of ten million Serf families, six millions have become purchasers of their allotments, thirty-one per cent of this number became so by their own voluntary choice, and sixty-nine per cent were obliged to purchase by the choice of their old masters, who elected to accept the redemption with State Funds. It appears from detailed statements that the State has advanced fifty-one million Pounds Sterling for the compulsory redemption of thirty-five millions of acres, allotted to about three and a half millions of freed Serfs. The price paid for redemption by the State was about 20s. per acre. In the case of voluntary settlements accorded to nearly two millions of Serfs, the Landlords obtained twenty per cent more from the Tenants than the State assignment. The money advanced by the State to redeem the Serfs, together with six per cent interest, is made recoverable in forty-nine years by an annual payment of two shilling and a half per acre, which he pays to the Officers of the Redemption Board. Peasants who have not elected the quarter allotment, or who have not been forced to redeem with State help, and have agreed to continue to be Perpetual Tenants, generally prefer Service rents to Money rents, and the Metayer form of Tenancy, which agrees best with the economical condition of the country, is coming extensively into vogue in respect of these properties.

The total extent of settled lands throughout Russia proper occupied by perpetual Tenants or proprietary Free-Holders, is about sixty millions acres, while the Landlords occupy on their own account two hundred and forty millions. The Crown Peasants come under a different category, but their condition is being daily assimilated to that of the redeemed Free Holders. The total sum advanced by the State, and secured on the lands of the Peasants, up to the end of 1869, was sixty-five millions Pounds Sterling out of which the State had foreclosed mortgages to the extent of fifty-three millions. The whole of this money has been raised in the first instance by the issue of State Banks Bills and Government Stock at five or five and a half per cent and the receipts from the Peasants, spread over forty-nine years at six per cent per annum, are expected to clear off the whole of these heavy liabilities. The Capitation Tax, the Imperial Territorial Tax, and the Redemption payments, taken together, average from 27s. to 35s. per head of the Rural population, or 1s. 6d. to 3s. 3d. per acre.

We trust these details of the progress of the Emancipation of the Peasantry in European Russia will prove of interest for more reasons than one. There can be no doubt that, as a consequence of this Emancipation, the Russian people have thriven in material and commercial prosperity, notwithstanding the increase of taxation caused by Foreign Wars, and the responsibilities of an Empire which covers nearly a quarter of the area of two great Continents. The Russian Exports of raw Agricultural Produce have vastly increased in value and amount during the last twenty years. The Cotton Spinning Industry has become a power in Western and Central Russia. The resources, material and moral, of Russia were severely tried in the late Turko-Russian War, and she stood the test in a way to confirm her position as a First Class Military Power, which could at any moment send ten Lacs of Soldiers to any portion of her vast territory for defensive and aggressive purposes. The Nihilist Outrages and Siberian Exiles should not in any way be allowed to come in the way of our appreciation of the great strides which Russia has made both at home and abroad, in the arts of Peace and War, during the last twenty years, and although for the time Absolutism has triumphed, we may almost with safety prophesy that a Nation of Peasant Proprietors, with such Democratic Institutions as the Communal and Cantonal, and District and Territorial Assemblies, will not rest content till it establishes its control over national affairs to the displacement of arbitrary or Bureaucratic Power.

A few words more before we bring to an end this brief review of the revolution effected in Russian Agricultural Economy twenty years ago. One of the worst effects of Absolute Power is that it warps men's perceptions in regard to the innate dignity of human nature, and its Common identity under all manner of extraneous disguises. The representatives of a Ruling Class soon learn to lisp the shibboleth of the natural and inherent superiority of European over Asiatic Races. It is urged that heroic remedies like the Emancipation of Serfs in Russia, and the creation of Peasant Proprietors in France and Germany, can safely be undertaken by the State with Public Credit or Funds, but that out here in India, the State, while claiming a monopoly of Landlord's Rights, must not incur any such responsibility, because the Indian Ryot is an improvident, spiritless, and ignorant Peasant, whose condition has been wretched all along, and can never be improved. Our reply to this charge is that the French Peasant was not always the abstemious and prudent Citizen that he now is; there was a time when Arthur Young mourned over the condition of the Agricultural Classes of France. The magic of Property and of Free Institutions have worked all this wonderful change. The degradation from which the Russian Peasant has been freed by a National Government can scarcely be said to be realized in the case of the Indian Peasants. The Imperial Government there, ventured in a spirit of statesmanship and philanthropy to redeem its Serfs, and make them Free Men, regardless of cost. The power of the Sowcar and of the State Landlord in this Country cannot be compared in the continuity and intensity of its abuse, for one moment, with the tyranny of the Nobility of Russia. The depression, however, such as it is, in this Country is real, and becoming worse every day. Let the State interfere not merely with a minimum piecemeal dose of Judicial Reform, but by the wholesale dispensation of a large administrative relief. If it subsidizes or guarantees Private Banks against risk during the first few experimental years, and enables them to rid the Peasantry of their ancestral debts, and if at the same time it allows the Land Revenue to be redeemed or permanently settled at a moderate figure once for all, it will provide an ample fund for Agricultural Relief Improvement without the necessity of borrowing a single rupee of fresh loans. The Ryot once emancipated, and set on his feet, and inspired with a sense that the land is as absolutely his as his home or clothes, there need never be any apprehension of his running into debt again and not practising thrift. The awakening of two hundred millions of the earth's most gifted Races will be a triumph of beneficent Government by the side of which the Abolition of Slavery in 1833 in England, or the Slave Emancipation War in America of 1860, and the contemporaneous Serf Emancipation of Russia, will be but child's play. It only needs a Statesman to grasp the full height of this argument, and to restore India to its proud position as the garden and granary of the world.

12

FOREST CONSERVANCY IN THE BOMBAY PRESIDENCY*

There is perhaps no more ominous feature in the climatic and economic condition of this country than the increasing frequency with which scarcity has deepened into famine during the last twenty years. The terrible visitations of 1860, 1865, 1869, 1873, 1877, recurring with almost cyclic regularity, have shaken the *nonchalance* and emphasized the attention of the most easy-going rulers to the paramount duty of famine insurance, and have forced upon them the most serious consideration of preventive and remedial measures embracing within their sweep the whole length and breadth of the Peninsula. Among preventive measures the conservancy of our forest tracts and the reboisement of our denuded hills and plains, deservedly occupy the most prominent place, and the breathing time which a short interval of years of seasonable rainfall has providentially secured for us cannot be turned to better account than in elaborating with a scientific and careful forethought the great policy of raising barriers against the flood tide of destruction which was allowed too long to have its own way, silting up our rivers and lakes, drying up their tributaries, denuding our hills and topes, reducing the humidity of our atmosphere, exhausting our

JPSS, January 1883, Vol.V, No.3

vegetable resources, and turning our fairest provinces into arid steppes of treeless and waterless expanse. It cannot be too often urged upon the attention of administrative authorities and the people generally that no lasting prosperity can be secured as long as we commit the fatal mistake of seeking present advantage by drawing upon the capital account of our credit with Nature's reserve forces. Sooner or later our imprudence will be overtaken with its fitting retributive punishment; nay, one can with considerable truth aver that such a retributive punishment has already commenced as a necessary consequence of the imprudent extension of cultivation, under suicidal encouragement from the Survey Department, into the very sacred regions of our hills and mountains. There is nothing more definitely ascertained than the fact that forests react powerfully upon the well-being of a country by the influences which they bring to bear upon the condition of flowing and standing waters, upon atmospheric moisture, on the regularity and moderation of climatic variations, on the storage and distribution, if not the actual volume and frequency, of rainfall, and, owing to the joint action of these causes, upon the productive powers of the soil and the material prosperity of its inhabitants. Over and above the increasing frequency of famine visitations the gradual deterioration in the productive powers of cultivated land all over the country, and the diminution of our labouring live stock, are facts which cannot be gainsaid or laughed away as exploded myths. Notwithstanding the demurer of the Government of India the President of the Famine Commission has set his seal to this revelation of our weakness, so humiliating to the self-complacency of our optimist generation. It is not our present purpose to refer more at large to these almost scientific truths regarding the importance of forest conservancy; we have only alluded to them here to provoke more general attention to our review of the growth of the Forest Department and of the strong and weak points of its present arrangements. We wish particularly to guard ourselves from the absurd charge that we do not realize the full importance of forest conservancy as an element of national well-being.

It is only within the last 20 years that both the Local and Imperial Governments have accepted forest conservancy as an important state function of sufficient consequence to justify the creation of a separate department. It is true, timber depots had been established in the Northern and Southern divisions so long ago as 1841 and pass fees were levied in all the Ghaut districts even before that date. As far as this Presidency is concerned, however, Surgeon Alexander Gibson was the first officer who organized forest conservancy on a solid foundation about the year 1855. Dr. Gibson had the charge of the botanical gardens, and as such had to supply Indian Medical herbs and drugs in large quantities on Government account to English druggists. While travelling over the wild forests of the country with this object in view, Dr. Gibson's attention was forcibly attracted towards the prodigal waste of vegetable treasures that had been going on for years together under the combined effects of a thriftless extension of agriculture, the demand of the fire wood contractor, and the depredations of the nomadic graziers and *gowlies* ever in search of new pasturage. For four years 1856-60 he travelled over the whole of the forest area, and for the first time mapped out all the more eligible sites and tracts which demanded careful conservancy. The thoroughness with which this work was done has never been surpassed, and the department which owed its origin to his ceaseless labours has hardly been yet able to occupy the whole ground sketched out for it by its first pioneer. These were days, however, of small beginnings. The whole revenue obtained in 1856-57 was represented by the small sum of Rs.135,062, while the charge of establishments came up only to Rs.14,218 leaving a balance of one and a quarter lac of rupees. The receipts were chiefly made up of pass fee proceeds of Rs.80,000, and about Rs.50,000 represented the yield from the sale of Government timber. The Presidency forests continued to be under the charge of a single Conservator with two or more assistants during the administration of Dr. Gibson and his successor Mr. Dalzell down to 1873, in which year the Northern and Southern charges were for the first time separated and placed under the control of district officers, assisted by a strong staff of Assistant Conservators, one for almost each Zilla circle, with a middle grade of Deputy conservators, and a lower grade of sub Assistant Native officers and rangers and inspectors. This increase of staff was chiefly employed in demarcating reserved and protected forests all over the Presidency. This work grew upon their hands, for many private rights and easements existed chiefly for grazing and *rab* purposes, and coterminous Inamdars and native states had forests of their own which had to be determined and regulated, and before the work had advanced in any sensible degree it was found that express legislation was necessary to strengthen the hands of forest officers and settle the nature and extent of private rights or, when these had to be purchased out-right, to fix the compensation. With the increase of staff the establishment charges increased out of all proportion with the receipts. The work of new plantations also engaged the attention of the Department about this time; the combined effect of this extension of work on all sides was seen in the financial results of the department. The receipts in 1873 excluding the Sind division were $9\frac{1}{4}$ lacs, while the expenditure was $5\frac{1}{4}$ lacs leaving a net profit of nearly 4 lacs of revenue. Since then the enactment of a general forest law in 1873 gave further stimulus to the growth of establishment. The corresponding figures for 1880-81 were receipts 11 lacs and the expenditure $8\frac{1}{2}$ lacs leaving a net revenue of $2\frac{1}{2}$ lacs. Of the total $8\frac{1}{2}$ lacs of expenditure the permanent establishments cost $3\frac{1}{2}$ lacs in pay, the charges for conservancy consisting chiefly of felling timber and bringing it to the depots came up to $4\frac{1}{2}$ lacs, while new plantations had the modest sum of about Rs.21,000 assigned to them. If these figures are studied more in detail, it will be found that excluding the Tanna Khandesh and Kanara districts, which are exceptionally situated, the receipts are barely sufficient to meet the charges, and that in this respect the Department has gone from bad to worse during the last ten years. The following statement will make this position clear.

Name of District	Receipts from all sources		Establishment and conservancy charges	
	1873	1880	1873	1880
Tanna	70804	171934	44057	82521
Kolaba	41563	40762	25609	39828
Rutnagiri	4992	6113	4456	14210
Khandesh	34892	126157	19653	62910
Nasik	14117	77689	14283	52808
Nagar	13281	19759	12213	31676
Poona	48135	33973	40372	64865
Satara	11851	45326	11166	49157
Sholapur	2459	5166	2130	17397
Surat	34848	51832	37944	39182
Kaira	10007	32971	16730	24606
Ahmedabad	196	1080	85	8
Direction	420774	329663	20839	24019
Cauaree	58574	44400	236462	206182
Dharwar	84284	95375	45218	37211
Belgaum	770	13411	47595	36024
Direction			646	9432
			18712	21776
Total	876529	1099961	558614	815930

The total receipts in 1880, excluding the Tanna Kanara and Khandesh districts, were Rs.467,714, while the establishment and conservancy charges over topped them by several thousand rupees being Rs. 498,024. In 1873 the corresponding figures were $3\frac{1}{2}$ lacs of receipts against $2\frac{1}{2}$ lacs of charges for the same fifteen districts. The apparent increase of gross receipts is more nominal than real, for the value of stock in hand in 1873 was Rs.38,715 while the corresponding figure in 1881 was Rs.267,279 or nearly a lac and quarter of rupees less. Making the necessary deductions it is thus clear that the department financially is scarcely more remunerative than it was ten years ago. As regards the extensive and unnecessary employment of European agency in this Department, which is principally responsible for the overgrown expenditure of the Department, it is not more open to that charge than other Departments of State. We also know it as a fact that this is acknowledged by several experienced and conscientious officers of the Forest Department. We have been unconsciously led to lay an emphatic stress on this feature of the departmental arrangements than we had at first intended to do, but we find from a closer study of the reports that this defect lies at the root of much of the barrenness of results about which such outcry is raised at times against the existing arrangements for forest conservancy. There are several other shortcomings in the administration of the forest department which we may point to, but it is not our present purpose to refer to them in detail, because compared with the all-absorbing importance of the subject to which we propose to invite the particular attention both of the Government and the public, these shortcomings are in our opinion of less importance. It must not be understood that we do not sympathise with the agitation which the people of the Tanna and Colaba districts have commenced with unprecedented vigour and enviable persistency of character against the absurdly vexatious interference of the forest department with the private rights of individuals and with the *bona fide* requirements of the agricultural community. We yield to none in wishing success to the public spirited leaders of the Tanna and Colaba agitation in their attempt to curb the insane zeal of some district forest officers, and to check the revenue-increasing instincts of the Department. It must also be clearly understood that we do not approve of the action of that department, responsible for the demarcation and settlement of the forest area, so far as it concerns the grant of adequate compensation to those Rayat's whose lands may be required for forest conservancy; for we are aware, that several complaints have been recently made in the Indapoor Taluka on the ground of the inadequancy of compensation. We are of opinion that, in as much as government has now opened its eyes to the suicidal consequences of its own insane policy of encouraging cultivation even in those sacred regions intended for forest conservancy, government must pay an adequate compensation to those who brought such lands under the plough under encouragement from the Survey Department. The Government must disgorge the money it made by its utter disregard of the cardinal principles of forest conservancy, which require that all mountain lands, toplands, river basins and the banks of large streams should be strictly and sacredly conserved with of course due regard to the requirements of the agricultural population.

The forest officers needlessly swell the cost of establishment by arbitrarily attempting to establish forest ranges in the flat parts of the country which were never meant to be conserved, at the risk of neglecting the more favoured localities. The insane attempt to show good paper results must be abandoned. The Deccan plains may be replanted in parts, but the forest department agency is too costly and too sparsely distributed for this purpose. Large administrative measures dictated by a prudent foresight might encourage investors with suitable concessions to conserve the growth of trees in topes and along river banks, but to take away the Rayat's land for forest purposes and then make belief of casting seeds broadcast in parched up soils never caring to see whether they grew up or rooted is simply a scandal which can never be too soon put a stop to. In England, France and other European countries large private forests exist in great numbers, and we do not see any reason why the same state of things can not be brought about here, especially because there are no people in the world who, like the Hindus, have almost a religious reverence for trees. The Government departmental agency is, moreover, as already stated above, too costly for such purposes, and we would, therefore, most strongly recommend the adoption of assigning forest areas for conservancy to large capitalists, who would do the work much better than the Department, if only duly encouraged by Government making liberal concessions to them. The Government of India who have recently recognized to the fullest extent the necessity of encouraging private enterprise in various directions, does scarcely require to be told of the importance of encouraging private enterprise in this direction also.

Having thus noticed briefly some of the most glaring defects in our forest administration, we deem it necessary in justice to the officers who have the charge of the department to state their case fairly in respect of the conservancy of our most valuable forest preserves. The cardinal principle of real conservancy in regard to forests appears to us to be to let the dry Deccan plains to shift for themselves for a time but to have a firm grip of all the Ghaut regions and the valleys and river basins. The forest department has been in this respect more sinned against than sinning. Considerations of paltry revenue, and to some extent false sentiment has come in the way of Government supporting the department in its representations on this point. The Survey Settlement Department has been chiefly to blame in this respect. Except in Konkan, hill sides, ravines, and valleys which were intended by nature as our forest reserves were assessed and numbered and cut up in lots and made the private property of Rayats, and as the full assessment was invariably levied whether the area was brought up under cultivation or allowed to lie waste, direct encouragement was thus held out for wholesale denudation, with the results which we now all deplore. When population was sparse and waste lands in abundance, this evil did not manifest itself in all its potency. Year after year, however, the process has grown from bad to worse till now we have reached a point when the mismanagement threatens to inflict on us very grave evils. All our large rivers and their tributaries take their rise in these mountains and bifurcations eastwards, and the outlook of these denuded regions is any thing but welcome to those who can see into the future. Ancient tradition set apart these valleys and hill sides as sacred preserves. Most of these forests were attached to some hill fort, and the men who guarded the hill forts had Inam grants of land on the express condition of Military service in times of war, and preserving the forests in time of peace. These guardsmen of the hills were ousted from their hereditary charges or their Inams were confiscated and they were left to eke their living by cultivating the ground, which they could only do by extensive destruction. The Hill forts of Sinhagad, of Purandar, Rajmachi, Lohagad and many others might be mentioned as instances in points. These forests were jealously preserved by the old rulers as a means of protection in times of war. There were many other places which were dedicated to some shrine or mountain deity, and this religious dedication held back the hand of the marauder. The hills of Harischandragad, of Shivaner, the Pratapgad hills opposite Mahableshwar, the Karti hills, the Trimbak and Bhimashankar hills were preserved by this religious reverence. There was not a river which took its rise in these hilly regions whose source was not jealously protected by this guarantee. The Revenue Settlement Department, however, rode rough-shod over these traditional restraints, and year after year its officers indulged in vain boasts of the extension of cultivation on mountain sides, and up steep valleys, oblivious of all more paramount and far-reaching considerations, having an intimate bearing on the well-being of the people on the plains. The protests of the forest department were pooh-poohed and destruction went on. The inevitable consequences have overtaken us; our rivers and streams have been silted up; the fertility of the soil on the plains has decreased; the supply of fire-wood has diminished; the number of agricultural cattle is yearly decreasing; inundations have been more frequent and the loss of life and property great. At the first settlement a large extent of land was left unassessed as *gairan* for grazing and *rab* purposes to the villagers. Even this reservation was held to be against the spirit of the survey department, and each fresh settlement absorbed all *gairan* lands attached to the villages, and accelerated into destruction.

So encouraged and forced upon this downward path, the Rayats made sad havoc with their scythe and their sickle terracing the hill tops with a very rude cultivation, ripping up the bowels of the earth, and exposing them to the inclemencies of sun and rain. The mountain tribes and the aborigines under the same pressure freely resorted to *Kumri* or *Dahli* cultivation which consists in lopping off branches of trees and burning them to ashes for planting the seeds for one year's crop. Next year they shifted to another plot with equally destructive results. The graziers and *gowlies* with their wandering herds completed this havoc. These imputations have not been cast on the Survey Department without full and sufficient grounds. The alleged extension of cultivation which is invariably the burden of these settlement reports is our best evidence. The confiscation and assessment of Gairaṇ lands has been protested against by the Rayats all over the country and by none more strongly than by the officers of the Forest Department. As an instance in point we refer to the Mulshi Peta in the Haveli Taluka. In the villages of Maleh, Wadvathad. Nanded, Wadusta, Mulshi Budruk, Shergaon, Waluch and Dongargaon as many as 9226 acres had been left unassessed in 1854 as Gairan land to be occupied by the Rayats for grazing and Rab purposes. During the last 30 years the whole of this area with a paltry exception of 160 acres in two villages has been assessed and given for cultivation, and only 530 acres in one village have been made over to the Forest Department. The same Department which seeks to confiscate for forest extensions thousands upon thousands of plain lands in the Indapoor and Man Talukas acts on a contrary principle in those parts of the country where preservation is most needed. No wonder that people deprived of free land for grazing and Rab purposes, make the largest present use of their poor lots, tear up the trees by their roots, leaven the mountain soil, and turn smiling uplands into barren rocks. The Revenue officers take up the part of the *kumri* cultivators against what they are pleased to call the encroachment of the Forest Department. Mr. Lee-Warner wrote some months ago in the pages of an English Magazine a harrowing account of the pressure put upon these hill tribes by forest rangers. Of course it is a delicate question what to do with these hill tribes; Government must take thought of their needs and not punish them for their ignorance. While all this may be admitted to have much force, there are at the same time considerations which outweigh these humanitarian appeals. The well-being of the whole settled community of the plains depends to a great extent upon the preservation of luxurious vegetation on these uplands. We derive our supply of water and fuel and timber from these sources, and we must take due forethought of the present and future needs and necessities of many millions of people. If indeed *kumri* cultivation was the only alternative open to save these aborigines from utter destruction, there would be some force in the appeals made on their behalf. But it has been demonstrated that the branches of trees cut down and burnt for ashes are really less helpful to serve as Rab and soil to the seeds of Wari and Nachani than the dry leaves of trees which with profuse liberality Nature sheds annually for man's wants. *Kumri* cultivation is only possible in the most primeval conditions of nature when the excessive rainfall produces a luxuriant vegetation which has to be turned for immediate service, and vegetable matter burnt off hand produces humic acid. The same service is, however, more economically rendered by burning leaves, and the only difference is that the latter operation is more laborious, though less prodigal and wasteful. In the progress of civilization *kumri* cultivation must give way to Rab cultivation, and this last to a well selected system of vegetable and animal manures. It is self-evident that even the tropical prodigality of our vegetable world cannot stand the destructive effects of the first two systems of cultivation when man destroys more by fire and axe than nature can slowly and spontaneously revivify and recuperate in the course of a single year. Fallen and dry leaves and dead branches and twigs of trees yield from 8 to 25 times more ashes than the wild husbandman secures by the unstinted destruction of living trees and roots and branches. The following comparative statement of the respective proportion of ashes has been prepared after a long course of experiments.

	Ashes produced by burning fallen leaves and twigs &c.	Ashes produced by lopping and burning living trees.
Teak	3.35	.35
Mango	10.00	.40
Jambul	8.00	.40
Nim	6.50	.30
Nandoshi	5.50	.35

Dry leaves constitute nature's own provision for manure when the destructive hand of man has not presumed to defile its virgin innocence, and civilised man must respect this ordinance in his own interest. A vigorous mango tree, when matured, throws down 140,000 leaves which contain about 700 lbs. of inorganic matter. With 70 such trees for a 20 acres field 49,000 lbs. of inorganic matter or 4900 lbs. of ash containing salts of lime and potash might be secured with unfailing regularity or 245 lbs. per acre. Besides the dry leaves the mango tree produces a vast quantity of vegetable manure in its blossom season. The Kumri and even Rab cultivation destroys the tree which in 4 years sheds its own weight of dry leaves and blossom, and subserves man's other wants, gives him shade and fruit and timber and fuel and holds together the soil and shelters the stream at its source. These figures speak for themselves. They demonstrate clearly what is obvious in itself that Kumri and Rab cultivation when it interferes with vegetable growth and does not utilize dry and dead matter is suicidal. As the forests are thinned, the soil loses its excess of humic acid and its porous character. The temperature is not kept down as before to a point which attracts the rain clouds, and the rain water does not soak down gently into the bowels of the earth, replenishing its subterranean springs, but runs away with violence, tearing earth and roots and stones and sand from the uplands below into the plains. Every little shower causes inundations, and after the waters flow over, they leave a thick sediment of silt which fills up the water courses and impoverishes the soil. The floods near Navsari and in the Khandesh rivers of which we heard only the other day, when the water rose to a destructive height with a rainfall of ten hours duration, have become the normal type of our present river system. In the Deccan especially our large and small rivers constitute and regulate the territorial divisions. Every small river system forms a Talooka with a hill and water-shed separating it from other river systems. The lands in the valley depend upon the river stream, not indeed for any direct supply of water but for the subterranean supply. Protect and clothe the hills, where the rains fall and rivers and streams take their rise, fringe the river slopes on both sides, and if the Forest Department secures these vantage grounds, it may well reconcile itself to let the treeless and waterless plain lands in the Eastern Districts to the natural force of circumstances. Nature will take care of these distant regions if it is well stocked at its fountain sources. The streams that have disappeared will begin to flood again and the rivers and banks will not be silted. This is the sole and real key of the situation. As long as we do not master the situation in this light, no indiscriminate extensions can prove of the slightest consequence.

We have referred above to some of the mischievous consequences, destructive floods, the disappearance of streams and the silting of river beds, which our neglect of conservancy in the higher and mountainous regions where the rivers take their rise, inflicts upon us. On the western ghauts as much as 200 inches of rainfall pours down in four months. An inch of rainfall represents 100 tons of water per acre. Few persons realize to themselves what the terrific force must be of 20,000 tons of water poured on each acre of our uplands. All the immense supply of water which might be utilized to fructify the earth and replenish our streams is allowed to be a violent scourge, tearing along our hill sides with unrestrained violence. The short sighted policy of the Survey Department and Revenue authorities first opened these regions to the destructive fire and axe of the Kumri and Rab cultivator and the wood contractor, and the hill sides denuded of their vegetable carpet have now been laid bare by years of violent floods which have silted up our rivers and lakes as though it were child's play.

Lake Fife, built at such cost, will be silted in the course of the next 50 years as surely as the Katraj lake has been during the last 40 years. In this collectorate the small river Bhama which flows below Chakan and Khed and joins the Bhima further south is a typical example. The river bed is well likened to a cask of sand which can never retain water, but must let it flow over its increasing shallow basin devastating the bank on both sides. The destruction caused by the Krishna, the Koyana, the Tapti, Nerbada, Girna and Panjara rivers has inflicted infinitely greater loss on private and public property in a single year than the whole revenue which Government may have derived from the miserable Nachni and Wari fields planted along the terraces of the assessed occupancies along the hill sides and on the tops of the hills. The contrast presented by the Ratnagiri district with its bare rocks and horrid ravines, and the well clothed Tanna and Kanara hills to the North and South teaches lessons which no body can well afford to ignore. Of course Government alone can accomplish little in this work of restoration. It is doing its best to atone for the errors of its past neglect. The time has in our opinion arrived when the matter must be taken up by the public in their own hands. It is our sense of the grave issues involved in a proper settlement of this question of forest conservancy that emboldens us to appeal to all thoughtful persons in this, as some might deem it, over wrought strain. We feel no misgivings on this head. The Forest Department and the Government must give up all idea for the present of making forest extensions in the plain country. This work may well be postponed for another generation. All our present efforts must be directed for the next 20 years at least to the conservancy of our mountains, hills and uplands, and the river banks. The vested rights of present occupants must be bought over and adequately compensated and both the axe and the fire must be laid under ban. The Forest Department is not at present a revenue-paying department, and it cannot reasonably be expected to be so for a long time to come. With a diminution in the cost of its supervising establishment Government might earn more, or at least be enabled to employ a larger staff. We build our hopes chiefly, however, upon the encouragement of private capitalists to help Government efforts in this work. Government should retain its public interest in this great undertaking, but the work of planting and reboisement can never succeed in the hands of a stipendiary agency. Large areas should be made over to rich capitalists on 20 or 30 years leases on condition that the lessee should arrange to have his hundred or a thousand large trees per acre during that interval, and his abstinence and trouble should be rewarded by a free and permanent grant of the use of the same under proper regulations as to felling of the property he creates. At present Government pays a miserable fraction to a few Khots and Rakhavaldars, but this make shift can never lead to any permanent good. The work must be entrusted to more thoughtful and intelligent hands if it is ever to bear any fruit. And as we have already shown above, the natives of the country are better qualified, because of their instinctive and religious reverence for trees and vegetable kingdom, to take care of forest conservancy than any officer of the dominant race. The active cooperation of large private capitalists should be ensured by securing to them adequate concessions. These and other questions discussed by us in this paper make out a strong case for inquiry. We wish the Government of India will appoint a competent Commission to deliberate on these points, and thus strengthen the hands of the forest officers. The points which call for such investigation may be briefly set forth as below.

(1) Is the present policy of indiscriminate extension of forest area by the absorption of treeless and waterless plains in the Eastern Districts likely to do any good sufficient to compensate the loss caused to the vested proprietors.

(2) What steps should be taken to buy all private rights to cut and burn and graze on hill side slopes and uplands, and cannot the agency of large capitalists be availed of to protect existing and replant extinct forests under proper regulations for their

preservation.

(3) By what means can the disproportionate cost of the forest establishment in the higher grades be reduced, and its numbers strengthened so as to secure a better supervision.

(4) What practical steps should be taken to prevent the silting up of our river beds and lakes and replenish our subterranean streams.

These and other questions which might easily be multiplied call for the exercise of all our highest talent and most matured experience. Forests once destroyed cannot be so easily restored and it requires centuries before the bare mountain side reassumes the pristine vesture of shaded woods. What has occurred in Greece, Asia Minor, Spain and France, and what is occurring before our very eyes in the more distant United States and Canada, ought to be warning to the people of India. It is in no spirit of partisan advocacy that we have ventured to direct public attention to this subject. We have not spared to expose what appears to us to be the weak points in the present arrangements, but there can be no doubt that we should be untrue to ourselves if we did not reiterate our conviction that far more than railways and irrigation works, far more even than our Schools and Police organizations, the weal or woe of this country depends under Providence upon the use we make of our present opportunity to regulate the conservancy of our forests. Nature has been defied and trifled with too long, and now it will not fail to lay its heavy hands of retribution and scourge us with plagues worse than those which afflicted Egypt and condemn our fairest regions to barrenness and decay.

13

PRUSSIAN LAND LEGISLATION AND THE BENGAL TENANCY BILL*

In one of our former numbers we presented an outline of the great Reform achieved by the Government of Russia about twenty-five years ago, which resulted in the emancipation of many millions of the praedial Serfs on Crown lands and the estates of the large proprietors in the country. A similar Economical Revolution was effected in the early part of the Century on an equally large scale, and with equally beneficial results, in the Social and Agricultural Economy of the Kingdom of Prussia. To us in India, which is now in the active throes of a great agricultural crisis in every portion of its widely scattered provinces, the origin and progress of this enfranchisement of the Prussian Peasantry possess a more than mere historical interest and teach us lessons which in the interests of this country we may not ignore without exposing ourselves to a great social cataclysm. The agitation in Bengal in connection with the great question of the Tenancy Bill will soon come to a head with the return of the Viceroy and his Council to Calcutta, and the strife of Class against Class, and of Labour against Capital, will be fought out to the bitter end. We feel persuaded that the Land Legislation of Prussia in the early part of this Century furnishes

*Published in *JPSS*, October 1883, Vol.V, No.2, and in *Essays*.

the most striking and historical parallel to this great impending crisis. There, as in Bengal, the Government of the Country sided with the cause of the enfranchised Labourers as against the all-powerful Landlord; there, as in Bengal, the tradition of a free Peasantry in a remote past, smothered but not killed outright by a long period of depression, furnished the stimulus for renewed efforts on a grander scale. This same Problem is equally prominent in Contemporary Politics in other parts of India, but the Classes representing the interests of Capital have not the cohesion and power which the Bengal Zemindars possess, and which establishes the closest resemblance between them and the great Feudal Aristocracy of Prussia. Of course, there are deep underlying differences in the situation which we shall notice later on, but the resemblances are sufficiently great to warrant a careful study of the Prussian land question by Indian students. We propose, accordingly, to furnish a brief *resumé* of this great revolution, which, in its distant consequences, has raised Prussia from a Second Class Power to be a leading State of Continental Europe, and enabled it, with a Confederated Germany at its back, to control the destinies of modern civilization in the latter half of this Century.

In the following observations, we have in view the Prussia of the first half of this Century, before the great victories of 1866 and 1870 raised it to its present towering position. The seeds of Prussia's present advancement were sown in the great humiliation which overtook the country on the battlefield of Jêna, which annihilated for a time the power of the Hohenzollerns, and made Prussia the sport of Napoleon's victorious Armies. Alone of the Continental Powers, however, her Sovereigns and Generals took part with Great Britain in the great revenge on the battlefield of Waterloo. It was in this period of national humiliation that Prussia consigned her destinies to the great statesmanship of her Chancellor Stein and Hardenburg, who, more than Bismarck of Moltke, may claim the glory of having saved their country in the dark hour of her national humiliation. The Feudal System, and the Social Polity and Agricultural Economy based on its principles, were buried in the great overthrow at Jêna, and when the national energy had its upheaval, it refused to be bound by the old trammels, and urgently called for a change. The Cycle of Reform commenced in 1807, when Municipal independence was conferred upon the Towns, invidious privileges regarding taxation were abolished, monopolies and restrictions gave place to a more liberal system of local and general management, and a more equitable Administration of Justice. The foundations of a system of Universal Conscription, and general if not compulsory, Education, had been laid in the last Century by Frederick the Great, and were vigorously pushed to completion at this time under the stress of a great necessity. These Agencies have contributed, along with other reforms, to be more particularly noticed hereafter, to develop the burnt energies of the population in all directions. The Begut Provinces of the Kingdom, Prussia proper Posen Silesia, Pomerania, Brandenburg, Saxon, West-phalia, and Rhineland, were about that time subdivided into districts; these last command many departments, which were either made up of Townships or Rural Communes. These Unions, Departments, and Provinces have each their representative Councils, consisting of privileged Landholders, representatives of the old Nobility, and of elected Representatives of the Departments and Town Communities. The holders of privileged estates, who exercised vast Judicial and Administrative Powers under the Feudal system, have been allowed to retain a considerable predominance in these Provincial and Local Councils, as also in the Upper House of the Legislature, but then other powers were destroyed by the Agricultural Legislation in the commencement of this Century. These few remarks upon the general course of Prussian Reform will now prepare the reader to follow intelligently the great work of Liberation achieved in connection with the Agricultural Economy of the country which falls within the more immediate scope of our present inquiry.

A brief survey must here be taken of the condition of landed Property, and its distribution between the different classes of the population interested in the ownership and cultivation of the soil. The Feudal conception of land was that it determined the status of the owner, and too often, the land became the unchanging subject of fixed ownership, and did not follow the changing lot of the Cultivator, or of the Proprietor. Land in large areas, and bounded by the natural limits of rivers or mountains, was held in common by entire communities. Settlers, and this common right was affirmed by a common change of fallow with cultivated land after every five or six years. In course of time, the cultivated land was broken up into smaller lots for the large sections of the Tribe, and these subsequently became subjects of individual rights, while the pastures and forests were held in common as before, and, when the Feudal system was organised, became the Demesne Lands of the Sovereign, or Manorial Lands of the Barons.

The Western Provinces of Prussia, lying to the West of the Weser river, being each colonised by more civilised Dutch and Flemish settlers, gave more scope to the position and independence of individual Proprietors of farms, while Silesia, Posen and Pomerania retained more exclusively the old organisation of Village Lands being owned in common by entire communities of Cultivators. In these Provinces, the land was divided periodically into lots, which were redistributed after intervals of seven years, while the pasture lands were used in common. On this condition of things, the Feudal System of the Middle Ages impressed its stamp and effected great modifications. Its general effect was to destroy or subordinate the ancient rights of small farmers, as also of Village Communities, to the dominion of the Lords of Manors, who monopolized all the profits and privileges of the lands included in their domains, partly by gift of the Crown, partly by forcible dispossession, and partly by the imposition of hard conditions of military and personal Services, subsequently commuted into payments of tithes and other burdens of serfdom or slavery. The cultivating Peasant forfeited or surrendered his personal freedom, and became a fixture of the soil he cultivated, valuable only for the services he rendered. He could not rise superior to his low status, and the aristocratic Noble could never forfeit his high caste. Custom, as settled by general assent or judicial decree, was the only restraint to these exactions of the Barons, and gradually Rural Society crystallized under its force into distinct factors. The personal services were commuted into money payments, but the nobility continued to have the monopoly of the lands, which they let to the Peasantry to cultivate on most disadvantageous terms. The original distribution between the Eastern and Western Provinces thus reappeared under the steadying influence of custom. The powers of Landlords were less onerous, and the sense of property, at the best a more or less limited hereditary, or leasehold usufruct, and the rights of equal succession to the Peasants' farm, were more distinctly the freely recognized in the Western than in the Eastern Districts. But as a general feature, the old Customary Law was nearly effaced by the growth and abuses of the Feudal System so that about the middle of the last Century, when Prussia was blessed with a capable Ruler in the person of Frederick the Great, the largest proportion of Peasant-estates were subject to the crushing and unquestioned dominion of the Nobles, and their highest interest in these lands was a more or less limited usufruct. Only a very small proportion of estates were Free-holds, or customary copy-holds, but even here the owner's powers of alienation were very restricted. Such was the miserable condition of the Peasantry in the last century, and we have now to trace the gradual steps by which the Enfranchisement of many millions of the Peasants, and the bestowal upon them of full Proprietary Rights, were achieved by the genius of Stein and Hardenburg in the early part of this Century.

With rare statesmanship, they grasped the fact that the essential condition of rescuing the Country from its miserable helplessness was to effect a radical change in the relationship of the soil with the person who cultivated It. They laid hold of the principle of Individual and Independent Property in the soil as the cardinal point of their Reform, and subordinated all other considerations to this main end. In the words of the first Edict issued by Stein, the great underlying principle of all reforms was "to remove whatever had hitherto hindered the individual from obtaining that degree of well-being which he was capable of reaching by exertions, according to the best of his ability." This Edict, for the first time in Prussian Legislation, recognised the fact that land was made for man, and promised to encourage all facilities for the acquisition of absolute ownership, and the free use of the land. As a commencement, it was resolved that all personal Servitude should be abolished before 1810. *i.e.*, within three years from the promulgation of the Edict. The shackles thus fell off from the bodies and spirits of many millions of human Beings, and this inspiration of new energy helped the subsequent work of Reform. In 1810, Stein, the author of the Edict of 1807, was banished by the Emperor Napoleon, and Hardenburg became Chancellor of the Kingdom and his Edicts moderated the sweeping force of the first Edict by the adoption of a more cautious Policy, which effected the same end gradually, without the risk of disruption and violence. A gradual abolition of Services and Rights of Common was shown to be possible by these famous Edicts for the "Promotion of National Agriculture" and "for Regulating the Relations of Land-lords and Peasants." This legislation of 1807 and 1810 was subsequently carried out by numerous supplementary Edicts, and by the inauguration of plans for subsidizing, with the help of State Funds, undertakings for the promotion of agricultural prosperity which were beyond the means of the Peasant Proprietors so freed from their Feudal Bondage.

We shall now address ourselves to a closer consideration of the methods followed out by the Prussian Government in giving effect to these great Edicts, which abolished Serfdom or personal Services, consolidated the Peasant's common Rights, and encouraged credit Organizations. The guiding principle in regard to the first of these changes was that all that is common is hurtful to the individual, and that perfect freedom of agricultural organization constituted the strength of the Rural population, and of the Nation at large. To abolish all encroachments on personal freedom,—to remove restrictions on right of property in land—to relieve the Peasants from being the sole class liable to the payment of State charges—to buy out the rights of the Lords of Manors over their Peasant Serfs' services—and turn these Serfs into free Proprietors—to commute the Real charges and services—to consolidate rights of common—and to facilitate the improvement of farms and other landed properties—these were the manifold methods by which effect was given to the Edicts of 1807 and 1810. A brief notice of the Legislation in each of these directions will illustrate the greatness of the work done in Prussia.

Personal servitude was abolished in 1807, and all servitude attached to the land was made to cease from 1810. Real Charges, which constituted the conditions on which the Peasants held their lands, were not abolished at this early epoch. By the old customary law, the power of eviction was unhampered, except by the condition that the Landlord should find a new Peasant for the cultivation of the soil. When absolute freedom of alienation was allowed, there was a great danger that the Landlords would buy out or evict their old Tenants, and retain the vacated lands in their own hands. The Edict of 1807 accordingly restrained the freedom, with this condition in favour of all Peasants who had any hereditary or particular interest in the lands, that these lands could not be absorbed except by the free consent of the parties. If the Lord had satisfied all the claims of the Peasant possessors, he was permitted to convert such lands into large Peasant Farms. The Edict of 1811 introduced a further modification. In consequence of the operation of the former Edict, two parties were recognized as having co-equal interest in land, the Lord entitled to the real charges and services, but burdened with an obligation not to absorb Peasant properties, and the necessity of finding a cultivator for them, and the Hereditary or leasehold Peasant burdened with the charges and servitudes mentioned above. If the parties agreed to a mutual compromise, the State gave full liberty to the Landlords to carry out the agreement. The rights of Landlords to be compensated were (1) the right of property, (2) claim for services, (3) the dues in money and kind, (4) farm stock and (5) real services. The rights of the Peasant which had to be valued for compensation purposes were (1) claim for support in misfortune, (2) the claim for wood and forest produce, (3) obligation on the Lord to build and repair buildings, (4) obligations on the Lord to pay taxes, (5) and certain rights of grazing. As some of these rights were not capable of valuation, the parties were left to arrange their differences amicably, otherwise the State intervened. A balance was struck between these mutual rights and obligations, and as this balance was against the Peasant Proprietor, a commutation was effected by the Peasant's foregoing one-third of a Free or Copyheld Holding and one half of the other Holdings to his Lord, after which both parties were left free to act as their interests dictated. This commutation was also made payable in the shape of a rent charge. In valuing the interests of the Peasant, the farm buildings were not included. Money commutations were not thought of because the Peasants had no money to spare, while the land in their possession had little value. To check any sudden disturbance of properties, the liberty of commuting was at first, allowed to holders of hereditary and taxable properties, and was subsequently extended to smaller farms. In 1815, it was ordered that rents in kind and money rents should be extinguished, or made terminable by their possessors, who were permitted to receive twenty-five years' value by way of redemption. In 1849, a Commission, composed of Rent Receivers and Rent Payers in equal numbers, was appointed, who fixed the form of commutation, and the rates and prices so fixed were made obligatory on all parties. It was in these various ways that the benefits of personal freedom, free use and free transfer of land, the abolition of all personal distinctions of rank and status as regulating the capacity for holding lands, and the abolition of the rights of pre-emption, were secured, and restrictions on absorption of Peasant Properties were gradually lessened. It is to be noted that, as was the case later on in Russia, no compensation was allowed for the abolition of personal servitudes. The

Serfs on Crown Lands were similarly set free by an Act of State. All restrictions in the interests of State Policy, such as the requisition of sanction for alienation upon the transfer of land were abolished by the Edict of 1861. Restrictions as to the use of Private Forests were similarly done away with. It was this last Edict of 1861 that sanctioned the formation of Agricultural Associations of which so much use has been made in subsequent years. Of course, it is not to be supposed, that there were no alternations of Policy in respect of this liberal far-reaching Legislation. There were numerous examples of retrograde Amendments in 1815 and 1851, but on the whole the Policy of converting Peasant Holdings into Absolute Properties was honestly carried out, till in 1860 the final Legislation on the subject completed the work commenced sixty years before, and abolished all vestiges of Feudal Restraints upon the powers both of Landlords and Peasants.

The commutation of Real Charges was a more difficult problem, and the State had to intervene by appointing experts to act as arbitrators, and fixing official prices and rates of compensation when parties would not agree. When the Rent Charge so commuted did not exceed two-thirds of the value of the land, its payment was undertaken by the Rent Charge Banks. If it exceeded two-thirds the Bank authorities might refuse advances. The arrangements for the settlement undertaken in the early part of Century were carried out by an allotment of portions of Peasants' Holdings to the Landlords, varying from one-third to half of the lands in their possession. The Legislation of 1850 and subsequent years interposed the machinery of Courts and Arbitrators to determine money compensations for abolished Rent Charges, and provided the machinery of State-subsidized Rent Charge Banks to help the Peasant to liquidate his liabilities at his convenience, without any injustice to the Landlord. Of course, these great Reforms were not carried out all at once throughout the Country. Each Province was dealt with separately after due consideration of its circumstances.

The abolition of the Rights of Common and Forest Rights was secured on a principle similar to that which was applied so effectively in respect of Lands, Servitudes, and Rent Charges. The interest of every sharer in these Rights of Common was valued, and to the owner of the same an equivalent piece of land was allotted, and when the land was insufficient for such a purpose, a Rent Charge was created in his favour, and these Rent Charges were subsequently commuted at twenty or twenty-five years' purchase. In carrying out these arrangements, parties were encouraged to come to a settlement by which, as far as possible, their Holdings would be consolidated, and the views of a majority of the interested parties were allowed to prevail, in respect of such Consolidation or Exchange arrangements. This principle of subordinating individual to public rights and conveniences formed the basis of the compulsory Drainage and Irrigation Schemes of Improvement, as also of Forest growth and Conservancy which on a grand scale were at this time undertaken by Government, while smaller works were promoted by compulsory or voluntary Associations of interested Landowners. When the State did not undertake improvements, it, at first, subsidized them by handsome advances of Public Loans, and more than fifty Laks of Rupees were advanced in this way in seventeen years (1850—1867). The payments made in satisfaction of these demands as they came in, were again advanced by the Department of Agriculture, which had the charge of these Funds, for helping similar fresh undertakings. Besides these direct subsidies, more recently the Prussian Government has sought to create a spirit of self-help by securing to such advances, when made by private individuals for purposes of improvements, paramount rights even against mortgagees, for purposes of recovery and has also empowered such Associations to issue mortgage Debentures, which were at first secured by a minimum State guarantee. This condition, however, has of late been dispensed with as no longer necessary. The Land Tax, which pressed heavily in former times, was also established on a fair and certain basis, being two to four per cent on the value of the net yield, the incidence of the Tax on Land being made equal to the weight of taxation on other kinds of property. It is no wonder that, under such stimulus, real Credit Institutions, Mortgage Debenture Banks, Rent Charge Banks, and Self-help Associations of all sorts, were promoted all over the country, providing the machinery and the funds by which the great national aims of the Legislature were facilitated by a free exchange of Capital, with the least possible risk and the largest possible returns.

This brief summary of the Land Legislation of Prussia will not be complete without some reference to statistical figures, showing how far, during the last sixty years, that these great Agencies of Enfranchisement have been in operation, the work of Reform has been completed. The total acreage of the kingdom of Prussia has been estimated to be seventy-three millions of acres, and out of this vast total, nearly forty-five millions of acres of land were in some form or other brought under the influence of this special Legislation. Nearly thirteen Laks of persons have commuted Team or Hand Services, by consenting to land allotments or making money payments. This change alone represents a saving of the labours of the Peasant class for thirty millions of days. In respect of Rights of Common, seventeen Laks of owners consolidated or settled their Right of Common over forty-one and a half million acres during the whole of this period of sixty years. Only one-twentieth of this work remained to be done in 1867. The tendency towards dismemberment has been thus counter-balanced by the encouragement towards consolidation, and in the end it has been found that the danger of excessive subdivision of Land has been avoided. In 1860 fifteen per cent of the total area of sixty-five and a half millions of culturable land belonged to the crown, the State Forests, or to the Church, or to municipalities; forty-four per cent., or twenty-eight Millions to non-peasant Proprietors, *i.e.*, the holders of large estates; thirty-five per cent, or twenty-four millions, were Team Farms of Peasant Proprietors, and five per cent or three and a half millions, were smaller Holdings. The aggregate average of Peasant Properties is thus nearly the same as that of large Properties. The transfer of land effected by the Disfranchisement Legislation may thus be said to have roughly divided the land equally between the rich Landlords and the poor Free men. There are, now about fifteen thousand owners of larger estates, and more than four Laks of Peasant proprietors with only sixty thousand Laks of Peasant Proprietors with only sixty thousand Tenants of superior Holders, and about twenty Laks of Agricultural Labourers. The proportion of Rural to Urban population in Prussia is seventy per cent of the former to thirty per cent of the latter. Heavy indebtedness, the attendant evil of small Proprietors, has been found to prevail in Prussia as in other countries, though the redeeming feature about Prussian Economy, is, that this indebtedness has been due chiefly to the efforts of the people to liberate and improve their Holdings, and it has a tendency to diminish, as the charges created by the Land Legislation and by loans borrowed for improvement are being gradually redeemed. Taking the value of landed estates at seven hundred millions, the amount of mortgage debt was three hundred and seventy-five millions, of which about twenty-five millions were represented by the Loans made by Rent Charge and Debenture Banks, and the remaining three hundred and fifty millions were due to Private Creditors. The proportion of Mortgage Debt to the value of land was formerly two-thirds in place of the present proportion of one half. The figures given above, include the debts due from the Privileged Holdings as also from Peasant Properties. Peasant Properties are, in fact, in many parts of the country less heavily charged than Privileged Estates.

In the words of a Parliamentary Blue-book, from which much of this information has been gathered, it may be stated, in concluding this review of Prussian Legislation, that the Prussian Nation, in the early part of the century, found itself burdened by a cumbersome Feudal System, and writhing in the agonies of Serfdom. Prussian Statesmen, accordingly, set themselves to a manifold task, which in sixty years was fully accomplished, the task of converting the Feudal Serf into a Free Proprietor, of removing the restrictions which the Privileged Owners of land felt so heavily, and making them unencumbered Lords of their properties, of abolishing all the confusion of Tenures, Charges, and Services, of relaxing Entails, of commuting Rights of Common, and of encouraging improvements with State help and State compulsion, and facilitating the free exchange of land. And all these great Reforms have been carried out without imposing any serious burden on the State's resources, without any violent disruption of the economical relations of different Classes of Society, and without the shock of Revolution or internecine class struggles.

Here is India, we sadly need the help of similar statesmanship. With a growing Population, and limited resources, the struggle for existence is already being felt, as a strain on the Social System. Meanwhile, the experiments that have been undertaken to remedy these disorders are not suggested by any broad view of the future, or any just consideration for vested rights. We refer, especially, in these remarks to the proposed Legislation in the Lower Provinces of Bengal and Bihar, which present the largest analogies to the condition of Prussia in the early part of the Century. There, as here, the old customary rights of property have suffered a depression from long disuse, and the rise of a moneyed and privileged class of Landlords, who have invested in land on the faith of solemn pledges, and are naturally anxious to turn their bargain to their best advantage. This class often press heavily, as in Bihar, upon the Peasant majority of the population. There can be no doubt that remedial Legislation is urgently required to check these evils, and, quite independently of the saving Clause contained in the Law of 1793, which extended the Permanent Settlement to these Provinces, there can be no doubt that the Government, in its capacity as Sovereign, has every right to undertake Legislation intended to remove admitted and general grievances. We cannot, however, approve of the direction and spirit of the Legislation embodied in the proposals which will soon come in for discussion before the Supreme Legislative Council, in respect of this Bengal Tenancy Bill. The proposed Legislation is based on lines which are diametrically opposed to the principles we have described above, as having influenced the great Prussian Chancellors. While the one sought to disencumber Land, and encourage the growth of absolute property both in the Landlord class and in the Peasantry, the proposals embodied in the Tenancy Bill are intended to increase these mutual encumbrances and the existing complexity of rights and interests. While the Prussian Legislation was guided by the principle of allowing compensation for the abolition of all Rights, Services, and Charges which were not of the nature of personal slavery, the Bengal Proposals reject all idea of compensation. While the Prussian Statesmen have tried their best to minimize executive interference in the settlement of class relations, the theory, underlying the Bengal Bill, is that the State Executive and Judicial machinery must prescribe and regulate every little incident of the relations between the Owners and Tenants of land. The only result, and, to some extent, the intended result, will be that the existing confusion will be still more confounded, class will be set against class, the sacredness of former pledges will be violated, the Landlords ruined without compensation, and reduced to the class of Rent-receiving Pensioners, and the Rayats taught to look more and more to the State as their sole Landlord, without acquiring the training necessary to raise them to a sense of their position. We shall try to make our meaning more plain in the sequel of this paper. We shall only premise here, with a view to prevent all possible misunderstanding, that we do not side with the optimist advocates of the existing condition of things. We freely allow that an urgent Reform, and a radical Reform, is called for, but our contention is that the lines on which the Legislature proposes to proceed are radically mistaken, and will never lead to any real settlement of the present disputes.

The first portion of the Tenancy Bill is devoted to the consideration of Khamar and Rayati lands. What it seeks to do in this connection is not only to register existing Rights and Tenures, but to stimulate the growth of Rayatwari Holdings, and to contract the area of Khamar land, that is, the land in the actual possession of the proprietor, and not let by him to a Ryot for cultivation. The Law is to presume that all land not shown to be Khamar is Rayati land. The Landlord's powers over Khamar lands are absolute, while in regard to Rayati lands, his powers will be greatly controlled by the proposed Legislation. Even when Rayati land is forfeited for default in the payment of Revenue, and bought in by the Landlord, it cannot be divested of its Rayati character, unless the Landlord keeps it in his own hands. The moment he lets it to a Tenant, its Rayati character revives by force of law. So far as the record of existing rights is concerned, we see no reason to object to the proposals of the Government. But, this exaggerated value set upon the reduction of Khamar land, and the creation of new Rayati lands, appears to us to be thoroughly wrong in principle. It is true, some customary incident of ancient times is pleaded as an excuse for the revival of this Policy. But circumstances have so altered since then, that its revival cannot fail to be mischievous. Our own view of the matter is that, while respecting all existing ancient rights, there should be no artificial discouragement to the growth of absolute property in land. If the Rayati land is insufficient to meet the existing wants of an increasing population, by all means encourage the Ryots to buy Khamar lands for consideration, by paying compensation regulated on a system of Real Charges, and extended over a long term, to the Landlord class, who have invested in land on the faith of a strict observance of their purchased Rights. Rayati land pre-supposes a limitation and complexity of Rights, while the tendency of all remedial Legislation should be to make as many Holdings, Khamar or Jerait, as possible. Land gains in every way, and loses nothing by being made the absolute property of the owner. The Prussian Legislation was based on this principle, and we cannot but strongly deprecate the suggestion that a contrary Policy should be inaugurated in Bengal at this day. The proportion of Khamar land is actually so small, being less than ten per cent, that it appears to us to be extremely unfortunate that this apple of discord should be wantonly thrown as a temptation in the way of the agricultural population of Bengal and Bihar.

The next two chapters of the Bill relate to the rights of subordinate Tenure-holders and are open to the same objection, that the Bill seeks to make much more complex the relations of parties in place of simplifying them, and allows relief to one class at the expense of another without providing compensation. It is well-known that the Permanent Zamindari Settlement of 1793 was made on the basis of exacting nine-tenths of the average Revenue of the estate as Land Tax, and allowing one-tenth to the Zamindar for the expenses of collection, and the risk and responsibility he incurred on that account. The Zamindars created subordinate Tenure on the same principle of recovering a fixed and a much larger proportion of the Revenue. This reservation, it is now proposed to limit by fixing thirty per cent. as the limit of the profits of a subordinate Tenure-holder, which should not be encroached upon by any enhancement of the payment claimable by the Zamindar from him. In the case of Jangalbari, or waste lands generally reclaimed at the expense of the Zamindar, this limit is fixed at twenty per cent. Over and above these provisions, it is proposed to rule that no enhancement shall at once double the former rate, and that no enhancement shall take place except at the interval of ten years. At every stage of the process, the Civil Court's intervention is made compulsory, and in the matter of registering these tenure rights and their transfers, the Collector's authority is interposed at every step. It has been estimated by competent authorities that there are in all about eleven and one-third Laks of Tenure-holders against two and a half Laks of Zamindars and Revenue-freeholders, and that they represent an income of eight Crores of Rupees as against thirteen Crores, which is the income of Zamindars and owners of Revenue-free Lands. These Tenure-holders are thus a very important class, and are well able to take care of their own interests. By their education and intelligence, they are far removed from the state of helpless dependence, which to a large extent is pleaded as a justification for the active interference of the Government on behalf of the Ryots, or other cultivators of the soil. The change, if necessary, in their condition should have been in the direction of enabling these classes to become full proprietors by private arrangement with the Zemindars, or by permitting compulsory purchase on the basis of a fair and equitable compensation. A balance of mutual liabilities and advantages ought to be struck, and according as that balance turns in favour of the Zamindar or the Tenure-holder, a money payment should be made in a lump sum, or a Rent Charge spread over years, or an Allotment made of an equivalent portion of land, followed thereafter by an extinction of all the inconveniences of subordination and division of interests and rights. Any one of these arrangements would certainly have a more satisfactory result in the general advancement of the country, than the plan of tinkering with existing rights in the assumed interests of one class, to the prejudice of the Zamindars, as at present proposed. The perpetual interposition of Civil Courts and Revenue Authorities can only result in paralyzing private efforts, and increasing the sense of dependence on the State as the only regulator of private rights, than which nothing can in the end prove more prejudicial to all classes concerned.

By far the most important portion of the Bill relates to the position of the Ryots. The evident and avowed intention of the proposed Legislation is stated to be the creation of a large class of what are called occupancy Ryots. The old Khoodkhast Ryot, no doubt, did possess customary rights and interests in Land long before the Permanent Settlement was made, and he was not in principle subject to arbitrary enhancement and eviction. His position was seriously damaged by the Settlement, which, in order to secure the prompt payment of the Revenue under the Sunset Law, armed Zamindars with extraordinary powers, and these owners made serious encroachments on the Ryot's independence. The Khoodkhast Ryots were like the Mirasdars of the Deccan. Just as in consequence of the Bombay Survey Settlement, Mirasdars have disappeared, and the old *Upari* Tenants have been turned into Occupancy-holders, the old Khoodkhast

Ryots were by force of circumstances transformed to a large extent into Tenants-at-will. After a long period of depression, Act X. of 1859 first conferred Occupancy Rights on all Ryots who occupied any particular Holding for twelve years at a fixed rental, and it is now proposed to confer this Occupancy Right on all Ryots who are residents in the village for a term of twelve years. The status of the holder determines the status of the Holding, and confers on the land a privileged character, thus reversing all past traditions and invariable practice, by which the Tenure of the land regulated the status of the cultivator. The Bill further proposes to confer special privileges upon this class. Their lands will be hereditable as well as freely transferable, and they may also sublet the land without restrictions. Their rents can be raised, but the limitations are so many and so complicated, that private contract will cease to regulate these enhancements in the majority of cases, and the interposition of Settlement Officers and Civil Courts will become a *sine qua non* at every step. The occupancy Ryot's rent cannot be increased except after a resort to Courts ; he cannot be ejected even for default in payment, except by a similar interposition. The right of pre-emption, left to the Landlord as a counterpoise to these large powers, is similarly clogged with conditions, so that it can only be exercised with safety after a resort to the Courts. The very price is to be fixed by the Courts if parties do not agree, as they will not in the majority of cases. Even when the Landlord buys in the land, the moment he lets it to a third party, that party acquires the status of a Ryot as freely as though he had succeeded by transfer from the former occupant. In regard to enhancements of rent, it is provided that no rent can exceed one-fifth of the gross produce; that no enhancement can take place except by a contract approved of by the Revenue Collector, or by a decree of Court; and the Revenue Collector is to determine the rates of land up to which enhancements may be made, and these rates are to be accepted by the Civil Courts as conclusive in all cases. An increase of rent claimed by reason of a general rise of prices is to be shared half and half, provided the half is not more than the proportion of the rise of prices to old prices. No rate can be doubled at any single enhancement, and an enhancement once made must hold good for ten years.

These are some of the provisions intended to protect the interests of the Ryot classes. Our Objection to the change is not based on any indifference to the interests of the Ryots. These Ryots number more than ten millions in all and pay a rental of twenty-one millions to the Zamindars and Tenure-holders, and, as we have said, they hold ninety per cent of the lands owned by the Zamindars. Such stupendous interests claim all the protection which farsighted statesmanship can confer on them. Our principal contention is that the Landlord's rights, sanctioned by usage and by law, will be adversely affected by these classes, and that the permanent peace and advancement of the Country will not be promoted by provisions which at every step set Class against Class, and compel resort to the Courts, or to the Collector's agency. The interest and ownership in land will still continue to be as divided as before between quarrelsome partners, and no real improvement will take place. Our own proposal is that, as far as possible, the entanglement of private relations should be simplified, and the occasions of conflict and subdivided ownership should be minimized. We would confer full Proprietary rights on the Ryots of whatever degree who hold Rayati lands, *i.e.*, non-Khamar, but these full rights should extend only over a limited portion of the estate so held, and will have to be purchased for a proper equivalent in the shape of resigning in the Landlord's favour all rights over the other portion not so reserved. The liabilities and rights of the Ryots and the Landlords must be duly weighed one against the other, and on the principle of a sliding scale, we would apportion the land between the two classes, assigning one and the larger part absolutely to the Ryot, another to the Landlord, and if a balance is still left due, we would provide compensation in money Rent Charges, by which means all conflict will cease, and both the Ryot and Landlord will be made to feel increased interest in their absolute properties. The more practical question relates to the way in which this liberation of the land from its present entanglements can be brought about. Our own proposals are based on the recorded experience of similar undertakings which have been successfully carried out in other countries. In the first instance, we would encourage the redemption of rent and other charges paid by the Ryots to the Zamindars, and Revenue-free and Tenure holders. The present value of the payments made by them to these classes comes to about twenty-one Crores. These twenty-one Crores paid to the Zamindars and Tenure-holders are, on an average, one-fifth of the gross value of the annual agricultural wealth of Bengal, which has been roughly estimated by Major Baring—now Lord Cromer—at one hundred Crores. As there are about ten millions of Ryots, this represents an average gross production of one hundred Rupees for each cultivating Ryot's family, out of which he has to pay at present twenty Rupees or one-fifth share. Estimated in acres, and taking the yield per acre to be ten Rupees, it follows that each Ryot cultivates about ten acres, and pays two Rupees an acre out of a produce worth ten Rupees per acre. In the case of the Occupancy Ryot, we would divide his Holding into three parts, make two of these parts over to him in absolute right, and hand over the third as absolute Khamar land to the Landlord. In the case of other Ryots we would divide the Holdings half and half. As this arrangement will not settle the account of their mutual rights and liabilities, the balance will have to be made up by money Rent Charges. The Ryot, left in possession of his one half or one-third Holding, should be required to pay his old rent on the reduced Holding for a period of thirty or forty years, so as to repay balance of the purchase money with interest. If the parties cannot be made to agree to this slow method, the Government could easily render them this help by advancing the money wherewith the Ryots might be enabled to purchase out their Landlord's claims. The capitalized value of half of twenty-one Crores will be about two hundred Crores, and that of one-third of twenty-one Crores will be one hundred and forty Crores. The Government could safely float any loan at four per cent, and pay off the Zamindars for the loss of their rights over the reserved portions of the Ryots' Holdings, and recoup themselves by levying six per cent interest from the Ryots for a term of thirty-five years. Purchase on these terms will be compulsory, and the Landlords will more easily be reconciled to it than consent to see themselves deprived of a valuable property without any compensation, as the present Bill proposes to do. Thrifty Ryots might be allowed the option of redemption at an earlier period by the inducement of a considerable reduction in the total capitalized value. This latter plan has been successfully adopted in Russia, in respect of the Serfs who received one-third of their master's lands in Free-hold right. The other plan would set off the mutual liabilities and rights of the two classes, and according as the balance inclined in the Zamindars' favour, an equivalent allotment of land made once for all, or a Rent Charge created for a term of years with a provision for a Sinking Fund, would have to be arranged. This was the principal feature of the Prussian plan of Enfranchisement, and it has this advantage that no liability is thereby thrown on the Government. Even under the Russian plan, the liability of the Government is only nominal, as it only intervenes in place of private money-lenders because its credit is exceptionally good, and its powers of levy are proportionately more effective. In this way we could achieve the liberation of the Ryots in Bengal in a generation or two without any violence to vested rights, and our plan would above all train and educate the people by a slow discipline of thrift to retain their newly acquired status. The present proposals of the Bill simply confiscate the interests of one class to benefit another, and can only be justified on Socialistic or Communistic principles.

The elements of national prosperity are wanting in a country whose principal resource is Agriculture, and that agriculture is in the hands of a thriftless and poverty-stricken Peasantry, who are weighted down with heavy charges, and whose life and labours are not cheered by the charm and strength inspired by a sense of property. If this Country sadly wants a proud and independent Yeomanry as the backbone of its strength and prosperity, it no less equally needs the leading and the light of

Propertied men. A complete divorce from land of those who cultivate it is a national evil, and no less an evil is it to find one dead level of small Farmers all over the land. High and petty farming, with an upper ten thousand of the holders of large landed estates, and a vast mass of peasant farmers, this mixed constitution of rural Society is necessary to secure the stability and progress of the Country. The Bill under consideration robs Peter to benefit Paul, and at the same time, it creates an hostility of interest, where entire union should prevail, and it clogs the land with a variety of interests and ownership, and entangles mutual relations in such a manner as to drive both parties constantly into Civil Courts. We know our suggestion is so far out of the lines within which the discussion has been hitherto conducted, that it is not likely to attract favourable attention on the part of the extreme advocates either of the Ryots or the Zamindars. Our perception, however, of the perilous nature of an obstinate persistence in a *laissez faire* policy is so keen, and our disapprobation of the revolutionary proposals now made is so radical, that we have deemed it necessary to scatter this seed on the field of discussion, and wait to see if it falls on good soil. A settlement based on the plan advocated by us will successfully accomplish all the ends that the Government has in view, and the Zamindars will not be in a worse position than they are now. They will get full compensation for the loss of their rights over one portion of their estates, and their dominion over the other half will be of a character which could never hereafter be questioned. On the other hand, if the present Bill passes into law, the restraints on the Landlord's power in the matter of enhancements and evictions, in the levy of rent, in the claim for improvements, and disturbance, will soon succeed in gradually lowering the status of the Zamindars to the level of pension receivers. Such a state of things will keep up and intensify all the elements of strife, and just as the riots and disturbances in Eastern Bengal have paved the way for the present legislation, further disorders will suggest more drastic and retrograde remedies in the future. It is, above all, important to put an end to this irritation, and this can only be done by the adoption of one or other of the alternative plans of settlement which we have ventured to propose. Let each man's land be as much his absolute property as his house or clothes, and things will settle down themselves agreeably to the interests of all parties concerned. The British Government in India, powerful as it undoubtedly is, cannot command the power to retrace its steps in such matters, and throw the Country backwards a hundred years. This attempt to revolutionize in a retrograde direction is bound to fail, and will fail only to suggest a further repetition of the same unsuited remedies.

To sum up the points in which our proposal possesses undoubted advantages over the present Bill,—

(1) Both would effect a Redistribution of Land, but while the Bill would make this allotment without compensation, our proposals are based on the grant of adequate compensation to the parties who might be deprived of their existing rights; (2) while the present Bill would perpetuate the existing conflict, and create fresh confusion and complication of interests in Land, our proposal would simplify this entanglement, as far as may be possible; (3) while the Bill would create an artificially defined class of subordinate Tenants tempted on all occasions to throw off their subjection, and a Landlord class hemmed in on all sides by inconvenient obligations, we would create an entirely independent Peasantry trained by thrift to price its independence, and at the same time confer an absolute property in their lands on the Zamindars and Tenure-holders; (4) while the Bill would drive both classes into Civil Courts and the Kacheries of Revenue and Settlement Officers at every step, we would simply lock up the doors of these coercive Agencies by taking away the usual inducements for strife and dissension, and make Custom and Contract the measure of the obligations binding one class to another, instead of a harassing and penal Law; (5) while the Bill would create fresh Occupancies, and destroy Khamar land, we would increase the latter, and raise the former once for all, to their full status; (6) while the Bill

would in the end cover the land with one dead level of pauper Tenants, we would ensure their more hopeful existence, aspiring always to attain a higher standard of comfort, alongside of a rich Middle Upper Class of great Territorial Lords.

One word more before we conclude. The present Bill makes no provision for the rights of the Government Tenants in Khas Mahals. There is no indication that the Government is prepared to bind itself by the restrictions it so generously imposes upon Zamindars to receive less than one-fifth of the gross produce as rent, or to refrain from ousting Tenants without resort to the Courts, or from doubling the rent at once, or to pay for improvements, or give ten years' rent as compensation for disturbance. The condition of the Ryots in these Khas Mahals does not compare favourably with the Zamindars' Ryots in Eastern Bengal. The Ryots' advocates in Bengal should certainly not content themselves with partial Legislation, which makes it possible for Government to refrain from dealing towards itself the same strict measure of equity which it proposes to deal to others. And as we are on this part of the subject, we may well ask whether, under the periodical Assessments, the State Landlord is prepared to concede as against itself the same measures of restriction and moderation which it is so anxious to provide for the Tenantry of the Zamindars. Here in this Presidency, Government doubles and trebles, in many cases quadruples, the Assessment at a leap, the Assessment has to be paid punctually on pain of forfeiture of all interest in land, there is no limit that the Assessment in all cases shall not exceed one-fifth of the gross produce, and no payment is made for improvements or disturbance when a Ryot is ousted from his ancestral lands. In all these respects, the Revenue Administration in other parts of India must be put on a more equitable footing before Government can with clean hands ask the Zamindars in Bengal to surrender the Proprietary Rights guaranteed to them by one hundred years' continuous possession; and on the faith of which most of the settled estates have changed hands to such an extent, that the idea of depriving the present race of landlords of their advantages without compensation for the loss thus thrust on them,Savours very much of a Communistic and Latter-day Saints' Revolution, than which, in a country circumstanced as India is, nothing can be more disastrous and perilous alike to the people and to their Rulers.

14

PROPOSED REFORMS IN THE RESETTLEMENT OF LAND ASSESSMENTS*

The close connection which exists between the system of land tenure prevailing in a country, and the character and condition of its population, has been often noticed by economical writers, but we do not remember to have seen this point elaborated with greater precision and force than in an official minute recorded by Sir Louis Malet in February 1875, and published in an appendix to the Famine Commissioners' Report. The retirement of Sir Louis Malet from official life formed the subject of a very appreciative and sympathetic review in the London *Times*, but in our opinion the reviewer did scant justice to what may safely be pronounced as the most characteristic feature of Sir Louis Malet's official career, and which constitutes his strongest claim to be remembered as a far seeing statesman, and not a mere successful official. It is the peculiar weakness of bureaucratic minds to feel a rooted aversion to first principles, to regard all appeals to general considerations as sentimental madness, to hug the present and the accomplished fact with supreme self-satisfaction, and generally to act on the maxim that sufficient for the day are the evils thereof. Sir Louis Malet rose far above this tame subserviency and the usual shifts and expediencies of

---

**JPSS*, January 1884, Vol.VI, No.3

public life, which are too often worshipped in the name of practical common sense, and pass current as safe wisdom in high places. In the minute referred to above, Sir Louis Malet, anticipating the objection that it was of no practical use to arrive at, and act upon, definite principles in the matter of land revenue, so long as we obtained our money, observed that this indifference to accurate thought and expression has been, and is, a source of the greatest practical difficulty,and is self-condemned by the fact that those, who profess to feel an aversion to general principles, perpetually invoke the same on public occasions. Only these appeals are made as catch-words to suit the shifting purposes of the hour, and to play fast and loose with popular confidence. According to Sir Louis Malet, the relation of cause and effect can be clearly traced between the land policy of Government, and the prevailing habits and deficiencies in the character of the Indian population. Indolence, unthriftiness, helpless dependence on Government, extreme poverty, low conditions of existence, and the general absence of a spirit of enterprise, and initiation, and progress among all classes— these leading defects in the national character of our people can only be due to a cause operative on an equally large scale. In an inquiry as to the relative efficiency and strength of those agencies, which have thus deteriorated the standard of national life in India, what more potent influence for evil can be named than the land revenue policy which, in Sir Louis Malet's words, sweeps into the coffers of the state 50 per cent or more of the net produce of the soil, thus diverting a fund which in countries, where private property in land is absolute, finds its way back again into channels of agricultural improvement. This extreme pressure is made more mischievous by reason of its uncertainty. If security and permanence are the essential conditions of productive energy in nations as in individuals, the absence of these conditions must result in the depletion of all vital activity in the body politic.

Although Sir Louis Malet's views failed to obtain a hearing at the time, there can be no doubt that, as he himself prophesied, the Nemesis of neglect, and of wanton tampering with natural laws, must over-take the Government sooner or later, and end in a crisis which will baffle all attempts to palliate the outward symptoms, and will force it to grapple with the disease cankering at the heart with desperate remedies. It is, therefore, to us a matter of intense satisfaction that the Government of India has awakened itself to the importance of a radical change in its policy in this connection. There have been, however, so many alternations and ups and downs in the attitude of the Government on the question of its relation to the land, that it would be presumptuous to prophesy that the present change of front will result in immediate practical action. Towards the end of the last century, the tide of English opinion set in steadily in favour of a permanent settlement of the land revenue, and the whole of the Bengal Provinces, and a portion of the Madras Presidency, secured the boon of a permanent settlement under Lord Cornwallis' rule. This policy continued to be in the ascendant till 1810, when it received a check, and under the leadership of Sir Thomas Munro in the south, and of Bird and Thomason in North India, the rival policy of fixing the land revenue for a term of years, subject to periodical revisions, came into the foreground, and dominated over the counsels of Government for nearly 50 years. About 1860, there was another swing of the pendulum in favour of a permanent settlement of the land revenue. The Despatches of 1862 and 1865 were the out-come of this change of views, and if the temporary rise of prices, consequent on the Civil War in America, had not intervened at this time, those Despatches would long ere this have been given effect to throughout the older and more settled parts of British India. Owing to this unfortunate accident, the policy of periodical settlements received a fresh impulse, which has not yet spent itself, although the temporary rise of prices which dazzled the official mind, and led it to dream of progressive prosperity, has long since abated. The occurrence of famines and the great loss of life consequent on these visitations, and the disturbances in rural society caused by heavy indebtedness, as also the check in the upward growth of the main sources of revenue, all these causes have concurred in opening the eyes of Government to the mistake which was committed 20 years ago, when Lord Lawrence in Calcutta, and Sir Bartle Frere in Bombay, leagued together to thwart the action of the Secretary of State. Even at present, the Government of India finds itself hampered by its own past antecedents, and the reform now proposed by Lord Ripon's Government has necessarily the character of a halting compromise between extreme views, and does not travel over the whole ground covered by the Despatches of Lord Halifax referred to above.

Having anxiously watched these changes of front in the attitude of Government during the past 25 years, and through good and evil report maintained our opposition to the school which, under the guidance of a false political economy, has strained the rights of Government to share in the produce of the soil to a degree which we knew before-hand must end in discomfiture, we heartily welcome this tardy awakening of the Government to a sense of its responsibility in this connection, and can fully realize the difficulties which hamper the free action of the Government of India at the present day. It is much to be regretted that Lord Ripon, distracted as he is by the opposition of powerful classes, and the insubordination of the official hierarchy, in the matter of the Jurisdiction Bill and Local Self-Government Legislation, will not find an early opportunity to carry out this great reform on the lines sketched out by him. We, however, hope that this year, when the burning questions of the hour will have received their quietus, Lord Ripon will find time to devote his energies to the careful elaboration of his present proposals, than which no other reform undertaken by him will better secure the free liberation of national energies in all departments of progress.

Before we proceed further with our observations upon the proposed reforms, it may be useful to state here briefly the main out-lines of the scheme which has been enunciated by the Government of India in sufficient detail for the North-West

Provinces and Oudh, and which is now under the considerations of the various local Governments, whose opinions have been asked in regard to it. In May 1883, Mr. Buck, Secretary to the Government of India, addressed to his Honour the Lieutenant Governor of the North-West Provinces and Oudh, a letter in which the principles upon which in future resettlements of land revenue should be conducted are explained at length. With a view to guard against any misunderstanding, the Government of India has taken care to inform the local authorities that a permanent settlement, pure and simple, on the lines laid down in Lord Halifax's Despatch, was rejected as out of question under existing circumstances. What is now aimed at is a reform in the system of revising periodical assessments. These ever-recurring revisions are a very serious evil, as they, so far from settling, unsettle men's minds, and create uneasiness by reason of their uncertainty. They harass the agricultural classes, and engender discontent by mistakes in assessments, they check expenditure on improvements, deteriorate the standard of agriculture, and involve great delay and heavy cost. These evils being admitted, what is now aimed at is that, without sacrificing the interests of public revenue, the vexations, delay and cost of the present re-assessments should be obviated, and in their place confidence should be created among the people of India and a stimulus afforded to the improvement of agricultural industry. The method by which Government propose to bring about this change is to eliminate from resettlement operations all attempts to make periodical surveys and valuations of the soil. Periodical Land Surveys and valuations, to be thorough and satisfactory, must involve delay and cost, uncertainty and harassment. The Government of India is of opinion that these valuations and surveys have now been sufficiently long in operation to furnish a safe and fair basis for future resettlements, without recourse from time to time to fresh and minute investigations. The only justification for this detailed inquiry urged by settlement officers is, that it is necessary to correct mistakes, and to re-adjust the assessments according to the changing values of neighbouring properties. This justification can only hold good in cases where the first surveys were imperfect and inaccurate. As a matter of fact, Revision Surveys and valuations do not discover any startling errors, and the labour is thus mostly thrown away. Moreover, an absolutely equal assessment is impossible, both by reason of the natural imperfection attending such operations, and the equally natural changes caused by variations in surrounding circumstances. Fresh appraisements of individual plots of land necessarily tax improvements, afford a premium to indolence, discourage thrift, and disturb vested rights created by a sense of confidence in the continuation of the existing arrangements. It is not so much enhancements as such, as their unequal and uncertain character, that unsettles men's ideas, and creates discontent. A proportional enhancement all round on the basis of existing surveys and valuations would, as far as Government is concerned, secure the same increase of revenue that is now realised under the existing system, without unsettling values and creating mistrust.

The Government of India, with the concurrence of the Secretary of State, propose accordingly not to simplify the methods of re-valuation at present in use, but to dispense with them altogether, and in their place substitute a self-acting scheme of readjustment. The agricultural value of an estate, which has once been ascertained by a tolerately correct survey settlement, will hence forward be accepted as a basis for future adjustment, and no inquiry for the purpose of correcting possible mistakes will be undertaken in respect of settlements made after a period to be fixed according to the fiscal history of each district. The impossible attempt of correcting past mistakes, for the good it accomplishes in a few cases, leads to incalculable mischief all round, and will therefore be abandoned. On the basis of valuations so fixed all re-adjustments will be made on general principles. It is in laying down the principles on which the readjustments are to be made that the Government of India makes its most important departure from the present order of things, and the clear and practical statement of its views in this connection affords ground for hope that the suggested change will not prove abortive.

The principles of the new scheme of readjustments have nothing of a revolutionary character about them. The Government of India propose to base future enhancements upon a record of facts, noted in detail over a considerable period, rather than upon estimates which are too often guess-work, upon ascertained statistics rather than upon conjectural and calculated figures, dependant for their accuracy upon the judgment of individual officers. This work of collecting agricultural statistics from year to year will hence forth engross the attention of settlement officers. As present, the owners and occupants of land are not in a position to form an approximate idea of the possible enhancement of the assessment on their estates after the expiration of the current settlement. This uncertainty will be to a great extent obviated when the enhancements are based upon statistics collected from year to year, and made available in anticipation for general information. The problem is thus stated,—how to give this assurance of security to occupants and owners of land without involving an unnecessary sacrifice of public interest. In other words, the Government of India is anxious to extend the benefit of a modified permanent settlement to all settled estates. With a view to secure this end, an analysis of the principal causes which justify an increase of assessment has been instituted, and the Government of India lay down definitely that no system of re-settlement can be satisfactory which permits enhancements except on the three following grounds;—

(1) Increase in area.

(2) Rise in prices.

(3) Increased production due to improvements made from state funds.

All improvements effected by private parties will in future be exempted from liability to increased assessment. The theory of the Bombay system of settlement recognises this ground of exemption, but as a matter of fact the direction of law in this respect is seldom observed in practice. In the other Provinces, both the theory and the practice are opposed to such exemptions. In laying down, therefore, that private improvements shall not be taxed, the Government of India will have conferred a most important concession on owners of land, the value of which cannot be too highly estimated. In 1874, in Sir Philip Wodehouse's time, the Bombay Government proposed to exclude all Kharab unarable land, which was not taken into account in the first settlement, from being subjected to assessment on revision. The Government of India at the time overruled the action of the Bombay authorities, and the matter was rested on this footing for the last 10 years. We protested at the time against this interference on the part of the Government of India, and it is, therefore, a matter of no small congratulation to find that the Government of India has been at last persuaded to abandon its old policy, and to admit that it is false economy to discourage in any way the employment of increased skill and labour on the part of private owners. The Government is now prepared to resign in favour of private rights its share of revenue on the profits of private improvements, which play such an important part in the justification of enhanced assessments.

When this exemption is allowed, the first of the three grounds, on which increased assessments may be claimed, loses much of its importance. The error in actual measurements between the first and revised settlements is seldom more than nominal, and as no two measurements will exactly agree, the practice even at the present day is not to disturb old measurements where the difference is less than 5 percent in the total area re-surveyed. A more potent cause which leads to enhanced assessments is an alteration in the valuation of land, or, in the technical language of the department, in the classification of the soil and its advantages or defects. Without any marked change in area, the settlement officers in charge of revision work too often raise the class value of the land, and put a higher figure upon this class value in consequence of an alleged rise of prices. This involves a double enhancement, and lies at the basis of much of the evil complained of in regard to enhanced assessments. The system in the North-West Provinces of classifying and valuing land differs so considerably from that which obtains in this Presidency, and this portion of the Government of India's letter under consideration enters here into such minute details, that it is unnecessary to enlarge upon it here. Suffice it to say, that just as in respect of measurements, the work done by the settlement Department hitherto will be accepted as a final basis, so also in the matter of valuations, the existing classifications will be accepted as final, if they are reasonably adequate. A varying period, according to the fiscal history of each district, will be fixed behind which no attempt will be made to penetrate in all regularly surveyed Provinces. When the original valuation has been unreasonably low, this initial period will be brought down to a later date than in the other districts not so circumstanced, but once fixed the period will be accepted as final. In the North-West Provinces, the settlements are invariably made with entire village communities, and the settlement officers base their enhancements upon estimates of increased rents. The Government of India directs that, in place of estimated rents, the settlement officers should collect statistics of actual rents received, and use them as the basis of their calculation. In the Bombay Presidency, the settlements are not based on rents, but upon approximate guesses as to the nature and quality of the soil. The work of classification is more elaborate here than in the North-West Provinces, but the same principle can be carried out with a slight variation. The classifications made by settlement officers, must, after a certain date in each district, be accepted as final, and all further readjustments of assessment should be made without going over the whole ground again. Of course in this Presidency, the work of classification is distinct from that of valuation, but as the class determines the value as between one land and another, the fixity of classification will go a great way to diminish the work of valuation.

The area and the class being thus determined on a permanent basis never to be altered, future re-adjustments can safely be made to depend solely upon the two remaining considerations, namely, the rise of prices, and increased productive expenditure by Government, which improves the value of the land. This latter cause may be further eliminated from consideration, because if a large undertaking, such as an irrigation work, is constructed by Government, the right of Government to levy a tax in addition for the advantage supplied cannot be questioned, and needs no special regulations. In the case of Railway works, or the opening of new markets by good roads, the expenditure of Government, if really productive, necessarily leads to a rise of prices, and cannot legitimately be counted as an independent agent. The result therefore is that future enhancements will virtually depend upon the action of only one of the three causes set forth above, namely the rise or fall in prices. The initial cultivated area and the initial classification of the land, fixed in the way specified before, being accepted as final after a date varying with each district, its initial revenue, on which the re-adjustments are to be made, will also be determined once for all. By the side of this initial revenue, a schedule of prices covering a long period will be prepared, and an attempt will be made to fix initial or normal prices varying with the condition of each district. When the actual prices for a considerable number of years are found to exceed the rate of these normal or initial prices by a certain proportion, the Government of India propose that the initial revenue will be raised but so as not to exhaust the margin of higher prices. While securing to Government a good share in the increase, a fair share will be left to the private owner, to compensate him for increased expenditure. Famine years will be excluded from the schedule of prices so as not to unduly affect the average. The Government of India are prepared also to fix a point to which prices must rise before revenue is enhanced on this ground, and further to fix the limit of enhancements to 15 per cent, beyond which the revenue will not be raised at any recurring settlement for a period of 20 years at least. In the case of superior holders with tenants under them, enhancements of Government assessment will regulate the enhancements of rents due from the tenants, and if disputes arise between owners and occupancy tenants, the same considerations will guide the Courts, or settlement officers who have jurisdiction in such cases, as those with which the Government proposes to check the action of its own officers.

We have thus given in brief the substance of this most important Resolution, and touched upon the points which bear upon the Bombay system of revenue settlement. The Government of India, in forwarding a copy of this Resolution to the Bombay authorities, sought an expression of the views of the Bombay Government as to whether, and how far, the principles laid down in the Resolution could be made applicable to this Presidency. The harassment and expense inseparable from resurvey and reclassification of soils at each recurring settlement is an admitted evil, and the urgent necessity of affording facilities to the owners and occupants of land to anticipate approximately the increase of revenue, which will be demanded from them, cannot be questioned. The Government of India have also informed the Bombay authorities that, although they overruled the liberal policy proposed to be adopted in this Presidency by Sir Philip Wodehouse in the matter of excepting Kharab lands from assessment, they are now prepared to revert to the proposals of 1874, if the local authorities can see their way to renew their suggestion on this occasion. The year 1848 is suggested as a date which might be accepted as the basis of fixing initial areas and classifications, and all lands excluded on the ground of being Kharab (unarable) in settlements made after that date should not in future be assessed for purposes of revenue. The opinion of the Bombay Government is asked upon the policy of this exemption, as also upon the point whether in special areas the enhancements should not be made progressive, instead of being made all at once. As regards Famine tracts, it is suggested that an acknowledged and definite system of suspensions and remissions in bad years, which will not depend upon the discretion of individual officers, will be a very desirable reform.

The Bombay Government, we are glad, to see lost no time in giving its best consideration to the suggestions made by the Government of India. The matter was at once referred to Mr. Stewart, the Survey and Settlement Commissioner, and his report was submitted in June last. In this report Mr. Stewart has discussed rather discursively the many subjects referred to in the letter from the Government of India. As far as the work of eliminating the process of resurveying and reclassification in revision operations was concerned, the Survey Commissioner stated that the Bombay system of settlement fully recognised this necessity, and for many years past has been worked to a large extent upon the principle formulated in the suggestions made by the Government of India. He stated it to be his deliberate opinion that if the time was considered ripe for its wholesale adoption in this Presidency, there was nothing in the Bombay system which would stand in the way of giving effect to the wishes of the Government of India in this connection. Of course, there was considerable difference between the theory and the practice of settlement operations in the North West Provinces and that which obtains in this Presidency. The North West Provinces system requires its offices to institute elaborate local inquiries to ascertain actual or estimated average rent-rates, which must cause harassment and vexation. There is nothing corresponding to this element of disturbance in the Bombay system, where no rent inquiries are made, the only operation of which the ryot has any cognizance is that of reclassification. Moreover, tolerably accurate land valuations based upon a rough classification of soils may serve the purposes in the North West Provinces, but will not prove equally serviceable in this Presidency, where the classification has to be more minute and complete. A close reclassification of soils cannot for some years to come be dispensed within this Presidency, because the work done in the early years of survey settlement operations was very far from being accurate, and poorer soils were overvalued, while good soils had been to a large extent under-rated. These defects have been for the most part corrected in later operations, and the work which has been done since 1854 does not, in Mr. Stewart's opinion, stand in need of any general or detailed revision. Mr. Stewart accordingly proposes that during the next 7 or 8 years, the present establishments should be utilised in their full strength to complete the remeasurement and reclassification work, and that after this period the services of the survey and settlement officers might be safely dispensed with, and the work of revising the assessments on the basis of the corrected remeasurements and reclassifications might be handed over to the revenue officers. Mr. Stewart has furnished a tabular statement showing the different stages at which this improved reclassification work has been carried in the different districts in a way to be at once adopted as the basis of future revision operations. There are seven districts Poona, Sholapur, Nasik, Nagar, Dharwar, Kaladgi and Belgaum, where the revision of rates has been carried out, or is now being carried out, and in these districts there can be no objection to declare that the present valuations of the soils should be accepted as final, without the necessity of any future revisions for the purposes of revenue settlements. The second class embraces the five Gujerat districts, Khandesh, Satara, Kolaba and Thanna, in which the original settlements have not yet expired, and the work of reclassification and measurement cannot be entirely dispensed with. In the third class fall the districts of Ratnagiri and Kanara, which are being settled for the first time, and the work of measurement and classification must be carried out in detail. Even in these districts field operations have been nearly completed. Throughout the 18 districts, the work of general measurement and reclassification will be finished at the latest in 7 or 8 years, if the establishments are kept up at full strength, and after that period no further operations will be necessary.

With regard to the second suggestion of the Government of India as to the principles on which reassessments should be adjusted to the basis of the initial measurement and class valuations when these are finally fixed, Mr. Stewart emphasized the difference which exists between the Bombay and North West Provinces system. The classification of soils in this

Presidency only settles the relative value of lands, but does not govern the absolute incidence of the land revenue. This is fixed on quite different considerations, and the total thus fixed is then distributed over the entire area according to the gradations of the different soils. The maximum rate being once fixed, the rates for lower soils are arrived at by arithmetical calculations. In revision work, it is this maximum rate which is enhanced according to general considerations, and the enhanced maximum rate being thus fixed, the subsequent operations are simply mechanical. With regard to the three considerations suggested by the Government of India—namely, increase of area, rise of prices, and large works of improvement undertaken by the states, as justifying ènhancement, Mr. Stewart stated that Pot Kharab, that is unarable land excluded from assessment in the first settlement, might safely be exempted from assessment if it was recognized as such in all settlements made after 1854. The work done before that year was in his opinion very inaccurate, and cannot be accepted as a basis for future guidance. Since 1854, the work has been more scientific, and if any Kharab land has been excluded from assessment since 1854, its exemption should be guaranteed. As a matter of fact, very small areas have been so excluded since 1854, and there is, therefore, little chance of any loss of Government revenue resulting from a guarantee against enhanced assessment on this account. In this Presidency, waste lands are always measured separately from cultivated and assessed areas and are not included, as in the North West Provinces, in the total settlement of the village. As these waste lands come under cultivation, they necessarily bring an increase of revenue in this Presidency to the state. The first of the three causes may therefore be safely eliminated from consideration. As regards the second cause, the rise of prices, Mr. Stewart stated that there was no difficulty in the way of adopting the proposal. He, however, questioned the policy of limiting the discretion of Government in this connection, for the certainty which would arise from such a limitation would not benefit the Ryots, and would only encourage capitalists to strengthen their hold on land. The third cause requires no special consideration, for the right of Government to levy a tax for additional facilities of water has never been questioned, and was fully recognised under the present system. As regards the questions of remissions and suspensus of revenue, Mr. Stewart stated that the Bombay system of settlement recognised the full necessity of imposing differential rates according to the security or insecurity of lands in the matter of rain fall, inundations, and other catastrophic causes. Each Taluka was divided into groups of villages to which different maximum rates were applied according to the certainty or uncertainty of rain-fall. For all ordinary variations of seasons, therefore, a sufficient consideration was already shown, and no further action was necessary except to provide for abnormal failures of rain-fall and other calamities.

The Survey Commissioner summed up his observations by stating (1) that the general remeasurement and revaluation of land at each revision were not contemplated in the Bombay system, and no such operations would be necessary after the present work had been placed on a satisfactory footing, which would be done in the course of the next 7 or 8 years, if the present staff were kept up at full work; (2) that areas entered as Pot Kharab in settlements made subsequent to 1854 might safely be exempted from revaluation; (3) that with this exclusion, and the separate assessment of waste lands, there was no necessity for making special provisions regarding progressive enhancements in future; (4) that when the field operations were completed, there would be no necessity for a separate survey and settlement Department, and the work of fixing and tabulating revised assessments might be handed over to the Revenue Department; (5) that there was no objection to introduce greater certainty in future assessments, but the policy of doing so was open to question; (6) that the principle of ordinary remissions and suspensions was fully considered and provided for in the Bombay system, and required no special recognition except for abnormal seasons.

Strengthened by this expression of the views of its Settlement

Commissioner, the Bombay Government felt itself in a position to reply at once to the letter of the Government of India to the effect, that it was in entire accord with the Supreme Government on the general principles enunciated by it, as those principles were applicable to the Bombay revenue system with certain modifications. As regards the question of Pot Kharab, the Government of Bombay stated that, although in 1874 when the question was first raised by Sir Philip Wodehouse, the suggestion, if carried out at once, would have resulted in unnecessary loss of revenue, the position at present was, however, different, and the Government was prepared to sanction the concession as a general principle in all Talukas classified and settled subsequent to 1854. This concession would remove the necessity for providing progressive increases as suggested in the Government of India's letter. As regards the proposal to fix initial areas, values, and revenues, the Bombay Government stated that the considerations which applied to the North-West Provinces did not possess the same force in this Presidency. At the same time when the survey record is once completed on a satisfactory basis, it will be available for use permanently and after the revised maximum rate has been determined by Government on independent statistical information it will be easy to secure its rateable distribution over the whole area of the group. With regard to the taxing of water advantages conferred by large state undertakings, the Government of Bombay had power under the Irrigation Act to levy special rates. In regard to well improvements, the Bombay Government stated that, after much discussion it was finally settled that wells were not to be considered as improvements liable to be taxed in making revised assessments. This provides only for new wells, and old wells, constructed before the first settlement, were separately provided for by the imposition, not of a special water rate, but by the charge of the highest dry crop rate. Generally speaking, therefore, in future, after the survey record has been completed, revision enhancements will solely be based on increased agricultural profit resulting from a general rise of prices, or partial rise of prices due to local causes, such as the opening of new markets by Railways constructed at the public cost. The Bombay Government further expressed their opinion that it was not easy to formulate a rule of proportions between revenue enhancements and rise of prices. Differing, however, from the view of the Survey Commissioner, the Bombay Government stated that, in its opinion, some measure of certainty in the matter of prospective enhancements was desirable, and that as a question of policy, anything which could operate to hold back capital from agriculture was an evil. At the same time no change in the principles of revision, as laid down in the revenue code, could be safely carried out until the Survey record was completed. As regards the subject of suspensions and remissions, the Bombay Government concurred with the views of the Survey Commissioner in stating that the present system provides sufficient relief for ordinary or partial failures, and operates mechanically and independently of the varying views of individual revenue officers. The subject, however, was still under consideration, and has been referred to a Committee charged with the preparation of the provincial famine code.

On the receipt of this reply from the Bombay Government, the Government of India issued their final orders upon the whole reference. The future assessment of Pot Kharab, or land escaping assessment as unarable at the time of settlement, will be henceforth abandoned in all talukas classified since 1854, and there will therefore be no necessity for providing for progressive increases of revenue within the term of the settlement. The work of remeasurement and reclassification of soils should be finished in the course of the next few years, and after that period the majority of the districts will be guaranteed against any change in the measurement of areas and the valuation of soils. At the end of this period, the fixed valuations of the soils will be openly declared, and the percentage of enhancements will thereafter be the same for all classes of soils in revision settlements. The Government of India, while taking a note of the difference of views which exists between the two

Governments on the point of rates and a rise of prices, express their satisfaction that the Bombay Government realise the advantages of eliminating uncertainty as far as possible, and deprecate the policy of retaining present uncertainty of assessment as a deterrent on the money-lending classes. The Government of India trusts that when the time for decision arrives, the Government of Bombay will see its way to secure as close an approximation as may be possible to a fixed and certain method of assessment, and that any considerations of a rise in profits, apart from a rise in prices, is sure to lead to undue enhancements, by taxing the same advantage twice over. This closes the correspondence between the two Governments on this subject.

Our summary of the official correspondence has already extended to such a length that we have hardly left any room for detailed observations on the proposals of reform enunciated by the Government of India. We may however state in this place that the views which we have in this journal and elsewhere published from time to time have been too often misunderstood. We have never asked for a subversion of the Rayatwari tenure, or the substitution in its place of Zamindari Settlement either on the Bengal plan of individual Zamindars, or on the North-West Provinces system of collective Zamindar village holdings. The Rayatwari system has obtained in this Presidency from time immemorial, and it is the only one suited to the democratic constitution of our rural society. The old Mirasi tenure was one of permanent Rayatwari holding, and we have always sought for the re-establishment of this Mirasi tenure and the re-assertion of its permanent condition. We have agitated, and shall continue to do so till the agitation succeeds in persuading Government to alter its suspicious attitude; we have agitated for a permanent settlement of the assessment on the Rayat's holding in this Presidency. There is no possible reason why small proprietors, dealing direct with Government, should not enjoy the benefit of a permanent settlement. The old Mirasdars were full proprietors of their lands in every sense, and they have been declared to be so by the highest Courts in the land. The right of the state to levy a share of the produce as a tax for public purposes has never been questioned; we only seek that this right should be regulated by the old traditions of our law, and pre-Mahomedan practice. The theory that the state is the owner of all cultivated land, and that private persons can at best be only tenants or occupants, is entirely of Mahomedan origin, and has no application in this Presidency because the Mahomedan law did not prevail here under the native Maratha rule. This despotic maxim of Mahomedan conquerors has in recent years found support from Anglo Indian writers and the radical teachers of English political economy, but neither the old Hindu Governments, nor the English Government upto a recent date, ever asserted such pretensions. The right of the state extends only to a fixed share of the produce of cultivated lands, and we have always striven to confine the authority of the state to a distinct recognition of this limitation. We are aware that the Government hesitates to accept this view because it apprehends that it might affect its revenues by making it impossible to raise the land tax according to the exigencies of the times. We are not disposed to ignore the weight due to this consideration, especially in a poor country like India, where the land tax is principal resource and sheet-anchor of Indian Finance. We should never have pressed our own views in this connection with any persistency if their adoption had involved any unnecessary sacrifice of public revenue. There is, however, not the slightest ground for any such misapprehension. Our proposal has always been that the permanent settlement should be made not of the money payments or revenue, but of the payment in kind, which should be fixed in proportion to the natural productive capacities of different lands, and this kind payment should be, at every recurring interval of 30 years or more, turned into money values, which should remain fixed for the currency of the settlement. In this way Government would receive in money the value of the kind payment which is its proper share. The settlement department should fix the proportion of this payment in kind once for all, and the revenue authorities should thereafter commute it in money values according to the permanent changes in prices. Such an arrangement will involve no sacrifice of public revenue. If prices rise with the prosperity of the country, the Government share of the fixed payment in kind turned into money values will also rise, and thus compensate the revenue for increased demands of expenditure. People who invest their savings in land will always know the extreme limit of their liability, and will regulate their mutual dealings accordingly. The land does not produce money, and money rates must always be fixed in reference to the produce in kind. The right of the state under the Hindu law also extends to a share of the produce. Both the natural and political conditions thus obviously require that the permanent settlement should be made with reference not to money rates, but to the staple produce of land. We are aware that the conservatism of the Indian authorities is so deep rooted, that it will take a long time before these views find acceptance with the Government. Meanwhile it is satisfactory to note that the Government of India has substantially affirmed the correctness of these views in the suggestions of reform made by it to the local authorities, which we have briefly summarised above. Though the points of view are so different, there is substantial accord in the final conclusions. We trust that the local authorities will heartily co-operate with Lord Ripon's Government in giving effect to this noble policy, than which no more important work was ever undertaken by the British Government in India. In this, as in other respects, the Government must retrace its steps, forget its Mahomedan antecedents of absolutism, and return to the old Hindu traditions, where the king's power was restrained in all directions by the rights of the people, among whom the king was more of a father and a manager than a conqueror or a sovereign lord, and cultivated land belonged in absolute right to private owners who paid as tax a fixed share of the produce to the king like any of his other subjects for the expenses of protection.

15

A PROTEST AND A WARNING AGAINST THE NEW DEPARTURE IN THE LAND ASSESSMENT POLICY*

The recent Resolution in the Revenue Department dated 26th March 1884, containing an exposition of the policy of Government in regard to the question of Revenue Survey and Assessment, and offering certain concessions for the protection from assessment of the increased value of land due to improvements effected in it by the Rayat-holders, marks another stage of definite progress in the controversy on this long-disputed subject which has been carried on by us with the Government for the last twenty years. It supplements and confirms the promises and assurances held out from time to time, and notably by the famous Resolution of 29th October 1874, when Sir Phillip Wodehouse's Government first proposed a new and important departure in the current traditions and practices of the Survey and Settlement Department. Owing to the opposition of the Government of India, acting under the advice of Sir B. Ellis, the good intentions which then animated the Local Authorities were

*_JPSS_, April 1884, Vol.VI, No 4. This article is incomplete as its last nine pages were missing from the _JPSS_ issue available to me (Bipan Chandra).

frustrated, and the proposals of Sir P. Wodehouse were rendered abortive and cramped in their beneficial application by a succession of retrograde measures which found favour with his successor, Sir Richard Temple. The opposition which we have steadily maintained to this retrograde policy was emphasized by the results of the two Government Commissions, and, as the outcome of this deliberation, the Government of India has now given its adhesion to a more statesmanlike and progressive reform, the principles of which were shadowed forth in the discussions which took place in the Land Improvements Loans Bill of 1883. The outlines of this scheme of reform, as formulated by the Government of India, were published in anticipation in the last number of our Journal, and since then the whole correspondence has been placed at the disposal of the public by the Local Authorities, who have taken advantage of this opportunity to expound more fully than has been done since 1874 their own policy in this connection. Unlike its predecessor, this new Resolution of Government is not likely to prove abortive, as it is as much the outcome of the pressure of the Government of India upon the Local Authorities, as the spontaneous action of these same authorities, who apparently have profited to a considerable extent by the bitter experience of the past ten years of low prices, agrarian riots, and severe famines. The concessions now made may, therefore, be safely accepted as a permanent land-mark of the gradual liberation of the policy of Government from the hampering constraints of the great unsettling Department.

It is true that the unfortunate delay of ten years, which has taken place, has robbed to a great extent some of these concessions of much of their practical value. We refer notably to the assurance held out in regard to the exemption of *pot kharab* lands from further assessment, as also the equally binding promise given that the work of re-measurement and reclassification of lands shall in future be either minimised, or dispensed with. By far the most important concession which has any value to the Rayat in the present day is the pledge now for the first time vouch-safed by Government, that improvements effected by the Rayat shall not be liable to be taxed on the expiration of the settlement. The necessity for a distinct promise on this head was forced upon Government by the ambiguous wording of the provisos of Section 107 of the Revenue Code, and we are glad to see that Government is now prepared to remove this section, or rather its provisos, from the Statute Book. The Hon'ble Mr. Hope must be thanked for thus forcing the hands of the Bombay Government. In his place in Council, during the discussions on the Land Improvement Loans Bill, Mr. Hope relied upon these provisos, and attempted to give them a wider interpretation than what the words of the Act warranted, or met the approval of the Local Authorities here. It is a comfort to know that in this respect the Hon'ble Mr. Hope was not authorized to decide what the policy of the Bombay Government is to be. That Government has lost no time in throwing Mr. Hope over-board, with all his boasts of the prosperous results of this short-sighted policy. Even Mr. Robert Knight, who has been for twenty years the great Defender of the Settlement Faith, and the unpaid advocate of the state ownership of all lands, has forsaken the standard of the Survey Officers, and pronounced against the iniquity of taxing improvements effected by private holders. This policy is now definitively abandoned. In the words of the Resolution "if in some cases, not at once perceptible, an increase of land revenue might be claimed under Clauses B and C. without violating any of the pledges given by Government from time to time, His Excellency in Council feels satisfied that no such advantage is comparable to the dis-advantage of retaining on the Statue Book a proviso, which is of such doubtful significance as to be capable of discouraging the investment of capital in agriculture, and the repeal of Section 107 in whole or part will, therefore, be taken into consideration." This concession so wrung from an un willing Government marks, as we have said above, a distinct step in advance towards the final decision of the whole question on the lines suggested by the Government of India for the modified introduction of a fixed and permanent settlement in this Presidency.

Another concession of equal importance is represented by the limitations of enhancements in revision settlement. These limitations were first formulated by Sir P. Wodehouse's Government in 1874, and were intended by him to be applicable throughout the Presidency. His successor, however, presumed to read between the lines of Sir P. Wodehouse's Resolution, and narrowed its application to two Districts only. This bone of contention has now been removed by para 37 of the present Resolution, which lays down that "the limitations of enhancement shall be observed in the revision of all original settlements of which the term expires after the revenue year 1883-84." Paras 5, 6, 8, 9, 10 and 11 of Sir P. Wodehouse's Resolution are quoted with approval in Para 36 of the new Resolution, but para 7 of the old Resolution, which was subsequently cancelled under orders of the Government of India, has not been reproduced, though for reasons, which we shall state in detail further on, it deserved a more prominent recognition on the present occasion, and ought to have been reproduced, more especially as the Government of India are at one with the Bombay Government in regard to the wisdom and justice of excluding the *pot kharab* lands from fresh assessment on the ground of their having been brought under cultivation subsequent to the first settlement. With this exception, this concession made after ten years discussion, has still a practical value in so far as it imposes a check to the maximum enhancements of discretion of Survey Officers.

While in these several respects the new Resolution will be hailed and deservedly hailed as a considerable boon by the agricultural classes, we cannot but regret that the value of these concessions should be, to a great extent, nullified by a proposal, which apparently has found favour with Government, to levy a tax on subsoil water advantages by what is called "a scarcely noticeable increase" of the soil rates on lands possessing such advantages in place of special water rates which are to be abandoned. Such a principle was, it appears, laid down in 1866 and re-affirmed in 1868. In a Resolution of 1868 the views of the Government were thus expressed :— "In regard to special taxation of wells it is said "with truth that water is, like mineral wealth, fairly taxable by the land-lord when used by the tenant. His Excellency in Council however considers that the first principle of its taxation should be that which governs the taxation of the land itself, viz. the capability of being used, rather than the use itself. If water of good quality be easily available near the surface, it is more reasonable to tax such lands by a light additional rate, whether the water be used or not, than to levy an oppressively heavy tax on those who expend capital and labour in bringing the water into use." It is admitted, however, that these principles were in abeyance for the past 15 years, as difficulties were experienced in carrying them into effect, and as a matter of fact, except in the Panch Mahals, the plan of taxing sub-soil water advantages has not been resorted to The Government has not ventured to state the nature of these difficulties which obliged it to sleep over this assertion of its rights for so long a time. We shall, however, render this service to Government by quoting their own words, from the self-same Resolution of 1868, from which Government has only quoted a portion as given above. That Resolution goes on to state that "there is, however, a point at which this principle must be modified; for when the land is such that when the water is not brought to it, it will bear nothing, and when water is used, it will yield a fine crop, then even a light tax in the former case is impossible. It must be held accordingly that the right of government to levy a rate by virtue of the water below the surface is in abeyance, or dormant till the water is produced, but it is doubted greatly even in this extreme case whether it is politic, though it may be asserted to be just, to levy more than would be leviable from first class rice ground which enjoys also the benefits of water, not created, it is true, by the tenant, but utilized by means of his preparation of the ground." The suppression of this portion of the Resolution, which furnishes a satisfactory answer to the crude suggestion made in the portion quoted by the Government in its recent Resolution, appears to us to be a very unfortunate omission. Even the Survey Officers felt scruples on this head. Major Prescott, Settlement Officer for

Gujerat, expressed himself strongly against the proposal to levy well assessment either on the bag, well, or the soil, because as he said "we cannot make right in practice what is wrong in principle." Sir B. Ellis, who was Revenue Commissioner in 1865, indeed proposed to tax the capability of sinking a well by digging within a few feet of the surface, and his scheme was ordered to be tried experimentally, but, as might be expected, it broke down utterly in the trial. Mr. Rogers stated officially that the proposal could not be carried out but by going through the whole of the processes preliminary to the imposition of a well-assessment under the existing system, and then putting on that assessment on the lands under the well. Colonel Francis stated that "it was impossible to make an addition to the Jirayat dry crop rates of all lands possessing a water-bearing stratum, that it would be necessary to take an existing well as the guide, and consider only the lands under it as having a water stratum." Mr. Rogers asked, "how was the classer to tell the depth of water from the surface, or its quality, in any field in which there is no well to guide him. He cannot dig everywhere, and it would be throwing too strong a temptation in the way of a man drawing perhaps 20 to 40 Rupees a month to allow him to put down his surmises. Officers of higher rank, above all suspicion of temptation, would simply throw up the attempt in disgust." If we mistake not, Mr. Havelock condemned the proposal in still more strong terms. Now that this abandoned proposal is to be taken up again, and sub-soil water advantages are to be taken into account in fixing the assessment on lands, it behoves Government to think twice before it commits itself to any such hopeless scheme which can only end in reviving old controversies, in discrediting the whole of the survey work by the introduction of an uncertain element in the calculation of the qualities of the soil, and in disturbing the relative equality of the incidence of taxation on which Government lay so much stress. Practically, the recognition of this new principle will unsettle the work of the Department from its commencement, for the classification of dry crop soils is made to depend chiefly upon the depth and the admixture of, or freedom from, faulty ingredients, without reference to external influences affecting its productive powers, such as climate, or water for irrigation. The impracticability of the proposal is written on the face of it. Sub-soil-water can always be found at more or less depth in every part of the country. The Settlement Officers are not supposed to be, and cannot in the nature of things be, experts, and will have no means of judging except after trial whether water can be had at the depth of a few feet, or so far below the surface as to render the gift almost useless. Without any accurate knowledge to guide them, the temptations to tax all lands for supposed advantages will be irresistible, and the chances of abuse of authority, against which so many precautions were taken by the framers of the Joint Rules, will be multiplied beyond control. In the end, this proposal will lead to a more or less arbitrary enhancement on all soils to cover the loss of revenue from the taxation on wells, the sacrifice of which revenue Government is so unwilling to reconcile itself to.

A similar proposal was made in regard to canal irrigation when the Irrigation Act was passed by the Local Council. Under the law, as passed by the local Legislature, and ratified by the assent of the Governor-General in Council, all lands commanded by the water of the canal were liable to be taxed with a protective rate scarcely noticeable in the individual field, but calculated in the aggregate to make up a large amount, whether in fact the owners of the adjacent lands took water from the canal, or refused to take it. We protested at the time against this abuse of Legislation, but our protest was made in vain. The matter finally was referred to the Secretary of State, and that authority overruled the action of the Bombay Government, and directed that the Act should be amended by the striking off of the obnoxious Sections, and the Local authorities had to give up their crude proposal. We warn Government that in the present case their hasty proposals, if carried into effect, will as surely meet with the same fate.

We have so far confined our remarks to prove the nugatory

and impracticable nature of the proposal to tax sub-soil water advantages, and the inconveniences to which it will lead. It is, however, necessary to examine the subject more in detail, and to discuss the matter on first principles. The idea apparently originated with Sir George Wingate, the father of the Bombay System of Revenue Settlement. Sir G. Wingate was of opinion "that the application of the cultivator's capital to the construction of a new well or the repair of an old one, does not create water for irrigation, but simply provides means for raising the water stored in the sub-soil to the surface, and applying it to the land. The well is the production of the cultivator's capital, but the water is not. The operation is analogous to the opening of a new mine. When once capital supplies the means of bringing the minerals to the surface in a form suitable to men's wants, it acquires value, and yields rent or royalty to the proprietor of the land from which it is extracted. Water, like minerals, is a subterranean product of great value, and therefore capable of legitimately yielding a rent to the lord of the soil, who is the Government in the present case." We have quoted this extract at some length with a view that full justice may be done to those who differ from us in this discussion. We also think that a full statement of the case for taxing subsoil water advantages is sufficient refutation by itself of the fallacies which under-lie this view of the matter. It will however be seen from the extract that Sir G. Wingate did not contemplate the actual levy of any assessment till the so-called sub-soil advantage was brought to the surface, and made available for the improvement of land. If the new proposal finds favour with Government, we shall have thus made after 20 years' experience the extraordinary progress of taxing supposed sub-soil advantages, whether or not they are brought to the surface, and this is to be done notwithstanding the fact that, at the time when Sir G. Wingate expressed his views, the Government set them aside on the ground that the right is dormant, or in abeyance till the land is benefited, and its water advantages are brought to the surface. The analogy of mineral wealth does not hold good because water, unlike minerals, is of no value except so far as it is applied to the irrigation of the land, which cannot be said to be the case with gold or silver mines.

There is, however, a stronger objection than all these considerations. Sir G. Wingate apparently was misled into the supposition that the Government was the lord of the soil, and as such entitled to claim rent for all possible advantages, which distinguish one soil from another. It is this fallacious supposition which lies at the root of all the misconceptions on the subject, and as long as this erroneous conception of state rights in the soil finds favour with Government, so long there will be little chance of any fair settlement of this land controversy. We have always maintained, and will continue to maintain till there is no occasion left for it, that the state has no proprietary rights in cultivated or waste lands, and that its interest is confined to a claim for a share of the produce, which may be more or less onerous, but is not of the nature of a monopoly or differential rent. The law on this subject is clear enough. As early as 1795, in the preamble to Regulation it was stated that, "by the ancient law of the country, the ruling power is entitled to a share of the produce." In our own Presidency, the law on the subject will be found clearly laid down in the Revenue Code, which in this respect reproduces the text of the old Regulations of 1827, which were themselves based upon the ancient law of the country. "Section 45 of the Revenue Code simply states that all land, except such as may be wholly or partially exempted, is liable to the payment of land revenue to Government." Regulation 17 of 1827 and Act 1 of 1865 are, if possible, still more explicit, for they recognise a distinction between owners and occupants of land. They mention specifically various proprietary tenures, and while designating the payment made to the State as land revenue, appropriate the term rent to the payment made by the occupant or tenant to the owner or superior holder. In the correspondence which preceded the framing of the Regulation of 1827, this point was expressly raised. One of the drafts submitted to the Court of Directors in 1822 asserted that the proprietary right in the land vested in the sovereign. This draft was rejected by the Court of Directors, who approved of a second draft in which it was stated that the ruling power was entitled only to a certain share in the produce of the land. In introducing the Bill which became subsequently Act 1 of 1865, Mr. Inverarity, who was in charge of the Bill, stated that "the acknowledged principle of an equitable land assessment was that Government was entitled to a certain share of the produce, the deduction of which leaves the cultivator a wide margin of profits after payment of all expenses." The question was again raised in 1856, when the Court of Directors formally laid down in their Despatch, dated 17th December 1856, that "the right of Government is not a rent, but a land revenue only, which ought, if possible, to be so lightly assessed as to leave a surplus or rent to the Rayat, whether he in fact lets the land to others, or retains it for his own cultivation." This same principle was re-affirmed by Sir Charles Wood in 1862, and by Sir Stafford Northcote in 1865, when Despatches were sent directing the redemption of land revenue, and the extension of the permanent settlement in all the old settled districts.

It is true the report of the Famine Commission gave countenance to the prevalent fallacy when it stated (pages 89 to 93) that, "by immemorial and unquestioned prescription, the Government is entitled to receive from the occupier of the land whatever portion of the surplus profit it requires, and that the land revenue may be regarded as a rent paid by the tenant, rather than a tax paid by the owner to the State." It is to be noted, however, that this view of the majority of the Famine Commissioners was dissented from by one of their own members, who protested "against the process of reasoning by which it is sought to uphold the theory first put forward by Mr. Wilson, that the land revenue in India is of the nature of rent, and that the ownership of the soil vests in the State." The Famine Commissioners cannot under any circumstances be regarded as an authority on this question, when their views are so opposed to the highest governing authorities, *viz.* the Court of Directors, and the Secretary of State. Judicial decisions without number can be cited in support of the same view. The Judicial Committee of the Privy Council, in a case reported in 11 Moore's Indian Appeals page 345, held that "the relation of land-lord and tenant did not exist between the Government and the owner of the lands which paid Jama or tribute. The holder's interest is an absolute ownership of the land, and the title of the Government rather resembles a seignory than that of a leasor with a reversion." To come nearer home, Mr. Mountstuart Elphinstone, in his report of 1819 on the territory conquered from the Peshwas, stated that " a large portion of the Rayats were the proprietors of their estates subject to the payment of a fixed tax to Government." Reviewing all these authorities, the late Chief Justice of the High Court of Bombay held it to be proved, in the Canara land case, that "as far as the Hindu law is concerned, the proprietary right of the sovereign derives no warrant from the ancient laws or the institutions of the Hindus, and is not recognised by modern Hindu lawyers as exclusive, or incompatible with individual ownership." The Mahomedan traditions are no doubt of a more arbitrary character, but in this Presidency, fortunately for the country, the British Government succeeded to the rule of Hindu sovereigns, and Mahomedan precedents have therefore no application.

There is no doubt as to what the Hindu law is on the subject. More than a thousand years ago, a commentator on the great work of Jaimini, author of the Purva Mimamsa, in discussing the question of the King's rights in cultivated land, laid down.

दुष्टशिक्षाशिष्टपरिपालनाभ्यां राज्ञः ईशितृत्वं स्मृत्यभिप्रेतम् इति, नराज्ञो भूमिर्धनं किंतु तस्यां भूमौ स्वकर्मफलंभुञ्जानानां सर्वेषां प्राणिनां साधारणं धनम् अतोसाधारण खण्डस्य सत्यपिदाने महाभूमेर्दानं नास्ति.

Another commentary on the same text states

पृथिव्यां संभूतानां व्रीह्यादीनां रक्षगेन निर्विष्टस्य कस्यचित् भागस्य ईष्टे न भूमेः तन्निर्विष्टाश्च ये मनुष्याः तैरअन्यत् सर्व प्राणिनां धारणविक्रमणादि यत् भूमिकृतं तत्रेशत्वंप्रति न कश्चित् विशेषः तस्मात् भूमिर्नदेया.

Colebrooke's rough translation of the above passages is to the following effect. "The kingly power is for the government of the realm, and the extirpation of wrong-doers, and for that purpose he receives taxes from husbandmen, but the right of property in land is not vested in him. The earth is not the King's, but is common to all beings enjoying the fruits of their own labours." Yajnavalkya has even gone further than these authorities. He says that "the King has no particular property in unclaimed or uncultivated land. If a subject chooses, he may occupy it without leave, giving the Raja his due." In Manu's time, land as such was contemplated as a subject of taxation. The land belonged to him

16

INDUSTRIAL CONFERENCE*

At the desire of the Chairman, and on behalf of the promoters of this movement, I wish to bespeak your favourable attention to a few observations on the objects of this Conference. We are met here to-day, for a purpose which is eminently catholic and acceptable to all. The programme of the Congress gatherings is avowedly Political. Here we eschew Politics altogether, for there is really no conflict of interests between the Rulers and the Ruled, who all alike desire to promote the Industrial and Economic Progress of this Country. The object of the Social Conference, similarly, sets the Reformers and the Orthodox majority in apparent opposition. Here, on the Economical platform, all shades of opinion, all differences of views on Social, Political, and Religious subjects, may unite and co-operate. This is a point on which it is needless to dilate much. Our people in times of old set to themselves only one question, and all our Works on Philosophy and Science commence and end with the Problem of Deliverance from Evil—which is described to be three- fold—the Weakness and Sinfulness of our internal Nature, the Evils we suffer from others, whether Gods or men, and lastly, the Evils we suffer by reason of our Physical Surroundings. People will not easily agree as to the method of Deliverance

*Inaugural Address at the first Industrial Conference, Poona 1890, published in *Essays*.

from the first set of Evils—hence the diversity of Creeds. In their advocacy of their own particular Creed, they will not even admit the right of others to cross-question them about their Faith, and they are too often disposed to deny the existence of any sin or weakness when challenged by others. In respect of the Second class of Evils, different classes of men will necessarily disagree to some extent and proposals for co-operation are not always welcome. In regard to the Third class of Evils, however, presented by the poverty of our resources, and our physical weakness, all men are agreed, and all have a common interest in co-operating together for the common good. In this Country especially, there is no room for a difference of opinion. Hindus and Mahomedans, Parsees and Christians, the Rulers and the Ruled, the Privileged and the Unprivileged Classes, all stand on a common platform, and, as the constitution of the present meeting itself demonstrates, are prepared to work together. The work of this Conference thus possesses certain advantages which are denied to similar gatherings, for other more or less Sectarian and Party purposes.

The Problem we have met here to consider is one of Ways and Means. About the existence of the Evil, there is no difference of opinion among us. The highest Official authorities like Sir Evelyn Baring, Sir William Hunter, and others, with the highest Non-official authorities such as Professor Dadabhai Naoroji and Mr. Hyndman, are agreed in admitting that the Poverty of this Country is phenomenal. The existence of this Poverty needs no demonstration. We need only walk through our streets, and study the most superficial aspects of our Economic situation, and the fact forces itself upon us that we are a people of little resources. Many millions among us scarcely earn a couple of annas a day, many millions more are always underfed, and live on the borderland of Famine and slow Death, into which the failure of a single Monsoon precipitates them. Of course, this condition of things is not of yesterday, and is not the result Soiely of Foreign Conquest and Competition. It is an old, a very old Inheritance. If we feel it more keenly now, we feel it because we are being roused from the Sleep of Ages, and our eyes have learnt to see, and our ears have learnt to hear.

The question of our comparative improvement or decline under Foreign Rule is similarly a question of Antiquarian History. The practical question for us all to lay to heart is not the relative, but the absolute Poverty and the present helplessness of the Country generally. To a certain extent, the historical discussion of the situation is instructive. There can be no doubt that, whatever may have been our improvement in other respects, we have in recent times become more than ever dependent upon the Single resource of Agriculture, precarious and contingent as that resource is, upon influences we cannot control or count upon with certainty. The co-ordination of Industries, which regulates the due proportions of men who plough the soil and raise raw produce with those who manufacture this raw produce, and others still, who exchange and distribute it, and the interplay of whose three-fold activities makes a Nation thrive, was never a very strong factor of our collective Social Polity. We have been all along like most Ancient Nations, more or less exclusively agricultural. But our contact with the world outside, and the freedom of Exchange which has resulted in consequence, have produced one most undesirable result. They have aggravated the situation by making us more than ever dependent upon a Single and precarious resource. The Industry and Commerce of the Country, such as it was, is passing out of our hands, and, except in the large Presidency Towns, the Country is fed, clothed, warmed, washed, lighted, helped, and comforted generally, by a thousand Arts and Industries in the manipulation of which its Sons have every day a decreasing share. Foreign Competition, not because it is foreign, but because it is the competition of Nature's powers against man's Labour—it is the competition of organised Skill and Science against Ignorance and Idleness—is transferring the monopoly not only of the wealth, but what is more important, of skill, talent, and activity to others.

The increases of our Exports and Imports should not dazzle our vision. The increase is good so far as it goes; but it is not unmixed good, with that increase shows that we are only perfecting ourselves in the faculty of growing Raw Produce, and are forgetting by disuse, the skill and the wealth of resources which manufacturing and industrial activity brings in its train. Last year, we exported sixteen Crores of Rupees' worth of Wheat, Rice and Pulses, fifteen Crores Raw Cotton, ten and a half Crores Opium, nine and a half Crores Oil-Seeds, eight Crores, Raw Jute, nearly five Crores of Hides and Skins, one Crore of Raw Wool, three-fourths of a Crore's worth of Dye Stuffs, half a Crore of Spices, half a Crore of Raw Silk, and a Crore of Miscellaneous Produce. Out of a total of nearly one hundred Crores of Produce exported, seventy-five Crores were thus raw Goods, while of manufactured or half-manufactured Goods, Cotton six and one-third Crores, Jute nearly two Crores, Sugar half a Crore, Tea five and a quarter Crores, Indigo four Crores, and Coffee two Crores, making a total of only twenty Crores, were exported, and of these twenty Crores nearly twelve Crores were again the product of Foreign skill and capital. While we exported raw Cotton, worth fifteen Crores of Rupees and six and three-quarter Crores worth of Cotton Goods, we imported twenty-seven Crores of Cotton Goods, and nearly four Crores' worth of Twist and Yarn. This single Export and Import respresents the change in our condition typically, and in fact sums up the situation. India, fifty years ago, clothed herself with her own Manufactures, and now she is clothed by her distant masters. The same is the case with Wool, Silk and other Textiles, with Oils and Hides. In 1888-89 we imported forty-one Laks of Rupees' worth Umbrellas, fifteen Laks' worth of Children's Toys and Games, twenty-two Laks of Stationery, forty-one Laks' worth of Paper, ten Laks of Soap, twenty Laks of Matches, sixty-six Laks worth of Glass, ten Laks' worth of Clocks and Watches, Carriages worth seven Laks of Rupees, eight Laks Candles, ten Laks Furniture, fifteen Laks' worth of Arms and Ammunition, twenty-one and a half Laks of Books, sixteen Laks of Leather and Leather Goods, thirty-one Laks of

Paints, nearly two Crores' worth of Oils, both Kerosene and Seed Oils, nearly two and a half Crores of Railway Materials, two and one-third Crores of Machinery and Mill-work, and Iron, Steel, and Metals of all sorts worth five Crores in all. We imported even Flour, Salt, and Salted Fish, and lastly Grain and Pulse. This is our condition, and when the whole situation is thus taken in at one view we feel that we are standing on the edge of a precipice, and the slightest push down will drive us into the abyss below of unmixed and absolute helplessness. Our Shipping is not ours; not even the Coasting Trade is carried on in our Bottoms. The proportion of Native Craft to the total tonnage is two and a third per cent, and it is a stationary percentage. Our Banking is not ours, though to a large extent we find the money which finances the Exchange Banks. The Insurance and the Freight and the Commission Business are all foreign Monopolies, and the Foreign Merchant's hand is seen trafficking direct with our producers in the remotest and smallest Villages. The Railways are admittedly foreign Monopolies. We have, of course, no legitimate ground to complain about these Foreign Agencies. They do very useful work and they are our masters, and helpful masters too, if we are apt pupils. They all indicate one fact which our people should lay to heart, but which they are too often tempted to lose sight of. Political ascendancy is not the only particular vantage ground which we have lost. Commercial and Manufacturing predominance naturally transfers Political ascendancy, and in this our collapse has been even far more complete. Of course, the situation is not hopeless, for no situation is ever hopeless to those who master its real significance, and resolve to do their best to improve it. As stated above, the question at issue is one of Ways and Means, and it is this question which we have met to consider.

There are some people who think that, as long as we have a heavy tribute to pay to England, which takes away nearly twenty Crores of our surplus Exports, we are doomed and can do nothing to help ourselves. This is, however, hardly a fair or manly position to take up. A portion of the burden represents interest on money advanced to, or invested in, our Country, and so far from complaining, we have reason to be thankful that we have a Creditor who supplies our needs at such a low rate of interest. Another portion represents the value of Stores supplied to us, the like of which we cannot produce here. The remainder is alleged to be more or less necessary for the purposes of Administration, Defence and payment of Pensions, and though there is good cause for complaint that it is not all necessary, we should not forget the fact that we are enabled by reason of this British connection to levy an equivalent tribute from China by our Opium Monopoly. I would not therefore desire you to divert and waste your energies in the fruitless discussion of this question of tribute which had better be left to our Politicians.

Secondly, in certain quarters, it is feared that till we find in India Coal and Iron in abundance, our struggle with the present situation is hopeless. The answer to this is, that the resources of Iron and Coal that have been discovered are not utilised by us to the full extent. It will be time enough to complain when we have done our best with the existing Coal and Iron Fields. There can be no question that the success of foreign Competition is greatly helped by the abundance of these materials, but far more helpful than these materials is the spirit and skill which work them, and which conquered India long before Steam Power came into use, and which turned the balance of Trade against India. If we but acquire the spirit and the skill, the resources will be discovered in yet unexplored situations all over the Country.

Thirdly, people are also heard to ask in despair the question, Where is the Capital to come from which will enable us to buy the Coal, Iron, and Machinery, and hire Foreigners' skill, and make them do service for us here? Our resources are no doubt scanty, but they are abundant enough, in all conscience, if we would only use them as such, and not throw them away into the sea, as we do year after year, in deference to old traditions, and antiquated fears and mistrust. Every year we import in Treasure Bullion, Gold and Silver of the value of twelve Crores' worth, *i.e.*, three Crores of Gold and nine Crores of Silver. The whole of the Gold disappears, and is absorbed by the soil, and of the Silver seven Crores are sent by us to the Mint every year, and the rest is absorbed like Gold. Since 1834, this absorbing process has secured the virtual destruction of nearly four hundred and fifty Crores of Wealth, which might have been turned to better account. The saving of four hundred and fifty Crores in fifty-five years by twenty-five Crores of people is not a sign of great prosperity, but we have made our position worse by burying it or using it unproductively. This hoarding, at least, proves that nearly eight Crores of Rupees may be each year turned to capital account, if we were only resolved so to use it.

Fourthly, of course, in the choice of Ways and Means, it is not open to us to adopt certain plans of operation, which, however much they might be condemned on abstract grounds, have been followed with practical success in many of the most enlightened Countries of Europe and America. We cannot, as with the Government of these Countries, rely upon Differential Tariffs to protect Home Industries during their experimental trial. We cannot expect the Government here, to do what France or Germany does for their Shipping Trade, and their Sugar Industry, and ask Government Bounties, and subsidies to be paid out of general Taxes. These are heresies according to English Political Economy, such as is taught to us, and whether they be really so or not, it is useless to divert our energies in fruitless discussion, and seek to achieve victory over Free Trade. We may, however, fairly expect Government to try as an experiment the Policy of the Culture System which the Dutch Government actually worked for thirty years in its own Possessions in the East Indies with signal success, and the principle of which is acknowledged by the Government of India in its Policy of *Tagai* advances, and its Railway development. If the Government borrows Crores of Rupees every year and constructs Railways and Canals out of these loans, it can as well encourage the growth of new Industries, by guaranteeing or subsidising such Enterprises in their pioneering stage. It has done so successfully in pioneering

Tea, Cinchona, and Cotton Enterprise in certain parts, and it can well extend the scope of its operations in other and more fruitful directions. It can also very well be asked to produce its own Stores here, just as it produces certain minor articles required by its Military and Postal Department. It can also undertake to buy Leather, Woollen Goods, &c., from the Indian Producer, and thus secure the benefit of a sure custom at remunerative rates to new undertakings. It can, finally, help people to join their Capital together under such Guarantees and Official supervision and afford such special facilities as the Government of Europe have extended to Land Improvement Banks.

After all, Government help can do but little, save pioneering work. The Government of India is anxious to help us. It is prepared to encourage Emigration abroad, and Immigration from densely crowded to sparsely inhabited tracts. But, where are the men who are prepared to take advantage of this extended field of Colonization both in India, Burmah, and elsewhere? We have yet to realise the situation. We have to resolve to work earnestly and perseveringly with a purpose and an organization which will conquer all obstacles. The Evil is too great, and of too long a standing, to be brought under control by private individual efforts. We have to work with a will, to pull long, and pull all, and to pull till we succeed. It is on this account that we are met together. This is only a Preliminary Meeting. We have to move the other Provinces, and arrange for a General Conference of those who think with us on this matter, and when the men of light and leading from different parts meet together, we may hope to set the ball rolling. The Promoters of the movement have not hit upon this Conference on the spur of the moment, or as an agreeable distraction. The idea has been slowly developing itself. It first found expression in a speech made two years ago at Ahmednagar. Since then friends have worked, and tried to educate Public Opinion. A very thoughtful article covering the entire range of the Indian Economical situation, and suggesting Ways and Means, appeared in one of our Journals, and it has attracted extensive notice. The particular positions taken up in that article may be controverted, and have in fact been controverted, but its general accuracy as a description of the existing state of things has not been questioned, and if it promotes discussion, it may yet serve most important purposes. I think, I have placed before you the whole situation, and have also given you an idea of the lines on which I desire that the entire question should be discussed, now or hereafter. We have to keep in mind the following almost axiomatic Truths in all our deliberations.

1. The work of the Conference should be conducted, and its Constitution framed on Non-Sectarian and Non-Party lines, so that all Classes of people may take part in it.

2. What we have chiefly to avoid is the pursuit of impracticable objects. We should husband our little resources to the best of our power, and not exhaust them by vain complaints against the drain of the Indian Tribute, or by giving battle with Free Trade.

3. We must realize clearly our exact situation, *i.e.*, first, our phenomenal Poverty, and secondly, our growing dependence on the single and precarious resources of Agriculture.

4. Having realised this situation, we must strive to correct it with a full sense that we cannot do all that we wish in a single year or a decade, and that we can at the most create the spirit and the tendency, and initiate the Movement of Change and set it afloat.

5. The proper scope of the work to be done is to correct the disproportion between our engrossing production of Raw Agricultural Produce, and our backwardness in the production and distribution of Manufactured Produce

6. In the accomplishment of this aim, we should not forget that there are permanent advantages and disadvantages en-

joyed by certain Countries and Races, which regulate the distribution and choice of Labour, and that we cannot hope to accomplish impossibilities. And yet, within these limits, there is ample scope for good and honest work, for many a decade to come, in the utilization of our existing—relatively to us ample, though as compared with other Countries scanty,—resources of natural Agents and Capital, with our limitless Supply of Labour. The skill and patience of our Industrial Classes are a rich inheritance which cannot fail to help us, if we but provide a larger sphere for its growth and training.

7. Bearing these limitations and advantages in mind, our more immediate efforts should be directed to the improvement by Art and Industry of our raw wealth of Agricultural Produce, and of the articles which we send away as Raw Produce, and import as Manufactured Produce.

8. No Hand-made Industry can hope to thrive in competition with Industry moved by cheap Natural Agents. The free use of Natural Agents, moreover, makes large investments of Capital a necessity, and thus handicaps all individual efforts beyond rivalry. What we have to bear in mind is, therefore, the organization for Industry and Capital on the Joint Stock principle for collective and large undertakings.

9. The superior skill of the Foreigner must be availed of freely by importing it from other Countries, till we train up our own people for the work, first, in Technical Institutes here and in Foreign Countries, and further, in the far more practical discipline of Factories and Mills at work.

10. Our Resources of Capital are scanty, but if we only knew how to use such resources as we have, and brought them together, we have more Wealth and Capital than we can at present properly handle.

11. While we put forth our energies in these directions, we can well count upon the assistance of the State in regulating our

Co-Operative efforts by helping us to form Deposit and Finance Banks, and facilitating recoveries of advances made by them, by encouraging New Industries with Guarantees or Subsidies, or Loans at low interest, by pioneering the way to new Enterprises, and by affording facilities for Emigration and Immigration, and establishing Technical Institutes, and buying more largely the Stores they require here, and in many cases by producing their own Stores.

12. State help is, after all, a subordinate factor in the Problem. Our own exertion and our own resolutions must conquer the difficulties, which are chiefly of our own creation.

These are a few of the thoughts which occur to me at this moment. You are most of you far better and more practically versed in these matters than I can well hope to be, and if I were called upon to justify this presumption on my part, I can only appeal to the fact that it has been the Brahmin's Hereditary Privilege to formulate the Nation's Wants and suggest Remedies. With these observations, I shall, with your permission, conclude the speech and resume my seat.

17

NETHERLANDS INDIA AND THE CULTURE SYSTEM*

THE Economic Problem which the Government of India has to grapple with in the immediate future of this Country is of a far more peremptory character than even the question of Frontier Defences against Foreign aggression, and it presents difficulties and uncertainties by the side of which the difficulties and uncertainties of the military situation are but child's play. The problem of settling New Continents, and planting on virgin soil 'Greater Britains,' has been so satisfactorily solved by the patience and genius of the British race, that it might, at first sight, surprise the superficial observer that the comparatively easy task of reclaiming India from the ancient bondage of Feudalism and Status, and bringing it into line with modern civilization, with its freedom of Contracts and the increasing activity of Commerce and Manufactures, which supplement the ancient single resource of Agriculture in Western Europe should have baffled the best efforts of British Statesmanship. After a Century of rule, the situation is as blank and dreary as ever it was before, nay, in certain aspects, it has grown worse by reason of the impact of civilized Foreign Rule and unrestricted Exchange, and undreamed of facilities of communication. The

*Published in *JPSS*, April 1890, Vol.XII, No.4, and in *Essays*.

co-ordination of Industries, which establishes a healthy proportion between the Rural and Urban Populations, had been displaced to a greater extent than ever it was before, and has increased the dependence of multitudes on the soil exhausted by over-cultivation. The growth of Population does not represent to the same extent growth in material comforts, and has led to the absorption of waste lands till, in some parts of the Country, the last margin has been reached, and millions die or starve when a single Monsoon fails. The increased Trade and Commerce of the Country represents a steadily diminishing proportion of Native enterprise and skill engaged in it, and the monopoly of Political power is made more invidious by the monopoly of commercial Wealth and manufacturing activity. The Bible-promise that '*To him that hath, much shall be given, and from him that hath not, the little that he hath shall be taken away*' sums up the situation.

The Administration cannot be charged with neglect or indifference to these changes. It has been honestly trying to apply palliatives, it ensures peace, protects Property and Labour, and secures the administration of Justice to all. It encourages emigration to foreign parts, and immigration from densely peopled portions to sparsely inhabited tracts. It has endeavoured to develop new sources of Wealth by encouraging pioneering enterprise. Above all, it has tried to open up the Country and utilize its Water Supply in a way which commands admiration. Its powers of action are limited and controlled by higher Authorities, and it is not, therefore, free to adopt certain remedies which commend themselves to Self-governing Countries in Europe, America, and the British Colonies, to protect themselves against the effects of foreign Competition, but, with this exception, everything has been done that human prescience could suggest, as possible remedies. Finally, it is open to conviction, and even prepared to retrace its steps, if it were convinced beyond doubt of its mistake. This circumstance justifies hope, and encourages the efforts of those who think that, notwithstanding past failures, a way may be found out of the difficulty, which involves no serious departure from established maxims of Civilized Rule, and promises success at no distant date.

I propose in the sequel to give a brief sketch of a great Experiment worked out by a European Power to improve the Economic condition of its Asiatic Dependencies, under circumstances very similar to those which obtain in India. There, as here, a civilized European Power was entrusted with the rule of vast Territories inhabited by a comparatively barbarous people, and the experiment was undertaken and persevered in, not purely from philanthropic motives, which prove weak in the long run, but from motives of Self-Interest, and resulted in a success, by the side of which the comparative failure of the efforts of British Rulers presents a very suggestive contrast. After being worked for thirty years, the experiment has been abandoned, because the special purpose, which dictated its adoption, has been to a large extent accomplished. The parallel is not, of course, complete in all respects. The Country where the experiment was tried was a small one, as compared with the vast expanse of India. The people, among whom it was tried, were a more homogeneous race than those who inhabit this Great Continent. The previous historical traditions were also not the same. But after making all allowance for these differences, there remains a sufficient substratum of common conditions, which justifies the assurance that an experiment undertaken in the same spirit here, with the necessary adaptations to suit local conditions, has a reasonable chance of attaining at least qualified success, so as to justify the venture.

The Experiment, to which the foregoing remarks relate, was tried by the Netherlands Government in their possessions in the East Indian Archipelago, Java and the Islands surrounding it. Java, it may be noted, became a Dutch conquest in the best days of Dutch domination on the Seas. It was administered by the Dutch East India Company in its own interests. The Company had the exclusive right of the Trade with Java, and it monopolized the production of Spices, the most paying produce of the Island, by continuing the ancient system of Forced Labour and Forced Deliverances. The Dutch Company left the Native Chiefs to rule the people, and confined their direct administration to the European Settlers in the Ports on the coast. In the French Wars, the Islands were under British management from 1811 to 1816, in which latter year, they were restored back to the Dutch, on the conclusion of Peace. Sir Stamford Raffles was British Governor during those years. Under the administration of this British Governor, the Indian *Ryotwari* System of fixed cash rates on land was introduced, the Native Magistracy was displaced, and European Agency in the Administration of Civil and Criminal Justice was substituted, and he declared that land was freely saleable for debts and arrears of Revenue. He abolished Forced Labour, and Monopolies of export and production, and threw open the trade of the Islands to all the world. These lines of policy will be easily recognized to be the lines of policy which have been steadily followed in British India. When the Islands were restored back to the Dutch, they, however, preferred to reverse this policy. They declared the lands to be unsaleable for debts or arrears of Government Revenue. They abolished the *Ryotwari* System of small Holdings at fixed cash rates, and reverted to the ancient Native method of Joint Village Responsibility. The task of direct Government by means of an European Agency was given up, and the authority of Native Chiefs, or Regents as they were called, was utilized for the government of the Native population. They abolished Free Trade, and substituted Differential Duties on imports from foreign parts. The Old System of levying the Land Tax in the shape of one-fifth of the produce and one-fifth of the labour of Agriculturists for State purposes, was restored, with the modification that the Labour share was reduced to one-seventh, or one day in the week. The tax both in produce and Labour in respect of Government Land was paid to the Native Chiefs in Territories governed by Treaty Chiefs and to the Dutch Government in Territories acquired by conquest. In respect of these Government Lands, the Peasants who cultivated them had only the usufructuary interest, and could not sell or alienate their right of user. In regard to private lands, the Peasants paid the rent, in kind and labour, to the private Owners who could not raise the rent as fixed by Law, and the private Owner paid to Government one-fifth of the net income or rent, or three-quarters of one per cent on Value. The Private Lands were liable to sale, and could be freely mortgaged or alienated. They could not, however, be sold until movables were exhausted, and even then, the Judge fixed the price, and the creditor had to take it at that price, if no bid was made, or the bids were lower. The Peasant had recognized status both in the advantages and burdens of the Joint Responsibility System of the Village. If he reclaimed new land, no tax was levied for the first five years. The Tax of one-fifth produce was settled with the Village Chief (corresponding to our Patel), and he distributed the burden. The Labour-share of the rent, one day's work out of a week, was utilised on the Public Roads and Canals, and other Public Works, and Private Landlords used it for the cultivation of their own lands. Each Householder was required to furnish one adult male for Forced Labour, whatever might be the number of members in the family. In course of time, it came to pass that the Villagers jointly employed a certain number of hired hands at their own expense on State Works, and discharged this burden of Forced Labour. To a large extent these principles still regulate the Administration of the Dutch East Indies.

For the Native Territories, Residents are appointed, who discharge Judicial, Administrative, and Financial duties. These duties, however, are light. The judicial work especially is lightened by investing Native Chiefs with large powers of conciliation and arbitration. The Resident sitting with two Native Members, decides criminal cases as Session Judge. In regard to Europeans, there are separate Courts of Justice presided over by Dutch lawyers. The Resident's salary is £1,250 a year, and he earns by commission a similar amount. Assistant Residents receive £500 per year. The Resident's Secretary is also a European Official. He has charge of Registration work, and is a

Treasury Officer and Record Keeper. Besides the Residents and their Assistants and Secretaries, there are Controllers of two classes charged with the duty of watching the condition of the Peasants, and of promoting their welfare. The Comptroller exercises no Judicial Powers, but is expected to act as Arbitrator or Conciliator. He has charge of Government Stores and is paid a salary which rises from £225 to £375 a year. The Residents with the Assistants and the Comptrollers of the several Provinces are under the authority of the Governor-General in Council. The work of actual government is, however, carried on by Native Chiefs. European Officers make suggestions or inspection Reports, but have no power to issue orders or enforce execution. Under the Resident there is a Native Regent for the Province, and there are District and Village Chiefs under the Regent. If a difference of opinion occurs between the Residents and the Regents, reference is made to the Central Authority. The Regent's salary ranges from £800 to £1,500 a year, and he also obtains a Percentage or Commission. He holds a sort of a Court, and is not only the Civil Ruler, but also the High Priest for his Province. The Regent exercises both Civil and Criminal powers except as regards Europeans, and the Residents are, at least in theory, deputed by Government to the Court of the Native Regent. The Regents are assisted by a Council of Vazirs, and have their own Secretaries and Clerks. The Regents preside over the Police Force, and have in their hands the appointment and control of the subordinate Native, District and Village Officials and Chiefs. These subordinate officials are called Mantries in Villages, and Vedanas in Districts, and receive salaries and commissions. They exercise Revenue and Police functions, and act as Conciliators, and no suit is entertained till conciliation fails. The Governor- General has a Council of four, and there is a High Court of Judicature with jurisdiction over Europeans and Natives of rank in the Coast Towns.

It was necessary to give these details of land management and Government in Java for a correct understanding of the experiment of the Culture System about to be described. It will be seen from them that the Dutch Government have steadily adhered to the Native model of Government, and limited the foreign Agency to the work of inspection and report, except in regard to the Dutch or other foreign Settlements in the Coast Towns. The difference between the British Indian System and the Netherlands' method of Rule is radical, the latter being Conservative and Protective, while the former is based on modern ideas of equality and is worked out by a much larger foreign Agency, than is found necessary in the Dutch Indies. The one system is, therefore, necessarily costly, and requires checks upon checks, and a hierarchy of officials. Notwithstanding its costliness due to the larger employment of Europeans, there can be no doubt that in its educating influence the British Indian System compares favourably with the Dutch method of Rule. That method, however, has its own advantages. It does not dismember Native Society to the same extent, as is found to be the case in India.

To proceed with the narrative, the Netherlands Possessions in the East Indies cover an area of 30,000 square miles. The population in 1885 was estimated to be about thirty millions. The Revenues in 1826 were eighteen million Florins, or one and a quarter Crores of Rupees, and they rose to thirty millions, or two Crores of Rupees, in 1833. In the years which preceded the introduction of the Culture System, the expenditure exceeded the revenue by three million Florins annually, for many years. This involved state of the finances first suggested to General Von de Bosch, Governor of the Netherlands East Indies, the necessity of taking urgent measures for developing the resources of the Island, and the plan followed by him is known as the Culture System. It was first introduced about the year 1831-33, and continued in operation for more than thirty years. The Theory of the system was that all Government Lands not required for Rice cultivation, which afforded subsistence to the cultivators, were to be planted with crops for which there was a demand in Europe, by means of advances to be made by the State to private Contractors, who undertook to plant the particular crops, and sell the produce to Government at fixed rates, and liquidate the advance made to them by instalments in a fixed number of years. These advances were of several kinds. The first in order, was the advance for initial expenditure necessary to start the concern. It might be a Planting concern or a Manufacturing concern. The Contractor received this advance under due regulations. In the first place, the advance to any particular Contractor was not to exceed two hundred thousands of Florins, or about £14,000. Though no interest was charged on this advance, it was repayable in twelve years by instalments of one-tenth from the third year. Care was taken to see that the Contractor was not a mere speculator, and the money was advanced to him under Official superintendence, which helped him to a choice of the site, as also in selecting and buying the machinery, and fitting up the mill, or making the water power available. In regard to the labour required for managing the concern, Government at first transferred to the Contractor the gratuitous or Forced Labour due to it from the peasants. The machinery was allowed to be imported duty free, and timber and other materials from Government Forests were supplied without charge. The Official experts assisted him with their advice. The Superintending Officer's certificate was necessary to satisfy Government that the money was spent for the purposes for which it was borrowed. Next to this initial advance, a yearly advance for the production or manufacture of crops was made on condition of being repaid out of the produce raised, at prices which were fixed in a way to leave a margin of profit, both to Government and to the Contractor. The Farms seldom exceeded four hundred acres. At first the whole of the produce was made over to Government at one-third above the cost price. This plan was found not to work well, and later on, the Government agreed to buy the produce at contract rates, which were fixed, so as to repay the yearly advance, and one-tenth of the initial or the building advance. Generally, the rates were so fixed that the delivery of two-thirds of the manufactured produce repaid the yearly advance, and left one-third as profit out of which the initial advance was repaid. The areas adapted for particular crops were chosen by Government Officers, who left in each Village sufficient land for Rice cultivation for the peasants, and required the villagers to plant one-fifth of their lands with the Contractor's crops. When one-fifth area was thus set apart for the contractor's crops, no Land-Tax was levied from that village. If, after paying the yearly advance and one-tenth of the building advance, any surplus was left, the Contractor had to share it with the villagers. In course of time, experience showed that the practice of remitting the Land-Tax worked unjustly, and it was accordingly given up, and in its place another plan was adopted by which the full rent was collected from the Village, and the labourers were paid individually in cash for the work done. Under this new arrangement, out of the cash payments made for wages, the villagers were enabled to pay the Government demand without the necessity of borrowing. In short, the Java Culture System may be described as a system of encouraging the planting of remunerative crops, and manufacturing them for the European market, by private agency and at private risk, with Government advances, and under Government supervision, and with the Government as the sole customer. All the three parties who worked the System, the Government, the Contractor, and Peasants, benefited by it. The Government borrowed money, as it alone could borrow, on Public Credit, and bought the produce so raised by Contractors to whom the money was advanced at low rates of interest, and it repaid itself, both principal and interest, by buying at rates which left a large margin of profit on sale in Europe. The Contractor, after he paid off the advances made to him, became the owner of a large and flourishing Concern, while the Villagers or Peasant labourers received much higher wages than they ever could obtain before, or shared in surplus profits. The Culture System was worked to best advantage in respect of First Class crops, such as Sugarcane, Indigo, Tea, Tobacco, and Cochineal, which required high planting, and skill in manufacture. There were, however, certain kinds of produce such as Coffee, Cinnamon, and Pepper, of the Second Class, which did not require planting or manufacturing skill. The intervention of Contractors was, therefore, dispensed with in their case, and advances were made to the Cultivators direct, and as with our own Opium Cultivation in Behar, prices were fixed beforehand through the Official Agency in such a way as to leave a margin of profit to the Cultivators as also to the Government, which had a right to buy the entire crop at fixed rates. The Sugarcane crop was the most remunerative, and next to it was Tobacco cultivation. The vigilance of the Official Agency was secured by a percentage as commission paid to them on the quantity of produce raised. The self-interest of the villagers was sharpened by a rule, which directed that if the crops failed, they should get nothing. In 1854, while two and a half millions of acres were under Rice cultivation, one hundred thousand acres were planted under the Culture System. The Land Rent paid to Government on these one hundred thousand acres was assessed at the Rice rates. The Government looked to the profits realized by it, on sale of the crops in Holland, as their only return.

The first Contracts were made for twenty years, and at the end of that period were renewed for another term. About thirty to forty Crores of Rupees were in all advanced under this System, and when the first advances were repaid, they were reinvested on similar terms. During the last twenty years, there have been no renewals. At present Independent Planters are encouraged to settle on Government lands, out of which large plots of uncultivated lands, measuring three hundred to four hundred acres, are leased for twenty years. No rent is charged for the first few years, and afterwards rent of Rupees two to three is charged as cultivation extends. The Reports of Local Authorities show that, notwithstanding the experience obtained under the Culture System, and the obligation on Government to buy produce at fixed rates, the Independent System of planting does not prove as profitable as the old system of protected and subsidized Planting and Manufacture. The two main defects of the most recent arrangements are : Firstly, the high rate of interest which the Planters and Manufacturers have to pay; and secondly, the absence of Official guidance which was secured under the old System. A Sugarcane Plantation, which cost two hundred thousand of Florins under the old System, was worth nearly three times as much at the end of the period, after the loans advanced had been paid off. The Independent System works well enough in regard to crops which do not require high skill and care. But, in the case of Sugar and Tobacco, the results are decidedly in favour of the Culture System.

This brief description of the Culture System will suffice to convey a general idea of the way in which General Von de Bosch succeeded in developing the resources of the Island. The experiment was undertaken merely for Revenue purposes, but indirectly it helped the Netherlands East Indies to attain a high degree of material prosperity. The deficits, which had, previously to 1831, been almost continuous for many years, were changed into surpluses of many millions of Florins. The Land Revenue, which was eighteen million Florins in 1817, and thirty millions, or two Crores of Rupees, in 1833, rose to one hundred and thirty-six million Florins in 1860, that is, nearly nine and a half Crores of Rupees. The advances required for the Culture System were made out of sums borrowed by the State, and this National Debt was repaid with interest in forty years out of the large profits which the State made by the sale of produce in Holland, so that in 1871 the Government of the Netherlands India had no National Debt. The surpluses of Revenue between 1831 and 1871 amounted to the large figure of seven hundred and twenty-five million Florins, or fifty-two Crores of Rupees. An official report submitted to Lord Dufferin by Von Den Berg, the Governor of Java in 1885, admits that the Culture System greatly contributed to the development of Java in growing Tropical produce. In 1871 there were ninety-seven Mill-owners with whom Government had contracted for the production of Sugar. These ninety-seven Contractors planted seventy thousand acres with Sugarcane, and employed two hundred and twenty-five thousands of labourers. The Exports and Imports in 1860 were nine million pounds Sterling worth of Exports and five million pounds Imports. Since 1871, as observed above, the Java

Government have discontinued the Culture System of encouraging production, and as a result of this change of arrangement, the prosperity of the Island has been almost at a standstill, and during the last eight years, from 1876 to 1884, there have been deficits of nearly seventy-five million Florins, which have had to be met out of the surpluses of one hundred million Florins of the first five years-1871 to 1876. The profits made by the sale of Government produce in Holland, which under the Culture System ranged from fifty to seventy million Florins, and were nearly equal to the Revenue raised in the Island by taxation, declined from sixty million Florins in 1871, to forty millions in 1884, and thirty millions in 1885. In consequence of this reduction, new Taxes had to be imposed, with the result that the Revenue raised by taxation, which was seventy million Florins in 1871, was one hundred and one millions in 1884, and one hundred and four millions in 1885. This increase of taxation has not, however, enabled the Government to avoid deficits. Financially speaking, therefore, neither the Dutch Government nor the people in Java, have benefited much by the change of System. There have been certain special circumstances which have contributed to produce this effect, notably the war with the Achines, and the efforts made by the Holland Government to shift a portion of her own burden of Debt to the Dependencies. The planting and manufacturing Industry encouraged under the Culture System has also suffered a collapse, and is not now as prosperous as it once used to be. The change of System was ostensibly introduced in the interest of the Native population, but the results do not show that the subjects of the Netherlands Government, both European and Native, have benefited much by the change, wages have gone down in most parts of the Island, while prices, both wholesale and retail, have not been kept up.

We have thus attempted to furnish in outline the leading Economic features of the condition of the Netherlands East Indies during the past sixty years, and contrasted, as far as published Records permit, the prosperity of the first forty years, when the Culture System was in force, with the comparative decline during the last twenty years when the Independent System has been more or less adopted in these Islands. This contrast is suggestive in itself, but it becomes more suggestive still when we compare Netherlands India with British India, and measure their relative progress under Foreign Rule. The Netherlands India is, as stated above, about thirty thousand square miles in area. The area of British India is thirty times more, being nearly nine hundred thousand square miles. The population of Netherlands India, however, is two and three-quarter Crores, or one-eight of the population of British India. In other words, the Netherlands India is four times more populous than British India. The Exports and Imports of British India in 1885-86 were sixty-seven and eighty-five Crores of Rupees, respectively. The Exports and Imports of Netherlands India were in 1885 and 1886, one hundred and sixty and one hundred and ninety million Florins, or nearly twelve and fourteen Crores of Rupees, respectively. Seeing that British India has a population eight times that of Netherlands India, and an area thirty times as large, the Imports and Exports together of British India ought to be at least twelve times as large as those of Netherlands India. But the actual figures show that our Exports and Imports were only six times as large as those of Netherlands India. Netherlands East Indies had no National Debt in 1871. In 1876 the Dutch Government transferred a portion of its Home Debt, about thirty Crores, to the Dependencies, and it was the only debt charged on Netherlands East Indies in 1884. The British Indian Debt represents a charge which exceeds two hundred Crores of Rupees. The Dutch Government derived a Revenue of nearly forty million Florins, or of three Crores of Rupees in 1884 from Sales of Produce, which did not represent taxation proper. The Indian Government has no such resource except the Opium Revenue, and Railways, which, however, being constructed out of borrowed capital, do not, yet, pay their expenses and the full interest charged on the Loans. The Opium Revenue in British India, after deducting charges, represents a profit of six Crores of Rupees only. The Dutch

Government, on the other hand, realises on sale of Government produce, Coffee, Sugar, Cinchona, Spices, etc., forty millions Florins by an expenditure of twenty-five millions, and as regards Opium, that Government has a monopoly which yields twenty-one million Florins, or nearly one and a half Crore of Rupees. Opium and Government Produce thus yield three Crores of Rupees out of a total Revenue of ten Crores. Like the British Government, the Dutch Netherlands Government have a Monopoly of Salt, but the Revenue realised is only half a Crore against eight Crores realised in British India. In this respect the Dutch Government does not tax Salt, a necessary of life, to the same extent as the British Government. The Land Revenue, including Land Rent, yields to the Netherlands Government twenty-two and a half million Florins, or one Crore and sixty Laks of Rupees. The Land Revenue in British India is nearly twenty-two Crores. In other words, while the population of British India is eight times as large as that of Netherlands India, the Land Revenue is thirteen times that of the Netherlands India. The Forced Services, which have now been for the most part commuted into a Poll Tax, yield about twenty-five Laks of Rupees to the Dutch Government. Even if this source of Revenue were included in the Land Tax and Land Rent, the land Revenue in British India still shows a higher percentage, being nearly one Rupee per head, while in Netherlands India it is about three-fourths of a Rupee per head. The Salt Tax is in British India six Annas per head, while in Netherlands India it is three Annas per head. Our Customs Revenue, having been needlessly sacrificed to Lancashire interests, scarcely yields one and a half Crores of Rupees. In the Netherlands India, the Customs Revenue exceeds seventy Laks. The taxes on Trades and Professions yielded in British India a Crore and a half of Rupees and in the Netherlands India the yield was thirty Laks of Rupees. Our Stamps Revenue Yielded more than four Crores of Rupees or three Annas per head of the population. In the Dutch East Indies, the Stamps Revenue was only eight Laks, and even adding Legacy and Transfer Duty, the Stamp Revenue was thirteen Laks, or less than one Anna per head. The Forest

Revenue represents a charge of one Anna per head in British India, which it was less than half an Anna in the Dutch East Indies. It will be seen from this that the pressure of the Land Tax, Salt, Stamps, and Forests, is much heavier in British India than in the Netherlands India, whilst the Customs, Duties, and the Trade or Income Tax were much higher in Dutch East Indies than in British India. The net Interest charge in British India ranges from four to five Crores of Rupees or three to four Annas per head. In the Netherlands India this charge is almost nominal. In the Dutch East Indies, one-third of expenditure is met without taxation. In British India one-tenth of the expenditure is so provided for. Out of a total Export of one hundred and fifty-four million Florins, the Netherlands India exported to the extent of one hundred and twenty-five million Florins' worth of manufactured produce. The chief articles exported were Sugar worth seventy-two million Florins, Tobacco sixteen and a quarter millions, Tin four millions, Tea two millions, Oils three and a quarter millions, Indigo four millions, and Coffee twenty millions. In British India, out of a total Export of ninety-nine Crores, manufactured Agricultural Produce was valued at about twenty Crores of Rupees. The chief articles exported were cotton manufacture worth six and one-third Crores, Tea five and a quarter Crores, Indigo four, Jute three and a half, and Coffee two Crores. We exported little or no Sugar or Oils. In other words while the proportion of Raw to Manufactured Produce exported from British India was four to one, the proportion in Netherlands India was one to four.

These contrasts between the Economic condition of the two Countries will be sufficient to convey a general idea of the way in which the development of the resources of the two Countries has been carried out under the influence of two different Systems. We have developed only the faculty to produce Raw goods to send them to be manufactured in other Countries, and to bring them back again for our use. In Netherlands India efforts have been made not only to grow more raw produce of a high order, but to manufacture it, and this result is due to the working of the Culture System already described. All this change has been wrought without charge to Government, and to the evident benefit of the people at an expenditure which, at the highest, did not exceed thirty to forty Crores of Rupees. The British Government in India has spent in Railways and Canals four to five times as much, but so far from helping the Country to be more self-dependent in regard to its Manufactures and Commerce, it has only tended to increase our dependence on the single resource of Agriculture to a much larger extent than before. Excluding Canals, the Railway Expenditure of nearly two hundred Crores has only made competition with Europe more hopeless over larger extent than before. Excluding Canals, the Railway Expenditure of nearly two hundred Crores has only made competition with Europe more hopeless over larger areas, and facilitated the conveyance of Foreign Goods, to an extent not otherwise possible. The Government of India, when it adopted the Policy of constructing Productive Works out of Borrowed Capital, did in fact affirm the principle that, in the peculiarly backward condition of the Country, the development of its resources could not be left to independent private enterprise, and that as representing the general public, it was bound to utilise Public resources of Credit and its superior intelligence and organization, for the advantage of its Subjects by undertaking to be the great Railway and Canal Constructors in the Country. The principle of the Culture System was thus, tacitly affirmed more than twenty years ago. The difference lay only in the objects for which this State Credit was used and pledged. The success of Railway Policy, thus undertaken twenty years ago in Lord Mayo's time, has been questioned in some quarters. For our own part we are prepared to admit that this success, though not commensurate with the expectations formed at first, has been considerable, and taken along with the Political and Military advantages of Railway Construction, there can be no doubt that the borrowed money has been well laid out. The Policy which requires the State to be its own Railway Constructor, though formally acted upon twenty years ago, was really first initiated when Lord Dalhousie's Government sanctioned the System of Guaranteed Railways. The State Credit was pledged under that plan as effectively as under the arrangements adopted in 1870. In regard to Canals the same observation holds good. If the State assumes to itself the functions of Landlord and Sovereign, its duties naturally assume a wider scope, and no defence is, therefore, necessary for the position thus taken up. The State, as representing the Public, has a right, and is under corresponding obligation, to undertake all functions which it can best perform to public advantage. The principle underlying the Railway Policy of British India and the Culture System introduced in Netherlands India by Von de Bosch is thus one and indentical. The difference lies only in the choice made of the objects of that Policy. The comparative figures given above show clearly that in the interests of the Dependencies, the objects kept in view by General Von de Bosch were of more paramount interest than those followed by the British Government in India. Facilities of communication are certainly desirable advantages, but more desirable still is the capacity to grow higher kinds of produce, and develop manufacturing and industrial activities. The sole dependence on Agriculture has been the weak point of all Asiatic Civilization. Contact with superior races ought certainly to remedy this helplessness, and not to aggravate it, as has been to a large extent the case in this Country. As the result of the two Systems at work in the two Countries, our proportion of Raw Produce to Manufactured Produce exported is four to one, while it is one to four with our Neighbours. The construction of Railways can never be compared, in their educating influence, to the setting up of Mills or Steam or Water Power Machinery for the production of Manufactured Produce in all parts of the Country. A Railways runs from one end of the Country to the other, and leaves no permanent impression upon the face of the Country, at least none so durable and penetrating as that which surrounds a great Manufactory. Now that the work of intercommunication has been well nigh completed, it seems to us that the time has come when Government should turn a new leaf, and venture upon a departure from its present received policy, on the model of the Culture System with suitable adaptations to Indian wants.

It cannot well be said that the policy thus recommended is entirely foreign to the genius of British Rule in India. In regard to Cinchona, Tea, and Coffee, the Government of India at great expense, pioneered the way for the introduction of these foreign products among the agricultural resources of the country. These pioneering efforts were made entirely at State expense. What is now suggested is that similar efforts in other directions than Agricultural Development should be made, not at State expense departmentally, but on the plan followed in the case of Railways by Guaranteeing or subsidising private efforts, till private enterprise could support itself, or better still, by the plan followed in Netherlands India by advancing loans to private Capitalists at low interest, and helping them in the choice of places and the selection of the form of investment. The British Government in India recognizes the principle of making advances for improvements to agriculturists, known as *Tagai* advances, but this power is so niggardly exercised that it may virtually be said to have been ignored in practice.

Those who counsel non-interference in such matters on the authority of writers of Political Economy forget that Political Economy, as a hypothetical *a priori* Science, is one thing, while Practical Political Economy as applied to the particular conditions of backward Countries is a different thing altogether. American, Australian, and Continental Political Economy, as applied in practice, permits many departures from the *a priori* positions of the abstract Science. If authority were wanted for this assertion, we could refer to Mill's Political Economy. The quotation is peculiarly appropriate as it lays down the duties of Government in Countries circumstanced like India.

"A good Government will give all its aid in such a shape as to encourage and nurture any rudiments, it may find, of a spirit of individual exertion. It will be assiduous in removing obstacles and discouragements to voluntary enterprise, and in giving whatever facilities and whatever direction and guidance may be necessary. Its pecuniary means will be applied when practicable in aid of private efforts rather in supersession of them, and it will call into play its machinery of rewards and honours to elicit such efforts."

"Government aid, when given merely in default of private enterprise, should be so given as to be, as far as possible, a course of education to people." Government must undertake to do "the things, which are made incumbent upon it by the helplessness of the public, in such a manner as shall tend not to increase and perpetuate, but correct this helplessness."

These principles justify a departure in the directions suggested above. The Railway Policy pursued by Government has, as a matter of fact, except in a few Presidency Towns, killed out Local indigenous Industries, and made people more helpless than before, by increasing their dependence and pressure on Agriculture as their only resource. The Policy adopted by the Dutch Government sixty years ago, has produced the opposite effects, and made Java export four times less Raw Produce and four times more of Manufactured Produce, than has been the case in British India. Mr. Mill recommends pecuniary assistance in aid of private enterprise, and the Government recognizes this duty in its *Tagai* advances. So far, therefore, as authority is concerned, there is no heresy in the recommendation of a departure of Policy in the direction suggested by the experience of Java. We are aware that objection will be taken to the proposals made above on the ground that, finding Capital for Industries and Manufactures is a function which does not belong to Government. This is no doubt theoretically true, but at the same time, it does not lie in the mouths of those who advocate a vigorous Railway Policy to urge this objection, for, if the principle be accepted, it follows that Government has no business to find Capital for Railways or Canals, or for Pioneering Tea or Coffee Enterprises. Those who urge this objection forget that the great want of India is Cheap Capital ready for investment in large Enterprises. The Savings of the Indian population are but scanty. A large proportion of these Savings is taken up by Taxation, a still larger proportion is hoarded or buried under one form or another, and there is but a fraction less than four or five Crores of Rupees, all over the Country, left for industrial investment on a large scale. A large portion of these five Crores is in the hands of men in Presidency Towns, who have little relations with the Country at large. The habit of forming Joint-Stock Organizations is not developed, and the savings are invested in Government Stock or in Post Office Banks and bear no productive efficacy. Just as the Land in India thirsts for water, so the Industry of the Country is parched up for want of Capital. The evil is not of to-day, but is an old inheritance. Capital desirous of investment and content with low interest is a National want, and this want cannot be adequately supplied by any partial or local private efforts. These last are good as far as they go, but after all they are a drop in the ocean. The want being National, the Nation has a right to expect their Rulers to supply the want, more especially as these Rulers are not Afghans or Turks, but men belonging to a race the most gifted and the best endowed with material possessions, and lending their surplus Wealth to all the countries of the world, and capable of applying that Wealth in the most Productive channels. In the case of Java, the Contractors to whom Government advanced loans were all Dutch Adventurers, but when these settlers went and settled in Foreign Lands, and invested their money and talent in local industries, the evils of Foreign Absenteeism were not felt to be so great as in the case of the Railway investments. In borrowing a lesson from the Dutch Method of conducting these operations, the British Government here need not confine their loans to British Capitalists only. Native enterprise, where the security was satisfactory, might well be allowed to share in the new undertakings. This would remove one of the admitted evils of the Dutch plan of action. The loans need not be advanced free of interest, as was the case in Java. The British Nation will not tolerate any action on the part of Government here, to have a

Monopoly of sale of certain products. The East India Company had such privileges, but they proved a source of discontent, and the Monopolies had to be abolished in favour of Free Trade. These portions of the Dutch arrangement will, therefore, have to be dropped, but they do not form essential parts of the Scheme. The System of Forced Labour was, even in Java, given up, and in its place cash payments were substituted. The wages of labour in India are so low that there is no advantage in, or occasion for, this assistance of forced labour. These accidents of the Culture System thus eliminated, what remains for Government to do is to encourage Native and European enterprise in starting New Industries by advances, limited, as in Java, to maximum amounts, and made repayable at low interest in a certain number of years. The disbursement of these advances in the most profitable way should be subjected to the superintendence of Official Experts, who should help and guide private efforts, and watch the interests of Government by preventing abuse.

In the choice of Industries, Government may well prefer those in the prosperity of which it has a large stake, and in respect of which India possesses special advantages. As instances, the Iron and Coal Industries may be safely taken up for first trial. In regard to the Iron Industry, Mr. O'Connor observes in his last report that 'No practical development of the Iron Industry has as yet been made in India. The Barakpore works, where an industry of the first magnitude might be created by the expenditure of Capital and skill, are still limited to the production of Cast Iron in trifling quantities, although the State and Public require an import close on a quarter of a million of tons of Iron and Steel yearly, without including quantities imported as Machinery, Mill work, and Railway Material.' In regard to Coal, Government has for a long time worked the Warora Mines on its own account. In place of this costly departmental work, it may be suggested that private enterprise duly subsidised, or guaranteed, or helped with loans, should be substituted. Similarly, in regard to agricultural produce, Sugar is one of the

Industries which needs help. Private efforts to establish Refineries fail on account of the difficulties placed by the Abkari Department, in utilising the refuse or non-saccharine matter, for purposes of Rum or Liquor. Our competition in this article is not with England, but with China, Mauritius, and the Straits Settlements. With the Government assistance in money, and freedom from Abkari difficulties, India would produce its own Sugar. Similarly, in Oils, our competition chiefly is with Ceylon, Mauritius, and the Straits Settlements. We export Seeds of all sorts to the extent of eight Crores, and import Cocoanut Oil from the Mauritius and from Ceylon, Ground Nut Oil from Java, and Linseed Oil from England. In the case of Beer, there has been a considerable development of Indian Breweries, but the importations are still many times the quantities produced in India. Woollen manufacturing Industries and the Tanning of Hides and Skins and the Manufacture of Paper and Glass also afford large scope for the springing up of new enterprise.

We might multiply the list, if it were necessary to go into details, but it is unnecessary to do so, for the struggle, at present, is to secure the recognition of the principle advocated. All that I contend for is that on the principle followed by Government of borrowing two to three Crores each year for so-called productive Railways, it should borrow or divert this amount for the encouragement of New Industries in the Country by means of advances, or subsidies, or guarantees according as circumstances require.

Even if the Government be not prepared to take this risk on its own shoulders from fear of English criticism and jealousy, a way might be found, giving effect to arrangements proposed on a small scale by empowering the existing Local or Municipal Boards, or creating Special Corporate Boards of Trade and Commerce, to borrow from the Government at low interest the moneys required, and advance them as loans for the improve-

*Since reduced to $3^1/_4$ per cent. and $3^1/_2$ per cent.

ment of Rural and Urban Industries. The Savings deposited with Government, are at present wholly unproductive. The Depositors are paid $3^3/_4$ * per cent. by investing their moneys in Government Stock at 4 * per cent. This benefits nobody. If instead of the present arrangement, the District and the City Deposits were lent by Government to Municipal and Local Boards or District Corporate Banks, and these Bodies, empowered to make advances, say at five or six per cent to private persons with skill and energy to turn them to account, an annually increasing Fund of four to five Crores will be at the disposal of the Government for purposes more calculated to benefit everybody than the present plans. Each District might thus have a Fund to develop its resources in its own way, and several Districts might combine together to support a strong undertaking for common advantage. If the powers of these Boards were thus enlarged, there would be no risk of loss to Government, and the Boards might make considerable profit by the use of the money, and thus relieve the burden of Local Taxation. Of course, the Government through its Officers would have a potent voice in the proper disbursement of these borrowed moneys, and with judicious supervision the whole face of the Country might be changed in the course of a few years. The Government might also help these efforts by giving its own custom to these manufacturing concerns in respect of the articles required for its Stores. When the Country was thus enabled to obtain a new start, and Factories and Mills on a small or large scale were set up all over the land, the present paralysis would give way to a play of energies which would far more effectively than Schools and Colleges give a new birth to the activities of the Nation. This then is our plan. The alternative suggested above may do as an experiment, but it would be far better if the Government recognized this function of developing New Industries in the Country, to be as legitimate a part of its duty as it now regards Railway Construction to be. The principle underlying both functions is the same. The one has been tried and

*Since reduced to $3^1/_4$ per cent and $3^1/_2$ per cent.

has attained its success, but has not cured the particular weakness which has crippled the growth of the Nation. The experimental trial of the other principle in a Neighbouring Country has to all appearances supplied this defect, and this experience warrants a similar trial in this Country.

18

THE RE-ORGANIZATION OF REAL CREDIT IN INDIA*

No fact in the economic condition of this Country arrests attention more forcibly than the contrast presented by the hoards of unused Capital, stored up in the vaults of the Presidency and other Exchange Banks, and the high premium Government Securities command on one side, and on the other the utter paralysis of Industry in rural India, due to the poverty of the resources of the Classes engaged in the production of wealth. It would appear as if some impenetrable barrier intercepted the overflow of Wealth, and barred the channels of communication between the reservoirs of Capital and the parched fields of Industry, dried up for want of the wealth-bearing and fertilizing moisture. This is not a fancy picture. It is a stern reality which has to be faced by all who feel an interest in the well-being and progress of the Country. The Presidency Bank of Bombay alone, has at this moment more than Fifty Millions of Rupees of Deposit Receipts, which it does not know how to use, and which drives it in despair to refuse Municipal and other Private Deposits except as Current Accounts which bear no interest. Nearly Twenty Millions of Rupees are locked up in the Post Of-

*Read before the First Industrial Conference, at Poona, in 1891, and published in *JPSS*, July 1891, Vol.XIV, No.1 and in *Essays*.

fice Savings Banks in this Presidency alone, and as many as Fifty Millions of Rupees are similarly locked up all over India, which the Government cannot turn to account except by buying its own Paper, and maintaining from the interest proceeds its Paper Currency Department. Government 4 per cent. Paper sells for Rupees 107 or 108, and 5 per cent. Municipal Loans fetch Rupees 111-12 per nominal value of Rupees 100. The average for ten years of Gold imports has been Forty Millions of Rupees and of Silver Seventy Millions of Rupees, the latter chiefly coined into Rupees, the former chiefly absorbed in ornaments. Meanwhile, the Cultivating and Artizan Classes can get no loans, except at rates of interest ranging from 12 per cent to 24 per cent. In the four Deccan Districts, Poona, Satara, Nagar, and Sholapur, with a population of three millions and a-half, for which information is available the amount of annual borrowings on the mortgage of land exceeds four millions, and of simple loans one million and six hundred thousand, the interest rate on mortgage Loans being generally 12 per cent and on simple Bonds 24 per cent. The slightest irregularity or delay in the annual rainfall deprives the whole population of food, and, what is far worse, leaves them without work, and Government finds it necessary to strain all its resources to arrest not only the Food Famine, but the Work Famine as well. Less than 3 per cent of the land in the Presidency proper, excluding Sind, is protected by Irrigation. This is the actual situation, and it is clear that it is alarming enough. If there were no Capital in the Country seeking investment, there would be reason for despair. But as things stand, the situation is not hopeless. There is Capital ready to hand awaiting secure Investment. There is the broad dreary expanse of Industry which is thirsting for Capital, and offering the most secure Investment for its fruitful employment. What is wanting is the necessary skill and patience which will adjust the capacity of the one to the wants of the other, and make both work in a spirit of harmony and co-operation.

In this connection it is very unfortunate, that the Economic conditions of England are so widely divergent from those of

India that the Rulers of the Country, brought up in the traditions of their Native Land, find themselves more or less unprepared to grapple with the difficulties created by this novel situation. With its land owned chiefly by a few Landlords, and its Peasantry representing a very small proportion of the Wage-earning Classes, with its large accumulations of Capital, and the vast development of its Manufacturing and Commercial activities, Great Britain is most peculiarly circumstanced, and its Economic History furnishes no guide for dealing with the difficulties of the situation in India, where, except in a few Provinces, the State claims to be the sole Landlord, and Agricultural Classes from 80 per cent of the total population and there is no accumulation of Capital; and Manufactures and Commerce are in their rudimentary stage, and in that stage also, chiefly monopolized by strangers. On the Continent of Europe, however, Indian Problems are fairly reproduced with Indian conditions of life and property, and the lessons to be derived from the study of Continental Economy have a more practical bearing than the maxims contained in the usual Textbooks of English Political Economy. The task of re- organizing Credit, both Real and Personal, on a sound and progressive basis has been undertaken by Continental Statesmen and Thinkers during the last fifty years, and they have succeeded in bridging the gulf which separates the saving few from the producing many in a way which commands attention. If this task were undertaken in the same spirit by those who feel its importance here in the promotion of National Well-being, and a *modus operandi* established by which people seeking secure investment can be brought face to face with those who need their help and are prepared to offer that security, the Nation would soon start upon a new race of life with its powers invigorated, and its energies awakened in a way no other single agency can accomplish. This Conference will not have met in vain, if it succeeds in drawing public attention to the subject as one of paramount importance, and if it prompts to suggest ways and means for practical adoption, based on principles which will, in course of time, find their further development in far-reaching beneficial consequences.

With this view, it is proposed to give a brief history of the growth of the Organization of Real Credit in the Countries of Hungary and Austria, France and Italy, Belgium and Switzerland, during the past fifty years.

To take up the history of the movement in Hungary, it is noticeable that two important developments in the condition of the Agricultural Classes forced this subject upon the attention of the Ruling Classes in Hungary. As these developments find their counterpart in India, they deserve special notice. In the first place, after the Revolution of 1848, the Hungarian Peasants found themselves in the possession of personal freedom, and of proprietary right which they had only imperfectly enjoyed before. They were Serfs before, and though partially emancipated under Maria Theresa, their complete emancipation took place after the Revolution of 1848. The old serfs were made proprietors of the lands they held under their Landlords, who were bought off to give their consent by suitable compensation. Compulsory labour was abolished; Rents, Taxes, and Tithes were consolidated together, and the Nobles were taxed like any other Classes, and had to pay wages to their old Serfs when they employed them on their diminished Farms. Copy-hold and Serf-hold Property became Freehold. As many as five lacs (Five Hundred thousands) of families were thus restored to Freedom, and, on an average, their Holdings were about fifteen acres each. This, it may be noted, fairly corresponds with the change which has been brought about over the greater part of India by the Survey Settlements, except that the State in India has stepped into the position of the Private Landlord, and claims to be owner of all cultivable and cultivated land. The next change which took place in Hungary was also reproduced in the history of our own Country. Owing to increased facilities of communication, new Markets were opened, and the Export trade was developed to a large extent. Old methods of cultivation, which did well enough under old conditions, were felt to be inadequate, and it was found necessary to abandon the old system. Owing to the poverty of good waste land, the cultivation had to become intensive in place of the old system of extensive cultivation.

Under the double influence of these two causes, the problem of reorganizing real credit, *i.e.*, of securing loans on easy terms on the security of Real Property, first presented itself for practical solution, and Real Credit Institutions, worked on divergent principles, were started, either in the interest of the borrowers who clubbed their resources together, and founded such institutions as the Boden Credit Institute, or in the interest of the lenders who opened departments for real advances in the great National Banks, such as the Austro-Hungarian Bank or the Provincial Savings Banks. The first Boden Credit Institute was started in 1863 by two hundred and nine land-owners who subscribed among themselves a large amount of Capital, about fifteen millions of Rupees, of which one-tenth was paid up in cash, and the remaining nine-tenths was represented by Bonds passed by the Founders in favour of the Bank, which were gradually withdrawn as the Reserve Fund increased. Every borrower had to become a Member, and guaranteed with others, who joined with him, the solvency of the concern to all who had dealings with the Bank as Bond-holders or Depositors. The ordinary rate of interest on mortgage loans was much higher, but the Institute made its advances at a fixed rate of interest—six and a half per cent—which was gradually reduced to four and a half per cent. The advances made were limited to half of the assessed value of the property mortgaged. No property was taken in mortgage which did not yield a fixed and certain income, and no loan was made except by way of a first and sole charge. The rates of interest stipulated included interest proper, and one per cent for the sinking fund or for the amortization charge, and twenty-five to fifty per cent for the expenses and the Reserve Fund. The repayment of principal and interest was secured by spreading the payment over a period of thirty-four to forty-one years. The Bank issued its Bonds of one Hundred or one Thousand or ten Thousand Florins at 4.85 per cent, and these Bonds were made payable to bearer, and, being negotiable, freely changed hands, and a portion of them was withdrawn by lot as each debt was paid off in part. The Bank was required by law to keep its Bonds strictly within the amount of the value of the mortgaged property. Besides this guarantee, the creditors had a first charge on the ten per cent. paid-up capital of the Founders, and on the Reserve Fund, and the Mutual Guarantee Fund, and the subsidy paid by Government to help the Reserve Fund. It is very important to note the concessions granted to this Bank by the Hungarian Government. The Government granted a subsidy to the Reserve Fund of five hundred thousands of Florins. It exempted the Bank's profits from the income-tax, and its operations from all stamp duties. It lent the help of its officers for assessing the value of the property mortgaged. It ordered inspection of accounts with a view to secure obedience to the rules, and, finally, it permitted the Bank to foreclose or sell the mortgaged and also unmortgaged property of its debtor on default being committed in payment without requiring it to go to law, and take its chance of justice, with all its delays and costs. The borrower was required to pay six-monthly interest in advance, and the Bank also paid the coupons on its Bonds to the holders thereof after every six months. In consequence of these exceptional privileges, few defaults were committed, and it has been estimated that out of some fourteen millions advanced by the Bank to eleven thousand borrowers, the Bank had to suffer loss to the extent of twenty- five thousand pounds sterling only. The borrowers were allowed freedom to pay off their debts in anticipation, and a considerable minority took advantage of this privilege. The Institute has thus fully realized the leading ideas of its promoters. It acts as intermediary between the borrower and the lender; while procuring for the borrower easier terms, and teaching him self-reliance and freedom, it favours the lender by offering its own guarantee for the money he advances to the borrower through its agency. These facilities have greatly helped the prosperity of all Classes in the Country, and lowered the rate of interest all round.

The Boden Credit Institute also deals with Communes and Municipalities, and advances loans on special terms favourable to these Corporations and to the Bank. This Bank is the best type of institutions worked in the interests of the borrowers, as the founders are content with five per cent interest on paid up capital, and its Directors receive no payments. There are other Institutions worked on the same principles in the interest of the lenders, and in their case dividends are declared as in ordinary Banks, varying according to the conditions of each year's operations. The Principle of all these Banks which make advances on Real Property is to interpose the Bank between the borrower and the lender, to guarantee the lender against all risks, and thereby secure a reduction of the rate of interest so as to help the borrower with loans at a slightly enhanced rate of interest, and provide for a Reserve Fund, and for the expenses of management, and by spreading the payment over a long number of years, generally forty years, provide for a gradual but certain satisfaction of both principal and interest. The Austro-Hungarian Bank is the chief of these Banks, which carry on business in the interests of lenders. Besides doing the regular work of a National Bank, it has a Real Credit Branch managed by a separate Committee. In consideration of the special privilege of obtaining speedy execution of its claims, and exemptions from Stamp Duties conferred on it, the Government has a hand in the supervision of the management of this Branch. A Government Commissary is appointed to this duty. The Bank issues Bonds at four per cent. and charges four and a half to five and three-quarters per cent according as the period of amortization is long or short.

There are other Banks such as the Hypotheken Bank or the Credit Foncier, the Commercial Bank of Buda-Pesth, and the Savings Banks, which do not enjoy any special privileges, but do a large amount of work.

A smaller Boden Credit Institute was founded in 1879 to help poor Land-holders. The Government granted a subsidy of half a

Million Florins to its Reserve Fund, and its other rules and privileges, and the powers of Government control are very much the same as those described above in regard to the bigger Institution. It has helped land-holders with loans amounting in all to ten Millions of Rupees, secured on a total value of twenty-five millions, and has, in course of time, reduced the rate of interest from seven and a half per cent to four and a half per cent.

All these Banks in Austro-Hungary have lately been empowered to advance loans for improvement purposes, and such loans are advanced at four and three-quarters per cent including the sinking fund; and the period for extinction of liability ranges from thirty to fifty years. These advances are exempted from Stamp Duties and other charges, and the technical execution of these improvement works, which involve expenditure over a certain amount, is entrusted to the State Engineers as a portion of their charge. Default or difficulty of collection rarely occurs as advances are by rule limited to half the value of the assets. In Austria, the Provincial Boden Credit Anstallen receive subsidies from the Provincial Governments, and in return the Governments exercise control and supervision through their Commissaries.

To come next to the Countries of the Latin Union, France, Italy and Belgium it is to be noted that the establishment of a Crédit Foncier, or Mortgage Bank for lending money on the security of lands, forced itself upon the attention of the French people about the time of the Revolution of 1848. Inquiries made at the time elicited the fact that the usual rate of interest on mortgage loans was nine to ten per cent, and the idea of the promoters was to remove the difficulties in the way of finding Capital on the credit of land felt by the Peasant Proprietors created by the French Revolution.

In 1852, three great Institutions were founded in Paris and in two other places, but they were soon amalgamated into a Central Institution with its head-quarters at Paris, and with an exclusive right to operate throughout France. The object of such Institutions was laid down to be the advance of loans to small land-owners at moderate interest, and provide for the repayment of the principal and interest of the same in a long period of forty or fifty years. The capital of this Central Bank was raised to sixty millions of Francs, one half of which was paid up. In consideration of the exclusive privileges conferred on the body as the sole National Bank for the mortgage of Real Property in France, Government has insisted upon retaining in its hands considerable powers of control and supervision. The Governor and two Sub-Governors are appointed by the President of the Republic out of the larger shareholders, and there is a Council of Shareholders. In 1860, the Credit Foncier was authorized to lend money to Communes and Departments, secured on Municipal and Local Funds. The Credit Foncier cannot issue its Bonds over and above the value of the mortgaged property, and it must keep a Reserve of twenty per cent of the total of the sum advanced. The capital of the Credit Foncier has been gradually raised from sixty millions to one hundred and eighty millions.

The amount of its mortgage advances rose from eight hundred and fifty-two millions in 1852 to two thousand and four millions in 1888, and its loans to Communes rose similarly from four hundred and seventy-eight to nine hundred and fifty-three millions. The net profits realized were seven and one-third million Francs in 1878, and twenty-two and two-thirds million Francs in 1889. No loan is advanced unless the property mortgaged yields a certain and durable return. It is not advanced beyond one-half of the value of the property as assessed by the Bank's experts. The expenses of negotiating the loan and satisfying the Bank about the title deeds come to about 3 per cent, and are borne by the borrower. The interest charged is 4.85 per cent, and the period fixed for repayment may be either a short or a long term. The debtor may pay off the loans in anticipation. In all, three thousand and four hundred millions of Francs have been advanced as loans since 1852, and default was committed only in respect of debts amounting to eighteen millions, in regard to which the Bank found it necessary to buy the property itself. As a consequence of this improved organization of Credit, the rate of interest has fallen throughout France from nine or ten per cent. to five per cent The Government guarantees the Credit Foncier against competition and lends it the assistance of its officers.

France is pre-eminently a Country of Peasant Proprietors with small Holdings like those of India, and its agricultural interest is of considerable importance. Of course the French people are differentiated from our countrymen by their remarkable thrift, industry, and forethought, and their powers of organization and mutual help. These habits are, however, essentially the creation of the change that took place in the early part of the Century, when the estates of the Nobles and the Bishops and Monasteries were escheated to the State and parcelled out among the Peasant Farmers.

The accounts of the French Peasantry as given in the narratives of Mr. Arthur Young in times which preceded this great change do not show that there was then any such advantage enjoyed by them over our people. The French peasant is besides the proprietor of his Holdings; and has no Land-Tax to pay. Barring these differences of history and character, the conditions in France are like those of Western India. The French peasant is heavily in debt, more than half the land being mortgaged, but his debts sit lightly on him, because they represent improvements made in the land, which cannot be said with equal truth of the debts due by our peasants. The reorganized system of Land Credit which has worked these wonders in France, and Austria, and Hungary, may therefore be safely expected to achieve equal success in India.

In regard to Italy, these observations apply with still greater relevancy. In 1861 it was ascertained that the average rate of interest on mortgage loans was eight to ten per cent, and the amount of the debts charged on the land in Italy, excluding

Venice and Rome, was two thousand six hundred and ninety millions, while the net income was four hundred millions, and the Government charge on the land was one hundred and fifteen millions. Deducting Government and other charges, one hundred and twenty millions, and the interest amount, one hundred and forty millions, the owners had only one hundred and forty millions of revenue at their disposal. With the increase in Government taxes and in the interest charges, the balance left in the hands of the Landowners grew less each year, and this drew the attention of the Italian Statesmen to the necessity of taking early action on the lines followed with such brilliant success in France.

In 1862 it was accordingly proposed to start a Central Credit Foncier for the whole Kingdom with a Capital of four millions of Pounds Sterling, and invested with exclusive privileges, and helped by a Government subsidy of four Hundred thousand Pounds Sterling. It was not found possible to float the scheme in its huge proportions, and in 1866 a compromise was adopted by which the Agency of seven existing Banks was utilized, and powers were conferred on them to operate exclusively within their defined Zones, and deal in mortgage business. The rules of business were the same as those of the kindred Institution in working order in France. Loans were to be advanced up to half of the value of the property mortgaged, and gradual liquidation of principal and interest was to be provided for. The interest rate was to be a uniform one—five per cent, and the Banks were to issue Negotiable Bonds, and withdraw them gradually as instalments were paid or satisfied. Between 1866 and 1885, thirteen millions of pounds were lent to eight thousand three hundred and fifty-five borrowers. After 1885, the Zone System was done away with, and any Bank of Association with a Capital of four hundred thousand Pounds Sterling was permitted to transact mortgage business under the condition mentioned above. The rigidity of a uniform rate of interest was also done away with, and discretion was allowed to charge four, four and a half and five per cent interest according as the period was long or short; the rule of limiting advances to half the value was also relaxed and loans were permitted up to three-fifths of the value. Under this New Law, the National Bank of Italy and seven other Banks carry on mortgage dealings in addition to their other business at Naples, Rome, Sienna, Bologna, and some other Towns. The Municipal Authorities of Sienna were the first to work the celebrated Monte Pia System of loans on pledges nearly three hundred years ago. The Italian Law allows to these Banks great facilities for the speedy and cheap recovery of mortgage debts, and the Government does not, as in France, exercise any active control in the management of the Banks' affairs. The Banks which issue these Bonds undertake to sell them on commission; the Bonds are made payable to bearer, and the holder has no claim against any private mortgagor, but only against the Bank. All the eight Banks cash each other's Coupons.

In Belgium, the First Institution of the kind we are now considering called Le Caissa Hypothecain, was established in 1855 with a view to offer facilities to capitalists for investing their monies safely, and to borrowers for borrowing money at low rates, and enabling them to clear off the principal and interest amounts by instalments spread over a long period. The powers of the Bank were enlarged in 1886, and it has since taken the name of Credit Foncier de Belgique. There are other Institutions which do the same business. The Belgian Authorities had under contemplation the creation of a Central Institution which was to have power to advance money on Houses, Forests and Woods up to one-fourth their assessed value, and on lands up to a half. The borrowers were to pay five and a quarter per cent interest, which rate was to include the Sinking Fund and expenses of management and registration, and the period fixed for repayment was to be forty-one years. The Bank was to issue four per cent. Bonds fully covered by the value of the property mortgaged, and the Belgian Government agreed to undertake the work of collecting the instalments due by the Bank's debtors through its Treasury Agents, and in case of arrears special facilities were to be allowed for realizing the monies due, the Bank's Debts being allowed a priority over all other debts, and the transactions of the Bank were to be exempt from all taxes and duties. The Bill was passed by the Lower House, but before it received the assent of the Senate, a Political crisis occurred, and no further action was taken in the matter. The concessions proposed and accepted by the House of Representatives deserve, however, to be specially borne in mind, as they indicate the extent of support which Continental Governments are prepared to give in the work of Re- organizing Credit.

The Federal States of Switzerland furnish equally interesting examples of this same liberal policy. In these States, Private Capitalists seldom lend money on their own account. The Mortgage and Savings Banks virtually monopolize the business. These Mortgage Banks are either purely State Institutions, or of a mixed character. The Mortgage Bank of the Canton of Berne is a State Institution, and is the most important Institution of its kind in Switzerland. These State Institutions are more successful than Private or Mixed Banks. Of course the State Banks do not satisfy all demands, and there is thus full scope for private enterprize. The State Institutions have this advantage over Private Banks that, they do not screw up the rates of interest, while their ample means enable them virtually to regulate the rate of interest all over the Country. The Berne Bank has reduced its rate of interest within the past fifteen years from five to four per cent, and has thereby doubled and trebled the volume of its business. The deposits have increased from £1,119,629 to £3,032,389, and the Loans from £1,600,000 to £3,200,000. Most of the Swiss Cantons have each their separate Mortgage Bank, and though Savings Banks, which deal in Personal Credit, are generally private, yet in many parts of the country the Communes assist even these Banks by taking a certain number of shares. Swiss Mortgage Banks lend by way of first charges only, and compel borrowers to discharge all previous claims. The amortization arrangements enable the indebted Agriculturists to pay off their debts, and free their lands from encumbrances with certainty and ease. Under the direct system of lending, creditors exercise a moral tutelage or dominion over the debtors who sink in dignity. The relations between a private debtor and creditor have a tendency, in course of time to develop mutual misunderstanding and bitterness. The Emancipation of the population from this source of moral degradation by interposition of the Banks has proved of the highest value as an agency for the Education of the people in the best virtues of Citizenship. The Bank's relations to its debtors are of the simplest character and involve no useless expense. The men who have money, and want to invest it safely, find that they have not to hunt after their debtors, inquire into their solvency, and go to law to test the result. The man who has saved money which he wants to lend goes to the Bank, pays down his money as a Depositor, or buys the Bonds of the Bank, and when the six-monthly instalment falls due, he signs the Coupon, and encashes it. An immense waste of power, time, and money is thus saved to him and to the debtor. The business becomes specialized, like any other business, all risks are avoided, and all the benefits of a secure investment and cheap loan are secured to the monied and needy classes. These Swiss Mortgage Banks furnish, perhaps, the best example of genuine co-operative effort that is seen in any part of the world. Farmers club together for the purchase, in a joint way, of Agricultural Cattle, of Seeds, of Manure, Pasture Lands, Cheese Dairies, or for draining Marsh Lands, and constructing Country Roads, and the Banks help them to do so on very easy terms.

This principle of co-operation for common purpose was first worked out in Germany on lines formulated by Raiffeisen, but they have been developed most widely and beneficially in Switzerland. Each Member contributes a fixed sum per month or year, and the Association also receives Deposits. Out of the Collections and Deposits, Loans are made to those who need them for buying Cattle or Seeds or Manure. The Association has a charge on the Cattle etc., so bought, and the Swiss Law provides that if any one of the Members breaks his engagement to the

Association, and sells the Cattle, the act is not only a civil but a criminal offence, of which a Magistrate takes instant cognizance. The engagement has in this case to be executed before the Magistrate so as to avoid all future complications. These small Associations receive help from the State Governments, and in return their accounts are open to inspection by State Officials.

This completes the summary I proposed to give of the most recent history of the Re-organization of Credit in some of the principal Continental Countries of Europe. The Present circumstances of this Country demand that the efforts made by the Statesmen of so many countries, and which have been attended with such success, should be carefully studied by us with a view to practical action. There can be little doubt that, if similar attempts had been made in England, the Rulers of India would not have failed to take upon their shoulders the work of Reorganizing Credit on these lines in India long ago. The circumstances of England are, however, peculiar. The vast mass of her population consists mostly of Wage-earners, who possess neither lands nor houses nor appliances of their own. The rich Capitalists and Landlords own the lands, and houses, and machinery, and factories, and being intelligent and well organized, need no special help. It is these peculiar circumstances which have made it superfluous for the Statesmen of England to devote their attention to these matters. They are naturally disposed to take care of their wage-earning Classes, to feed, clothe, and house them properly, to provide for smaller hours of work, to arrange for the compulsory safeguarding of the comforts and conveniences of Factory Hands. These traditions impel them also to turn their philanthropic attention to Factory Legislation here, which, though reasonable in its way, affects but a drop in the ocean of Humanity in India. Our agricultural and artisan Population are not wage-earners. They own their lands and houses, and implements of trade, and their small shops, and factories, and their cattle and carts. They mostly work on their own account, and if they have no store or savings of their own, as they generally have not, they must borrow money, and repay it as they best can. The necessity of Re- organizing Credit transaction is thus not confined to Agriculturist Classes. It is a general necessity created in this Country by its circumstances and habits, and any measures which tend to rescue this business from its present chaos, and restore certainty and honesty in it, are sure to put new life and energy in the body politic. The question of Credit, as observed above, does not concern Agriculturists alone. It equally concerns Spinners and Weavers, Carpenters, Smiths, Dyers, Potters, Brass and Copper, Silk and Embroidery workers, Shopkeepers, Carriers, and all the Trades and Professions that are now practised in this Country. It will have been seen from the summary given above, that the Statesmen of Europe have realized their duties in this matter of affording facilities for the Re-organization of Real Credit, and given it practical effect in various ways, (1) either by lending the help of its Officials for control or management or inspection work, or (2) by subsidies, or (3) by undertaking Collections, or (4) by giving a Monopoly of business, or (5) by facilitating the work of Recovery, or (6) by exempting their business from all Stamp Duties and Income Tax and other charges. The circumstances of India furnish strong grounds why the Government here should help this work of Re-organizing Credit in all these ways according as local difficulties or aptitudes may suggest or justify. An effort was made in this part of the Country to start an Agricultural Bank on the lines laid down above. The Scheme was well supported by the Local Government, and by the Government of India also, acting under the advice of Sir E. Baring, now Lord Cromer. It was, however, negatived by the India Office Authorities. No blame need be laid at the door of any body for this untoward result. The English Rulers in India are brought face to face with the specialities of Indian life, and realize their responsibilities. In England the Authorities have not the advantage of this touch with actual life, and their English traditions naturally predispose them to regard that the State, as such, has no functions or responsibilities in this connection. The promoters of the Agricultural Bank desired that

Government should sanction the experiment in one *Taluka* by undertaking an inquiry into the previous debts of the Agriculturists, which, when ascertained, were to be paid off by the Government, the Bank undertaking to make good the sum so paid on conditions of its being allowed a first charge on the mortgaged Estates of the *Ryots* so benefited. The Bank undertook to charge very low rates of interest, and to recover them in instalments fixed with the approval of Government Officers. To prevent all disputes, it agreed to leave this work of Collection of instalments due, in the hands of the Village Authorities, who were to realize the instalments as they now realize the Assessment of Government or its *Tagai* advances. Lastly, the Bank prayed that Assessment within the area so dealt with should not be raised, so as to disturb the arrangements they might enter into, and that their transactions should be exempted from all taxes and charges. In consideration of their undertaking to finance and work the concern, and charge low rates of interest, the Government was to help them to obtain speedy and cheap execution. It will be seen that none of the special privileges and concessions asked for were without their precedent in the Credit Fonciers and Land Mortgage Banks subsidized and helped and controlled by the European States. The Scheme, however, fell through then, for reasons which it is needless now to relate. The difficulties of Indian life are, however, too serious and peremptory to be satisfactorily disposed of in any other way, and the question is sure to force itself soon upon public attention. Already we hear that the Madras Government has appointed a Special Officer to inquire into the subject, and the time, therefore, seems opportune to press the matter once more upon the attention of Government. State help is needed for the very cogent reason that State control and supervision are necessary to inspire confidence. No other organization in the Country has such a diversified, intelligent and widely diffused Agency at its disposal. The interests of the State also, are materially involved in the matter of the well-being of the most numerous and least helpful Classes of the taxpaying population.

The State need not expend its Funds. The Funds will be forthcoming to any amount if it only promises to organize the Agency, and set it at work. The Post Office and Savings Banks deposits are ready to hand. All that Government has to do is to organize District or City Committees of Indian Capitalists, to empower them to receive deposits at fixed rates and lend them at slightly higher rates to the borrowers on the security of lands, or houses, &c., the excess rate providing for a gradual amortization of the debt in a definite period, as also, Insurance charges and working expenses. The Loans of these District Committees should be allowed priority over all other debts, and exempted from all duties, and certain and speedy execution should be permitted to them. The experience of the working of similar bodies in Europe, and it may be noted in Egypt also, justifies the hope that the losses will be very trifling, and the benefits incalculable. What holds true of Agriculture holds equally good in this country about every other Trade and Industry. The recuperative powers of Nature and Art are limited, and cannot stand the dead weight of prohibitive rates of interest, made necessary by disorganized Credit, and the uncertainties and delays and expenses of Civil Proceedings. Remove these difficulties and hindrances, and Credit will rise to its natural and healthy level. The glories of peace are far nobler than those of war. The whole Country is looking up with wistful eyes for a Statesman who will guide its destinies in this great struggle, and help it to win the race of life and revived health, and national well-being.

19

INDIAN POLITICAL ECONOMY*

In the Beginning of this year before a similar gathering in Bombay, a master-hand sketched the outlines of the influence of Nature on Literature and Politics, and in a few bold touches showed how, from time to time, the aberrations and evil tendencies observable in English thought and action were counteracted and corrected by an appeal to, and a diligent Study of, the standard of Nature—the Final Source of all True Knowledge, and the only Guide to wise conduct. The same master-hand drew also the moral to be learned from such a Study—the moral being that our growth could only be in strict correspondence to our aptitudes and surroundings, and that we should be on our guard against precipitation and hot-house Culture, which can never lead to permanently beneficial results. There can be no doubt that the Historical line of Thought so developed is to some extent the Chief characteristic feature of the latter half of the present Century. It occurred to me at the time that if the Law of Relativity and Correspondence holds good in Politics and Social Sciences generally, it ought to hold good equally in all kindred subjects, including, among others, the Science of National Wealth, or as it is more popularly described, Political Economy. As a matter of fact, however, what do we see about

*Lecture delivered in the Deccan College, Poona, in 1892, and published in *JPSS*, January 1893, Vol.XV, No.3, and in *Essays*.

us? The same Teachers and Statesmen, who warn us against certain tendencies in our Political aspirations, forget this salutary caution when the question at issue is one of Indian Economics. They seem to hold that the Truths of Economic Science, as they have been expounded in our most popular English Text-books, are absolutely and demonstrably true, and must be accepted as guides of conduct for all time and place whatever might be the stage of National advance. Ethnical, Social, Juristic, Ethical, or Economical differences in the environments are not regarded as having any influence in modifying the practical application of these Truths. If Free Trade is good for England, it must be equally beneficial to all Countries, and prohibitive or Protective Duties, Bounties and Subsidies, Restrictions and Regulative Control, are absolute Evils, and no thought need be given to the relative differences in Civilization, or the possession of natural advantages, or disadvantages in matters of situation, climate, soil, National aptitudes and wants. If Factory Legislation is good in one Country, it must be equally needed to protect Labourers everywhere. If Laws in restraint of Usury are out of place in Centres of Commercial and Manufacturing activity, they must be equally pernicious in backward, antiquated, and agricultural Communities. If the State finds no occasion to help Credit Institutions in England the demand for such help, in Countries where the spirit of private enterprise is feeble, is also held to be preposterous. If the Government of advanced Countries do not undertake certain functions with a view to direct Industry and help enterprize, the Government out here is equally precluded from taking any new line of departure in these matters. If direct Taxes suit English conditions of life and property, they must be equally suitable to Indian conditions, and Octroi and Transit Duties must be kept down rigorously as sources of our Local or Municipal Income.

I might multiply these instances without number, but those given above will, I hope, serve to illustrate my present purpose. Even if Statesmen had stopped here, there would have been some extenuation for the line of conduct adopted by them. The absolute Truths of Political Economy, however, are appealed to as a justification for a curious change of front. Men, who come from a Country where private property in land is most absolute, develop on their arrival here a taste for Socialistic Doctrines. The State aspires to relegate all Private Property in land into mere superior and inferior Holdings. A love for Capitalists farming on a large scale gives way to a taste for *petit culture* by poor Tenants. In England the Landlords as such pay no special Tax to the State, but here Land is taxed on the ground that there is an unearned increment based on the Theory of Economical Rent, and that this unearned increment belongs of special right to the State. While the Nationalization of land is but a Socialist dream in England and Europe, it is in full swing here, and furnishes a scientific justification for periodical Revisions and Enhancements. Status and privilege form still the very cornerstone of English Social arrangements, but here every member of Society is only a mobile atom, without differences marking him off from others, so far as the State is concerned. The Middle Class is the backbone of English Supremacy, but here there is no room for a Middle Class between the State and the poor Tax-payers. This change of front is a curious study by itself. For my present purposes, it is not necessary to cite more instances. Of course, if Political Economy is a Science of general and absolute Truths, like Physics or Astronomy, the tendency noted above to push its principles to their logical conclusions in all times and places, even when English Statesmen halt midway in their practical application of these principles, is intelligible, and may be even wise. There can be no doubt that those who thus give effect to these principles honestly believe in the scientific and absolute character of these Economical conclusions. But it is certainly a fair subject for consideration whether this belief is well-founded. If in Politics and Social Sciences, time and place and circumstances, the endowments and aptitudes of men, their habits and customs, their Laws and Institutions, and their previous History, have to be taken into account, it must be strange indeed, that in the Economical aspect of our life, one set of general principles should hold good everywhere for all time and place, and for all stages of Civilization. This conflict was one of the reasons which induced me to take up this subject for consideration on the present occasion.

Another reason which also influenced me in the choice of this subject was the fact that at this time, when an appeal is being made to the popular will in two great Communities to declare itself, the questions at issue are more Economical than Political in their character. The dreams of Cobden and Bright, of Ricardo and Mill, that the civilized world would, in a few years, with one accord embrace their principles, has not been realized. In America the issues are solely Economical. One party favours Free Trade, and other favours Protection. One party favours Silver Legislation, the other denounces it. In England also, as you are aware, the present Prime Minister has declared himself in favour of what is called Fair Trade, which is a modification dictated by Political Economical considerations of the extreme doctrine of Free Trade with a view to restrict the freedom to those who reciprocate it, and the Liberals have denounced this lapse from orthodoxy as unpardonable heresy. Even in Ireland, the Political issue is really at its base an Economical Dispute, which centres round the question of the extent of the rights of Private Property and Free Contract as between the Landlords and the Tenants. Similarly, here in our own Country, the Currency Association is also running a tilt against Economical Theorists, and boldly denies the universality of the equation of Supply and Demand as the best and only regulator of the exchange values of the precious Metals. On the Continent of Europe, and in the English Colonies, the same protest is being practically urged against the extreme rigour of the current theories of orthodox Political Economy. The Americans dispute the rights of the Chinese to settle in their Country, the Australians fear the same scare, and even in England, Legislation was contemplated against the immigration of alien Jews, on the ground that they were likely to under-bid the indigenous labourer. The Trades-Union and Strikes, and the Knights of

Labour of which we have heard so much recently, furnish another form of this same general protest. This conflict of practice with theory, not in one, but all points, not in one place or country, but all over the world, which distinguishes Contemporary History, furnishes another reason which appeared to me to justify a reconsideration of the question on broader lines than those you will find enunciated in the ordinary Text-books.

In justice to some of these Writers, it must be admitted that they have taken good care to prevent many of the misapprehensions which are popularly entertained about the absolute and general character of the Economical Doctrines taught by them. Mr. John Stuart Mill, for instance, states in his preface that "for practical purposes, Political Economy is inseparably intertwined with many other branches of Social Philosophy. Except in matters of mere detail, there are perhaps no practical questions, even among those which approach nearest to the character of purely Economical questions, which admit of being decided on Economical premises alone." You will also recollect that one characteristic feature of Mr. Mill's work is his frank recognition of an essential difference between the Laws relating to the Production of Wealth, which he deems to be Universal and not arbitrary, and those which regulate its Distribution. The Laws of Distribution, Mr. Mill admits, are partly of Human institution. Mr. Mill, and Mr. Cairns more clearly even than Mr. Mill, affirmed the hypothetical character of the Science. Mr. Mill contented himself with suggesting the necessity of verification to establish the soundness of the hypothetical demonstration, but Mr. Cairns went further, and asserted that "Economical Laws are not assertions respecting the character or sequence of phenomena, and that they can neither be established nor refuted by Statistical or Documentary Evidence." It is true this was not the position of the earlier Teachers, Adam Smith, Ricardo, Senior, James Mill, M'Culloch, and Malthus, who never doubted that in all their reasonings they were dealing with Human Beings as they actually exist. Adam Smith, for instance, believed that Nature had made provision for Social Well-being by that principle of the Human Constitution which prompts every man to better his condition, and in aiming at individual good, every man is led by an invisible Hand to promote general good. Human Institutions only interfere with this tendency, and when all restraints are removed, the obvious and simple system of natural Liberty establishes itself. Ricardo and Malthus were, if possible, still more dogmatic and absolute in their assertion of these necessary tendencies, and made no allowances, or at the best gave scanty recognition to, the one-sided character of their premises. Mr. Senior seriously thought that the whole Science could, like Geometry, be reduced from four axiomatic propositions. It will be useful at this stage to note the general features of these assumptions of the earlier Economists, which they believed to be as necessarily and universally true as the First Law of Mechanics, that Bodies move in straight lines, or the First Law of Physics, that they attract each other directly according to their mass, and inversely according to the square of their distance. These assumptions may be thus briefly stated :—(1) that National Economy is essentially Individualistic and has no separate Collective aspect; (2) that the Individual, or typical Economical man, has no desire but that of promoting his own Self-interest, or at least that this is his strongest motive power; (3) that this Self-interest is best promoted by the largest Production of Wealth, *i.e.*, articles with value in Exchange, at the least trouble; (4) that such Pursuit of Private Gain by each individual promotes best the general good; (5) that the free and unlimited Competition of individuals in the race and struggle of life is the only safe and natural regulator; (6) that all customary and State Regulation is an encroachment on natural Liberty; (7) that every Individual knows best his Interest, and has the capacity and desire of acting according to this knowledge; (8) that there is perfect Freedom and Equality in the power of contract between individuals and individuals; (9) that Capital and Labour are always free and ready to move from one employment to another, where better remuneration is expected; (10) that there is a universal tendency of Profits and Wages to seek a common level; (11) that Population tends to outstrip the means of subsistence; (12) and that Demand and Supply always tend mutually to adjust each other.

These assumptions lie at the root of all dogmatical treatment of the subject. It need not be said that they are literally true of no existing Community. To the extent that they are approximately true of any state of Society, the assumptions furnish valid explanations of its Economical Statics. Even then they furnish no suggestion as to its dynamical progress or development. As these assumptions do not absolutely hold good of even the most advanced Societies, it is obvious that in Societies like ours, they are chiefly conspicuous by their absence. With us an average Individual man is, to a large extent, the very antipodes of the Economical Man. The Family and the Caste are more powerful than the Individual in determining his position in life. Self-interest in the shape of the desire of Wealth is not absent, but it is not the only nor principal motor. The Pursuit of Wealth is not the only ideal aimed at. There is neither the desire nor the aptitude for free and unlimited Competition except within certain predetermined grooves or groups. Custom and State Regulation are far more powerful than Competition, and Status more decisive in its influence than Contract. Neither Capital nor Labour is mobile, and enterprising and intelligent enough to shift from place to place. Wages and Profit are fixed, and not elastic and responsive to change of circumstances. Population follows its own Law, being cut down by Disease and Famine, while Production is almost stationary, the bumper harvest of one year being needed to provide against the uncertainties of alternate bad Seasons. In a Society so constituted, the tendencies assumed as axiomatic are not only inoperative, but are actually deflected from their proper direction. You might as well talk of the tendency of mountains to be washed away into the sea, or of the valleys to fill up, or of the Sun to get cold, as reasons for our practical conduct within a measurable distance of time.

This hypothetical character of the entire fabric of Doctrinal

Economy has been more or less freely recognized, as stated above, by Mr. Mill, Mr. Cairns and other Teachers of Political Economy; and in our own time, Mr. Bagehot has gone so far as to assert that the traditional system rested on assumptions which were not only not true generally, but were true only of England of the present day. He calls it the Science of Business done in large and trading Communities. It does not explain the Economic life of earlier times, or of our own times in other Nations. It is insular, and has not obtained general recognition, by reason of its being chiefly a convenient series of deductions from assumed axioms which are in many times and places not true, and are only true in England, where Capital and Labour can freely transport themselves from one employment to another. Mr. Sidgwick, another contemporary writer, has expressed the view that the abstract method is useful only for the statical study of Economy, and that its conclusions, even within this province, are only hypothetically valid. In the dynamical study of the Progress of Wealth the value of the deductive method is almost nil. Mr. Cliff Leslie has expressed himself in stronger terms. The Economy of every Nation, according to this writer, is the result of a long growth in which there has been continuity and change, and the economic side of this change is only a particular aspect. The Laws of Social Progress in Wealth must be sought in the history of the general Social Evolution which is different in different countries. Professor Jevons was filled with such despair by the sterile character of the hypothetical system that he thought the only way to cure its defects was to fling away, once and for ever, preposterous assumptions of the Ricardian School. It will be thus seen that in the land of its birth and highest development, the claims of Political Economy as ordinarily taught in the Text books, have been seriously questioned, and its value as a guide to practical conduct greatly discounted.

You will naturally desire to know how this revulsion of thought has been brought about in the course of a hundred years. It becomes necessary in this connection to take a retrospective view of the progress of the Science in Western Europe during the past two or three hundred years. Such a retrospect will help us to judge for ourself how far the development of the Scientific Theory of Political Economy can be regarded as even now complete. The ancient conception of Political Economy had regard chiefly to laying down the practical rules of prudent conduct for each private individual who desired to be rich. The conception of it as a Principle of Social Polity was more or less ignored. The general feeling in those days was that manual labour was below the dignity of a Free man. Such work was done by Slaves, or as we would in this country describe them, by the Lower Castes. A Free-man could only devote his attention to Agriculture. Commerce and Manufactures were later developments. This circumstance also explains the interdict on Usury which was a common feature of all Ancient Institutes, excepting those of our own Country, which in this respect were more advanced than the Greek, or Mahomedan, or Christian notions on the subject. Gradually Slaves became Serfs, and then Freemen, who worked for wages. These Serfs, seeking refuge in ancient coast towns and Roman Colonies, developed them into the Free commercial cities of the Middle Ages about the times of the Crusades, and later on into great manufacturing centres. The discoveries of the 15th Century gave a stimulus to trade, and later on to Colonization. The large imports of Gold and Silver helped to encourage the greater circulation of Money. The gradual rise of European Monarchies, and the decay of the Church and the Nobility, removed the pressure of Feudal ideas, and raised the status of those who were engaged in Commerce. The Republics of Italy developed Banking and Credit. It was when the national activity of Europe took such a varied from, stimulating Agriculture, Commerce, Manufactures, Banking, Currency, Exchange, Co-operation, Taxation, Colonization, and Foreign Conquests, that the ground was prepared for a systematic study of the Theory of the Laws which regulated Economical arrangements, and made Nations prosperous and strong, or the reverse. And the first speculative explanation attempted is known in history as the Mercantile

Theory. It is too much the practice of Text-writers to cry down this Theory as one which confounded Wealth with Money and Bullion, and made the possession of precious Metals the test of National prosperity. This is however, an utterly unfair and one-sided view of the subject. The leading feature of the system was that it set a higher value on Commerce and Manufactures than on Agriculture, and on Foreign over Home Trade. It encouraged Exports, but desired to check Imports with a view not to retain money so much as to develop Home Manufactures. Lastly, it prescribed the directive control of the State in the way of stimulating domestic Manufactures and encouraging Commerce. Each State competed with the rest in Foreign Markets, and sought to secure the most advantageous terms, and it sought also to extend its Colonies and Dependencies with a view to increase the sphere of open Markets, for its produce. It is enough to state that men like Colbert, and Oliver Cromwelll, Raleigh and Childe, could not have encouraged a system which had not some solid justification in the then circumstances of Europe. Cromwell's Navigation Laws have admittedly been the foundation of England's Naval Supremacy, and Colbert made France in his day the most prosperous State on the Continent. He had a keen perception that State protection and control were but crutches to teach the Nation to walk, and that they should be thrown away when the necessary advance had been made. It was under the influence of the same ideas that the Great East India companies of Holland, France, and England were formed, and received the support of their respective Governments. Charters and Monopolies, Bounties and Subsidies, were freely granted under the influence of same ideas, and State help and regulation did their work remarkably well.

In the next Century the natural progress of events made Nations alive to the abuses of the old system and men began to feel the necessity of freedom in the Economical as well as in the Political field. This work of destructive and negative criticism began in England with the teachings of Hobbes and Locke, but was more earnestly taken up in France previous to the Revolution. The enormous abuses of State control and direction, of monopolies and restrictions, led to a reaction in favour of a theory which was founded on the idea of Natural Liberty. In this negative Philosophy individual man was moreover, conceived as being solely guided by Private Interest, which it was supposed he understood better for himself than others could do for him, and the removal of all restrictions and prohibitions became the watch-word of this School. The previous preponderance of State support in favour of Commerce and Manufactures was condemned and a preference for Agriculture as the only true source of all Wealth was developed into a mania. In grasping the conception that money alone was not Wealth, and that all Wealth is created by human Labour applied to Natural Agents, people ran to the other extreme of classifying Commerce and Manufactures along with service and professions under the head of Unproductive Labour. In protesting against Protection and Prohibition, the extreme view went so far as to hold that Government itself was only a necessary evil, and that the State had no concern with Industry, and must confine itself to its sole function of keeping the public Peace. This conception of the domain of Natural Liberty in Economics was but a part and parcel of the great movement of Freedom which culminated in the French Revolution. Quesnay, Guorney, and the great Statesman Turgot, were the advocates of this New School of Thought which is known as the School of the Physiocrats.

Next in order of time we have Adam Smith, who was the direct product of the French negative School of Quesnay, but he improved upon his model and exposed the weakness of that School in two important respects. He established the fact that Agriculture was not the only source of wealth, and that Manufactures and Commerce were equally efficient in this respect, and that Nature helped man equally in all the three departments. While accepting the *laissez faire* doctrine of Free Trade as a general principle, Mr. Smith was alive to the fact that restrictive Navigation Laws had helped greatly to ensure English Commercial Supremacy, and he justified these Laws on the express ground that defence was of more importance than opulence, and he advocated what are known as Fair Trade views, *i.e.*, views which permit retaliation by way of Differential Duties against non-reciprocating Countries, on condition that such retaliation produces its desired consequences. He also approved of temporary concessions by way of Monopolies to Chartered Companies in enterprizes which involved risk and expense. Adam Smith never separated Economical from Social considerations, and thus occupied a position of advantage, which his Successors gave up by their too absolute assertion of his doctrines. I have already spoken of the rigid character of the system of Ricardo, Malthus, Senior, James Mill, Torrens, McCulloch and others and shown how this dogmatic feature provoked a reaction in England, at first faintly represented in the protests of John Stuart Mill and Mr. Cairns, but more decidedly formulated by Bagehot, Leslie and Jevons. This strong reaction of feeling among English writers was due to the influence of the great French and German Teachers. August Comte was the first who denied the name of Science to the doctrines taught by the Deductive School, and he elaborated his own system of the Historical Method of Research, and these hints were taken up by the German and English Thinkers of our day. Sismondi was the first economical writer who gave expression to the dissatisfaction felt in France at the conclusions of the English Economists. He charged the Individualistic School with tendencies by which the rich became richer, and the poor were made poorer. He protested against the abuses of the *laissez faire* Policy, and invoked Government intervention for protecting the masses against the classes, and the weaker races against the pressure of the stronger and more advanced Nations under the *régime* of Competition. Sismondi declared that the State was not merely an agency for keeping peace, but that it was an organization for securing the progress of the people as widely as possible, and for extending the benefits of the Social Union to all. Another French writer, Dunoyer, defined Liberty not as a mere negation of restraint, but a positive effort to increase efficiency of Labour in all its grades.

Two American Thinkers, Hamilton and Carey, sounded the same note of difference in more distinct terms. Hamilton was one of the Fathers of the American Constitution, and he stated that the English doctrine of Absolute Freedom was practicable only if all Nations accepted Free Trade views simultaneously, and he suggested a scheme of Protective Duties which were later on adopted as the leading feature of American State Tariffs. The Hayleybury Professor Jones had before Carey attacked the Ricardian Theory of Rent as being true only of Farmers' rents, and as wholly inapplicable to the Indian Ryots' rent or the Metayer or Cottier rents. Carey went further, and denied that there was any Economic Rent proper, and contended that Rent was only a remuneration, in the same way as profits, of past invested Capital or Labour. Carey justified Protection to domestic Agriculture on the ground that the waste products of land must return to the soil to restore its powers, and this restoration was not possible where Raw Products were exported to and consumed by distant Countries. Like the French Sismondi, Carey regarded the State as a co-ordinating power in Society, which checked the tendency of individuals to seek immediate gain at the sacrifice of permanent National interests, and he asserted that Protection was justified as being the only means by which the obstacles, thrown in the way of younger and less advanced Communities by more advanced Nations could be removed. The immediate loss to the Nation was, like the sum spent on the Education of youth by individuals, which more than re-pays itself in the long run.

Like the French and American writers, the Italian Economists of the modern period, Gioga and Ludovico, also advocated State Regulation of Industry, and asserted the Doctrine of Relativity as being an essential factor of all true Economic Theory. The work of positive exposition was, however, most successfully taken up by the German Professors. Müller first suggested that Adam Smith's system, as elaborated by his more dogmatic disciples, was essentially English and Insular. It succeeded in England, because the national life of England was preserved intact by its favoured situation and past history and conservative instincts, while it was unsuitable to the Continental Countries, because, with them the preservation of the National existence was a subject of greater importance than mere individual prosperity. It was the writings of List, which gave the fullest expression to this rebellion against the orthodox creed. He urged that the permanent interests of Nations were not always in harmony with the present benefit of individuals. National well-being does not consist only in the creation of the highest quantity of wealth measured in exchange value, independently of all variety of quality in that wealth, but in the full and many-sided development of all productive powers. The nation's Economic Education is of far more importance than the present gain of its individual members, as represented by the quantity of wealth measured by its value in exchange. In a sound and normal condition, all the three departments of national activity must be fully developed. Commerce and Manufactures are, if possible, more vital in their bearing on the education of the intelligence and skill and enterprize of the Nation than Agriculture. In a purely Agricultural Country there is a tendency to stagnation and absence of enterprize and the retention of antiquated prejudices. The function of the State is to help those influences which tend to secure National Progress through the several stages of growth, and adopt Free Trade or Protection as circumstances may require. In this view Free Trade may be good for a Country like England, but not for America and Germany.

The subsequent German Teachers further elaborated this historical view, and under the stimulus of the success of the comparative method in Philology and Jurisprudence, proposed to reconstruct Economy by the help of the new method. Raw, Knieys, Roscher, Hildebrand, Wagner and others worked on these lines. Their influence made itself felt on English thought, and Leslie and Jevons were directly influenced by these teachings. They advocated that Economy was only one branch of Sociology, and like all Social Sciences, it must be studied both in its statical and dynamical conditions, and that the basis of a hypothetical economic man, guided solely by one motive of Self-Interest, must be given up, and man as he is, both selfish and altruistic, possessing rights as well as being bound by duties, must be studied in History, both Ancient and Modern. In brief, this German School regards that Universalism and Perpetualism in Economic Doctrine are both unscientific and untrue.

This resumé of the past and contemporary history of the growth of Economic Sciences in England, France, Germany, Italy, and America will satisfy the student that modern European thought does not at all countenance the view of the English writers of the Ricardian School, that the Principles of the science, as they have enunciated them in their Text Books, are universally and necessarily true for all times and places, and for all stages of Advancement. Modern Thought is veering to the conclusion that the Individual and his Interests are not the centre round which the Theory should revolve, that the true centre is the Body Politic of which that Individual is a Member, and that Collective Defence and Well-being, Social Education and Discipline, and the Duties, and not merely the Interests, of men, must be taken into account, if the Theory is not to be merely Utopian. The Method to be followed is not the Deductive but the Historical Method, which takes account of the past in its forecast of the future; and Relativity, and not Absoluteness, characterizes the conclusions of Economical Science. There are those who seek to get over this difficulty by differentiating the Science from what they are disposed to call the Art of Economy. This divorce of Theory and Practice is, however, a mischievous error, which relegates the Science to the sterility of an ideal dream or a puzzle, and condemns the Art to the position of a rule of the thumb. Theory is only enlarged Practice, Practice is Theory studied in its relation to proximate Causes. The Practice is predetermined by the Theory which tests its truth, and adapts it to different conditions by reason of its grasp of the deep-seated, permanent, and varied basal truths. I hope thus to have shown that the nature of the subject itself as a branch of

Social Science which is best studied historically and not deductively, the actual Practice of the most Civilized Nations and the history of the growth of its Theory given above, alike establish the Doctrine of Relativity, and the predominant claim of Collective Welfare over Individual Interests, as the principal features in which the highest minds of the present day chiefly differ from the Economical Writers of the Old School, with their *a priori* conclusions based on individual self-interest and unrestricted competition.

We have next to consider the bearings of this enlarged view of the Science in its Indian aspects. The characteristics of our Social Life are the prevalence of Status over Contract, of Combination over Competition. Our habits of mind are conservative to a fault. The aptitudes of climate and soil facilitate the production of raw materials. Labour is cheap and plentiful, but unsteady, unthrifty, and unskilled. Capital is scarce, immobile, and unenterprizing. Co-operation on a large scale of either Capital of Labour is unknown. Agriculture is the chief support of nearly the whole population, and this Agriculture is carried on under conditions of uncertain rainfall. Commerce and Manufactures on a large scale are but recent importations, and all industry is carried on, on the system of petty farming, retail dealing, and job working by poor people on borrowed capital. There is an almost complete absence of a landed gentry or wealthy middle class. The land is a monopoly of the State. The desire for accumulation is very weak, peace and security having been almost unknown over large areas for any length of time till within the last Century. Our Laws and Institutions favour a low standard of life, and encourage subdivision and not concentration of Wealth. The religious ideals of life condemn the ardent pursuit of wealth as a mistake to be avoided as far as possible. These are old legacies and inherited weaknesses. Stagnation and dependence, depression and poverty—these are written in broad characters on the face of the land and its people. To these must be added the economical drain of wealth and talents, which Foreign subjection has entailed on the country. As a compensation against all these depressing influences, we have to set off the advantage of a free contact with a race which has opened the Country to the Commerce of the world, and by its superior skill and resources has developed communications in a way previously unknown. If we wish to realize our situation fully, we may not overlook this factor, because, it represents the beam of light which alone illumines the prevailing darkness. It cannot well be a mere accident that the destinies of this Country have been entrusted to the guidance of a Nation whose characteristic strength is opposed to all our weaknesses, whose enterprize, chiefly in Commerce and Manufactures, knows no bounds, whose Capital overflows the world, among whom Contract has largely superseded Status, and Competition and Co-Operation play a predominant part, whose view of life is full of hope, and whose powers of organization have never been surpassed.

The first point which illustrates the divergence between the orthodox English doctrine and the enlarged views I have attempted to set forth, as characterizing the more developed modern European thought on the subject, relates to the so-called system of the territorial Division of Labour by which the orthodox economists assign to the backward Torrid Zone Regions of Asia the duty of producing Raw Materials, and claim for the advanced European Temperate Zone Countries the work of transport and manufactures, as a division of labour in production which is fraught with the highest advantage to all, and is almost a Providential dispensation, against which it would be foolish to rebel. Of course, as far as the natural advantages of climate and situation force our hands, economically backward races must submit to such an arrangement, but it is fairly open to question whether there is any such inevitable necessity which justifies a line of separation, which has a tendency to accentuate natural deficiencies, and make them a source of permanent weakness. (1) In the first place, the Torrid Zone people may fairly appeal to past history, when their skilled products found a ready market in temperate kingdoms, and excited such jealousy as to dictate prohibitive sumptuary laws both in ancient Rome and in modern England. (2) They may also urge that the natural fitness of things requires that the manufactures should spring up where the raw materials grow, and where besides, there is demand for the manufactured produce, rather than that bulky goods should be transported many thousands of miles over land and sea, and re-consigned the same way back. (3) The differences in favour of temperate regions are all modern growths due to the employment of Steam Machinery, and the abundance of cheap Iron and Coal. This is a real advantage, and has to be faced, but if it can be faced, there is no natural incongruity in an arrangement by which Industry would return to its ancient home with a double saving in time and cost. (4) Neither Mr. Adam Smith, nor even Mr. John Stuart Mill, recommend absolute freedom in such matters. Adam Smith was a Fair Trader, and Mr. Mill distinctly recognizes an exception to the general rule of Free Trade, where time is required to see whether new industries are or are not adapted to the natural resources of new countries. The late controversy between Mr. Blaine and Mr. Gladstone chiefly turned upon this point, Mr. Blaine contending that, with a large Continental Country like America, with all shades of climate and soil and position, the conditions of the problem were different from those of an isolated small territory like England. The Australian Colonies also justify their departure from the orthodox policy on this same ground. India may fairly claim the benefit of the experience and practice of these self-governing Communities, and demand breathing time. (5) It is further to be noted that such a division of Production, if permanently stereotyped, consigns Asia to an Industry which is under the bane of the Law of Diminishing Returns, while the West of Europe appropriates to itself those forms of Industry which are not subject to any such Law. The orthodox view thus condemns the poor to grow still poorer, and helps the rich to become richer—"it giveth much to him that hath, and taketh away from him that hath not the little that he hath." (6) Lastly, people forget that the Agricultural Industry in the Torrid Regions has to work under the disadvantage of an uncertain rainfall, and suffer from famine visitations, which, when they come, paralyze

Production, and condemn millions to violent or slow death. A due co-ordination of the three-fold forms of industrial activity, even if it be not immediately most advantageous to individuals in any one period, is a permanent National Insurance against recurrent dangers, and as such is economically the most beneficial course in the interest of the Community.

(2) The point noticed above has reference chiefly to Foreign Trade. In domestic interchange also, the same law operates, and every Nation which desires economical advance has to take care that its urban population bear an increasing ratio to its rural masses with every advance it seeks to make. Mr. John Stuart Mill has expressly laid down that no Agriculture can be really productive which is divorced from a neighbouring non-agricultural market represented by thriving Towns and Cities. Under Native Rulers there was a sort of a rude adjustment made in this direction, when the Courts of the Petty Sovereigns afforded so many centres of urban activity in industries patronized by the Court and its dependents. Mr. Mill suggests that in the absence of such near markets, the next available substitute is a large export trade to Foreign Countries. This substitute cannot, however, be accepted as really answering the purpose in view. The progress of ruralization in modern India means its rustication, *i.e.*, a loss of power, and intelligence, and self-dependence, and is a distinctly retrograde move. The growth of the sea Ports and of the few Military and Railway Stations is not enough to counterbalance the enormous loss that has been inflicted by this retrograde movement. Every class of artizans, the Spinners, Weavers and the Dyers, the Oilsmen, the Paper-makers, the Silk and Sugar and Metal workers, etc., who are unable to bear up against Western competition, resort to the land, leave the Towns and go into the Country, and are lost in the mass of helpless people who are unable to bear up against scarcity and famine.

(3) The highest Statesmanship may well feel aghast at this rapid change, and I know as a matter of fact that this subject

weighs heavily on the conscience of the British Administrators in India. They, however, feel powerless to act under the influence of the all-pervading doctrine that these matters lie outside the province of Government. A regular system of Immigration from thickly populated poor Agricultural tracts to sparsely peopled new and virgin districts is a desideratum. The halting efforts made in this direction produce no good, for the concessions are not liberal enough, and there is no prescience about it. The Ancient Rulers who settled waste districts, and founded towns with flourishing and extensive Industries, made no difficulty about granting the most liberal concessions. Anticipating Mr. Wakefield's colonization proposals, whole Village Communities with their varied elements of life were encouraged to move *en masse*, and were made comfortable in their new places. Powerful Guilds of Traders and Artizans from distant places were similarly induced to settle in new Towns by free gifts of lands and houses and privileges. Stray settlers attracted by a few years' leases can never accomplish the end the Rulers have in view, and such attempts are bound to fail. A Colbert or a Peter the Great is wanted to give effect to such a scheme, and the ordinary doctrines of *laissez faire* must be set aside in view of the great interests at stake.

(4) Conquest, consolidation, and conciliation have had their heroes in British History. Systematic Colonization and the promotion of varied culture are the next stage of development; and it may be hoped that, before long, with Africa and Australia and the East and West Indies literally starving for Indian Labour, and Burma, at our door opened up, the ravages of periodical famines, carrying away our thousands and millions for want of work when Agriculture fails will become impossible, as soon as the policy of let-alone is given up, and an active effort made in all directions to stimulate productions both of raw and manufactured products. If the State can legitimately undertake from borrowed funds the construction or subsidization of Railroads and Canals, if it can afford to sell the Fee Simple of waste lands at nominal rates to European settlers on the hills, the road

is certainly open for a further development of this same industrial effort on new lines. The Dutch Netherlands Government have shown the way in Java, and with less selfish motives the same method might well be tried in regard at least, to the Industries allied with Agriculture, Sugar Refining, Oil Pressing, Tobacco Curing, Silk Rearing, etc., all of which can certainly be made to thrive in this torrid land under skilled supervision.

Proceeding next to the department of Distribution, the enlarged view of Political Economy stated above does not accept the position of the unearned increment as a leading feature of the Law of Rent in India. The Unearned Increment Theory fits in only where landed property continues for generations in the possession of the same family. If the land changes hands, the incoming purchaser buys it at its market value, and he enjoys no unearned advantage, and the so-called rent is but a return by way of fair profits on his investment. The English conditions of Land-lordism, where the land under a complicated system of entails and settlements and primogeniture, continues in the same family for generations, allow free play to the law of the Unearned Increment. Here, in this country lands and houses are not so tied up, and they change hands frequently and largely, In every twenty years, the Registration Returns show that the value of sales comes up to the total value of landed property. In one generation, property thus changes hands, and when new men come in as purchasers for value, they do not enjoy any unearned increment of the past, but have to pay full value for the differential advantages of superior productiveness and vicinity. In the same way the Ricardian Theory that Economic Rent does not enter as an element of price, admittedly does not apply when all occupied land has to pay Monopoly Rent to the State Landlord. There is no competition among Landlords in this country, for there is only one true Landlord and the so-called Land Tax is not a tax on Rents proper but frequently encroaches upon the Profits and Wages of the poor Peasant, who has to submit perforce to a loss of Status and accommodate himself to a lower standard of life as pressure increases.

Lastly, the Advanced Theory expounded by the Modern School fully justifies the attempts made by the Government here and in England to check the abuse of Competition among poor tenants by conferring Fixity of Tenure, by adjusting rents judicially for a term of years, and imposing limitations on its increase. In this matter the Tenants of Government claim the same consideration as those of private Zamindars. The justification for this active interference is as valid in regard to Agricultural Labourers and Tenants, as it is in the case of Factory Labourers and Miners in Europe. These people are unable to combine for self-protection, or at least their combination is not so effective as that of the Employers of Labour, and when their efforts fail to obtain regular redress, disorder and misery result as consequences, and threaten public peace and general well-being. In the same spirit, the regulation of the Freedom of Contract in regard to the fixing of rates of interest in transactions between the poor disunited indebted classes and the money-lenders, and the protection of immovable property from being sold away for improvident debts, not secured on the same, are all legitimate forms of protection of the weak against the strong, and do not affect the real freedom of Distribution. The Advanced Theory concedes freedom where the parties are equally matched in intelligence and resources; when this is not the case, all talk of equality and freedom adds insult to the injury. It is in this spirit that the Distribution of Produce among the needy many and the powerful few has to be arranged, *i.e.*, in a spirit of equity and fair play, and the orthodox Views of Finality in such matters must be reconsidered in all the relations of life.

Lastly comes the great department of Governmental interference. The meddlesomeness of the Mercantile System provoked a reaction against State Control and Guidance towards the end of the last century in favour of Natural Liberty. The Doctrines of this Negative School have now in their turn been abused by a too logical extension of its principles. There is a decided reaction in Europe against the *laissez faire* system. Even in England, the recent Factory Legislation, the qualified recognition by law of Trades-Unionism, the Poor Law System, and the Irish Land Settlement, are all instances which indicate the same change of view. Speaking roughly, the province of State Interference and Control is practically being extended so as to restore the good points of the mercantile system without its absurdities. The State is now more and more recognized as the National Organ for taking care of National needs in all matters in which individual and co- operative efforts are not likely to be so effective and economic as National effort. This is the correct view to take of the true functions of a State. To relegate them to the simple duty of maintaining peace and order is really to deprive the Community of many of the advantages of the Social Union. Education, both Liberal and Technical, Post and Telegraphs, Railway and Canal Communications, the pioneering of new enterprize, the insurance of risky undertakings, all these functions are usefully discharged by the State. The question is one of time, fitness, and expediency, not one of liberty and rights. In our own Country, the State has similarly enlarged its functions with advantage. The very fact, that the Rulers belong to a race with superior advantages imposes this duty on them of attempting things which no Native Rulers, past or present, could as well achieve, or possibly even think of. This obligation is made more peremptory by the fact that the State claims to be the sole Landlord, and is certainly the largest Capitalist in the Country. While the State in India has done much in this way in the working of Iron and Coal fields, and in the experiments made about Cotton and Tobacco, and in Tea and Coffee and Cinchona Plantations, it must be admitted that, as compared with its resources and the needs of the Country these attempts are as nothing by the side of what has been attempted with success in France, Germany and other countries, but which, unhappily, has not been attempted in this country. Even if political considerations forbid independent action in the matter of differential duties, the pioneering of new enterprize is a duty which the Government might more systematically undertake with advantage. In truth, there is no difference of principle between lending such support and guidance, by the free use of its Credit and superior Organization, in pioneering Industrial Undertakings or subsidizing private Co-operative effort, and its guaranteeing minimum interest to Railway Companies. The building up of National, not merely State, Credit on broad foundations by helping people to acquire confidence in a free and largely ramified Banking system, so advantageously worked in Europe under different forms, has also not been attempted here. There is, lastly, the duty cast on it of utilizing indigenous resources, and organizing them in a way to produce in India in State Factories all products of skill which the State Departments require in the way of Stores. These are only a few of the many directions in which, far more than Exchange and Frontier difficulties, the highest Statesmanship will have a field all its own for consideration and action. They will, no doubt, receive such consideration if only the minds of the Rulers were once thoroughly freed from the fear of offending the so-called maxims of rigid Economical Science. It is time that a new departure should take place in this connection, and it is with a view to drawing public attention to this necessity that I have ventured to place before you the results of modern economic Thought. In this, as in other matters, the conditions of Indian life are more faithfully reproduced in some of the Continental Countries and in America than in happy England, proud of its position, strong in its insularity, and the home of the richest and busiest Community in the modern industrial World. If the attempt I have made leads to a healthy and full discussion of the change of policy I advocate, I shall regard myself amply repaid for my trouble.

The following extracts will show that the views embodied in the foregoing paper are not confined to the Native Community only, but that Anglo-Indian Thinkers of note are also becoming every day more and more alive to the evils of the present *laissez faire* Policy of the Government of India. The first extract is taken from "A Modern Zoroastrian," by S. Laing, sometime

Financial Minister to the Government of India. The second extract is taken from "A Study in Indian Administration," by Sir William Wilson Hunter and it represents the views entertained by the late Sir Maxwell Melvill on Indian Political Economy.

Extract from Mr. Laing's "A Modern Zoroastrian."

"When Sir Robert Peel some forty years ago announced his conversion by the unadorned eloquence of Richard Cobden, and Free Trade was inaugurated, with results which were attended with the most brilliant success, every one expected that the conversion of the rest of the Civilised World was only a question of time, and that a short time. Few would have been found bold enough to predict that forty years later England would stand almost alone in the world in adherence to Free Trade principles, and that the Protectionist heresy would not only be strengthened and confirmed among Continental Nations such as France and Germany, but actually adopted by large and increasing majorities in the United States, Canada, Australia, and other English-speaking Communities. Yet such is the actual fact at the present day. In spite of the Cobden Club and of arguments which to the average English mind appear irresistible, Free Trade has been steadily losing ground for the last twenty years, and Nation after Nation, Colony after Colony, sees its Protectionist majority increasing and its Free Trade minority dwindling.

"It is evident there must be some real cause for such a universal phenomenon. In Countries like France and Russia we may attribute it to Economical ignorance and the influence of cliques of manufacturers and selfish interests; but the people of Germany, and still more of the United States, Canada, and Australia, are as intelligent as ourselves, and quite as shrewd in seeing where their interests really lie. They are fettered by no traditional prejudices, and their Political instincts rather lie towards Freedom and against the creation of anything like an Aristocracy of wealthy Manufacturers. And yet, after years of free discussion, they have become more and more hardened in their Protectionist heresies.

"What does this prove? That there are two sides to the Shield, and not, as we fancied in our English insularity, only one.

"Free Trade is undoubtedly the best, or rather the only possible, policy for a Country like England, with thirty millions of inhabitants, producing food for less than half the number, and depending on Foreign Trade for the supplies necessary to keep the other half alive. It is the best policy also for a Country which, owing to its Mineral resources, its accessibility by sea to Markets, its accumulated Capital, and the inherited qualities, physical and moral of its working population, has unrivalled advantages for cheap production. Nor can any dispassionate observer dispute that in England, which is such a Country, Free Trade has worked well. It has not worked miracles, it has not introduced an industrial Millennium, the poor are still with us, and it has not saved us from our share of commercial depressions. But on the whole, National Wealth has greatly increased, and, what is more important, national well-being has increased with it, the mass of the population, and especially the Working Classes, get better wages, work shorter hours, and are better fed, better clothed, and better educated than they were forty years ago.

"This is one side of the Shield, and it is really a golden and not an illusory one. But look at the other side. Take the case of a Country where totally opposite conditions prevail: where there is no surplus population, unlimited land, limited capital, labour scarce and dear, and no possibility of competing in the foreign or even in the home Market with the manufactures which, with Free Trade, would be poured in by countries like England, in prior possession of all the elements of cheap production. It is by no means so clear that Protection, to enable Native Industries to take root and grow, may not in such cases be the wisest policy.

"Take, as a simple illustration, the case of an Australian Colony, imposing an Import Duty on Foreign boots and shoes. There is no doubt that this is practically taxing the immense majority of Colonists who wear and do not make these articles. But, on the other hand, it makes the Colony a possible field for Emigration for all Shoe-makers of Europe, and shoe-making a trade to which any Australian with a large family can bring up one of his sons. Looking at it from the strict point of view of the most rigid Political Economist, the maximum Production of Wealth, which is the better policy ? The production of Wealth we must recollect, depends on Labour, and productive labour depends on the Labourer finding his tools—that is, employment at which he can work. A labourer who cannot find work at living wages is worse than a zero; he is a negative quantity as far as the accumulation of wealth is concerned. On the other hand, every workman who finds work, even if it may not be of the ideally best description, is a wealth-producing machine. What he spends on himself and his family gives employment to other workmen, and the work must be poor indeed, if the produce of a year's labour is not more than the cost of a year's subsistence. The surplus adds to the National Capital and thus Capital and Population go on increasing in Geometrical Progression. The first problem therefore, for a new or backward Country, is to find 'a fair day's wages for a fair day's work,' for as many hands as possible. The problem of making that employment the most productive possible is a secondary one, which will solve itself in each case rather by actual Practice than by abstract Theory.

"This much, however, is pretty clear, that in order to secure the maximum of employment, it must be varied. All are not fit for agricultural work, and, even if they were, if the conditions of soil and climate favour large Estates and Sheep or Cattle Runs rather than small Farms, a large amount of capital may provide work for only a small number of labourers. On social and moral grounds, also, apart from dry considerations of Political Economy, progress, intelligence, and a higher standard of life are more likely to be found with large Cities, Manufactures, and a variety of industrial Occupations than with a dead level of a few Millionaires and a few Shepherds, or of a few Landlords and a dense population of poor Peasants. If Protection is the price which must be paid to render such a larger life possible, it may be sound policy to pay it, and the result seems to show that neither it nor Free Trade is inconsistent with rapid progress, while, on the other hand, neither of them affords an absolute immunity from the evils that dog the footsteps of Progress, and from the periods of reaction and depression which accompany vicissitudes of Trade."

Extract from Sir W.W. Hunter's "Study in Indian Administration."

"But Sir Maxwell Melvill, or Max Melvill as he was affectionately called throughout his career, was an important personality and a living influence quite apart from his official work. In Economics he did not shrink from declaring himself a Protectionist of the American type, that is to say, an advocate for Protection not for a single isolated Country, but for a great Continent like America or India made up of a number of States, possessing within them the resources for almost every kind of Production, indeed for almost every form of human industry, and capable of a self-sufficing economic development. One of those who knew him best believes that it was this consciousness of holding views not in accordance with the prevailing doctrines of the Government of India, which influenced him in declining the seat in the Viceroy's Council."

20

IRON INDUSTRY—PIONEER ATTEMPTS*

I have in my Essay on Indian Political Economy endeavoured to lay down a few general principles which should regulate the action of the State, in respect of the development of Industrial Enterprise in India. I propose on the present occasion to illustrate these principles by an historical review of the efforts made to develop the production of a particular Indian Product, which is closely associated with the revival of Indian manufactures, and which may well be described as typifying the Resources of Wealth, on which our future prosperity mainly depends. The history of the successive attempts made by Private and State Agencies to develop the Iron Industry in India has a mournful interest, and yet it is full of instruction. As Captain Townsend of the Ordnance Department has observed in his work on the Mineral Wealth of India, nothing strikes the stranger who studies Indian Economy so much as the contrast between the bounty of Nature and the poverty of Man in the matter of this Iron Industry. Endowed more richly in Iron ore than almost any other country in the world, India has in a commercial sense, no Iron Industry at all. There are only forty-two Iron and Brass Foundries in the Country, working chiefly on Foreign Imports, and employing twelve thousand men. Mr. Ball, Deputy superintendent of the Geological Survey, in his work on

*Read at the Industrial Conference, Poona, 1892, and published in *Essays*.

Economic Geology, and Dr. Watt, in his Dictionary of Indian Economic Products, have described the extent and richness of the Iron ores which occur in all formations, in the metamorphic rocks, semi-metamorphic or transition rocks, in the conglomerates, in the cretaceous rocks, in the Deccan trap, in the sand-beds of rivers, and in the detrital ores of sub-recent Age. In respect of Geographical distribution, there is absolutely not a Province or even a large District in all India, which is not favoured with rich Iron ore deposits of one kind or another, and in which there are not traces of Iron manufactured by Native Methods down to very recent times.

The Iron Industry not only supplied all local wants, but it also enabled India to export its finished products to Foreign Countries. The quality of the material turned out had also a world-wide fame. The famous Iron Pillar near Delhi, which is at least fifteen hundred years old, indicates an amount of skill in the manufacture of Wrought Iron, which has been the marvel of all who have endeavoured to account for it. Mr. Ball admits that it is not many years since the production of such a Pillar would have been an impossibility in the largest Factories in the world, and even now, there are comparatively very few factories where such a mass of metal could be turned out. Cannons were manufactured in Assam of the largest calibre. Indian Wootz or Steel furnished the materials out of which Damascus Blades with a world-wide reputation were made, and it paid Persian Merchants in those old times to travel all the way to India to obtain these materials, and export them to Asia. The Indian Steel found once considerable demand for Cutlery even in England. This manufacture of steel and Wrought Iron had reached a high perfection at least two thousand years ago.

All this is now changed. The Native Furnaces all over the Country have stopped work. The Domestic Manufacture has been, in most places, crushed out by foreign competition, and complete extinction in the near future is the fate with which it has been cursed. This fate has overtaken it contemporaneously with an enormous increase in the demand for Iron Goods. The measure of this increase will be gathered from the fact that in 1888-89 India imported nearly four million hundredweight of Iron, worth two and a half Crores of Rupees. The Imports of Steel were a quarter of a million hundred weight, worth thirty-four Laks of Rupees, Hardware and Cutlery Imports exceeded one Crore of Rupees. Railway Plant and Stock were worth two and a half Crores of Rupees, and Mill Work and Machinery two and one third Crores of Rupees, while Government Imports came to one Crore. In all, about eleven Crores' worth of Iron Goods were imported in 1888-89. The Imports twenty years ago, under all these heads, were about two and a half Crores only, and the difference between the two totals to a large extent measures the displacement of Home Manufactures.

Of course, it is but fair to note that, besides the effects of Foreign Competition, the collapse of the Iron Industry has been brought about by the increasing scarcity of Fuel. The Native Furnaces have all along used Charcoal fuel, and their processes involve great waste of power and resources, as much as fourteen tons of fuel being required to produce one ton of Iron. As a consequence, the production of Iron by the old Native Methods cannot be continued, except at a cost which is prohibitive. This question of cheap fuel lies at the bottom of the success of any organized attempt to revive the Industry under modern conditions. In this respect, Nature has not been equally munificent in her gifts. While the Iron ore is to be found all over the Country, the only cheap fuel which can enable India to compete with England, namely, Indian Coal, is not so widely distributed, but in the region where it is found, the resources of India are by no means stinted or poor. The Coal-bearing area is estimated to exceed thirty-five thousand square miles. The regions of the Wardha-Godavari Valleys, the Valleys of the Soane and its Tributaries, and the Valleys of the Damuda and its Tributaries, and the Lower Range of the Vindhya and the Himalaya Mountains, represent the Coal Region of India, and these Coal resources, thanks to the action of Government, and the Railway Companies, have been largely utilized. It was estimated in 1879-80 in Official Reports, that out of a total consumption of some one and a half Million tons, one Million tons were raised in India, and about five Laks of tons were imported. During the last fourteen years the consumption and Home production has nearly doubled. More than two Million tons of Indian Coal were produced and consumed in India, and the Foreign Imports were about eight or nine Laks of tons in 1888-89. Besides the convenient vicinity of cheap Fuel, another equally essential requisite for the successful manufacture of Iron is, abundance of Lime-stone to serve as Flux, and of Fire Clay for the Furnaces. This resource generally accompanies Coal Formations. At least, this has been the case in India. The need of proximity to Sea or Railway, and abundance of Coal and Lime-stone, limit the possibilities of successful Indian Manufacture of Iron to a few favoured regions. Mr. Ball has with some hesitation expressed his opinion as follows:—By adopting improved processes of manufacture in the Raniganj Field, Iron and Steel of high quality might be manufactured under proper management at a probable cost which would admit of their underselling the English Iron in the Bengal Markets. With improved communications, this same result may be predicated of the Palamow Field in the Hajaribag District. The Chanda field with improved processes of reduction will be in a position to supply the Central Provinces and Bombay with Iron at an average rate lower than that paid for English Iron, and this remark holds true of some of the localities in the Narbada Valley and in Upper Assam. As regards the rest of India, there does not appear any solid ground of hope, under existing conditions, of manufacturing cheap Iron, which will compete in price and quality with the English imported article. Captain Townsend is equally, or if possible more, discriminating in his forecast. According to him the Raniganj Field possesses all the auxiliary advantages, though its Iron ore is not of the best. The Wardha Valley, in the proximity of the Warora Coal Mines has superior Iron ore, but its Coal Supply is not equally good. He mentions the Hazaribag Field as in every way eligible, as its Coal is richer than Raniganj and Warora. The Southern Indian Iron Field near Salem is the richest in all India, and though it does not enjoy the advantage of Coal deposits in the vicinity, Captain Townsend thinks that this difficulty is not insuperable, especially, if the manufacture is limited to the higher classes of Iron, while the Raniganj and Wardha Fields might confine themselves with advantage to the cheaper and inferior classes. Mr. Ball also suggests, that when there are extensive jungles, the absence of Coal Mines does not matter much, since the unrestrained annual jungle-fires consume a much greater amount of timber than any number of Charcoal Burners could do, and with a judicious system of Forest Conservancy, it should be possible to allow Native Furnaces near such jungles. Sir George Molesworth, writing in 1882, gave it as his opinion "that Charcoal-made Iron will never be able to compete with English Iron, but a well-organized system of Forest Conservancy ought to be able to secure Charcoal Fuel at a low price for smelting purposes, and within close proximity to the Iron Works." Such a Conservancy is not easy to secure, and there is no great prospect of help in this assurance. Dr. Watt, after a careful examination of all existing sources, arrived at the conclusion that the Bengal and Jabalpore and China Fields offer, under existing circumstances, the only possible opening for large Iron Works.

Dr. Watt, in his Dictionary, quotes the testimony of an Official Expert, from which it appears that the price of Iron is increased fifty per cent. by reason of Freight and Landing Charges, about one mile of Iron Railway Sleepers costing in England £2,000 and in India Rs.31,000. The difference is due to £1,000 charge for Freight and Landing. The railway carriage charge and during recent years the heavy loss by Exchange raise this difference fully fifty per cent. more. It has been estimated that about one hundred and fifty Crores' worth of Iron has been imported into India during the last thirty years, and fifty Crores of Rupees at least have thus been paid for Freight and Landing Charges alone, which would have been saved if the Industry had been started here. Mr. Ball observes, that if the Government had started the manufacture of Iron on an extended scale at the time of the first opening of the Railways, great benefits would have accrued to the State. If the State was justified in undertaking the construction of its own Railways, there was nothing inconsistent with principle in its undertaking the manufacture of its own Iron any more than in its manufacture of Salt or Opium. The effect of its establishing Factories for Iron manufacture throughout India would have, in Mr. Ball's opinion, enabled the State to keep vast sums of money in circulation, and would have given employment to large numbers of people who now resort to Agriculture as their only resource. This golden opportunity was allowed to pass, and we find ourselves in the anomalous situation that after one hundred and fifty years of British Rule, the Iron resources of India remain undeveloped, and the Country pays about ten Crores of Rupees yearly for its Iron supply, while the old race of Iron Smelters find their occupation gone.

It must be admitted at the same time, that the Government of India has not been altogether oblivious of its duties in this connection. The Government, through its Geological Survey Department has carefully, and at considerable expense, surveyed the Regions which abound in Iron Ores. The value of this service can never be overestimated. Next to these Surveying operations, it has also from time to time, spent considerable sums on experimental trials, it has subsidized Companies to whom concessions more or less favourable have been granted, and lastly, it has directed its various Departments to obtain their supplies from Local sources, and thus helped the efforts of these Companies. There is thus no question of principle involved in the matter. The principle of State-help and guidance in pioneering new enterprize has thus been accepted and acted upon by the Government here. The only fault one can lay at its door, is that this Policy has been followed with half-heartedness and oscillations of purpose, the result of which has been that as a rule most of the private attempts made on various occasions have proved more or less failures, serving only to discourage all enterprize in this direction.

The object of this paper is to give a brief History of these attempts, and to ascertain the cause or causes why they turned out failures :—

1. I shall first take up the Salem Iron Field. In 1825 Mr. Heath obtained a Government advance for the purpose, and he succeeded in 1833 in forming a Company called the Indian Steel, Iron, and Chrome Company. The Lease-hold rights of this Company extended over four Districts of South Arcot, Coimbatore, Malabar, and South Canara, and it established three Factories, at Porto Novo in South Arcot, at Beypore in Malabar, and at Palampetti near Salem. The Steel manufactured by this Company was very highly thought of, and it established a depôt at Chelsea, through which the Steel was tested and passed before being sold. The business of Mr. Heath's Company was after some years taken over by another Company, who continued to work the Porto Novo and Beypore Factories till 1859. The Company had in those days great difficulties to encounter. They consumed Charcoal Fuel, which had to be brought from a distance of more than twenty-five miles, and the Flux used was Sea-Shells, and both Fuel and Flux had to be taken to long distances. Notwithstanding these difficulties, the Pig Iron produced was pronounced by Sheffield Iron Workers to be superior to any produced in England and Sweden, and it commanded a good price, £6 10s. per ton, in London for conversion into Steel, and two Bridges, the Britannia Tabular and Menai Bridges, were built with this material. Next to the difficulties about Fuel and Carriage, there were in those days difficulties about Shipping. The Furnaces were seldom at work for more than four months, and stocks accumulated. The hold on the English Market could not be retained by reason of this irregularity of supply, and the cost of management increased proportionately to the stoppages. As a consequence of these drawbacks, the Company never declared a dividend, and the Sheffield Ironmonger's prophecy

that India would ultimately become one of the largest sources from whence Sheffield would draw her supply of Raw Materials, remained unfulfilled. The Company appears to have stopped work about 1860-61, so far as the Porto Novo Factory is concerned.

2. The Beypore Factory of this same concern was started in 1833, but it changed hands frequently. The Factory was working in 1857, and the Gun Carriage Department pronounced favourably upon the Iron turned out, as being suitable for their purposes. Ultimately, owing chiefly to deficiency of Fuel and the bad roads, the Company had to bring wood Fuel from Ceylon by sea. The German employees left service in 1859, and though improved processes were introduced in 1861, the resuscitation was only temporary, and the Works were shortly after abandoned. It will be seen from this account that the quality of the Iron turned out was in every way satisfactory, and the attempts of the Company failed chiefly by reason of the smallness of their capital, which did not permit of their insuring a regular supply, and the difficulty about Fuel.

As far as the difficulty about Communication is concerned, the last thirty years have effected great changes, and this difficulty may almost be said to be minimized. The difficulty about Fuel is also likely to be overcome. Captain Townsend suggests that the distance between the Singareni Coal Field and Salem is not so great that a Light Coal Tramway would not pay a really large firm consuming its hundreds of tons a day. He, indeed, cautions any new Company against limiting its ambition to the manufacture of Pig Iron only. He would insist upon a really large undertaking, complete with all the necessary Plant on the spot, the Puddling Furnaces, the Rolling Mills, the Steam Hammers, and all the other appliances of a First Class Factory and Foundry able to turn out finished Bars, and even finished Steel. This means a very large undertaking, and as no dividend can be expected for the first few experimental years, no Capitalists would venture, unless the concessions are liberal, and a subsidy promised on the plan which helped the Guaranteed Railway Companies to obtain their capital.

3. In 1874 a fresh attempt was made to form a Company in Madras to work the Iron ores of Chingulput. The difficulty in the way of that Company was chiefly that of obtaining Fuel which they expected to secure from the Godavari District. Nothing came of the venture, as apparently, the necessary capital could not be secured, though, as far as local consumption was concerned, there was an ample field, as more than eighteen Laks of Iron was imported annually into Madras City alone.

4. We next turn to the Bengal Presidency. The Districts of Beerbhum and Hazaribag and Raniganj are the chief places where rich Iron ore is found in close proximity to Coal deposits. In Beerbhum, so far back as 1774, one Native Trader, Indra Narayan Sharma, asked for a concession covering the Beerbhum Iron sources, and he agreed to pay five thousand Rupees as rent. The offer was accepted but no lease was taken out.

5. In 1777 Messrs. Motte and Farquar and Messrs. Summer and Heatly obtained concessions, the former of the Districts to the West of Burdwan and the latter in parts of Beerbhum and Pachete, to produce Iron and sell it free of Duty. Messrs. Motte and Farquar undertook to cast Shot and Shells for the Government at three-fourths of the cost in Calcutta of imported goods. Mr. Farquar obtained the concession, and entered upon the possession of his Districts. He also obtained an advance of fifteen thousand Rupees from Government to complete his Furnaces. The Factory was carried on from 1779 to 1789, in which last year the concession about Gunpowder Works was resigned, and the lease was allowed to expire in 1795. While the Works were open, Mr. Farquar's Iron was sold for five Rupees a Maund against ten Rupees a Maund of imported Iron in Calcutta.

6. Dr. Oldham was appointed by the Court of Directors in 1854 to inquire into the Iron resources of Beerbhum, and he pronounced an adverse opinion, chiefly on the ground of the scanty supply of Economic Fuel. But notwithstanding this pronouncement, Messrs. Mackay and Co. of Calcutta started in 1855 the Beerbhum Iron Works Company. It was very favourably reported upon in 1856. Mr. Sowerby in 1858 made an adverse Report, and Messrs. Mackay and Co. replied to Mr. Sowerby's criticisms. They stated that they turned out two tons a day, and they were able to sell Iron at thirty-seven Rupees a ton. Notwithstanding this favourable account the Work was frequently interrupted, and in 1860, Mr. Blanford was appointed to report upon the Factory. His Report showed that, though the Factory was carried on at present at some loss, the cost would be considerably diminished, if production was increased by the employment of additional Capital. He also reported that the estimated prices were lower than those of imported Iron and the quality of the Iron turned out was superior to that of ordinary English Pig Iron. He also stated that the supplies of Iron, Coal, and Flux were sufficient for works of moderate size, but not for large Works.

7. Notwithstanding this Report, the Works appear to have been abandoned, and their place was taken up by Messrs. Burn and Co.'s' Factory, which commenced operations in 1875, but this new Company soon found it necessary to abandon all idea of enlarging the Works, and ultimately gave them up. The chief difficulty in the way of these Beerbhum attempts was that of Fuel, and this difficulty has since increased. This difficulty makes it impossible to work the Iron ores, which are richer than those of Rániganj, with the same advantage as that of the inferior material supplied by Raniganj, because of the abundance of Coal Fuel in that locality.

8. We next come to the Rániganj Field. The Bengal Iron Company was formed in 1874, and it continued to work till it stopped business in 1879. The Company committed the initial error of

starting with an insufficient capital of ten Laks, out of which it had to pay a large sum for the land taken up. The Company asked Government to help them to raise additional Capital from the public on moderate terms, but these arrangements fell through, and the money had to be raised on Debentures at high rates of interest. Government, indeed, gave a large order for Castings, but owing to financial difficulties, the work had to be stopped, and the men employed were thrown out of work, and the Shareholders lost their money. The Iron ore worked was of the best quality, and the Flux and Coal were conveniently to hand. As many as twelve thousand and seven hundred tons of Pig Iron were turned out by this Company before it stopped business. Its daily out-turn of twenty tons was secured by a charge of thirty-seven tons Iron ore, twenty-seven tons Coke, and twenty-three tons Lime-stone, the yield of Pig Iron being thus twenty-three per cent. The average cost was forty Rupees per ton, and it might have been reduced to thirty-three Rupees. In Mr. Ball's opinion, if the Company had been helped through its early financial difficulties, Iron cheaper and better in quality than is imported from abroad would have been turned out. Captain Townsend states that the failure of this Company proves nothing except that success in the enterprise is not possible with small Capital.

9. Three years later, this concern, since called the Barakor Works, was taken up by Government, and placed under the management of Ritter Von Schwartz. One Blast Furnace was started in 1884, and produced down to 1889 more than thirty thousand tons. A second Blast Furnace has been since added, and arrangements made to smelt from fifteen thousand to twenty thousand tons a year. Pipes, Sleepers, Bridge Piles, and Ornamental Work, Railway Axle Boxes, and Agricultural Implements, are made in large quantities here. The success of this Work has demonstrated the fact that Iron could be smelted in large quantities on European principles in India.

10. Since 1889, these Works have been again made over to a New Company by the Government of India.

11. In the Jabalpore District, one Mr. Olpherts has obtained a concession, and is making experiments with a view to the production of Charcoal Iron by the use of European methods. The Umaria Colliery has been recently opened in this vicinity, and the rich Iron Ore to the North-East of Jabalpore will soon be taken in hand.

12. The Narbada Iron and Coal Company has obtained a concession of a lease of the Tendarkhera and Omarpani Iron Mines, together with the Coal Mines of Mopani. The Company has not yet worked the Iron Mines, though the conditions of its lease made it obligatory upon the Company to produce five thousand tons within five years from the time the Railway reached Jabalpore. It may be noted here that this ore also is very rich, and a Suspension Bridge over the Bias near Sagar was built so far back as 1830, with metal prepared after Native methods from this Mine.

13. The Chanda District surpasses all others in the richness of its Iron ores. Their superiority consists in their total freedom from Phosphorus. Government appointed Mr. Nees to make an experimental trial of the Iron Ores. In 1875 he made the first trial, but it did not succeed owing to the large quantity of Coal Ashes which prevented liquefaction. The second trial proved a better success. While the Iron ore is of the best quality, the Warora Coal is not so suitable as Raniganj, as the percentage of Carbon is less, and of Ashes is unusually large. Captain Townsend believes that there are certain superior varieties of Coal in the Wardha Valley, and that they would enable the work to be carried on under favourable conditions.

14. In Central India in the Narbada Valley near Barwai Station, Colonel Keatings arranged with the sanction of the Government of India to start an Iron Factory. Colonel Keatings

was deputed by the Secretary of State to go to Sweden, and study the processes there, and he engaged a Swedish Engineer named Mitandar, and brought him over with him to India in 1861. The Fuel used was Charcoal, and the Flux was conveniently near. A Blast Furnace, Rolling Mills, Charcoal Ovens, Calcining Kilns, were all set up, and after two and a half Laks of Rupees had been spent, the Government refused to incur further expenditure, and declined to give the help of more European hands to Mr. Mitandar, who consequently left India in 1864, and the Works could find no purchaser even for five Thousand Pounds.

15. In the Punjab the Native Ruler of the Nahun State has incurred considerable expenditure in starting at Sirmur a Factory supplied with European appliances, and in 1880 the Works were opened with great *Eclat* by His Excellency the Viceroy.

16. We shall next turn to the History of the Kammaon Iron Mines. In 1855 the Court of Directors sent one John Henwood to report on the Iron and Copper ores of Kammaon, but nothing came of this deputation. Mr. Sowerby was, at the same time, employed by the East India Railway Company to explore the resources of the Country in Upper India. General Strachey in 1856 framed a Scheme estimated to cost fifteen and three-quarter Laks of Rupees, on which it was expected that six and a half per cent. interest would be earned by the manufacture of thirteen hundred tons of Cast Iron, and three thousand five hundred tons of Wrought Iron per year. Mr. Sowerby was appointed by Government in 1857 to take charge of this Work. About the same time a Company was formed which took over the Government Works at cost price in 1860. It did not work satisfactorily, and Dr. Oldham was appointed to report on the cause of the failure, and he ascribed the failure to the extravagance and incompetency of the men employed. In 1862 two Private Companies, Messrs. Davies and Co., and Drummond and Co., which had been working separately before, were amalgamated and called the Kammaon Iron Work Company. A License was promised by Government, but two years elapsed

before it was issued, and in the meanwhile the Company had come to grief, as they were unable to raise the capital required, by reason of the delay in granting the License.

In 1877 the Government again took up the question of Iron manufacture in Kammaon, and spent money considerably, but there was no great improvement.

17. The latest attempt in the way of direct Government manufacture of Steel for Shell and Shot purposes was made at the Cossipore Factory, and the Pioneer reports that it was in every way a success. In the interests of Military Defence, the necessity of the Indian Government being provided with its own Arms and Ammunition, is so obvious, that it is not likely to be disputed. The same justification exists for the manufacture of the Rolling Stock and other Materials likely to be required for State Railways. For commercial success the extension of the Works, so as to meet private demand, will be soon forced upon Government.

We have thus passed in review the History of seventeen attempts made by Private and State Agencies to start Iron Manufactures on a large scale, and this brief survey of previous attempts leads one to the conclusion that the failures were due:—

1. To the smallness of the Capital employed, and the poverty of the financial Resources of the Private Companies.

2. To the scarcity and heavy cost of good Fuel.

3. To the inaccessibility of some of the places chosen, in respect of Railway and Sea Communication.

4. To the oscillations of purpose shown by the Government which made them impatient of results.

5. To the want of skill and good management on the part of the persons employed to conduct the Experiment.

6. To the delays caused by Red Tape, and the unwillingness of Government to Subsidize or Guarantee Interest during the

experimental period of the concern. The failures are due to causes which can all more or less be provided against by proper care and prudence, and some of them have obviously ceased to be the obstacles they once appeared to be, by reason of improved Sea and Land communications.

The *Pioneer*, in some of its recent issues, has spoken in strong terms about the illiberal character of the Concessions offered in the way of Prospective and Mining Leases. Leases for Short Terms confined to very small areas will never answer the purpose. If the Manufacture is to be carried on, on a large scale, the Term must be a long one, exceeding fifty years or so. Such a concession may well be given to Companies which undertake to raise at least twenty-five Laks of Rupees of Capital. In the case of such Companies the detailed Surveying and Prospecting work must be completed by the Government, associating its own trained Officer with the private Expert. This plan was to some extent followed with success in the case of Gold Mining in Wynaad a few years ago. The necessary Capital being raised, Government should, when satisfied of the *bona fide* character and skilled management of such Concerns, guarantee a secure minimum interest rate during the first trial periods, on the plan so freely and advantageously resorted to in the case of Railway companies, and Government should reserve its right to share in the Companies' profits when they exceed a fixed minimum.

On the security of their Property and Machinery, Government should help the Company to float its own Debentures when necessary, or lend the money itself. The Companies should get their Lands free of cost, on condition that *bona fide* work is done within a given period. No Royalties and Fines should be charged till after the Company begins to earn a definite minimum of profits. The Factories should also be guaranteed continuous and certain demand for their produce at fixed prices, which should include not only the English prices in England, but Ship Freight, Landing and Railway Charges, and Insurance and Exchange. A separate Department of Commerce and Manufactures can alone devote itself to this work without frequent oscillations of purpose. These rules can only apply to large Concerns, which must be limited to places selected by Government Experts, as possessing all the advantages of good Ore, cheap Fuel and Flux, and easy Communication and near Markets. Smaller Concerns, to be worked with Charcoal Fuel near dense Forests in out-of-the-way Regions, will require separate treatment. The Lessees here may have a portion of Reserved Forest area handed over to their charge, on condition of their being required to replant fourteen times the area cleared in one year, or the Department may undertake to supply good Fuel at cheap rates on the spot. In all these various ways, Government may well help this new Enterprize on the development of which the Industrial Revival of the Country so largely depends. Government owns the Lands, the Mines and the Forests. It is also the largest Consumer, and the largest Capitalist and Manufacturer in the Country. There is no question of Protective Duties here. The Natural Resources are in unmeasured abundance, and the natural Demand is increasing every day in volume and urgency. Organized skill and direction are the only needs of the Country, and these the Government possesses or can command in a way which makes it their duty to step in, and assist the development of Local Enterprise, for which the necessary Capital will be forthcoming in this Country, if the early risks of such employment are reasonably assured against. In the words of Captain Townsend, where there is no Private Enterprize to interfere with, it is not any wisdom but a duty for the State to start the required Works. State Help and State Direction are required in India, when new lines of Industry are to be opened up, and if given freely, the expenditure will not only pay itself, but will enormously develop the Wealth of the Country.

21

TWENTY YEARS' REVIEW OF CENSUS STATISTICS*

The Decennial Census Report for 1891, for the Bombay Presidency, loses much of its interest by reason of the great delay that has taken place in its publication. This defect, however, sinks into insignificance by the side of another and more serious omission, for which apparently there was less excuse,-we refer to the disappointment caused by the total and studied neglect to bring together the facts and figures of the past three Censuses, in a way to illustrate the Social and Economical History of this Presidency, during the last twenty years. Attempts, indeed, have been here and there made to compare and contrast the Census figures of 1891 with those of 1881; but these attempts, being only half-hearted and unsystematic, lead to very inconclusive results. In the first place, India is not America, and a period of ten years is too short a term to measure any real or permanent changes in the condition of Indian Society. The figured results of 1881, moreover, had the additional disadvantage of recording the losses sustained, in consequence of the great Famine of 1876-78, and thus furnished no safe basis for a comparison of the normal conditions of life in this Country, and of its progress or otherwise in ordinary cir-

*JPSS, April 1893, Vol.XV, No.4, and published in *Essays*.

cumstances. Thirdly, the Census figures of 1881 were arranged and classified in many respects upon lines not observed in 1871, and these lines have been again abandoned in enumerating the results of the last Census. For these reasons, the Census Report of 1891 appears to us to be useful chiefly in its Appendices, and we propose, in the following pages, to make an attempt to present a connected view of the progress of this Presidency during the last twenty years, as far as it may be gathered from a comparison of the results of 1891, with those of the Census of 1871, only occasionally referring to the intermediate Census of 1881. Mere figured Statements, however detailed and numerous, have no suggestiveness about them, and it is necessary to study them in the lights and shades of contrast and comparisons to obtain practical lessons for the guidance of the Administration, and for the studies of the Political Economist. We shall confine our observations for the present to the purely British Districts of this Presidency, reserving our remarks upon the figured results for the Feudatory States to a future issue of this Journal.

The area of the British Districts has continued constant, being about 125,000 square miles. The Population Statistics, however, do not present stationary figures. The total Population, according to the Census of February 1871, was 16,228,774. The numbers were almost stationary in 1881, being 16,454,414, or an increase of only two and a half Laks-1.5 per cent. in ten years. In February 1891, the numbers returned were 18,857,004, the increase being over twenty-five Laks, or 16 per cent in twenty years, or about 0.8 per cent. per year. The Density of the Population, which was 130 per square mile in 1871, and 135 in 1881, has increased to nearly 151 per square mile. A comparison of these figures with those of England and Wales cannot fail to be very instructive. The area of England and Wales is 58,186 square miles, and its Population, which was 22,712,266 in 1871, rose to 29,001,048 in 1891, showing an increase of 6,278,782, or nearly 30 per cent. in twenty years, being nearly double our rate. This high rate of increase was, it must be noted, maintained notwithstanding the great relief given to the Population of England by an extensive system of Emigration, the like of which relief, we do not enjoy here. The actual density of the English Population increased from 389 per square mile in 1871, to nearly 500 per square mile in 1891. The rate of increase in this Presidency was only 8 per cent. against the English rate of 1.5 per cent per year, and the increase in our rate of Density is only 20 per cent. against the English figure of 110 per cent. In other words, the rate of Density in England, which was three times our rate in 1871, has now increased to three and a half times the average Density in this Presidency.

We have next, to examine the details for the several Divisions of the Presidency. For enumeration purposes, the Census Report of 1872 recognised chiefly four Divisions based on the principle of distinctive physical and climatic peculiarities, namely, the Deccan, Konkan, Guzerath, and Sind. In the Census of 1881 this principle was not followed, and the grouping was made on the basis of five Divisions (Deccan, Konkan, Guzerath, Karnatic, and Sind) based partly on physical and partly on Language peculiarities. In 1891, the same principle was followed with this further change, that the Kanara District, which was classed under Karnatic in 1881, has been classed under Konkan this time. These changes make it impossible to compare the totals of one Census with another, and introduce a needless element of variation which should always be avoided in such enumerations. We have found it necessary in consequence of these changes, to take up the District figures separately, and then group them together, and the following Statement presents the comparative results of the ascertained totals of Population by Districts and Divisions in 1871 and 1891.

Division	Population 1871	Population 1891	Increase or decrease in 20 years	Percentage Increase	Remarks
1 Guzerath					
Ahmedabad	829,637	871,589	41,952	5.0	
Panch Mahals	240,743	313,417	72,674	30.0	
Kaira	782,733	871,589	88,856	11.0	
Broach	350,322	341,490	–8,832	–2.5	
Surat	607,087	649,989	42,902	7.0	
Total Guzerath	2,810,522	3,048,074	246,384	10.0	
Area in square miles	10,082	10,296	.....	.....	
2 Konkan					
Kanara	398,406	446,357	47,945	12.0	
Ratnagiri	1,019,136	1,105,926	86,790	8.6	
Kolaba	350,405 }	509,584 }	159,179 }	4.0	Due partly to transfer of Talukas
Thana	847,424 }	904,868 }	57,444 }	16.0	
Total Konkan	2,615,371	2,966,735	351,358	13.5	
Area in square miles	13,558	13,639	.....	.....	
3 Deccan					
Khandesh	1,028,642	1,460,851	432,209	42.0	
Nasik	734,386	843,582	109,196	14.0	
Nagar	773,938	888,755	114,817	15.0	
Satara	1,116,050	1,225,989	109,939	9.5	
Poona	907,235	1,067,800	160,565	18.0	
Sholapur	662,986	750,689	87,693	13.5	
Total Deccan	5,223,237	6,237,666	1,014,419	20.0	
[illegible]	[illegible]	38,390	.....	.....	

Division	Population 1871	Population 1891	Increase or decrease in 20 years	Percentage Increase	Remarks
4 Sind					
Karachi	423,495	564,880	141,385	33.0	
Hyderabad	721,947	918,646	196,299	28.0	
Thur-Parkar	180,761	298,203	117,442	65.0	
Shikarpur	776,227	915,497	139,270	18.5	
Upper Sind Frontier	89,985	174,548	84,563	90.0	
Total Sind	2,192,415	2,871,774	678,959	34.0	
Area in square miles	46,598	47,789	.....	....	
5. Karnatic					
Belgaum	938,750	1,013,261	74,511	8.0	
Dharwar	988,037	1,051,314	63,277	6.5	
Kaladgi } Bijapur }	816,037	796,332	–19,698	–2.4	Due partly to transfer of Talukas
Total Karnatic	2,742,824	2,860,907	118,090	4.0	
Area in square miles	14,853	14,928	.....	.....	
6. Town and Island of Bombay	644,405	821,764	177,359	26.0	

It will be seen from this Statement that the increase of Population in Sind has been nearly twice the average for the Presidency, it has been a little over the average in the Deccan, sensibly below the average in Guzerath and Konkan, and much below the average in the Karnatic. The surplus Population of Guzerath finds a convenient out-let in the Panch Mahals, that of the Deccan in Khandesh, that of the Konkan in Bombay, while in Sind the expanse of arable but unoccupied lands is almost limitless, being dependent upon the extension of Irrigation and not on Rain-fall, and there is apparently no outlet for such expansion in the Karnatic Districts. The relative densities of the several Divisions disclose the following variations in the proportion of increased Density during the last twenty years.

DENSITY

Divisions	Year		REMARKS
	1871	1891	
Guzerath	279	300	The largest absolute increase in Density occurs in the Deccan, and the least, in Karnatic.
Deccan	134	162	
Konkan, excluding City of Bombay	193	217	
Karnatic	185	191	
Sind	47	60	

If the Panch Mahals figures be excluded from those of the Guzerath Division, the increase of Population in twenty years in the older and settled Districts of Guzerath, has been only eight per cent., and in Broach there has been an actual decrease which requires to be accounted for. Excluding Khandesh, the increase of Population in the Deccan Districts has been about 14.0 per cent. in twenty years. The Sind rate of increase is nearly equal to that of England. The Konkan Districts show a rate of increase which is nearly equal to that of the Deccan, excluding

Khandesh, and the Karnatic Districts fare the worst of all-the increase being almost nominal-only 4.0 per cent. in twenty years. It is obvious that the small proportion of increase in these Districts is due to the after effects of the Famine, from which apparently, these parts of the Country have not yet recovered. The Population of Belgaum, Dharwar and Kaladgi or Bijapur in the years 1871, 1881, and 1891, will be seen from the following Statement.

Districts	1871	1881	1891
Belgaum	944,985	864,014	1,013,261
Dharwar	989,671	882,909	1,057,314
Kaladgi or Bijapur	816,273	638,493	796,339
Total	2,750,929	2,385,416	2,866,914

It will be thus seen, that these three Districts lost nearly three and a half Laks of their Population or 3.0 per cent. in the Famine, and they have been just able to make up that deficit during the last ten years. The actual loss of Population was, of course, more than three and a half Laks, for, the normal increase in ten years must be added to this figure of registered deficiency. This circumstance accounts for the small rate of increase in these Districts. Compared with the totals of 1881, the increase in the Karnatic Districts has exceeded 20.0 per cent. in ten years, the rate of increase being 2.0 per cent. per year. In the Deccan Districts, Khandesh and Nasik did not suffer a shrinkage of Population, in consequence of the Famine, and Khandesh showed an increase of over two Laks, and Nasik of 143,000 people. The other four Districts showed a falling off, of 27,109 in Nagar, 20,732 in Poona, 229 in Satara, and 136,888 in Sholapur, the deficiency being in all one and four-fifths of Laks between the totals of 1871, and 1881. The actual increase in these four Districts between 1881 and 1891 is about seven Laks, which raises the proportion of increase in ten years to nearly 20.0 per cent. In other words, the Deccan Districts, having suffered less severely, have rallied more rapidly than the Karnatic Districts-which now stand very much where they stood twenty years ago, in point of Population. The Guzerath Districts, excluding Panch Mahals, did not suffer in any way from the Famine, and the slow progress of Population there, appears to be due partly to external checks, such as Cholera and Fever mortality, and partly, to the operation of prudential and preventive influences. The advantages of a fertile Soil and industrious Population are fully utilized by the existing Population of three hundred Souls per square mile, and the available area for extension is so limited that the Ryots have no other resource but to emigrate to the Panch Mahals. There is a similar escape for the congested parts of the Deccan in Khandesh, and for the Konkan Districts apparently in Bombay.

Excluding Sind, whose climatic conditions are so entirely different from the rest of the Presidency, there are only four Districts where the extent of available arable land per one hundred of the Population exceeds ten Acres, and in two only, Khandesh and Panch Mahals, this provision exceeds twenty-five Acres per one hundred of the Population. In all the remaining Districts, the proportions are below ten Acres per one hundred of the Population, which, as everybody will admit, is a very nominal figure. These proportions will perhaps, not be quite intelligible without further amplification. As the chief Dependence of our increasing agricultural Population is on the land still available for cultivation, the following Statement has been prepared to show, what area of culturable unoccupied land is still available for further expansion of cultivation, to keep pace with the increase of Population.

District	Population	Acres of Cultivated Land	Land still Available for Cultivation
Ahmedabad	871,589	1,870,717	87,872
Kaira	871,589	747,565	74,132
Panch Mahals	313,417	480,716	177,800
Broach	341,490	649,477	25,868
Surat	649,989	740,266	65,260
Guzerath Total	3,048,074	4,488,741	430,932
Thana	847,424	953,993	115,046
Kolaba	350,405	704,786	57,914
Ratnagiri	1,019,136	395,877	5,403
Kanara	398,406	324,746	61,743
Konkan Total	2,615,371	2,379,402	240,106
Khandesh	1,406,851	3,187,064	779,864
Nasik	843,582	2,316,207	134,076
Nagar	888,755	3,079,555	123,263
Poona	1,067,800	2,451,806	18,188
Sholapur	750,689	2,456,513	23,031
Satara	1,225,98[illegible]	2,123,870	35,245
Deccan Total	6,283,666	15,615,015	1,113,667
Belgaum	938,750	2,087,353	105,157
Dharwar	988,037	3,113,655	103,899
Bijapur	816,037	2,314,014	72,953
Karanatic Total	2,742,824	7,515,022	282,009
Karachi	423,495	850,476	1,139,634
Hyderabad	721,947	2,198,200	2,300,263
Shikarpur	776,227	1,490,961	1,722,414
Upper Sind Frontier	89,995	522,390	154,781
Thur and Parkar	180,761	5,278,623	443,203
Sind Total	2,192,425	10,340,650	5,760,295
Grand Total	16,882,360	40,338,830	7,827,009

The average per head of the Population of cultivated area is one and a half Acres in Guzerath, one and four-fifths Acres in Konkan, two and a half Acres in the Deccan, two and three-fourths Acres in Karnatic, and two and one-third Acres in Sind. These figures give for the Presidency, an average of two Acres of cultivated land per head of the Population, or ten Acres per head of each Peasant Proprietor's family. As regards arable land available for cultivation, it is about five per cent. of the cultivated area in Ahmedabad, ten per cent. in Kaira, about thirty-seven per cent. in Panch Mahals, four per cent. in Broach, and nine per cent. in Surat, the average for the Division being nine per cent. of the cultivated area. In the Konkan, this margin is one and a half per cent. in Ratnagiri, twelve per cent. in Thana, eight per cent. in Kolaba, and nearly twenty per cent. in Kanara; this last figure brings up the average for the whole Division to nearly ten per cent. In the Deccan, this proportion of arable to cultivated land is twenty-four per cent. in Khandesh, five per cent. in Nasik, four per cent. in Nagar, less than one per cent. in Poona and Sholapur, and about one per cent. in Satara. The average for the whole Deccan is seven per cent. These same proportions are five per cent. in Belgaum, and three per cent. in Dharwar and Bijapur. The average for the whole Division is four per cent. In Sind the uncultivated arable land largely exceeds the cultivated land in Karachi, Hyderabad and Shikarpur. The average for the whole Division is nearly ninety per cent. It will be seen from these details that, excluding Sind, there is not much room left for extended cultivation except in Panch Mahals and Khandesh, and to a small extent in Kanara and Nasik. In Sind these conditions are reversed. In all the older and settled Districts of the Presidency, the Agricultural Classes must, henceforth, resort chiefly to intensive cultivation or improvements. As it is, about one Crore of the agricultural Population manage barely to support themselves upon the yield of about four Crores of Acres, including fallow and twice cropped lands, and have, except in Sind, Khandesh and Panch Mahals, less than fifteen Laks of arable land to fall back upon for extended cultivation. These figure results present a very dark future as looming before our vision, if our chief dependence were placed on extended cultivation, as the only resource for supplying the wants of our increasing Population.

The only escape from this danger lies in the direction of the gradual transformation of the chief means of our livelihood, and the growth of an Urban and Industrial Population, in other words the rise of Towns or Cities. A careful examination of the statistical results furnished by these Census Reports satisfies us, that there are indications which prove that such a change is operating strongly in our favour. Defining a Town, as a collection of over five thousand inhabitants, it appears (1) that there has been a large increase in the number of our Towns, and (2) that the increase of the Town population has been greater than the increase of the Rural population. In 1871, there were in the twenty-three Districts one hundred and seventy-eight Towns, excluding the City of Bombay, with a total population of 2,134,419. In 1881, a different principle was adopted, which did not accept the test of Population as the basis of distinction, and sixteen places below five thousand in Population were included, and twenty-eight places with a Population exceeding five thousand were excluded, from the definition of Towns, giving as the result one hundred and sixty-five as the number of Towns according to the Census of that year, with a Population of 2,925,190 inhabitants. This unnecessary refinement was dropped in the last Census enumeration, and applying the old test of Population, it was ascertained that there were in all two hundred and thirty-one places which had more than five thousand inhabitants, and which might, therefore, be regarded as Towns. Comparing the figures for 1871 with those of 1891, it will be seen from the following Statement that all the Divisions except Karnatic showed an increase under this head.

Names	Number of Towns		Population of Towns	
	1871	1891	1871	1891
Guzerath	35	46	592,459	665,856
Konkan	26	30	218,397	283,292
Deccan	65	96	724,862	957,499
Karnatic	43	34	412,268	387,863
Sind	9	25	186,431	342,295
City of Bombay	1	1	644,405	821,764
Total	179	232	2,778,822	3,458,569

The number of Towns has thus increased nearly thirty per cent., while the Population of these Towns shows an increase of nearly twenty-five per cent. The total increase of the Population in twenty years has been shown above, to have been about sixteen per cent., and it is thus plain that there is a slight tendency inclining the scale in favour of Urban over Rural increase. This last appears to have been about fourteen per cent., the actual figures being 13,553,962 as against 15,398,445, as the Population of the Rural tracts in 1871 and 1891 respectively. So far, the figures are not unsatisfactory. The percentages of the Rural and Urban population for the several large Divisions, according to the Census Reports for 1871, 1881 and 1891 will be seen from the following Statement.

Names	1871		1881		1891	
	Urban	Rural	Urban	Rural	Urban	Rural
Guzerath	21	79	19.9	80.1	21.5	78.5
Konkan	8	92	9	91	8.8	91.2
Deccan	13.8	87.2	14.3	85.7	15.4	84.6
Karnatic	15	85	12.2	87.8	13.5	86.5
Sind	9	91	10.7	89.3	12.6	87.4

The above Statement shows clearly that the progress is very

slow and not very striking. Guzerath retains an easy command over the other Divisions, and no District in that Division comes up to the level of Ahmedabad, which has twenty-five per cent Urban to seventy-five per cent. Rural population.

The Sind figures are more hopeful, and the Deccan also appears to be slowly but successfully struggling against ruralization. The Karnatic Districts, however, do not appear to have yet recovered from the shock they sustained during the Famine. Taking the several Districts in their order, while Poona, Dharwar and Karachi show large advances in the direction of urbanization, and Ahmedabad, Broach, Nasik, Bijapur and Belgaum show slight advances in the same direction, ten Districts, Ratnagiri, Surat, Thana, Kolaba, Kanara, Nagar, Satara, Thur and Parkar, the Upper Sind Frontier, and Hyderabad show slight decline, and Kaira, Panch Mahals, Khandesh, Sholapur, and Shikarpur show decided decline in the Urban elements of their Population.

Even in the Districts which show better results, the so-called Towns are only larger Villages, and are wanting in the essential element of industrial activity.

This partial and not very strongly marked tendency towards urbanization is also attested to by the figures which show the relative proportions of Villages of different sizes and Population. Excluding Sind and the City of Bombay, it appears from the Census Returns of 1881 and 1891 that, while the proportion of Villages inhabited by less than five hundred persons was 65.5 per cent. in 1881, this proportion fell to 60 per cent. in 1891. The proportion of the class of Villages next above it, with a population, ranging from five hundred to one thousand was 21 per cent. in 1881, and 23 per cent. in 1891; the proportion of the class next above it, with inhabitants ranging from one thousand to one thousand and five hundred, was 9.7 per cent. in 1881, and 11.3 per cent. in 1891; of the class next over it, with a Population ranging from two thousand to three thousand, the proportion was 2 per cent. in 1881, and 2.7 per cent. in 1891; and of the highest class of all, with Population ranging from three thousand to five thousand, the proportion was 1.3 per cent. in 1881, and 2.6 per cent. in 1891. It is not generally known, but is none the less true, that the proportion of Urban to Rural population normally stands higher in this Presidency, than in most of the other Provinces of India.

Of course, it must be noted that the residents of Urban Towns, as defined above, are not all really Urban, in respect of their profession or source of livelihood, and on the other hand the residents of Rural areas do not all of them derive their livelihood from the land. It thus becomes necessary to examine the Statistics about the occupations of the people given in these Census Reports. The Census Classification of Occupations given in the Report of 1891 departs so materially from the principles adopted in the two previous Reports, that no fair comparison can properly be made between their results. Both in 1871 and 1881 there was a large class, nearly fifty per cent. of the total Population, who, being dependent on other persons, were returned as having no profession or occupation. This principle was not followed in 1891, when all these dependents were counted as forming a portion of the class to which the male or female bread-earner, on whom they depended, belonged. This appears to us to have been a perfectly wanton innovation, and even if there were some apparent advantages in the new classification, the Report ought to have furnished columns of Comparative Tables contrasting the results of 1891 with those of previous years on the old basis.

In the absence of such Comparative tables, we can only present the results separately. In 1871, persons employed in Government and other Public Service were 184,332, and formed 1.1 per cent. of the whole. The Professions absorbed 135,340 persons, and were .8 per cent. of the whole. Those, who engaged themselves in Personal Service, were 281,216, and were 1.7 per cent. of the whole. The Agricultural Industry, including the care and breed of Cattle and Sheep, was followed by forty Laks, who thus constituted 24.7 per cent. of the entire Population. Those who were engaged in Trade and Commerce were about four and a half Laks, and were 2.6 per cent. of the whole. Artizans and Handicraftsmen came to about twenty-two Laks, and were 13.5 per cent. of the entire number. All these Classes made up forty-five per cent.; and the Unoccupied and dependent Classes came up to ninety Laks, being fifty-five per cent. of the total Population. In 1881 Government Public Servants and those who were employed in the Professions, made up 1.5 per cent., those rendering Personal Service were 1.1 per cent., and the Commercial and Trading Classes represented 1.2 per cent. The Agriculturists were thirty-two per cent., the Industrial and Artizan Classes were fifteen per cent., and the Unoccupied were forty-nine per cent. of the whole. In the Census of 1891 the heading of Unoccupied Classes was discontinued as a separate Class, and we find that sixty per cent. of the total, and sixty-nine per cent. of the Rural, populations are shown to be Agricultural. The Artizans and Handicraftsmen, or the Industrial Classes, are shown to be twenty-one per cent. Their proportion is slightly higher in Towns than in the Country. The two Classes between them absorb eighty per cent. of the Population. The Trading and Commercial Classes are shown to be 4.6 per cent. in Towns, and 3.5 per cent. in the Country. Those who rendered Personal and Domestic Service are shown to be 2.7 per cent. Those engaged in Public Service appear to be 3.8 per cent., and the Professionals 3.3 per cent. If we have these percentages, so as to exclude the dependent Population, mostly women and children, we shall arrive by a rough guess at what these proportions would be under the old plan of classification. The old proportions of those engaged in Agriculture and Handicrafts do not appear, thus, to have been sensibly altered in favour of the latter Classes; and the same remark holds good of the Commercial and Trading Classes. This seems to be the general impression left on the mind by a study of these figures-into the details of which, we cannot now afford to enter at greater length.

The Statistics relating to Occupied Houses are also vitiated by the innovations adopted at the last enumeration, of excluding Unoccupied (houses from) the Census definition of a House, and the omission to classify Houses according to quality, which attempt was made in 1871 with some success.

The Census of 1871 showed that the total number of Houses in the Bombay Presidency was 3,254,540, out of which about 336,629 were of the Better Class, and were occupied by 1,885,910 persons. The rest, about ninety per cent., 2,917,911, were of the Inferior sort, and were occupied by 14,342,842 persons. These figures furnish a safe basis for fixing the relative number of our Classes and Masses, which are as eight to ninety-two of the Population. In the Deccan Division, including Karnatic, the average number of persons per House was 5.43, in the Konkan it was 5.7, in Guzerath it was 3.6, and in Sind it was 4.9 per house. The superiority of Guzerath in this respect is further brought out by the fact that out of the Better Class of Houses fully fifty-eight per cent. are found in the Guzerath Division. The Deccan comes a long way behind, and Konkan and Sind follow at no great distance. The Census of 1881 showed the total number of Occupied Houses and other Buildings to have been 3,605,812, being an increase of two and a half Laks over the figure for 1871, but of these 2,822,731 Houses were occupied. Between 1881 and 1891 the several Divisions showed the following increases.

Name	1881		1891		Increase Per Cent.	
	Houses in Towns	Houses in Country	Houses in Towns	Houses in Country	In Town	In Country
Guzerath	1,35,293	4,99,082	1,60,737	5,36,209	19	7½
Konkan	42,465	4,30,144	46,667	4,90,320	11	14
Deccan	1,28,001	6,37,867	1,87,468	8,61,770	47	23
Karnatic	54,488	3,75,847	69,475	4,46,611	27½	17
Sind	42,223	3,91,331	64,804	4,52,216	53	15
Bombay City	28,310	....	56,959	....	100	....

Here, also, next to the Town and Island of Bombay, Sind heads the list; Guzerath, while it is absolutely at the head of the rest of the Presidency, shows no progress. The Deccan Districts take a high rank, and Karnatic and Konkan come last.

We have now passed under review all those points of the Census enumeration which have a bearing upon the Economical condition of the Country. The Statistics relating to Sex and Age and Civil Condition, Education, Religion, Languages, and Infirmities are interesting in themselves, but they have little or no direct bearing upon the Economical Well-being of the Population, and we must, therefore, resist the temptation of entering upon a consideration of these matters. We hope, however, to take them up in a separate issue of the Journal.

22

INDIAN FOREIGN EMIGRATION*

No object of National Economy is more directly practical in its bearings upon the prosperity of the people than the question of providing expansive and remunerative labour facilities commensurate with the natural growth of the population. The Report of the Famine Commission has emphatically drawn public attention to the fact that "at the root of much of the Poverty of the people of India, and the risks to which they are exposed in seasons of scarcity, lies the unfortunate circumstance that Agriculture forms almost the sole occupation of the mass of the population, and that no remedy for present evils can be complete which does not include the introduction of a diversity of occupation, through which the surplus population may be drawn from agricultural pursuits, and led to find their means of subsistence on Manufactures, or some such Employment." There can be no doubt that the permanent salvation of the Country depends upon the growth of Indian Manufactures and Commerce, and that all other remedies can only be temporary palliatives. At the same time, it is admitted that this diversity and change of occupation is a very arduous undertaking. It pre-supposes a change of habits, it postulates the previous growth of Culture and a spirit of enterprize, an alterness of mind, an elasticity of

*Read at the Industrial Conference, Poona, in 1893. Published in *JPSS*, October 1893, Vol.XVI, No.2, and in *Essays*.

temper, a readiness to meet and conquer opposition, a facility of organization, social ambition and aspiration, a mobile and restless condition of Capital and Labour, all which qualities and changes are the slow growth of Centuries of Freedom and Progress. It is the object of Associations, like those under the auspices of which we meet here to-day, to promote and facilitate this change and diversity of occupation, but it is clear that, as a present remedy, there is but little hope of relief in this direction. A vast majority of the surplus poor population of an agricultural Country can only be naturally fitted to work as Agriculturist Labourers, and the slow development of our Manufactures, borne down as they are by the stress of Foreign Competition, cannot provide at present the much needed relief of work suited to their aptitudes. Inland and Overland Emigration, the overflow of the surplus population from the congested parts of the Country to Lands where Labour is dear and highly remunerative, can alone afford the sorely needed present relief.

As regards Inland Emigration, we are all more or less familiar with the migration of our surplus Agriculturist hands to the large markets of Labour, especially to places like Bombay and Karachi. The last Census Reports have demonstrated the fact, that the disinclination of the Natives of this Country to leave their ancestral Homes has been much exaggerated, and that a much larger proportion of our population show migratory habits than we were disposed at first to believe. The Districts of Khandesh and Panch Mahals are being thus settled before our eyes. The same process is going on in the other Provinces of India, particularly in the Punjab and the Central Provinces. A further development of this same system is supplying Ceylon in the extreme South, and in the North-East Assam, Cachar, Sylhet, and latterly the Districts of Upper Burmah, with the overflowing population of this Country. The whole of the Tea and Coffee Industry of the Country depends for its prosperity on the success of this Inland Emigration. Male and Female Recruiting Agents are employed to secure the services of Indentured Coolies, and Special Laws have been passed for their protection. There is, besides, a considerable flow of Free Emigrants also to these parts. From the congested Districts of Bengal, Behar and Orissa, as many as forty Thousand Coolies migrated in 1890, and thirty Thousand people emigrated in 1891, to Assam, the proportion of Free Emigrants showing a large increase over the Indentured and Sirdari Labourers. Of course, all who emigrate do not abandon their Native Homes. Three-fourths return back to India, but about one-fourth become permanent residents in their new Settlements.

Inland Emigration however, cannot be, in any way, compared in its volume, or in its immediate and remote bearings on national prosperity, with Foreign Emigration to the British and French and Dutch Colonies beyond the Seas. I propose in this paper briefly to give a summary of the History and Progress of Indian Foreign Emigration. Few people are aware of the comparative magnitude of this relief, thus afforded to our surplus population, and of the magnificent field for extension which is opening before our vision in the possibilities of the future. In this respect, the expansion of the British Empire in Africa is a direct gain to the mass of the population of this Country. The permanent opening up of the heart of Africa and of the Central Regions of Australia would not be possible or advantageous even to the indomitable resources of British Skill and Capital, if it did not secure the help of the unlimited and intelligent Labour and Skill of Indian Emigrants. Of course, there are difficulties in the way, as there will be difficulties in the way of all great enterprises. But the certainties of the future are too imperative to be much interfered with by these present dangers and inconveniences. The tastes, habits, temperaments, and prejudices of our people have acquired an inveterate force which makes it no easy task to adapt themselves to new surroundings, and yet if the old thraldom of prejudice and easy self-satisfaction and patient resignation is ever to be loosened, and new aspirations and hopes created in their place, a change of home surroundings is a standing necessity and a preparatory discipline, whose material and moral benefits can never be too highly estimated.

Mr. Draper, the American Philosopher, in his History of the Intellectual Development of Europe, went so far as to say that the Dotage and Death, which had paralyzed Oriental Races, could only be cured by the Free Transplantation of these people into Foreign Lands, or by Free Intermixture in blood with more Energetic Races. We are ourselves witnesses of the undesirability and hopelessness of the second Remedy proposed. The other Remedy is more hopeful, and it is on this account that I have ventured to take up this subject for discussion at the present Conference.

The First Question we have, therefore, to consider in this connection, is the extent of this Foreign Emigration and the Localities to which it has spread. The Localities where Indian Coolies emigrate are Mauritius, Natal, Jamaica, Trinidad, St. Lucia, Grenada, St. Vincent, St. Kitts, the Fiji Islands, British Guiana, French and Dutch Guiana, the French Possessions of Martinique, Guadeloupe, Réunion, the Danish Island of St. Croix, Ceylon, and the Straits Settlements. In 1874, the Government of India appointed a Special Officer to report upon the question of Coolie Emigration from India. That Report gives a detailed account of the condition of these Settlements, and I shall first try to summarize its leading features, and then bring down the information to more recent times, with the help of such Official Publications as were made available to me.

MAURITIUS

Mauritius is the largest, I am speaking advisedly, of our Indian Colonial Settlements. It is an Island, which lies on the East Coast of Africa, about 20° South Latitude and 57° East Longitude, and has a total Area of seven Hundred miles, thirty-seven miles long, by thirty-four miles broad. The Temperature of this Island ranges from 70° to 80° Fahrenheit. It has the closest affinities to India in its Climate and its Seasons. Out of a total Population of 3,10,000, nearly two Laks were Indian Coolies in 1861, and the rest partly Europeans,

Negroes, Arabs, and Creoles. The number had increased to 3,16,000 in 1871, the addition being due chiefly to the increase of the Indian Population, while the non-Indian Population actually diminished by nearly 18,000 Souls. The latest Returns for 1881 show, comparatively, still better figures. The Indians were 1,50,000 Males, and about 1,00,000 Females, out of a total Population of 3,60,000 Souls. More than two-thirds of the Population of the Island is thus of Indian Origin. The Males naturally preponderate over the Females, being in the proportion of nearly one and a half to one. Of the two Laks and more Indian Residents in 1871, a Lak and a half were Indentured Emigrants from India, about two Thousand had gone of their own accord, and fifty Thousand were the children born to these Emigrants in the Colony itself. The Indian Emigrants have no competitors in the Island in the matter of Agricultural pursuits, and they also find considerable employment in Domestic Service and in the Docks and in Trade, and latter chiefly Retail Trade. There are also eleven Indian Planters, and one Managei of a Plantation. The Chief Industry of the Colony is the production of Sugarcane, and the Manufacture of Sugar. The Indentured Indian adult Coolies get, besides their rations and houses free of rent, five to seven Rupees a month, and have to work six days in the week, and nine hours each day. Medical care is free of charge, and there is a free return Passage provided at the end of the Term of Five Years. There were about two hundred and fifty Sugar Estates in 1871 in the Island, which gave employment to 1,20,000 Labourers, chiefly Indians. Of this number, nearly 50,000 had emigrated from the Calcutta side, about 27,000 from Madras, and about 7,000 from Bombay. Since 1871, Emigration from Bombay has apparently fallen off, owing to the rise of the Mill Industry in this Presidency.

The History of Emigration to Mauritius commences with 1834. Between 1834 and 1838, as many as 25,000 Indians emigrated to that Island. From 1838 to 1844, there was a prohibition in consequence of some well-founded complaints of abuses. In 1842, Act XV. of 1842 was passed, which reopened

Mauritius to Indian Emigration. In 1884, the Government of the Island took up the work of the protection of Indian Emigrants in their own hands. A bounty was paid out of Colonial Revenues for each labourer imported, and the Government received the orders of the Planters, and sent them to their appointed Agents in India. The Government of India appointed besides, a Protector of its own to check the abuses of the Colonial Agents.

These arrangements lasted from 1844 to 1859, when, owing to the accounts of fearful mortality on board the Ships which took the Emigrants to Mauritius, Government enforced a temporary prohibition, which was subsequently removed on satisfactory assurances being given that the abuses complained of would not be again permitted. In 1859, there was a Commission appointed under the Presidency of Dr. Mouat, to frame Regulations for the convenience of Emigrants on board the Ships, and fresh Regulations were enforced for the protection of the Indians. There was another Commission of Inquiry in 1866-67, which inquired into the Causes of an Epidemic in Mauritius, which proved fatal to a large number of the Indian Settlers. Notwithstanding, the beneficent interference of the Government of India, the Official Report for 1871 states that the tendency of Mauritius Legislation has been towards securing a complete dependence of the Indian Labourers upon the Planters who employ them, for Free Labour is both directly and indirectly discouraged, while the Indenture System is more and more extended. The condition of affairs in 1883 is thus described: "While the Government of India have taken great care to secure the satisfactory regulation of the Emigrant Ships, the Laws of the Island have been so unjust to the Coloured People, and so much to the advantage of the Planters, that gross evils and abuses have arisen from time to time. In 1871, a Royal Commission was appointed to inquire into the abuses complained of. Various Reforms were recommended and some improvements have been effected. But the Planters are not remarkable for their respect of the rights of the Coloured People, and the system is liable to gross abuse, unless kept under vigilant control by higher Authority."

The total number of Schools—Government and Aided—in the Island, was ninety-two, attended by about nine thousand and five hundred Scholars. Out of this number, fourteen per cent. were Hindus, five per cent. Mahomedans, seventy-three per cent. Roman Catholics, and eight per cent. Protestant Christians. There were seven hundred and twenty-five Scholars in all, of Indian parentage in 1871, attending twenty-five Schools. Much, therefore, remains yet to be done for the Education of the Hindu Population of the Island. The Labour Ordinances are very stringent, and are strictly enforced. The Indian Population on the Island follow, besides Agricultural Labour on the farms, the occupation of Carpenters, whose wages are on an average £3 a month, of Blacksmiths, Washermen and Tailors, who earn half that rate of Sugar-Makers whose wages are £2, and of Mill-drivers who earn £2-10s. There are also Masons, Gardeners, Cooks, Coachmen, and Grooms with wages ranging from fifteen to twenty-eight shillings. The Deposits to the credit of the Indian Immigrants in 1871, were nearly £83,000, and their Remittances to India amounted to Rs.20,000 in 1871.

The Laws of the Island, as shown above, place some restraints on the liberty of Indians to settle down as Free Citizens. A considerable number, about twenty thousand in all, have, however, settled down as Free Men, and earn their living as market Gardeners, Artizans, Tradesmen and Job Contractors, and a few have even attained the position of Managers and Owners of Plantations.

The latest Report of Immigration in Mauritius, furnished by the Government Protector in that Island, which I could secure, is for 1890. It shows that about two thousand Emigrants came to Mauritius in 1890, from Calcutta, Madras, and Bombay, and about one thousand and fifty-four returned back to India. The Females were about thirty- six per cent. of the Males. The number of those who returned to India during the past five years has ranged from one thousand and fifty-four to two thousand three hundred and fifty, giving an average of sixteen hundred per year. Among those who returned in 1890, three hundred and seventy-seven went to Calcutta, three hundred and forty-seven to Madras, and three hundred and twenty- one to Bombay. The total amount of Savings brought by the returned Coolies was Rs.32,394 in 1890. In some previous years, this total was as high as Rs.1,40,000, Rs.1,03,000 and Rs.1,23,000 in 1886, 1887, and 1888 respectively. The Savings in Deposit Banks to the credit of the Indian Coolies resident in the Colony show an average of Rs.16,50,000 during the three years 1888-1890. Out of the one and a quarter Lak of the Indian population residing on Sugar Estates, more than half do not work on the Plantations, while less than half are employed on the Plantations, which numbered about one hundred and twenty-seven in 1890. This completes our review of the Indian Settlement in Mauritius.

BRITISH GUIANA (DEMERARA)

This Colony lies along the North Coast of South America between 7° and 8° North Latitude and 57° to 60° West Longitude, and has a rich alluvial soil. As in Mauritius, the cultivation is confined chiefly to Sugarcane. The Seasons are, as in India on the Coast, only two, the Rainy and the Hot Season. The Temperature is seldom below 75°, and rises to 90° Fahrenheit, and the average Rainfall is 100 inches. Out of a total population of one and a quarter Lak in 1851, there were only 7,682 Coolies from India, and about 2,100 Europeans, the rest were Natives of the Country, and Negroes. When Negro Slavery was abolished in the West Indian Islands, it was proposed to transplant the free Negroes to British Guiana, but the attempt failed, and in 1838, the first importation of 400 Indian Coolies took place. In 1844- 45, the number of Indian Coolies imported was 4,616. Between 1850 and 1870, about 65,000 Indian Coolies were imported, out of whom 7,000 returned to India during the same period. In 1871, the total population of the Colony was two Laks, out of whom 43,000 were Indians, half of them working on the Plantations under Indentures, about 9,000 were Free Labourers, and the rest, about 10,000, were otherwise employed in Towns and Villages. The Labour Laws in Guiana are as stringent and one-sided as those of Mauritius. The Labourers have no summary remedy for the recovery of their wages except by a civil suit, while the Planters' remedies in case of the absence or desertion of the Coolies are most ample and strict. The Coolies are employed in one hundred and twenty-three Plantations, out of which number, eighty five are either owned by Absentee Landlords in London, Liverpool, and Bristol, or are mortgaged with Absentee Creditors. This is a peculiar feature of the Sugar Industry in British Guiana which distinguishes it from the Mauritius estates which are generally owned by resident French and Creole Owners. Owing to this peculiarity, task work is much preferred, and is rigidly enforced in preference to day-work. The Task Masters employ Overseers and below them are Head-men who are called Drivers, who supervise the gangs of Labourers. The Drivers in charge of Indian gangs are chiefly Madrasees. The Indian Coolie does not get through the same task as the Negro Labourer, but the latter never works continuously. The Indian Coolie is more regular in his habits, and he is thrifty by nature, and saves money. The Guiana Coolies are independent in their bearing. The Chinese Labourers, however, surpass both Indian Coolies and Negroes in their several excellences. There were on the Plantations in 1871, about 44,000 Indian Coolies, 1,250 Africans, 6,600 Chinese, and about 1,700 Portuguese and West Indies men. Out of the 44,000 Indian Coolies about 9,000 men were not indentured. The Wages earned by an adult Coolie range from seven to ten Annas per day, and the cost of living was six Annas a day. More recent Legislation enforces the payment of twenty-five Cents, or ten Annas per day, as minimum Wages, of an adult Male over sixteen years, and twenty Cents for each Female labourer. Notwithstanding the hardships of the Labour Laws, the high wages earned have induced nearly fifty per cent. of the Labourers to reindenture themselves on the expiration of their first Term. About 18,000 Labourers out of 40,000 so indentured themselves on receipt of fifty Dollars as bounty. There are besides, 8,000 or 9,000 Free Coolies who have saved money, and earn their own wages. The agriculturist Labourers have, as in Mauritius, free lodgings and medicine, and free rations in their first year of settlement. The fact that there are thousands of Indians who do not care to return to India, even after a stay of fifteen or twenty years, goes to show that, on the whole, these Indian Settlers are well-off in the Colony. While the majority of the Indian Settlers are employed on the Farms, a few keep Cows and ply Carts, and there are Lodging Houses and Shops owned and managed by the Indians. A few have also enlisted in the Police, and in the Army. About 2,820 Immigrants who returned between 1839 and 1869 brought with them 95,000 Dollars to India. The men are to women in the proportion of three to one. The Mahomedans and the Hindus settled in the Colony observe Mohoram, and the Hindus have built two Temples. As might be expected, the marriage tie sits loose with these men, and they also indulge in excessive drink.

The Report of British Guiana for 1890, shows that there were in all 1,07,424 Indian Coolies—62,000 Males, 23,000 Females, and 17,000 Children. About 73,000 of the number were indentured, and the rest not residing on estates were about 35,000. Out of 72,000 on the estates, 46,000 were Males, and 26,000 Females. These Indian Settlers owned 21,000 Cattle and 5,200 Sheep. About 2,125 Coolies returned to India in 1890, and brought with them 25,000 Dollars worth of jewellery, and 1,17,000 Dollars worth of Savings. The Deposits of 6,323 Indian Depositors were 1,16,000 Dollars in Savings Banks, and 259 Depositors had 10,283 Dollars in Post Office Banks.

TRINIDAD

This Island lies off the Coast of Venezuela in 10° to 11° North Latitude and 61° to 62° West Longitude, and has an area of two thousand square miles. The Temperature ranges from 71° to 85°

Fahrenheit and there are only two Seasons—the Rainy and the Dry season, and the heat is considerable. Sugar, Coffee, and Cocoa are the chief articles produced in the Plains, which intervene between the three high chains of hills that traverse the length of the Island. Cotton, Tobacco, and Indigo are also produced in large quantities. Sugar is the Chief Export, and its value rose from nearly fifty Laks to seventy-five Laks between 1856 and 1867. The total population of the Island in 1856 was 68,000, of whom 4,000 were Natives, and about 2,000 Africans, and 4,000 Indian Coolies. In 1871, the Indian Immigrants had increased to nearly 23,000 Souls, besides 454 Indian Children born in the Island. There is, as usual, a Government Agent who inspects the estates, and reports to the Government of the Colony the condition of the Coolie Employees. He allots the Coolie labourers to the estates and cancels the Indenture of any Immigrant whose employer disobeys the law, and abuses his power. The contracts for service are generally, for a term of five years, and the work days in the year are 280, and the hours of work nine hours a day. As in British Guiana, the task work system finds most favour with the employer. The prescribed minimum rate of wages is twenty-five Cents, or ten Annas per day, for an adult Male Labourer. Wages are paid fortnightly, and may be summarily recovered by an application to a Justice of the Peace. The laws against vagrancy and absence and desertion are very stringent, and strictly enforced. Free rations are paid in the first two years of the Indenture, and afterwards they are paid in money. On completion of the five years' term, a certificate of industrial residence is given, and after ten years, a man is allowed free passage back to India, or he may in lieu thereof, claim a Ten Acre Grant of Crown Land. In this respect, the condition of the Trinidad Coolies compares favourably with those of Mauritius and British Guiana. Children under ten are not indentured. Out of 18,556 men employed on the Estates in 1871, 10,616 were indentured, and 7,949 were unindentured. The average arrivals for each year between 1867 and 1871, were 2,000 Coolies per year. There were 12,000 Male against 6,500 Female Indians in the Island in 1871. The general rate of Wages is considerably over the minimum of twenty-five Cents, and ranges from thirty-five to forty-three Cents, or fourteen to sixteen Annas per day. The number of Coolies who returned to India in 1869, was 372, and they brought with them 16,000 Dollars as Savings. In 1870, about 408 men returned, and brought back nearly 13,000 Dollars. Up to 1871 about 285 Indians commuted their back passage by claiming Grants of Land, and 253 purchased exemption from compulsory work under the Indenture for the last two years of their term. In one Province, 357 adult males, 199 Females, and 246 Children are now settled on their own farms. Besides the 18,000 people employed on the Estates, there are 9,000 Indians absorbed in the general population. About 7,000 people have forgone their privilege of a back passage. About 131 Indian children attended the schools in Trinidad in 1871.

In 1884, the Trinidad Indian Coolies celebrated their Mohoram festival and a riot took place, which was punished with such severity that it formed the subject of an Official Inquiry. The dispute arose from the rivalry of the partizans of opposite bands of Tabut processionists, and more than twelve thousand Coolies took part in the riots, and the Police had to fire with a view to disperse the rioters. Twelve Coolies were killed, and four hundred injured in the tumult. Sir Henry Norman, a retired Anglo-Indian, once Governor of Jamaica, was appointed to report upon these disturbances. His Report shows that of the total number of Indians in Trinidad, less than one-fifth are Mahomedans, and the rest are Hindus. The Hindu Coolies took the chief part in the Tabut processions, and some of the Mahomedans had actually asked the Government to put a stop to the disorderly conduct of the Hindu processionists on religious grounds. The Tabut procession is turned to account by the Hindus as a day of National demonstration. The Indians in Trinidad formed two-thirds of the entire population. In one district where the riots occurred the Indian Coolies were four-sevenths of the population. Sir Henry Norman officially reported that residence for some years made the Coolies independent, and even overbearing. A large portion elect to remain in Trinidad when they are entitled to Free Passage back to India. Those who go to India take large sums of money with them, and not a few return back to Trinidad. Occasional cases of ill-treatment might occur, but in the opinion of Sir H. Norman, the Coolies are very well treated. In 1890-91, Coolies numbering about 3,800 landed in Trinidad, Men about 2,400 and Women about 1,400. About 685 returned back to India, taking with them nearly 11,000 Dollars as Savings. Between 1851 and 1891, about 12,000 Coolies returned, and brought twenty-four and a half Laks of Rupees as their Savings. The annual remittances to India by Trinidad Coolies range from £15,000 to £23,000. Between 1871 and 1881, about 24,000 Coolies went to Trinidad, and about 3,500 returned to India. About 600 Coolies commuted their Free Passage, and settled in the Island. Since 1869, about 1,168 Coolies have received their land allotments of ten Acres each, 1,475 have each received a five Acre allotment, and about 3,100 took their £5 bounty in lieu of Return Passage. The total population in Trinidad in 1891 was 71,533 of whom nearly 55,000 were Coolies. There were 2,750 Coolies who had deposits in Savings Banks, and this amount was in all 31,000 Dollars. The number in 1881 was 1,500, who had 24,000 Dollars in deposits. There were fifty-three Schools attended by about 2,900 Coolie-children—both boys and girls—in the Island.

FIJI

Fiji is an Island in the South Pacific, where Emigration appears to have commenced within very recent times, since 1874. In the first year, 480 Indian Settlers landed on the Island. Since then, nearly 10,000 Indian Coolies have been imported into Fiji. The actual number resident in 1891 in the Island was 8,000. The number who went to Fiji in 1891 was 1,050 in all. Out of the total number about 3,000 were Indentured Labourers, and the rest had completed their term. The Births in the Island were about 151, and the Deaths 229 in the Indian population, and there were four Marriages. A Special Law for the Registration of Indian Marriages was passed in 1891. The Chief Industry in the Island is the cultivation of Sugarcane. The working days are six and a half in the week. The term of Indenture is five years. The minimum rate of wages is one Shilling for adult Male, and nine-pence for Female Labourers. Rations are provided at the rate of five-pence for each person above ten years of age, for six months after arrival. Lodgings and medical relief are provided free. Free Return Passage is given after five years' service. In 1891, there were 343 Coolies who had deposited 10,638 Dollars in the Savings Banks in Fiji. The number of depositors and the amount deposited have both steadily risen, since 1885, when there were 106 depositors with 3,470 Dollars to their credit. Similarly, as against ten Coolies who remitted £84 to India, there were in 1891 as many as 102 Coolies who remitted £546 to India.

ST. VINCENT

St. Vincent is a small Island in the Antilles group, and lies in 13° North Latitude and 61° West Longitude. Its area is 130 square miles. It produces Sugarcane, Arrowroot, Cocoa and Cotton. The term of Indenture is for three years, though it may be extended for two years more, and at the end of eight years, the Indian Immigrant Coolie is entitled to a Free Passage. For re-Indenturing, bounty is given at a rate fixed on a sliding scale, according to the number of years of residence. The minimum rates of wages are fixed by law at ten-pence a day for adult males, with lower rates for women and children. Free rations are only given in the first month, and by special arrangement for two months more, and after that period, the wages earned cover all payments. The work-days and working-hours are the same as in the other Colonies. The Owners of the Estates are required to provide convenient lodgings and free medicines for their Indian Labourers. In the year 1891 about 1,273 Indian labourers earned 8,821 Dollars in the first six months, and during the next half year 1,442 Indians earned 18,000 Dollars. This gives an average of eight to twelve Dollars per man per month. The Indian Coolies numbered 552 in 1864, and rose to 1,442 in 1871, out of whom 792 were adult Males, 338 were Females, and about 300 Children. Since 1871 St. Vincent is not much favoured by Indian Coolies, and Emigration has fallen off in this Colony.

GRENADA

Grenada is the Southernmost Island of the Antilles group, and lies 12° 20' North Latitude and 61° 20' West Longitude. It has an area of 133 square miles. Coffee, Cocoa, Cotton, Sugar, Indigo, and Tobacco are the chief products of the Island. The provisions of the Immigrant Legislation are the same as those of the Colony of St. Vincent. Indentured Immigrants agree to work for five years. Free Passage is earned by five years' industrial or ten years' total residence. In 1871, there were 1,863 Indians in this Island, nearly 1,000 being adult Males, about 400 adult Females, and 450 Children. These were settled on forty-six Esta s. There were, besides, some free Settlers, but their number was not large. The able-bodied men earn one Shilling and three-pence per day, but the minimum rate of wages fixed by Law is eight-pence.

In the Census of 1881, the number of Indian Immigrants was shown to be 1,052, and in 1891, this number was reduced to 1,013. The Coolies are, for the most part, engaged in agricultural operations. Many of them, however, are Proprietors of small Holdings of Land, and some are tolerably large ones, and a good many are engaged in business. About 500 of the Indian Coolies were shown to be Hindus by Religion, 72 were Mussalmans, and the rest were Native Christians. The Missionary Schools are largely attended by the children of the Indian Settlers, and this circumstance accounts for the large percentage of Native Christians. Most of those who are now living in the Island were born there, or have come from other neighbouring Islands.

ST. LUCIA

St. Lucia is an Island in the Windward Group and lies in 13° 50' North Latitude and 61° West Longitude, and has an area of 245 square miles. The Temperature ranges from 71° to 83° Fahrenheit, and the average Rainfall is about 94 inches. It had a population of 24,123 Souls in 1854, out of whom 947 were Whites and the rest persons of Colour. Sugarcane cultivation is the chief industry of the Island. The laws regulating Labour are clearer and more stringent than the laws of any other Colony. The Immigration Agent, who is a paid Government Officer, inspects the Ships on their arrival, and assigns the Immigrants to the Planters. The wages are required to be not less than those paid to free labourers, and as far as possible, the allotments are made so as to keep husband and wife, child and parent, together. The Indenture is then drawn up and signed before a Magistrate, and the Agent visits the Estates to see that the laws passed for the Protection of the Coolies are strictly enforced, and that the Labourers are fairly treated. The contracts are for five years, but the Immigrant may redeem the last two years by payment of a fixed sum of money. After five years of industrial service, he obtains a Certificate of Discharge, and after eight years, he is entitled to a Free Passage, which he may commute into money, or he may accept a Grant of Land instead. The rate of wages ranges from one Shilling to one Shilling and four-pence per day, for adult Males and ten-pence a day for Females. The Employer is required to provide proper lodgings for the labourers, and each house has an acre of Provision Ground. For the first three months free rations are allowed, according to a fixed scale. The Penal provisions against absence from work and desertion are stringent and strictly enforced. Up to 1862, in all 1,535 Immigrants were imported into this Island. After 1862, no Immigrants were imported for many years. In 1864, the number of Indian Immigrants in this Island was 1,316, and they were reduced to 1,079 in 1868. Though all had become entitled to free passage back to India, only 460 accepted the boon. The rest chose to take the bounty and become permanent Residents on the Island. Immigration to this Island has been resumed in recent years, since 1881. In 1891, there were on the Island in all 2,500 Indians, out of whom 1,640 were employed on twenty-two Estates and 225 of these Indians possessed twenty Horses, four hundred and eighty Cattle, and two hundred Sheep and Goats. Some of the more enterprizing of these Immigrants had begun to purchase land with the object of forming a purely Indian Settlement of Peasant Proprietors on the Island. There were five Schools attended by the children of the Indian Coolies, which received Grants-in-aid from Government.

JAMAICA

Jamaica is an Island in the West Indies, and lies between 17° 40' and 18° 50' North Latitude, and 76° 10' to 78° 30' West Longitude. It has a surface area of 6,400 square miles. There is a mountain range of considerable height which runs right through the middle of the Island, and the plains gradually slope down its sides to the sea. Its chief products are Sugar, Rum, and Coffee. Cotton and Indigo were formerly produced in large quantities, but these industries have either much declined or disappeared in recent years. The Indian Coolies are employed chiefly in Sugar and Coffee Plantations and in the Breeding Pens on the hills, where excellent Cattle and Horses are reared on the rich grazing grounds that cap these hills. The Indian Immigrants were first introduced in 1845. In the first three years, about 4,000 Indians were imported into the Colony. For the next twelve years Immigration was stopped by reason of internal troubles in the Colony. It was resumed in 1859, and during the next twelve years, about 9,000 Indian Coolies were imported. The Immigration Agent allots the Immigrants to the Estates according to their wants after satisfying himself that the conveniences of the Coolies will be duly looked after. The period of Indenture is five years. As elsewhere, the Agent is required by law to see that wives and husbands, and parents and children, shall not be separated. Before the allotment, the Immigration Agent feeds and supports the Coolies at Government expense. The Planters contribute to this Fund, and the Government assigns the yield of certain taxes to the same purpose. The Agent has also the power of cancelling the Indenture in case the Employer ill-uses his work-people, or abuses his powers. In 1871 the number of Indian Coolies was nearly 10,000. Free rations, clothes and lodgings have to be provided by the Employer, according to a scale laid down by the Government. Rations are stopped after the Immigrant has been for some time on the Island, and the Agent is satisfied that he can easily procure within his earnings his own supplies. In this case, money wages are paid to the Immigrants. The usual rate of wages is one Shilling a day for each adult Male, and nine-pence for a Female adult labourer. There are six working days in the week, and the hours of work are nine per day. Special arrangements for Task-Work are permitted with the sanction of the Agent. The laws against absence and desertion are, as in the other Colonies, severe, and strictly enforced. In case of sickness, Medical Officers of Government attend upon the sick person, and look to his wants. Out of the whole number of Indian Coolies in the Colony in 1871, about fifty per cent. *i.e.*, 4,608, were indentured Labourers, and worked on eighty-seven Estates. After the indentured term of five years is over, the Indian Coolie is free to follow any calling he likes. A few become Shopkeepers, but many continue their employment as free labourers on the Estates. After ten years' residence, the Immigrant becomes entitled to a Free Passage, which he may commute by accepting a Grant of ten Acres of Crown Land. Out of 2,140, who became entitled to a return passage in 1872, 925 returned to India, but 1,215 commuted their privilege, and settled permanently in Jamaica as Residents. Up to 1871, as many as 14,400 Indian Coolies came to Jamaica, and only about 2,773 returned during the same period. About 925 Coolies returned to India in 1870, and they carried with them

Savings estimated at 17,000 Dollars. If a labourer becomes permanently disabled or sick during the term of his Indenture, free Return Passage is given to him. The conditions of employment are thus, on the whole, very satisfactory. Between 1860 and 1877, a period of seventeen years, about 16,000 Coolies have been imported, sixty per cent. males, and Forty per cent. Females. Out of the whole number, 1,952 have returned during the same period, and 12,600 were in the Colony in 1877, and worked on 103 Plantations. The total number of Indians in the Colony in 1892 was 14,000, of whom 4,100 were working under Indentures, and 10,000 had completed their ten years, and were working as Free Labourers. There were 667 Indian Depositors in the Savings Banks, and the amount to their credit was 14,054 Dollars, against 145 Depositors who had 16,758 Dollars in 1871. Among the new arrivals in 1892 was one Chandra Kumari, who claimed to be of the Jung Bahadur Family, and she stated that she had run away with one of the Palace servants. About 450 Coolies returned to India in 1892, and brought with them £1,748 worth of cash, and £500 worth of Jewellery.

NATAL

Natal is a tract on the South-East Coast of Africa, 200 miles long and 100 miles broad, with a total area of 17,000 square miles. There are three Zones or Strips; the Coast Strip, about 15 miles broad, is sub-Tropical, and Sugarcane, Coffee, and Indigo are grown there largely, as also Mulberry, Vine, Olives, Oats, Beans and Potatoes. Maize is, however, the chief grain crop. The second Zone is more Temperate, and Cereals grow there. The third Zone is hilly, and on its Western Side the range of mountains rises to 8,000 feet above the level of the sea. This portion is best fitted for pasturing Sheep and Cattle, and is also suited for the Growth of Cereals and Fruits of Temperate Regions. In the Coast Strip the Temperature ranges from 77° to 85° Fahrenheit in the Summer Season, and from 85° to 70° in Winter. The Temperature in the Central Region is more mild.

From 1842 to 1856, Natal was administered as a Dependency of the Cape Colony, but in the latter year a separate Administration was formed. In 1860, the total population was 1,25,000, out of whom 8,000 were Whites, and of these last one-third were Dutch Boers, who occupied the Territory before the British invaded it, in 1842. in 1872, the Indian Immigrants were estimated to be 5,700 adults, and they had all served out their term of Indenture. Nearly one-half of this number were employed on Sugar and Coffee Estates. The other half were Traders, Shop-keepers, Gardeners, Fishermen, and Domestic Servants. Some of the Coolies had also become Land-Holders themselves, and cultivated Sugar-cane and Maize. Some 400 Indians had gone further west to seek their fortunes in the diamond fields of the Transvaal. Ordinary workmen get 15s. a month, skilled workmen earn from 30s. to £2. One Indian earned as much as £4 a month. On the Railway, Indian Coolies get 20s. to 30s. a month. In all cases rations are given in addition to money wages. About 6,445 Indians were imported as Coolies in Natal up to 1866. The children of the Coolies live and thrive better in Natal than in India. The death rate is lower, and the general state of health is better. The Coolies build their own houses out of materials supplied by their Employers, and small garden grounds are attached to the houses in which Tobacco is grown. There are four Schools for Coolie children, which are aided by Government Grants. In recent years very few Coolies go to Natal under Indentures. The general Law of Master and Servant is found to be sufficiently protective of their interests. The percentage of Women is low, Males being sixty-seven per cent. against thirty-three per cent. Females. There were 231 Indian Coolie Depositors in the Savings Bank in 1871, who had deposited £6,000. A large portion of the Savings has been invested in the Colony in Vegetable and Tobacco Farms, and many Coolies earn their living as Boat-owners and Fishermen. After retiring from the position of labourers, many Indians take up Crown land, and grow Sugar-cane on their own farms. In 1891, as many as 3,183 Indian Immigrants landed in the Ports of this Colony, and about 774 Immigrants returned to India, bringing with them in all £13,387 worth of cash and jewellery. Indian labourers are now employed throughout the length of the Colony, and no complaints are made in respect of them. The Indians introduced in recent years compare very favourably in physique and general health with those who were formerly imported. The Indian population has increased from 10,625 in 1876 to 38,365 in 1892. The births in this Community in 1892 were 966, and the deaths 617. Out of the total of 38,365 Indians in Natal, 24,010 were free Indians, and 14,325 were Indentured Labourers. There were nearly 19,000 Male adults, 8,500 Female adults, and about 11,071 Children. Immigration into Natal first commenced in 1860. Since that date 50,101 Indian Immigrants entered Natal. Out of this total number, 5,172 died, 7,115 returned to India, and 4,552 left the Colony otherwise, in thirty-two years. Out of 10,150 children born in the Colony, about 2,300 returned to India, about 2,000 died, and about 700 left the Colony otherwise. There were 130 Indian Marriages registered in 1891, but no case of divorce was instituted in the Courts. In 1891, about 641 Immigrants completed their indentured term, and obtained the Certificate of Industrial residence. A considerable number of them have taken to Farming and Gardening on their own account. They are also Hawkers, Traders, Fishermen and Fruit-sellers. Many have left the Colony for the Transvaal Gold Fields. They generally form a prosperous and orderly section of the population of Natal. The relations between the employers and the Employees are reported to be very satisfactory. In the Up-country Districts, the Indians have the exclusive charge of ploughing, stock and agriculture entrusted to them by the farmers, and they are allowed to sell Potatoes, and Vegetables, Mutton and Milk in as large quantities as they need, in addition to their wages. Their reputation for reliability and Industry is thoroughly established, and without them the Industry of the Colony could not be carried on. In the Savings Bank 225 Depositors had nearly Rs.50,000 to their credit, and a few more prosperous Indians remitted Rupees 5,000 besides to India.

This account extracted from the latest Official Reports would go to show that the alleged misunderstanding between the Whites and the Indian settlers, of which we hear so much, is of recent growth. As might be expected, there must be, in the nature of things, considerable conflict of interests between the Indian Traders and the White population, and things apparently have gone from bad to worse during the last few years.

NON-BRITISH COLONIES

Of the non-British Colonies, Dutch Guiana appears to attract a large number of Indian Emigrants. Indian Emigration appears to have commenced soon after the Abolition of slavery. It was not till 1870, however, that a Convention was made between England and Holland, and a Dutch Government Agent for Surinam, the Capital of Dutch Guiana, was appointed at Calcutta. In 1873, 2,448 Emigrants were imported into this Colony. In 1874,1,405 Coolies were imported. In December 1875, there were about 3,000 Indian Coolies in this Colony. During the last four years for which information is available about 3,200 Indian Coolies were despatched from Calcutta to this Colony. The Indenture term is for five years, the working year being of 313 days, and the minimum hours for work are seven hours in the fields, and ten hours in Building work. The minimum rate of wages is twenty-five Cents for Male adults and sixteen Cents for Females and Children. Rations are provided on a fixed scale for three months after arrival; provision for free lodging and medical relief is also enforced, and free return Passage can be claimed at the end of five years. In 1891 about 570 Coolies returned to India bringing with them aggregate Savings of the value of Rs.81,461. In 1889, the number returned was 587, and they brought with them aggregate Savings of the value Rs.1,10,000.

The Colony of French Guiana also imports Indian Coolies, so also do the French Islands of Guadeloupe and Martinique, but detailed information about these settlements is not available.

The only French Colony about which information is available is the Island of Réunion, which lies 90 miles to the South-west of Mauritius. The Island is 40 miles long and 27 miles broad. Cotton, Coffee, Cloves, and Sugarcane are the chief products of the Island. In 1861, the number of Indian Immigrants was about 40,000, of whom 33,000 were adult Males, 4,300 adult Females and 2,000 Children. In 1863, the number of Indian Settlers had risen to 46,411. The Employers have to supply free rations, clothing, lodging, and medicines, and pay besides Rs.5 a month as wages to each adult Male, Rs.3 to each Female, and Rs.2 to each Child. After completing five years, Free Passage is allowed back to India. The Coolie Emigrants are well off, and some own small Holdings and Gardens of their own, and others manage Shops. The working hours are nine and a half per day. In recent years Emigration from British Indian Ports has been stopped on account of complaints about mismanagement and abuse of powers. A few Coolies still emigrate from the French port of Pondicherry. Negotiations have been opened by the French Government with the Government of India to allow the resumption of Coolie Emigration from the British Ports to this Island, and Mr. MacKenzie was sent by the Government of India to arrange the terms on which this concession could be granted with safety.

CEYLON

Nearer home, the Island of Ceylon attracts a considerable body of Indian Coolies from the Madras Presidency. As many as 75,000 Coolies leave Indian Ports for Ceylon each year. Three-fourths of them return back to India, and the rest stay permanently in Ceylon. It has been estimated that between 1843 and 1867, nearly fourteen and a half Laks of Coolies went to Ceylon, out of whom eight and one-third Laks returned to India. The rest remained in the Island as permanent Settlers. Out of the total population of Ceylon, estimated in 1871 at twenty-four Laks, as many as six Laks, or twenty-five per cent., were

Indian Coolies, and others settled in that Island during the previous forty years. The Straits Settlements, Singapore, Penang, and Malacca also attract a considerable number of Coolies from India. About 40,000 Indians are found in these Settlements, employed chiefly as agricultural labourers, though a considerable number of them also follow other pursuits.

This completes our review of the British, French, and Dutch Colonies and Possessions to which, during the past fifty years and more, the surplus labour of India has been exported. Taking a general view of the question, it will be seen that Foreign Emigration from India represents a large and most important interest. As the result of the past fifty years of protected Emigration, as many as 12,00,000 of people are to be found scattered throughout these Settlements. The popularity of Foreign Emigration is evidenced by the following facts which can be gathered from the Reports:—(1) The number of Emigrants has been steadily increasing. (2) The proportion of Women to Men is also more favourable in recent years than it was in the first half of this period of fifty years, 1842-1892. (3) The number of those who return back to India has always been smaller than those who left each year. (4) Among those who return to India, a good many re-Emigrate with their Families. (5) Of those who go out of India as Indentured Labourers under contract, nearly one half settle in these Colonies as Free Labourers. (6) Of those who so settle, a small proportion acquire land of their own, or become traders, or pursue other callings, indicative of their attainment of a higher social status. (7) Notwithstanding the severity of the laws against desertion and absence from work, the Indian Coolies thrive remarkably well, and acquire habits of thrift and independence for which they are not much noted during their residence in India. (8) The Wages earned are from two to three times those obtained in India, and the climate appears generally to agree with the Indian Settlers and their Families. (9) Their general prosperity is fully attested to by the large remittances they make to this Country, and the Savings they bring with them when they return, as also by the increase of their Deposit accounts in the local Savings Banks. Of course, there are difficulties and obstructions in the way. Without a strict enforcement of the Protection Laws in their interest by the Government of India, the Coolie Emigrants would not be able to hold their own against the greed of their Employers, the Planters, who are not generally noted for their humanity. The Magistracy and the Government machinery in these Colonies, being entirely in the hands of the White population, are not very impartial in their treatment of the Indian Settlers, and there is not much scope allowed for the independent growth of the Coloured Races. Notwithstanding these disadvantages, there can be no doubt that the System of Protected Emigration has, on the whole, been very beneficial, and that it will, in course of time, lead to further developments in the interest of the Indian Settlers in those Colonies, at least, where, as in Natal, Trinidad, Mauritius and British Guiana, the Indians already represent a considerable proportion of the population.

The most hopeful feature of this stream of Foreign Emigration is represented by the fact that the Higher Castes of Hindus occupy no small place among those who emigrate. The Emigration Report for 1889 showed that, out of 11,000 Emigrants who left the Port of Calcutta in that year, 1,315 were Brahmins and men of the Higher Castes, 3,356 were Agriculturists, 958 Artizans, and the Low Caste Emigrants were 4,152. The Hindus in all made up nearly 9,800, while the Mussalmans were 1,154 and the Christians 15. The Emigration Report for 1890 shows that, out of some 13,000 persons who left the Calcutta Port in that year, as many as 1,234, or ten per cent., were Brahmins and men of the Higher Castes, about 4,100 were Agriculturists, about 800 were Artizans and the Low Caste Emigrants were 5,200, in all. The Hindu Emigrants were 11,345, while the Mussalmans were 1,623, and the Christians 89. Similarly, out of nearly 16,000 Emigrants who left Calcutta in 1891, 1,170 were Brahmins and men of the Higher Castes, 6,000 were Agriculturists, and about 900 Artizans, while the Low Caste Emigrants were 6,200. The Hindu Emigrants were in all 14,000; the Mussalmans were 1,558 and Christians nine. This feature of Hindu Emigration is the most hopeful, seeing that it is not the Low Castes alone who emigrate. Out of nearly 47,000 people who emigrated from the Port of Calcutta during the three years, 1889 to 1891, about eleven per cent. were mahomedans, and eighty-nine per cent. were Hindus; and out of this eighty-nine per cent. less than forty-five per cent. were Low Caste people, and the rest were Artizans, Agriculturists and Brahmins and men of the Higher Castes.

It only remains now for me to indicate briefly the lines on which Associations like those under the auspices of which we meet here to-day, can make themselves practically useful. In connection with these twelve Laks of people settled in Foreign Parts, if people in Bombay, or Madras, or Calcutta would venture to go out of their usual track, they could easily establish thriving Agencies in all these ten or fifteen Colonies, where such a large number of Indians are settled, and are presumably well off. The Bombay Mill Owners, for instance, could not find a better market for their Native made cloth than in the outlying possessions. The Emigration business is one which Native Shippers could well undertake with advantage, especially with Mauritius and Natal on the African Coast. It should be the business of Associations like these to obtain the latest information from, and keep up communication with, these distant Settlements. The School-master, the Doctor and the Lawyer, the Artizans of all classes, and even the Priests of different Sects, have here a most favourable field for their operations and enterprize among people who are their kith and kin, and on whom sympathy would never be wasted. The Government of the Queen-Empress extends its common protection to us and to them, and the Government of India is most conscientiously alive to its duty of protecting the interests of these Indian Settlers. If we could send out our young men to these Possessions of the Crown, they will surely be able to earn their living, and do a great deal of practical good. A little organization and some enterprize are alone needed for utilizing this vast force which lies scattered about in distant Possessions. It is with a view to rouse interest in the welfare of these people, and enable us to do our duty by them, that I took up this subject for this year's Conference, and I shall be amply rewarded, if among those who hear me the Merchants, Manufacturers, Traders, and Representatives of different Provinces, any one or more feels himself moved by the spirit of enterprize and sympathy, and is led in consequence to cultivate better relations of Trade and Industry with these twelve Laks of people established in Foreign Parts.

23

PRESENT STATE OF INDIAN MANUFACTURES & OUTLOOK OF THE SAME*

Dr.Watts, Reporter on Economic Products to the Government of India, has, in his recently published Memorandum on the Resources of British India, devoted an entire chapter to the consideration of the "Present State of Indian Manufactures and Outlook of the same" for the future which is eminently suggestive, and deserves most careful consideration by the Members of an Association, such as that under whose auspices we meet here to-day. The political domination of one Country by another attracts far more attention than the more formidable, though unfelt domination which the Capital, Enterprise, and Skill of one Country exercise over the Trade and Manufactures of another. This latter domination has an insidious influence which paralyzes the springs of all the varied activities which together make up the life of a Nation, and this influence was so paramount at one time in British India, that there were grave reasons to fear the worst consequences of this inevitable change. In the Eighteenth Century, England, like the other Countries of Europe, desired to have Colonies of its own race in all parts

*Read at the Industrial Conference, Poona, in 1893. Published in *JPSS* October 1894, Vol.XVII, No.2, and in *Essays*.

of the World, chiefly for the command of the markets, thus opened up to the Home Manufacturers and Traders. The Colonies were looked upon as, and in fact were actually called, Plantations, where raw produce was grown to be sent to the Mother Country, to be manufactured and exported again back to the Colonies and to the rest of the World. This Policy suggested restrictive measures of action intended to foster domestic Trade and Arts at the sacrifice of the best interests of the Colonies. The American War of Independence put an end to this scheme of Economic Government, and since then, though the sphere of English colonization has been multiplied during this Century beyond all previous record, yet these new Colonies have from the first been allowed to work out their own destinies, free from the leading strings of domestic control. The great Indian Dependency of England has, during this Century, come to supply the place of the Old Colonies. This Dependency has come to be regarded as a Plantation, growing raw produce to be shipped by British Agents in British Ships, to be worked into Fabrics by British skill and capital, and to be re-exported to the Dependency by British merchants to their corresponding British Firms in India and elsewhere. The development of steam power and mechanical skill, joined with increased facilities of communication, have lent strength to this tendency of the times, and, as one result of the change, the gradual ruralization of this great Dependency, and the rapid decadence of Native manufacture and Trade, became distinctly marked. Even now the danger is not over. It is, however, a most fortunate circumstance that, during the last twenty years, there has been a clearly distinguishable departure from the till then unimpeded process of ruralizing a vast Continent long known for its great resources and aptitudes. The rationale of the existence and working of such a body as the Industrial Association of Western India is that it seeks to encourage this tendency, and check rustication. It is, no doubt, a struggle of a very unequal character, a struggle between a Giant and a Dwarf, and yet the struggle has to be maintained against great odds; and those who are engaged in the struggle cannot do better than note from time to time, whether the direction of the movement is correct, and its velocity satisfactory. I propose in this paper to bring together certain facts, chiefly based on Official Publications, which will, I hope, satisfy you that, on the whole, we have reasons to congratulate ourselves upon the result, that the tendency towards rustication has been checked, and India under British Rule has been gathering up its forces, and marshalling them in order to ward off the evil effects of the first surrender that it had to make by way of homage to British skill, capital and enterprize.

Dr. Watts has in his Memorandum noticed one side of this counter-movement, which has become clearly visible during the last twenty years. A careful analysis of the Trade Returns of British India for 1892-93 discloses the fact that, out of a total of one hundred and sixty-four Crores' worth of Exports and Imports, excluding Treasure and Government Transactions, we imported nearly sixteen Crores of Raw Produce against nearly thirty-six Crores of Manufactured Produce, while we exported eighty-five Crores of Raw Produce against sixteen Crores' worth of Manufactured Articles. In a word, our Exports to Foreign Countries showed that eighty-five per cent. of them were represented by the bulky agricultural produce, which gave no employment to local skill and capital, except such as was represented by the rude methods of Agriculture, while in the Imports we did not know how to supply our wants in regard to seventy-two per cent. of the articles we received from foreign Countries. These proportions of seventy-two per cent. Imports and eighty-five per cent. Exports are sufficiently expressive of the present condition of things. In 1892, we exported twenty and a half Crores of Cotton and Jute Fibre, another twenty and a half Crores of Grain, eleven and a half Crores of Seeds, ten Crores of Opium and Tobacco, about nine Crores' worth of Tea, Coffee, and Indigo, nearly three Crores of Hides and Skins, Horns, etc., three-fourths of a Crore of Dye Stuffs and Spices, about two-thirds of a Crore of Raw Silk, two-thirds of a Crore of Timber, a quarter of a Crore of Manure, three-fourths of a Crore of Lac, and one-third of a Crore of Catechu or Cutch. These articles make up in all eighty Crores. The principal raw materials which India imported in large quantities in the same year, were the Metals,—Iron and Steel of about three and a half Crores, Copper two Crores, and the rest about a Crore,—one and three-eighths Crores' worth of Coal, other Minerals three-fourths of a Crore, one-third of a Crore of Stone, marble and precious Jewellery. The rest of the imported articles were all more or less the products of skill and capital engaged in manufactures, including from twenty-five to thirty-one Crores of Rupees' worth of Cotton Goods, three Crores of Silk and Woollen Apparel, two and a half Crores of Sugar, one and half Crore of Wines, six and two-thirds Crores of Machinery and manufactured Metals, three Crores of Dyes, two Crores' worth of Oil, and about a Crore of Tea, Coffee, and Sundries. This state of things was the growth of the last half Century. In 1853 Cotton Goods and Yarn imported into India were worth less than sixty Laks of Rupees, and in forty years they swelled to the enormous amount of twenty-five Crores. Silk and Woollen Goods imported in 1853 were worth only five Laks, and they rose to two and one- third Crores in forty years. Similarly, raw Jute and Grain exported from India were about four Laks each in value in 1853, and were respectively worth five Crores and six Crores in 1892.

About twenty-two years ago, I had occasion to notice this collapse of domestic Industries, and the gradual rustication of our chief occupations, in a series of Lectures which have been published, and it was about this time that a welcome change took place, whose effects are now perceptibly visible. Things were as bad as could be about 1870-75; since then the tide has turned, and India has shown signs of a revival which marks its first step in the transition from a purely agricultural into a partly manufacturing and trading Country. Dr. Watts has in his Memorandum clearly brought out into prominence the chief features of this change. Of course, no change has taken place in the absolute disproportion between the Exports and Imports of raw and manufactured produce, but their relative proportions have changed in a way which marks the beginning of this new departure from the old traditions. The chief features of this change may be thus described. Firstly, our Exports of manufactured or partly manufactured goods have risen from five and a quarter Crores to sixteen and a half Crores in the past fourteen years, 1879-1893, the increase being thus two hundred and eleven per cent. in fourteen years. There is a steady annual increment of fifteen per cent. with only two exceptional years, during that whole period. Secondly, our Exports of raw produce have also risen absolutely, but the relative rise is measured by the difference between sixty Crores and eighty-five and a half Crores, which means an increase of forty-two per cent. in fourteen years, or an annual increment of three per cent. per year, against an annual increment of fifteen per cent. in the export of manufactured produce. Thirdly, the increase of manufactured articles imported into India, has only been thirty per cent. in fourteen years, rising from twenty Crores to thirty-six Crores, which gives an annual increment of two per cent. per year. Fourthly, the increase in the imports of raw produce has been about a hundred per cent., rising from thirteen and three-fourths Crores to twenty-six and a half Crores' worth in fourteen years. This gives an average increment of six and a half per cent. The following Table sets forth the several points noticed above in a very clear manner.

	1879	1892	Percentage increased.	
			Total	Annual.
Manufactured Imports	Rs.25,98,65,827	36,22,31,872	39	2.8
Raw Imports	Rs.13,75,55,837	26,38,18,431	91	6.5
Manufactured Exports	Rs. 5,27,80,340	16,42,47,566.	211	15
Raw Exports	Rs.59,67,27,991	85,52,09,499	43	3

It will be seen from this Table that while the absolute disproportion still continues to be very marked, there is a very healthy change in their relative proportions. Fifthly, while the

Imports of manufactured articles were sixty-five per cent. of the total Imports in 1879, this proportion has fallen to fifty-seven per cent. in 1892; similarly, while the proportion of manufactured Exports was only eight per cent. of the total Exports in 1879, they were in 1892 nearly sixteen per cent. This change is a steady tendency which characterises the returns of most of the years included within the period noted above. Sixthly, the above conclusions are based on the Official Trade Returns. Dr. Watts, however, questions the principle of the official classification which relegates such Goods as Spirits, Flour, Sugar, Oils, etc., to the head of Raw Produce; while Coir, Cordage, Oil-cakes, Hides and Skins, Lac, are shown as manufactured. The growth of the Industries concerned in the production of Indigo, Tea, Coffee, Oils, Sugar, Beer, Tobacco, Cigars, etc., marks the first step in the progress of India from a purely agricultural into a partly manufacturing Country, which is quite as important as the actual multiplication of Jute, Cotton, Silk, Woollen, Paper, Flour, and Oil-Mills, and Leather and Sugar Factories. By reclassifying the details of the Official Returns on this more correct basis, it is shown that our Manufactured Exports bear to our Raw Exports the proportion of thirty to seventy, instead of sixteen to eighty-four per cent.

The question naturally arises,—how has this change for the better been brought about? It has been brought about silently and surely by the efforts of the Indian people, assisted to a large extent by the influx of British capital and enterprize. A few illustrations will best explain the working of this double Agency. Taking Cotton Goods in the first instance, it will be noted that the Imports of Cotton Goods and Yarn were valued at nineteen and a half Crores in 1875, and though they rose as high as thirty-one Crores in one or two years, they have been almost steady during the last fifteen years at a figure which averages twenty-five Crores. The Exports in the meanwhile have risen from less than two Crores, to nearly ten Crores, during the same period of eighteen years. The export of Raw Cotton stood at five and a half Crores, in 1860, rose to thirty-five Crores in 1865-1866, and has since fallen to about sixteen Crores in 1868, fourteen Crores in 1878, seven and a half in 1882, and was thirteen Crores in 1892. These changes in the Exports and Imports of raw and manufactured Cotton have been contemporaneous with the development of the Cotton Mills in India, which have risen from fifty-eight Mills with 12,983 Looms and 14,36,464 Spindles in 1878, to 130 Mills with 26,347 Looms and 33,78,903 Spindles, giving employment to one hundred and fifty thousand hands. The capital sunk in these Mills was less than two Crores in 1875, and is now estimated to be nearly ten Crores. This vast Industry has all grown within the last forty years, and the Bombay Presidency takes the lion's share of the benefits secured thereby, inasmuch as no less than 88 Mills are in this Presidency, besides 380 Presses, and a still larger number of Ginning Factories.

The place which the Cotton industry occupies in this Presidency, is taken up in Bengal by the Jute industry. There are twenty-seven Jute Mills, and twenty-three Presses, and many private concerns, with a capital of six and a half Crores, with 9,000 Looms and 1,80,172 Spindles, giving employment to over seventy-seven thousand men. The Exports were over ten Crores of Bags, and the home consumption is equal to the foreign demand. The export of raw Jute still amounts to fifty-two Laks of hundredweights.

There are eighty-one Silk filature concerns in Bengal, which give employment to 8,000 hands permanently, and an equal number temporarily, and produce five Laks of pounds of Silk. There are two Mills, one in Calcutta, and another in Bombay, which supply chiefly the Burmese markets. There are other factories which produce Tasar, and Chora silk for the local market. The Silk Mill in Calcutta exported sixteen Laks of Rupees worth of Silk goods to England and France. The exports of raw Silk were worth sixty Laks of Rupees.

There are five Woollen Mills with 532 Looms and 17,210 Spindles, and they give employment to over three thousand hands. The capital employed is thirty Laks, and the annual out-turn of goods is worth twenty-one Laks of Rupees, chiefly for the supply of local and departmental wants. The Woollen and Silk Piece-goods imported were of the value of nearly three Crores of Rupees, which shows what scope there is still left for further expansion. The exports of Cashmere Shawls, which at one time were nearly thirty Laks of Rupees in value in 1868, dwindled down to two and a quarter Laks in 1890-91.

There are ten Paper Mills with a capital of nearly twenty-five Laks of Rupees. The out-turn had quadrupled in ten years, and was twenty-six Million pounds in 1892. There is considerable scope for extension here also, since the value of imported Paper of all kinds averages about fifty Laks of Rupees.

There are forty-seven Tanneries, thirty-three out of which are in the Madras Presidency, nine in Sind, two in Calcutta, two in Cawnpore, and one in Agra. The Export trade in tanned Hides has increased from three Crores to five and a half Crores in eighteen years. In tanned Leather manufactures, these Indian Tanneries compete with the imports from Europe.

There are in India twenty-three Breweries, all started since 1850. The capital employed is seventeen Laks, the out-turn is fifty Laks of Gallons, out of which nearly twenty-seven Laks were purchased by Government for the use of soldiers. The remaining twenty-two Laks are consumed by the civil population. Till within the last three or four years, there was practically no import of beer for the use of the Army. Latterly, since 1891, this monopoly has been destroyed, and imported Beer is again coming in in large quantities. Altogether one Crore's worth of Wines and Spirits is imported into India, and about half a Crore's worth of Beer and Cider was imported in 1892.

There are, besides, two Soap Factories and ten Rope Factories at work in this Country, chiefly supplying local and departmental wants.

There are fourteen Sugar Factories and Refineries, five in Madras, seven in Bengal, and two in the North-West Provinces. The capital of two of the more important Factories, that of Casipore near Calcutta, and the Rosa Factory in Shahjahanpur, is twenty-six Laks of Rupees. The Imports of Sugar are, however, seven times as large as the Exports. The competition of Beet Sugar has checked the local production for export markets, as also for home consumption. The wants of local consumption are chiefly satisfied by the use of the Jaggery. The value of imported refined Sugar was two and two-thirds of Crores in 1892, and its quantity two Million Tons. Raw Jaggery exported was worth forty-five Laks.

Next in order come the Flour Mills, of which we have forty-six at work in India, nineteen being in the Bombay Presidency. The capital employed by five of these, which are Joint Stock concerns, is sixteen Laks of Rupees, and the total capital of all the Mills might come up to thirty Laks. There are, besides, several Tobacco Curing Factories, Bone-crushing Factories, Iron and Brass Foundries, Oil Mills, Saltpetre Refineries, Saw Mills, Potteries and other Companies. In the words of Sir Edward Buck, they all indicate that "India is entering upon an important period of manufacturing activity. Already a substantial commencement has been made in Cotton and Jute Goods, followed by manufactories of Wool, Paper, Leather, Sugar, Oil, and Tobacco."

Side by side with this expansion of Indian manufacturing Industries, we have to note the great development of the Tea, Coffee, Indigo, and Cinchona Plantations. The capital sunk in these industries is chiefly European, and the management is also in European hands. The total area under Tea cultivation in 1892-93 was 3,34,825 acres, out of which half the area is cultivated by Private Concerns, and one Lak of acres belongs to Companies started in England, while half a Lak of acres belongs to Companies started in Calcutta. The total exports were one hundred and twenty million of pounds in weight worth six Crores of Rupees in all.

The total capital employed by the registered Tea Companies in these concerns exceeds eight Crores. The Capital of the Private Tea Concerns may be assumed to be as much. This Industry gives employment to ten Laks of people. The land occupied was waste land, which yielded nothing before European enterprize turned it to account.

The Indigo Concerns at work in India in 1892 were represented by 2,702 Factories and 6,032 Vats, which gave employment to three and a half Laks of people, solely in the production of the manufactured article of commerce. The Agriculturists who produce the Raw material are not included in this number. The average exports are fifteen Million pounds, valued at nearly fifty Laks of Rupees.

Coffee Plantations cover 1,27,648 acres in British India, besides large areas in Mysore, Cochin, and Travancore. The total area under the Coffee crop may safely be put down at two Laks of acres. The total export of Coffee is nearly three Laks of hundred-weights. There are thirty-seven Coffee Works in the Madras Presidency, which give employment to 1,379 permanent and 5,433 temporary hands. There are besides numerous Lac Factories, many Native, and a few under European management, giving employment to 2,614 permanent hands, and 1,600 temporary labourers. The Catechu or Cutch Trade is also considerable. The value of the exports in 1892 was nearly forty Laks.

Next to these Plantations and Mill Industries, an important development of the resources has taken place in the Mineral wealth of India, and notably in the use of Indian Coal. The value of the Import of Foreign Coal was as high as two Crores of Rupees in 1888, but has fallen to one and a quarter Crores in 1892. The Imports have not expanded with the increase in demand, and this is entirely due to the working of Indian Collieries. The Bengal Collieries alone have quadrupled their output, chiefly as Exports by sea to other Provinces, in five years, the Exports having risen from four Laks of Tons in 1888 to twenty Laks in 1892. In 1892 there were eighty-two Collieries at work in India, of which seventy-three were in Bengal, one in the Punjab, three in Assam, one in Central India, one in Deccan Hyderabad, and one in Beluchistan. The output has doubled itself in ten years, and was two Million Tons in 1892, more than one Million Tons being made up by the Bengal Collieries alone. Out of these two Million Tons, one Million Tons were used by the Railway Companies. Burma also has large Coal deposits which are being brought into use. Bombay, Madras, and the North-Western Provinces have no Coal Mines.

Gold Mines have been re-opened by the help of British capital and enterprize in Mysore, and Wynaad and the out-turn in 1892 was nearly worth nine Laks. The average of the imports of Gold in five years was more than four Crores per year, being nearly twice the figures in 1872, and thrice the figures in 1852, which were respectively two and a half and one and one-third Crores. One hundred and fifty Crores' worth of Gold has been imported into India since 1835 for hoarding purposes.

The success which has attended the flow of English capital in respect of Coal Mines has not rewarded the efforts made to develop the Iron resources of India. Not that India is wanting in this natural source of Wealth, but it is not possible to work these resources in the face of European competition. The great difficulty in the way is to find Iron deposits near enough to Coal Mines which can produce cheap and good fuel. The Baragor Iron Company in Bengal is, however, progressing satisfactorily. The imports of Iron, and Iron-ware, including Railway materials and Mill machinery, in the meanwhile, have remained stationary at the high figure of nine or ten Crores, during the past five years.

The amount of salt produced in India was over nine Laks of tons in 1892, and the Imports were three and a half Laks of Tons. The total duty levied was eight and a half Crores. Saltpetre was an Indian monopoly in former times. Owing to the discoveries of a substitute by artificial processes, the demand for Indian Saltpetre has fallen off, and Saltpetre worth only five Laks was exported in 1892.

India imported from sixteen to twenty Laks of Pearls during the last five years, while its own Pearl Fisheries yielded but a poor return. Since the conquest of Burma, Ruby, Jade, Amber, Sapphire and other Precious Stones have become a new source of wealth, but as yet these resources show no great development.

I have thus passed in review all the principal Manufacturing, Planting, and Mineral Industries which have sprung up in India during the last forty years, and which have shown a very healthy development during the last twenty years. They represent an investment of nearly fifty Crores of Rupees, and afford new and varied employment to nearly twenty-five Laks of people all the year round. This is an humble beginning, but it is a very hopeful one, and its effects are plainly visible in the altered relations which have come to subsist between Indian Exports and Imports of Raw and Manufactured Goods.

It might appear to some that it is not very safe to rely upon Statistics of Trade or Industry of a general character, and to base conclusions thereon which might or might not hold good of particular parts of the Country, in the welfare of which we may be more intimately interested. It is with this view that I desire you to turn to some Local Statistics of this Presidency, about the correctness of which we need have no misgivings, and which also point in the same direction as those I have already examined. In another place I have noted the proportion of Rural and Urban populations in this Presidency, as they are disclosed by the two Census enumerations of 1872 and 1891. The Census of 1872 disclosed one Hundred and seventy-nine Towns with a population of more than five Thousand inhabitants in the Bombay Presidency. This same number rose to two hundred and thirty-two in the Census of 1891. The population of one Hundred and seventy-nine Towns was in 1872 shown to be 27,78,822, or seventeen per cent., while the population of the two Hundred and thirty-two Towns was found to be 34,53,569, or nearly nineteen per cent. of the total population. The number of Towns had thus increased by thirty per cent. in twenty years, and the population of these Towns had increased twenty-five per cent. The total increase of population during the same period of twenty years was only sixteen per cent., and the Rural Areas showed an increase of fourteen per cent. in their population. The increase of Towns, and the higher rate of increase in the population of Towns, as also the slight increase in the relative proportions of Urban and Rural populations, show clearly that the tendency towards rustication had been checked, and that gradually but surely, the first signs of the new Civic Life were manifesting themselves. The difference in the relative percentages of the Town and Country population shows slight and scarcely perceptible Progress, but that slight Progress was in the right direction.

The same fact is brought home to us by a careful study of the Census of Occupations. Unfortunately no fair comparison can be instituted between the results of the Census of 1872 and those of 1891, because of the different principles on which the Census Tables in each of these years were prepared. However, taking the last Census enumeration as a basis, we find that in 1891, out of a total population of 1,88,84,704 enumerated, 1,10,08,233 were returned as Agriculturists, which gives a proportion of nearly fifty-nine per cent. The division of Town and Country is not sharply marked out in this land. The Town has a considerable Agricultural population, and the Country has its own Village Industries. It is therefore useful to note the relative proportions of the different Classes of Occupations in Town and Country.

The Agriculturists, who are fifty-nine per cent. of the whole population, were returned as forming fifteen per cent. of the Male, and nineteen per cent. of the Female population, in Towns, and sixty-seven per cent. of the Male and Female population in the Country. The Purveyors of Vegetable Food were five to seven per cent. and of animal food one to two per cent., of the entire population. The Dealers in Building Materials and Artificers engaged in Building were about two per cent. in Towns, and less than a half per cent. in the Country. The Cotton Industry engaged three per cent. of the entire population, being distributed, however, in the proportion of nine per cent. in Towns, to about two per cent. in the Country. The Woollen, as also the Hemp and Flax Fabrics, engaged less than a quarter per cent. of the population, both in Towns and Country. The Silk Industry had no representatives in the Country, but engaged in Towns one per cent. of Males, and one and a half per cent. of the Female population. The Dress-makers were one and a half per cent. of the entire population, but predominated in Towns, where they were four and a half per cent. as against less than one per cent. in the Country. Gold and Silver-smiths were nearly one per cent. of the entire population, being however, two per cent. in Towns, and less than a half per cent. in the Country. Brass, Copper, and Tin-smiths were found in Towns only, but the Iron workers or Blacksmiths were nearly equally distributed between Town and Country, with a slight preponderance in the Towns. Wood, Bamboo, and Cane Work engaged about two per cent. of the population, these classes being nearly three per cent. in Towns, and less than one per cent. in the Country. Leather-workers and Shoe-makers were almost equally distributed, both in Town and Country, their proportion ranging from one and a quarter per cent. to one and a half per cent. of the population. Money Lenders were a luxury of the Towns, being nearly one and a half per cent. there, against less than half per cent. in the Country. Merchants, Brokers, Contractors were exclusively confined to Towns, where they formed one and a half per cent. of the population. Lawyers, Doctors, Priests and Engineers, were conspicuous by their absence in the Country, and their comparative importance in Towns was not great, since they together made up less than a half per cent. of the population. Music was almost equally distributed over Town and Country, but Prostitution was a feature of it which belonged to Towns only, where it figured as high as half per cent. of the Female population. Retired Pensioners and Owners of property, who lived on interest, were also Town luxuries, being half per cent. there, and altogether absent in the Country. If we bear these relative percentages in mind, we shall find that there are a number of Industries, especially those concerned with the working of Metals, Leather, Dealers in Books, Paper and Stationery, and in Hard-ware of all kinds, also Lamps, Matches, Timber, Stone-workers, Watchmakers, Railway Employees, Cartmakers, Butchers, Toddy-drawers and Liquor-sellers, Jaggery and Sugar-makers, Contractors, Builders, Lawyers, Doctors, Engineers, Factory hands, which show a tendency to increase, while men engaged in Oil-pressing, Weavers and Spinners of Cotton and Wool, Potters, Grocers, Peddlers, Woodcarvers, Embroiderers and Dealers in Gold and Silver, and Jewels, Priests, Musicians, Military Classes, and Carriers, of all kinds, have a marked tendency the other way. Industries which flourished by the favour of Courts, and their dependents, have a tendency to disappear, while the Industries which concern themselves with the comforts and convenience of the Middle Classes, have a tendency, as indicated above, to develop in course of time. As regards the majority of the Lower Classes, they are generally unaffected by either of these changes. Whether we wish it or not, the transformation of Industries sketched out above is inevitable, and we must make the best of it. I have tried to study the question from all sides with the help of Trade Returns, Census Statistics, and the Official Publications bearing upon the general welfare of the Urban and Rural population. I have placed before you what appear to me to be good grounds for the hope I entertain that India has now fairly entered upon the path which, if pursued in the same spirit which has animated its Capitalists hitherto, cannot fail to work out its Industrial salvation. What we have to do in each case is to learn by organized co-operation to compete with the Foreigner, and take in as much Raw Produce from Abroad as we need, and work it up here, and to send in place of our Exports of Raw Produce, the same quantities in less bulky, but more valuable, forms, after they have undergone the operation of Art manipulation, and afforded occupation to our Industrial Classes. I might illustrate this by the following table.

IN PLACE OF EXPORTING	CONVERT THEM INTO & EXPORT
Oil Seeds	Oils
Dye Stuffs	Dyes and Pigments
Wheat	Flour
Unhusked Rice	Husked Rice
Jaggery	Sugar
Raw Cotton	Cotton Goods
Raw Wool	Woollen Goods and Shawls
Raw Silk	Silk Goods
Jute and Flax	Gunny Bags, Ropes
Hides and Skins	Prepared and Tanned Leather
Raw Tobacco	Tobacco Cured, and Cigars
Fish	Cured and Salted Fish
Rags	Paper
Wood and Timber	Carved Wood and Furniture

I might multiply this list without end. This is the practical work which Providence has set down for us to learn under the best of teachers. We have already made fair progress. We have to improve our Raw Materials, or Import them when our Soil is unsuited to their production. We have to organize Labour and Capital by co-operation, and Import freely Foreign Skill and Machinery, till we learn our lessons properly and need no help. We have rusticated too long; we have now to turn our apt hands to new work, and bend our muscles to sturdier and honester labour. This is the Civic Virtue we have to learn, and according as we learn it or spurn it we shall win or lose in the contest. We have to work against great odds, which are represented by our Old Traditions, our Poverty of Resources, and the hostile Competition of Advanced Races, whose industrial organization has been completed under more favourable conditions than our own. My object in reading this paper before you is chiefly to show you that, notwithstanding these disadvantages, and the Free-Trade Policy of the Government, we may win, if we will only persevere in our efforts, and direct them by co-operation on a large scale into the proper channels. We cannot afford to be dreamy and self-contained, and turn back from our present opportunities to a past which cannot be recalled.

Natural aptitudes, undeveloped but unlimited resources, peace and order, the whole World open to us, our marvellous situation as the Emporium of all Asia, these priceless advantages will secure success, if we endeavour to deserve it by striving for it. This is the creed for the propagation of which, by exhortation and example, the Industrial Association of Western India was started, and I feel sure it will soon become the creed of the whole Nation, and ensure the permanent triumph of the modern spirit in this Ancient Land.

24

LETTERS TO GOVERNMENT ON THE DECCAN DACOITIES*

No. I

No. 79 OF 1879.

SARVAJANIK SABHA ROOMS.
Nagarker's Wada near Vishrambag.
Poona 25th April 1879.

To,

THE CHIEF SECRETARY TO GOVERNMENT,
Bombay.

We have been directed by the Managing Committee of the Poona Sarvajanik Sabha to submit for the favourable consideration of His Excellency the Governor in Council the following representation in connection with the great insecurity to person and property now prevalent throughout some of the Deccan Dis-

JPSS, July 1879, Vol.II, No.1. Drafted or supervised by Ranade

tricts consequent upon the unarrested progress and the increasing daring of bands of dacoits, who have been infesting the said Deccan Districts, and harassing their peaceful inhabitants for the last two months and upwards, and to request you to place the same before His Excellency in Council at as early a date as possible.

2. The present disturbances prevail chiefly in the three Districts of Poona, Sattara and Sholapoor though occasional outbreaks of similar lawlessness have been reported in the Tanna, Nasik and Khandesh Districts also, and they have certainly struck great terror into the hearts of the peaceful inhabitants of the adjoining British Districts and the Native States. The inhabitants of that portion of the territory of His Highness the Chief of Bhor, which is contiguous to the disturbed districts of Poona and Satara, as well as those of the State of Kolhapoor and a few other states in the Southern Maratha country, appear to have been stricken with terror. During the last three months no less than 29 dacoities have been reported in the newspapers and the value of property stolen and destroyed is close upon one lac of rupees. Dacoities have been reported at Dhamori, Walhe, Saswar, Poona, Talegaum, Indapoor in the Poona District, at Sholapoor in the Sholapoor District, at Nandoshi and Gharsandi in the Satara District, and at Haranai and at Chal in the Sachiva's territory. A statement is hereunto appended giving the names of the villages, where dacoities and high-class robberies have been reported in the newspapers. Government will thus have some idea of the extent of uneasiness caused by the present disturbed condition of the three Districts of Poona, Satara, and Sholapoor. The sufferings of the peaceful inhabitants of these districts are aggravated by the fact that they are so thoroughly disarmed, and the Police force is so inconsiderable that they have no means to defend themselves against the dacoits. The dacoits are fully conscious of this fact which has made them so daring and bold, that sometimes they commit dacoities in open day light and ill-treat both the male and female inmates of the house that many happen to

fall a victim to their lawlessness. It is some relief, however, to find that, except in one or two cases, these disturbances have not been attended with any loss of life, though instances are not wanting in which these dacoits committed outrages on the persons of their defenceless victims. The Police arrangements appear to be so defective that though it is nearly two months and upwards that the present disturbances commenced, yet the Police have not been able to give any great confidence to the people of the disturbed districts by bringing to justice the real offenders against law; for hitherto only few dacoits have been punished. The consequence of such a state of things is that well-to-do people have for the most part either removed or are in the course of removing themselves, their families and their movable property to centres of population. During the past few weeks the city of Poona has received large accessions of this nature to its population, who, finding it unsafe to continue at their homes in the country, have been forced to resort to this extreme step as a precautionary measure. As an instance of the foregoing assertion we may be permitted to state for the information of His Excellency the Governor in Council that most of the well-to-do families in the villages of this district, marginally noted,* have deserted their houses in the said villages and have removed themselves to places of security. This fact the truth of which can be easily ascertained by instituting strict inquiry speaks anything but creditably for the efficiency of the police arrangements in imparting security of life and property to those who rely upon them for both. The people even of large cities like Poona are not without apprehension for the security of their life and property, firstly on account of the general disturbed condition of the three above mentioned districts, and secondly because not long ago, that is, in the early part of the present disturbances a daring dacoity attended with loss of life was committed in one of the suburbs of this city. This locality is situated almost midway between the cantonment on the one side and a police chowkee on the other. The dacoits who committed this daring act have not yet been apprehended, and

* Siwapoor
Wadgaum
Sonapoor
Tallegaum

this fact has naturally enough considerably shaken the confidence of the people in the efficiency of those who are entrusted with the guardianship of their material interests.

3. The Committee of the Sabha gratefully acknowledge the promptitude with which the Government appointed a special officer to deal with these dacoits summarily, and the officer who has been deputed to this work possesses rare qualifications to carry out successfully the work entrusted to him. It is to be regretted, however, that the force at his command is much too restricted in point of numbers and efficiency of arms. The Committee think that the time has come for the temporary employment of detachments of a regular military force which should be quartered at convenient centres till the disturbances are settled and confidence restored. The dacoits belong chiefly to the criminal classes who have been impoverished and thrown out of employment by the famine and scarcity for the last two or three years, and the stoppage of the great public works. Till the next monsoon rains fall and secure employment to the agricultural classes in the country, the present state of unsettled things might continue unabated. The police force must therefore be strengthened in number and supplemented by small military detachments. The Committee of the Sabha learn from the news-papers that the Government has already appointed a commission of executive officers to inquire into the origin of these disturbances and to suggest remedies. The Committee of the Sabha humbly submit that it is rather too early in the day to try to reasonably account for the disturbed condition of the districts, and feel the necessity of the executive authorities directing their undivided attention towards restoring order and giving confidence to the frightened people by hunting down these bands of dacoits from their hiding place and bringing them to condign punishment.

4. When the present disturbances manifested themselves for the first time, the Committee of the Sabha felt and hoped that the executive authorities of the districts concerned would lose no time whatever in promptly restoring order and dispersing

the bands of dacoits at an early date. The Committee, however, regret exceedingly to have to observe that though it is now two months and upwards since these troubles commenced, that hope has not yet been realized to any appreciable extent. On the other hand it appears from the daily reports that appear in the newspapers that dacoities are on the increase. It may be that owing to the insufficient strength of the police force at the disposal of the executive authorities of the Districts concerned they are not equal to the task before them without receiving accession to their establishment. The Committee of the Sabha can well understand that a Police force, which may suffice for the requirements of any given district in ordinary times, may be quite insufficient and unequal in such exceptional times as the present. It appears, however, that beyond patrolling the roads with Police Swars and establishing Chowakies in a few places, the executive authorities have taken no active steps to master the situation. The Committee of the Sabha hope that, even if the Government should not deem it expedient at the present time to sanction the employment of detachments of regular force against the dacoities, there can be no objection to adopt the usual precautions which have been adopted on similar occasions before, and which it is in the power of the civil authority to carry out without increasing any great responsibility. It is well known that the general disarmament of the people encourages the dacoits in their lawlessness by rendering their victims entirely helpless to protect themselves. The best way to inspire confidence among the people would be to issue licenses to the head men of the villages to retain swords and matchlock guns in their possession and to arm them with these weapons at their own cost. Another precaution which would have an equally beneficial effect would be to revive the ancient system of requiring the adult males of the villages to watch their villages by turn during the night time. This volunteer police system was found very effective in old days and by encouraging people to help themselves and to have mutual confidence cannot fail to produce the best result. The old practice was to require the villages to attend the Chawari by turns during the night and keep watch and ward in turns. The third precaution sanctioned by old usage is to keep muster rolls of the criminal tribes settled in the villages. Each man belonging to these suspected classes was required to be in personal attendance at the village Chavakee during the night when the muster was taken and his absence or presence was duly noted. The muster rolls when regularly kept afford important clues to trace the whereabouts of the suspected inhabitants. These three precautions taken together will go a great way to relieve the Police force of their present duty, and the Committee accordingly pray that Government will issue instructions to the District Officers to carry them into effect at the earliest opportunity. Rewards for the apprehension of the more noted dacoits should also be publicly notified, as has been already done in the case of one, as such a measure would be useful in sowing disunion among these people. The adoption of these measures will, the Committee hope, to a great extent render it unnecessary to strengthen the Police establishments. The ordinary expedient adopted by the Government of quartering punitive posts at the expense of peaceful inhabitants will not be found to be very effective in the present juncture, and it only aggravates the misfortunes of the peaceful classes who are punished for no fault of theirs with permanent burdens. The several expedients suggested above have the advantage of enlisting the people on the side of Government and secure their cooperation in the preservation of order and tranquillity, and the Committee hope that by their early adoption these unhappy disturbances will soon be checked and the country restored to its normal condition of peace and progress.

We have the honour to be,
Sir
Your most obedient servants,
SHIVARAM HARI SATHE,
Secretary Poona Sarvajanik Sabha.
S. H. CHIPLONKAR,
Editor of the Quarterly Journal,
Poona Sarvajanik Sabha.

Statement to accompany the letter No. 79 dated 25th April 1879 giving the names of villages where dacoities were committed and the amount of property reported to have been lost or destroyed.

No.	Name of the place where the dacoity was committed	Name of the district	The amount of property lost or destroyed
1	Ranajoo	Khandesh	3000 Rs. property.
2	Palusdeva Road	Poona	30 Rs. property.
3	Nandosee	Satara	15 to 20 thousand Rs. property.
4	Baramati Peta	Poona	Not known.
5	Kharsoondi	Satara	Not known.
6	Between Baramati and Dicsal	Poona	Looted the post. (Tapal).
7	Janai Mala	"	Ornaments.
8	Wadagaum Sheri	"	25 to 30 Rs. worth.
9	Between Poorundher & Poona	"	2 horses and some property.
10	Dhamari	"	$2^1/_2$ to 3 thousand Rs. property.
11	Boregaum	Satara	200 to 300 Rs. property.
12	Másal	Mogalayee	15 to 16 thousand Rs. property.
13	Sholapoor	Sholapoor	Some property on the Railway gate there.
14	Narsingapoor	Poona	3000 Rs. worth property.
15	Nirnimba	"	Not known.
16	Bawade gate	"	Arms and dresses.
17	Veeravhale	"	3000 rupees worth.
18	Harnai	Bhore	Not known.
19	Mangdari	Sholapoor	14 to 15 thousand Rs. worth.
20	Rooyi	Poona	Documents &co. burnt.
21	Sonapoor	"	Not known.
22	Chandakhed	"	Not known.
23	Kelawada	"	400 rupees property.
24	Chal	Bhore	Documents &co. burnt.
25	Tembhooni	Poona	2 to 4 thousand Rs. property.
26	Hamodi	Bhore	1200 Rs. property
27	Jawale	Poona	500 Rs. property.

No. II.

No. 81 OF 1879.

SARVAJANIK SABHA ROOMS.
Nagarker's Wada near Vishrambag.
Poona 20th May 1879.

TO,

THE CHIEF SECRETARY TO GOVERNMENT,
Bombay.

SIR,—In continuation of our letter No. 79 dated the 25th April last, we have been directed by the Managing Committee of the Poona Sarvajanik Sabha to express their most grateful acknowledgments to Government for the promptitude with which the authorities have adopted rigorous measures to suppress the dacoities in this part of the country, and they feel confident that they represent the public feelings of satisfaction for the considerable success which has attended the efforts of the District authorities.

1. It is true that the measures of precaution adopted have not yet been crowned with that complete success which is necessary for the re-establishment of peace and order. In the early part of the last week matters seemed to have gone from bad to worse. For while hitherto the peaceful inhabitants of this city were mainly concerned for the security of life and property in the unprotected districts, the news of the dacoity at Palaspe on the other side of the Bombay harbour, the largest of its kind since these troubles began, and the fearful conflagrations in Poona on the night of Tuesday the 13th May, by which two public buildings of the utmost value to the inhabitants were completely destroyed, have struck terror into the hearts of the citizens, and have caused quite a panic amongst them. The Committee of the Sabha in common with the people of this ancient and historical town have viewed with profound sorrow the destruction by fire of two such Public Palaces as the Vishrambag and Boodhawar wada and the irreparable loss which both the Government and

the people have sustained thereby. The Sabha beg to express their sincere abhorrence of this wicked and fiendish act and their deep sympathy with Government for the heavy loss sustained. In addition to the historical traditions which were inseparably connected with both these important buildings in the estimation of the inhabitants of this town, there were associations of a more potent character which made people cherish them as their most valued possessions. Since the establishment of the British power in this part of the country, both these buildings, but more especially the Vishrambag Wada were consecrated to learning, and most of the men of the present generation and of the rising generation have received their education in these two buildings. These associations had so far endeared the buildings to the people of Poona that when the news of their being set on fire spread through the town, every one repaired to the scene of the conflagrations prepared to do his utmost to put out the fire and save these noble palaces,—palaces with which the memory of his earliest days was inseparably associated,—and when all efforts proved of no avail, many hundreds of people were struck with dismay as they took a last view of the burning piles and shed a tear over their ruins. Many an educated native worked as hard as any other man, whether official or non-official, to save the buildings from destruction and rendered material aid. With them it was a labour of love combined with duty. In fact the two back quadrangles of the Vishram Bag Palace were saved mainly through the exertions of the Assistant Masters and the students of the Poona High School.

2. These conflagrations along with the great Palaspe dacoity and the rumour of many smaller disturbances which have been reported in the news-papers as having occurred in the districts, marginally noted,* and a list of which is hereunto appended, have brought the sense of insecurity nearer home, and the people of this town feel the necessity of Government taking some strong measures at a very early date for

* Poona
Sholapoor
Sattara
Belgaum
Ratnagiri
Tanna

the special protection of the city. The police force of this town is lamentably and notoriously weak and inadequate in point of strength and numbers, and unless it is largely strengthened, at least temporarily, people are not likely to feel themselves secure against the lawlessness of these desperate outlaws and dacoits. The Committee of the Sabha earnestly pray government to act upon the suggestions made in their last communication on the subject and swear special constables from among the resident population of this city, and also issue arms to some of the threatened villagers that they may be enabled to defend themselves against these Ramosee outlaws.

3. The recent conflagrations have been popularly ascribed to the evil machinations of some incendiaries, set on to that kind of work probably by the dacoits in the Moffusil, and the circumstantial confession of one of the parties arrested on suspicion strongly confirms this belief. Government will be exceedingly glad to learn that the parties, who now confess to have set fire to the Vishram Bag and the Boodhawar Palaces, were first discovered by the united efforts of some of the leading members of the Sabha and of the native community generally, and handed over by them to the City Magistrate.

4. As a set off to these troubles and anxieties the Committee of the Sabha have learnt with sincere pleasure the news of the capture by the Poona Police of a large gang of dacoits and of the recovery of all the ornaments and the treasure taken by them at the great Palaspe dacoity. Major Daniell, the special Police Officer appointed by government, has by this signal service vindicated the choice made by Government when he was first appointed to this arduous duty. The Sabha and the people generally feel confident that now that the first blow has been struck home, the gang will be soon brought to bay and hunted down till it is dispersed, and the tranquillity of the country assured beyond all risk of such disturbances. The active cooperation of the people of the districts with the efforts of the Police is a duty which the entire civil population owes to itself

and to the Government, and it is prepared to offer loyal help that might be required in this crisis and it is only their helplessness which has hitherto prevented them from rendering much resistance to the dacoits. If the measures of self-defence and precaution, suggested in their previous letter, be carried out, the Committee of the Sabha feel sure that the efforts of the out-laws will soon collapse and that they will be handed over to the judicial tribunals for condign and exemplary punishment.

We have the honour to be,
Sir
Your most obedient servants,
SHIVARAM HARI SATHE,
Secretary Poona Sarvajanik Sabha.
S. H. CHIPLONKAR,
Editor of the Quarterly Journal,
Poona Sarvajanik Sabha.

STATEMENT to accompany letter No. 81 dated 20th May 1879 giving the names of villages where dacoities were committed and the amount of property reported to have been lost or destroyed.

STATEMENT OF THE SABHA

No.	Name of the place where the dacoity was committed	Name of the district	The amount of property lost or destroyed
1	Banere	Poona	40 rupees worth.
2	Near Ambeel Nala	"	200 " "
3	Kalose	"	500 to 600 rupees worth.
4	Kalagaum	"	200 rupees worth.
5	Dhoolkhed near Taklee	"	One Surveyor's whole property.
6	Between Tembhoorni and Kandher	Sholapoor	100 rupees worth.
7	On way to Kandher	Poona	100 rupees worth.
8	Asawali	Satara	Not known.
9	Dhamni	Poona	3 to 4 thousand Rs. property & two police persons wounded.
10	Barsi	Sholapoor	100 rupees besides ornaments.
11	Dawadi	Poona	9,300 to 9,400 rupees property.
12	Nimbgaum	"	3,000 rupees property.
13	Mahaloonge	"	Not known.
14	Near Mhaisgaum	Sholapoor	600 and 2,000 rupees property of two men respectively.
15	Ten miles from Nandagada	Belgaum	3 to 4 thousand Rs. property.
16	Nera	Tanna	5 to 6 " "
17	Palaspe	"	1,50,000 rupees property; two men killed.
18	Vaijanath	"	100 rupees cash, besides some property.
19	Alegaum	Poona	1,500 rupees property.
20	Poladpoor near Deval and Borad	Ratnagiri	5,000 " "
21	Hadapsar	Poona	5,00 " "
22	Sholapoor	Sholapoor	Did not find anything.
23	6 miles from Matheran	Tanna	Not known.
24	Chikhaly	"	3 to 4 hundreds worth.

25

LETTERS TO GOVERNMENT ON THE DECCAN DACOITIES*

No. III.

No. 121 OF 1879.

SARVAJANIK SABHA ROOMS,
Nagarker's Wada, near Vishram Bag.
POONA, *31st December* 1879.

TO,
THE CHIEF SECRETARY TO GOVERNMENT,
BOMBAY.

SIR,

In continuation of our letter No. 81 dated 20th May 1879, we have been directed by the Managing Committee of the Poona Sarvajanik Sabha to submit this third representation to you on the subject of the Deccan Dacoities, and to request you to place

JPSS, April 1880, Vol.II, No.4. Drafted or supervised by Ranade.

the same before His Excellency the Governor in Council for their most favourable consideration.

1. At the outset the Committee of the Sabha beg to congratulate the Government on the capture and the subsequent conviction of Wassudev Balwant Phadke, the fool-hardy mover in one of the bands of dacoits that infested these Deccan Districts in the early part of the current year. The Committee of the Sabha are glad to find from the Administration Report of the last year recently published that the impression about the connection of the educated natives with the dacoity troubles which for a long time found favour in certain quarters, has been openly declared by the Government itself to be quite unfounded, and that the movement had little or no hold whatever on the sympathies of the entire population, educated and uneducated, and that, except among the criminal classes and half starved unemployed wretches, and a few giddy school boys Wassudev had no help and found no followers, that he was only one very insignificant leader, and that even the outlaws left him very early to shift for himself till he was hunted down and captured. Moreover the fact that these troubles were not at an end with the capture or death of Wassudev, Daulatia, Omia, and others of the outlaws, but still continue in portions of the disturbed districts, and that the dacoities were not confined to any one district but were spread over five districts and contiguous Native States, will it is hoped convince Government that it was not, as was suggested in some quarters, the artful scheming of any one or more individuals that brought them on, but that, like the Deccan Riots of 1875, they were the spontaneous result of a number of concurrent causes of long and wide operation.

2. Soon after the commencement of the disturbances in the early part of the current year, the Government contemplated the appointment of a Commission of Inquiry under the presidency of the Commissioner Central Division to inquire into, and report upon, the origin and causes of the disturbances, and to suggest remedies. The Committee of the Sabha in their letter No. 79 represented at the time, that it was too early in the day

then to appoint such a Commission of Inquiry, as it was a matter of the first importance at the time, that the District Officers should devote their undivided energies to the effectual suppression of the evil. The Committee of the Sabha are grateful to Government for their having taken their prayer into favourable consideration. Although the country is not yet restored to its former condition of undisturbed tranquillity, yet now that the neck of the troubles may be said to be broken, they think the time has come for the appointment of a Commission of Inquiry to inquire into and report upon, the origin and causes of the disturbances. The occurrence of so many serious outrages in such a short space of time is happily now so rare that it becomes necessary in the interests of public peace to ascertain what were the pre-disposing circumstances which led to these troubles and which gave them such long impunity. The utter helplessness of the disarmed country people, as disclosed by these sad occurrences, to defend their homes and possessions against the dastardly attacks of the outlaws, and the total insufficiency of the Police protection, which required to be supplemented by military aid to quell the disturbances, make it incumbent on the Government to take early action in the matter.

3. This inquiry becomes the more necessary and obligatory when it is remembered that there is a wide divergence of views among the officials themselves, and a wider still between the views of the officials and the people most intimately affected by these troubles, and there are already indications that strong measures of repression find favour in certain quarters, although public opinion is strongly pronounced against them as both unjust and injurious to the general interests involved in the satisfactory settlement of these troubles. For the Committee of the Sabha think that it is opposed to all principles of justice and good rule that the defenceless and innocent inhabitants of the Moffusil villages, who have been, in consequence of their dis-armament and the failure of the Police to protect them against the lawlessness of the criminal classes, made to suffer great loss and injury to their persons and possessions for which they have ob-

tained hardly any redress, should further be required to defray the expenses of additional punitive posts, which are only justified when the disorderly conduct of the villagers generally render them necessary. It cannot be maintained for a moment that the villagers acted in concert with those who looted and killed them. Moreover it should be remembered that unlike the village communities of olden days those of the present day have no hand whatever in the preservation of order and peace, and the control of the criminal classes in their respective limits, the whole of which responsibility has been taken upon itself by the Government in the Police Department. Such being the case it is manifestly hard upon the villagers in the Purandhar and the other Talukas that they should be held responsible for the lawless acts of their criminal and starving classes, and taxed an additional rate which represents a sum in many places nearly equal to one third the land tax they pay to Government, and many times the yield of the license tax. The Committee of the Sabha, therefore, submit with, due deference that Government should not finally commit itself to such stringent measures before the whole subject has been properly inquired into, and the imposition of a special Police rate recommended by an impartial Commission.

4. The Committee of the Sabha feel the more anxious in this matter because unfortunately before there was time to form a deliberate opinion on the matter, authoritative declarations were hazarded of course on the basis of reports made by the District officials by the Head of the Local Government and endorsed by the Government of India, denying the truth of the views held on this subject by the Sabha and by independent public opinion generally, that the troubles resulted from the pressure of famine times and the simultaneous operation of enforced economy in the Public Works Department and the extension of forest laws and the rigorous exaction of the land revenue. All the evidence accessible to the public tends to show that agricultural distress has been the principal source of the disturbances. This evidence is of a two-fold nature—the first part being based upon the im-

pressions formed by Government Officers and the second part on the facts elicited during the course of judicial investigation before the Sessions Judge of Poona. Under both heads we shall mention several facts whose importance cannot be over-rated:-

(1) The Counsel for the prosecution in Empress *versus* Wassudev based his own theory of the motives which prompted the misguided followers of Wassudeo to join him more on this admitted distress of the agricultural classes than the efficacy of Wassudeo's seditious preachings.

(2) One of the inspired organs of the English Press the *Bombay Gazette* which has throughout maintained the correctness of the official view, has been at last obliged to confess that the forest extensions are to some extent responsible for these troubles. This confession is professedly based on official sources of information.

(3) It would appear further from the last instalment of Mr. Cairds' "Notes by the way in India," published in the October number of the *Nineteenth Century* that long before the actual breaking out of the dacoity disturbances, the Police Department thought that the stringent application of the Forest Regulations had aroused great discontent which would most likely lead to crime and might become a source of danger. It is to be noted that this impression was formed by the Police officers in the Deccan long before the actual breaking out of the disturbances. They thought the matter of sufficient importance to communicate the same to the Famine Commission during their sojourn in the Deccan. Mr. Caird was himself so convinced of the importance of this fact that he deemed it necessary to supplement the statement quoted above by a piece of advice to the authorities concerned to the effect that though the preservation of forests is to a certain extent most desirable, "their extension by the Forest officers in reckless manner and with too high a hand should be most carefully guarded against." This observation shows that Mr. Caird at any rate, if not his colleagues also in the Famine Commission, has been convinced of the reckless ex-

tension of the Forest Regulations by the officers of that Department. In the opinion of the Committee of the Sabha the over-stringent application of the Forest Regulations did not itself create the dis-order, but it aggravated the mischief brought on by the agricultural distress of the past years. The rigorous exaction of the land revenue during the last two or three years, even when little or no crops were harvested, and when all the savings of thrift and providence had been exhausted by an unprecedentedly protracted season of scarcity, as also the abrupt stoppage of all public works forced on Government at a time when they were most needed to give employment to the starving population must also have lent considerable help to bring on these disorders and swell the ranks of the outlaws.

(4) This view of the case is supported by the second class of evidence, which is alluded to above, and which, as previously remarked, is based upon the facts elicited during the judicial investigations before the Sessions Judge of Poona. Up to the end of October last the Sessions Judge of Poona tried in all thirty-four cases of dacoities committed to the Poona Sessions. From the two statements hereto appended, it will be seen that the number of the accused put on their trial was 243, of whom 166 belonged to the Poona District, 66 to the Sholapur District, 3 to Satara District and 8 to the Ahmednagar District. It will also be seen further that out of the 34 cases of dacoities tried by the Poona Sessions Court, 21 occurred in the Poona District, 11 in the Sholapur District, and one each in the Satara and Tanna Districts. It will further appear from the second statement that out of the total number of 243 accused put up on their trial for committing dacoities, 104 were Cultivators, 28 Ramoshi watchmen, I Village Patel, 67 labourers, 19 petty dealers and artizans, 19 village Mahar servants, 1 trader, and 4 Mangs. Now when it is borne in mind that almost the entire population of our villages is directly or indirectly connected with agriculture, the Committee of the Sabha think that those entered under the second,third, fourth, sixth and eighth columns can be, some wholly and some partially, regarded as agriculturists. Thus it

would appear that more than four fifths of the total number of the accused in these 34 cases of dacoities were wholly or partially agriculturists. These figures lend strong and unexpected support to the soundness of the views held by the Sabha from the first on this subject.

5. But even if it be admitted that these figures do not completely establish the case of those who, like the Sabha, have all along maintained that nothing more or less than pure agricultural distress was at the bottom of these disturbances, they most strongly disprove the position taken up by some of the District Officials and endorsed too summarily by the higher authorities that the troubles were not due to agricultural distress but to the machinations of a few men. The Committee of the Sabha have no doubt that the Government will feel relieved that the statistics herewith appended together with the other evidence and notably the strongly expressed opinion of Mr. Caird of the Famine Commission are more than sufficient to clearly prove that the dark and vague, though sufficiently expressive, language in which H. E. the Viceroy in July last hinted at the existence of causes other than agricultural distress as being the sources of these disturbances, was unjustified by facts, then perhaps not within the knowledge of government. The autobiography of Wassudeo Balwant Phadke produced in evidence by the prosecution, goes to support the same view. In one part of that document he says that he had been working more than half a dozen years to incite the Ramoshis and other criminal classes not only of the Deccan but other parts of this Presidency to actively assist him in his mad project for the overthrow of a Government which is not only one of the best, but taking all things into account absolutely *the best* Government that India can ever hope to have under existing circumstances. He, however, failed till the commencement of the current year to induce even the Ramoshis to co-operate with him. This circumstance has, in the opinion of Committee of the Sabha, a two-fold significance; it proves in the first place that the Ramoshis and other criminal classes of other parts of this

Presidency, other than the four Districts of the Deccan proved deaf to the last to the preachings and inducements of Wassudeo, while in the second place it equally proves that even those who actually joined him were influenced less by the preachings and inducements of Wassudeo, than by the necessities of their condition, being without any resource wherewith to earn even the scanty livelihood which constituted their competence. The frequent desertions and returnings to their ordinary pursuits after having joined him in two or three dacoities of which Wassudeo charges several of his following both in his autobiography and his diary, point to the same conclusion and show, that many who joined him deserted him the moment they became possessed of means sufficient to enable them to tide over a season of general agricultural distress, depression and scarcity of employment. These facts are of great importance and significance and should not be treated of lightly or under-valued.

6. It will be thus seen that unless based upon facts to which the public has yet had no access, the "very different causes of these troubles," of which the Viceroy spoke in July last, do not appear to have any foundation in fact, and the cause of these troubles which both His Lordships and His Excellency the Governor of Bombay discarded as not proved appears to be the probable, if not the only, explanation of the troubles. A clear case is thus made out for the appointment of a Commission of Inquiry to inquire into, and report on, the origin and the causes of these disturbances. The Committee of the Sabha are not aware up to this moment of the nature or character of the evidence on which His Excellency the Viceroy relied as being of sufficient force to point to a very different cause of these troubles. This evidence, whatever it be, will have to be submitted to the Commission of Inquiry and to be sifted by them in the same way as they will sift the evidence which is now forthcoming in support of the hitherto discredited cause of these troubles.

7. The Commission of Inquiry will have to inquire in connection with these disturbances, whether any or all of the following causes had influenced those who resorted to dacoity:—*(a)* the

land revenue policy of the Local Government which reversing its hitherto traditional liberality in the matter of remissions recovered the assessment during the last three years without allowing any substantial remissions; *(b)* the extensive application of the Forest Regulations by the officers of that Department; *(c)* the Licence tax which is reported to have been over-assessed in the case of several petty dealers, and to have been assessed on those whom the Legislature never thought of including; *(d)* the general depression brought on by a series of bad seasons; *(e)* the violent and abrupt suspension of all public works this time last season when they were needed most to secure employment to the needy and the hungry. The Committee will also inquire *(f)* whether the existing Police organization is defective and *(g)* how far the villagers need greater protection by a distribution of arms being made to the village authorities and the more substantial Ryots by a requisition of voluntary watch service from all land-holders, and by keeping a careful register of the criminal and suspected classes.

8. In conclusion the Committee of the Sabha trust now that a clear case in favour of the appointment of a Commission of Inquiry to inquire into and report upon, the origin and the causes of the Deccan Dacoities has been made out, the Local Government will be pleased forthwith to appoint such a mixed commission composed both of official and non-official elements, before committing itself finally to any definite course of policy in regard to the adoption of preventive or repressive measures.

We have the honour to be,

Sir,

Your most obedient servants,

SHIVARAM HARI SATHE,

Secretary of the Poona Sarvajanik Sabha

S.H. CHIPLONKAR,

Honorary Secretary of the

Poona Sarvajanik Sabha.

N.B.—Want of space compels us to with-hold the bigger of the two statements of which the one that follows is a kind of analysis.—*By the Editor*

PROCEEDINGS OF THE SABHA

Number	Name of the Dacoity Case	District	a. Cultivators	b. Ramoshi Watchman	c. Village Patels	d. Labourers	e. Petty artizans & dealers	f. Village Mehars	g. Traders	h. Manas	Total
1	Dhamari Case	Poona	7	3	0	6	3	0	0	0	19
2	Ambegaom Case	Sholapoor	1	0	0	0	0	2	0	0	3
3	Koregaom Case	Poona	1	5	0	2	0	0	0	0	8
4	Mouje Garvi Case	Sattara	0	1	0	2	0	0	0	0	3
5	Mouje Kadad Case	Poona	7	5	0	0	1	4	0	0	17
6	Mouje Rewasi Case	Poona	7	0	0	1	1	1	0	0	10
7	Mouje Kudal Case	Sholapoor	0	0	0	7	0	0	0	0	7
8	Mawodi Case	Poona	4	0	0	0	1	0	0	0	5
9	Shilawadi Case	Sholapoor	2	0	0	0	0	0	0	0	2
10	Bharab Case	Sholapoor	1	0	0	0	0	0	0	0	1
11	Pandharpoor Case	Sholapoor	2	0	0	2	2	0	0	0	6
12	Jagwagi Case	Sholapoor	1	0	0	1	0	0	1	0	3
13	Mouje Saraphwadi Case	Poona	0	1	0	8	0	0	0	0	9
14	Mouje Rewade & Garade	Poona	6	0	0	0	0	0	0	0	6
15	Bhaje Case	Poona	2	0	0	3	0	3	0	0	8
16	Sakurdi Case	Poona	3	0	1	0	0	0	0	0	4
17	Nere, Chikali & Palaspe	Tanna	9	2	0	7	2	0	0	0	20
18	Mouje Chisoli Case	Sholapoor	0	2	0	2	0	0	0	0	4
19	Pavgaom Case	Sholapoor	0	0	0	1	0	2	0	4	7
20	Mouje Wabal Case	Poona	11	3	0	10	8	1	0	0	33
21	Mouje Walhe Case	Poona	1	1	0	2	0	0	0	0	4
22	Walati Case	Poona	0	0	0	0	1	0	0	0	1
23	Mouje Parusa Case	Poona	6	0	0	0	0	0	0	0	6
24	Davadi Limbgaom Case	Poona	0	1	0	2	0	0	0	0	3
25	Mouje Walati Case	Poona	1	0	0	4	0	0	0	0	5
26	Mouje Nagerali Case	Sholapoor	4	0	0	2	0	2	0	0	8
27	Sarole Case	Sholapoor	1	0	0	2	0	4	0	0	7
28	Davadi Case	Poona	0	0	0	1	0	0	0	0	1
29	Narsingpoor Case	Poona	0	0	0	1	0	0	0	0	1
30	Poona Case	Poona	0	0	0	1	0	0	0	0	1
31	Donje Case	Poona	3	0	0	0	0	0	0	0	3
32	Sakurdi Case	Poona	1	0	0	0	0	0	0	0	1
33	Jabuta Case.	Poona	5	3	0	0	0	0	0	0	8
34	Kolgatwade Case	Poona	18	1	0	0	0	0	0	0	19
	Grand Total		104	28	1	67	19	19	1	4	243

Select Bibliography

Chandra, Bipan, (i) *The Rise and Growth of Economic Nationalism in India,* New Delhi, 1966.
(ii) *Nationalism and Colonialism in Modern India,* New Delhi, 1979.

Coyajee, J.C., "Ranade and After", *Indian Journal of Economics,* Jan. 1942, Vol. XXII, No. 3.

Datta, Bhabatosh, (i) "The Background of Ranade's Economics", *Indian Journal of Economics,* Jan. 1942, Vol. XXII. No. 3.
(ii) *Indian Economic Thought- Twentieth Century Perspectives, 1900- 1950,* New Delhi, 1978.

Dutt, R.C., *Economic History of India,* 2 Vols., London, 1901 and 1903.

Ganguli, B.N., (i) *Dadabhai Naoroji and the Drain Theory,* Bombay, 1965.
(ii) *Indian Economic Thought—Nineteenth Century Perspective,* New Delhi, 1977.

Gokhale, G.K., (i) *Speeches,* Madras, 2nd edition, 1916.
(ii) *Speeches and Writings of Gopala Krishna Gokhale,* edited by R.P. Patwardhan and D.V. Ambekar, 3 Vols., Bombay, 1962.

Gopalakrishnan, P.K., *Development of Economic Ideas in India,* New Delhi, 1959.

Iyer, G. Subramaniya, *Some Economic Aspects of British Rule in India,* New Delhi, 1988 reprint, originally published in 1903.

Jagirdar, P.J. (i) "Ranade and the Historical School of Economics", *Indian Journal of Economics,* Jan. 1954, Vol. XXXIV, No. 3.
(ii) *Studies in the Social Thought of M.G. Ranade,* Bombay, 1963.

(iii) *Mahadev Govind Ranade*, New Delhi, 1972.

Joshi, G.V., *Writings and Speeches*, Poona, 1912.

Karve, D.G., (i) "Ranade and Economic Planning ", *Indian Journal of Economics*, Jan. 1942, Vol. XXII, No. 3.
(ii) *Ranade- The Prophet of Liberated India*, Poona, 1942.

Kellock, James, (i) *Mahadev Govind Ranade*, Calcutta, 1926.
(ii) "Ranade and After", *Indian Journal of Economics*, Jan. 1942, Vol.XXII, No. 3.

Mankar, G.A., *A Sketch of the Life and Works of the Late Mr Justice M.G. Ranade*, 2 Vols., Bombay, 1902.

Minocha, V.S., "Ranade on the Agrarian Problem", *The Indian Economic and Social History Review*, October 1965, Vol.II, No. 4.

Naoroji, Dadabhai, (i) *Essays, Speeches and Writings*, edited by C.L. Parekh, Bombay, 1887.
(ii) *Foverty and Un-British Rule in India*, London, 1901.
(iii) *Speeches and Writings*, Madras, no date.

Nanda, B.R., *Gokhale, The Indian Moderates and the Raj*, Delhi, 1977.

Parvate, T.V., *Mahadev Govind Ranade- A Biography*, Bombay, 1963.

Pradhan, B.P. and Bhagwat, A.K., *Lokamanya Tilak, A Biography*, Bombay, 1958.

Ranade, M.G., (i) *Essays on Indian Economics*, Bombay, 1898.
(ii) *Miscellaneous Writings*, Bombay, 1915.
(iii) "Plea for Protection- Indian Sugar Industry", *Times of India*, May-June 1899, Bombay, no date.
(iv) *Minute of Dissent* to the *Report of the Finance Committee*, 1886.
(v) *A Revenue Manual of the British Empire in India: An Epitome of the Fawcett Committee Report of 1877*, Poona, 1877.
(vi) *A Note on the Decentralization of Provincial Finance*, Poona,

1894.
(vii) *Rise of the Maratha Power*, Bombay, 1961.

Ranade, Ramabai, ***Ranade, His Wife's Reminiscences***, translated from Marathi, by Kusumavati Deshpande, New Delhi, 1963.

Ray, Prithwis Chandra, *The Poverty Problem in India*, Calcutta, 1895

Singh, V.B. *From Naoroji to Nehru, 6 Essays in Indian Economic Thought*, London, 1975.

Sovani, N.V., "Ranade's Model of the Indian Economy", *Arth Vigyan*, Vol. IV, No. 1.

Stokes, Eric, *The English Utilitarians and India*, Oxford, 1959.

Telang, K.T., (i) *Free Trade and Protection from an Indian Point of View*, Bombay, 1877.
(ii) *Select Writings and Speeches*, Bombay, 1885.

Tucker, Richard P., *Ranade and the Roots of Indian Nationalism*, Bombay, 1977 edition.

Wacha, D.E., *Speeches and Writings*, Madras, no date.

A Bibliographic Note:

For a comparative study of the early nationalist as also British Indian economic thought, *see* Bipan Chandra's two books. D.G. Karve's work is unsubstantiated. P.K. Gopalakrishnan's generalizations are in some cases not borne out by his references. B.N. Ganguli's is the best of the existing analysis of Ranade's economic thought but, unfortunately, it is not comprehensive enough. For biographical details, the reader should consult Parvate, Tucker, Jagirdar and Mankar. These authors also discuss Ranade's economic thought.

Index